Everyday
Mathematics®

Student Reference Book

The University of Chicago
School Mathematics Project

 **Wright Group**

The McGraw·Hill Companies

UCSMP Elementary Materials Component

Max Bell, Director

Authors

Max Bell, Jean Bell, John Bretzlauf, Amy Dillard, Robert Hartfield, Andy Isaacs,
Deborah Arron Leslie, James McBride (Director), Kathleen Pitvorec, Peter Saecker

Technical Art

Diana Barrie

Photo Credits

Phil Martin/Photography; p. 2, Michael Newman/PhotoEdit; p. 3, Barbara Stitzer/PhotoEdit; p. 7, National Aeronautics and Space Administration; p. 115, Bruce Herman/Stone; p. 116, Myreleen Ferguson/Photo Edit; p. 121, ArcWorld; p. 149, John Edwards/Stone; p. 220, ©The British Museum; p. 237, Alfred Pasieka/Science Photo Library; p. 244, National Aeronautics and Space Administration; p. 313 (left center), The Pierpont Morgan Library/Art Resource, NY; p. 313 (right center), Scala/Art Resource, NY; p. 314, Foto Marburg/Art Resource, NY; p. 318 (center), Scala/Art Resource, NY; p. 318 (bottom), Werner Forman Archive British Museum/Art Resource, NY; p. 319, National Archaeological Museum head no. 1571; p. 325 (top), M.C. Escher's "Hand with Reflecting Sphere" ©1997 Cordon Art-Baarn-Holland. All rights reserved.; p. 325 (left and right bottom), M.C. Escher's "Symmetry Drawing E 88" ©1997 Cordon Art-Baarn-Holland. All rights reserved.; p. 327 (top right), Photo Courtesy of The Newberry Library, Chicago; p. 327 (center right), M.C. Escher's "Mobius Strip II" ©1997 Cordon Art-Baarn-Holland. All rights reserved.; p. 328, Copyright © Scala/Art Resource, NY; p. 332, AP Wide World Photo; p. 334, Alexander Calder's "Sea Scape, 1947" ©1976 Running Press, Philadelphia, Pennsylvania. "Courtesy of Whitney Museum of American Art."

p. 328, *The Leonardo* illustration reprinted with permission. Copyright ©1966 by Scientific American, Inc. All rights reserved.; pp. 329–331, Reprinted with permission of Simon & Schuster from *The Great International Paper Airplane Book* by Jerry Mander, George Dippel, and Howard Gossage. Copyright ©1967 by Shade Tree Corporation.

 The *Student Reference Book* is based upon work supported by the National Science Foundation under Grant No. ESI-9252984. Any opinions, findings, conclusions, or recommendations expressed in this material are those of the authors and do not necessarily reflect the views of the National Science Foundation.

Send all inquiries to:
Wright Group/McGraw-Hill
P.O. Box 812960
Chicago, IL 60681

Printed in the United States of America.

ISBN 0-07-600061-3

3 4 5 6 7 8 9 10 11 QWD 08 07 06 05 04

The McGraw·Hill Companies

Contents

Whole Numbers   1

Decimals and Percents   25

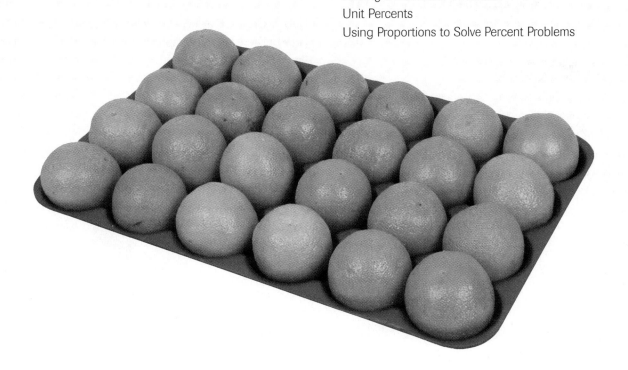

Geometry and Constructions 145

Measurement 189

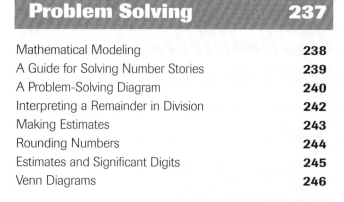

Games 273

Art and Design Activities 311

About the *Student Reference Book*

A reference book is organized to help people find information quickly and easily. Dictionaries, encyclopedias, atlases, cookbooks, even telephone books are examples of reference books. Unlike novels and biographies, which are usually read in sequence from beginning to end, reference books are read in small segments to find specific information at the time it is needed.

You can use this *Student Reference Book* to look up and review information on topics in mathematics. It consists of the following sections:

- A **table of contents** that lists the topics covered and shows how the book is organized.

- Essays on **mathematical topics,** such as whole numbers, decimals, percents, fractions, geometry, measurement, data analysis, and problem solving.

- Descriptions of how to use a **calculator** to perform various mathematical operations and functions.

- Directions on how to play some of the **mathematical games** you may have played before.

- A set of **tables and charts** that summarize information, such as a place-value chart, prefixes for names of large and small numbers, tables of equivalent measures, tables of equivalent fractions, decimals, and percents, and formulas.

- A **glossary** of mathematical terms consisting of brief definitions of important words.

- An **answer key** for every Check Your Understanding problem in the book.

- An **index** to help you locate information quickly.

This reference book also contains descriptions of **Art and Design Activities** you can do.

How to Use the
Student Reference Book

Suppose you are asked to solve a problem and you know that you have solved problems like it before. But at the moment, you are having difficulty remembering how to do it. This is a perfect time to use the *Student Reference Book.*

You can look in the **table of contents** or the **index** to find the page that gives a brief explanation of the topic. The explanation will often show a step-by-step sample solution.

In some essays you will see a small book symbol. The symbol gives page number references to essays that are related to the topic under discussion. For example, simplifying fractions involves finding equivalent fractions, so there is a reference to the page which contains a description of how to find equivalent fractions.

There is also a set of problems at the end of most essays, titled **Check Your Understanding.** It is a good idea to solve these problems and then turn to the **answer key** at the back of the book to check your answers to make sure that you understand the information presented on the page.

Always read mathematical text with paper and pencil in hand. Take notes, draw pictures and diagrams to help you understand what you are reading. Work the examples. If you get a wrong answer in the **Check Your Understanding** problems, try to find your mistake by working back from the correct answer given in the **answer key.**

It is not always easy to read text about mathematics, but the more you use the *Student Reference Book,* the better you will become at understanding this kind of material. You may find that your skills as an independent problem-solver are improving. We are confident that these skills will serve you well as you undertake more advanced mathematics courses.

Whole Numbers

Uses of Numbers

Try to imagine having even one day without using or thinking about numbers. Numbers are used on clocks, calendars, car license plates, rulers, scales, and so on. The major ways that numbers are used are listed below.

- Numbers are used for **counting.**

> **EXAMPLES** Students sold 147 tickets to the school play.
>
> The first U.S. Census counted 3,929,326 people.

- Numbers are used for **measuring.**

> **EXAMPLES** He swam the length of the pool in 32.9 seconds.
>
> The package is 30 inches long and weighs $4\frac{3}{16}$ pounds.

- Numbers are used to show where something is in a **reference system.**

> **EXAMPLES**
>
> | Situation | Reference System |
> |---|---|
> | Normal room temperature is 21°C. | Celsius temperature scale |
> | Shauna was born on July 23, 1991. | Calendar |
> | The time is 10:13 A.M. | Clock time |
> | Detroit is located at 42°N and 83°W. | Earth's latitude and longitude system |

- Numbers are used to **compare amounts** or **measures.**

> **EXAMPLES** The cat weighs $\frac{1}{2}$ as much as the dog.
>
> There were 2 times as many girls as boys at the game.

- Numbers are used for **identification** and as **codes.**

> **EXAMPLES** phone number: (709) 555–1212
>
> ZIP code: 60637   driver's license number: M286-423-2061

Mr. John Doe
1234 North Maine Street
Thome, Nevada
53207-4123

Kinds of Numbers

The **counting numbers** are the numbers used to count things. The set of counting numbers is 1, 2, 3, 4, and so on.

The **whole numbers** are any of the numbers 0, 1, 2, 3, 4, and so on. The whole numbers include all of the counting numbers and zero (0).

Counting numbers are useful for counting but not for measuring. **Fractions** and **decimals** were invented to name measures. For example, fractions are often used in recipes for cooking and for measures in carpentry and other building trades. Decimals are used for almost all measures in science and industry.

> **EXAMPLES** The package weighed 14 pounds 15.3 ounces.
>
> The recipe called for $2\frac{1}{4}$ cups of sugar.
>
> The window measured 1 foot $11\frac{3}{8}$ inches wide.

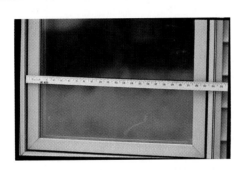

Negative numbers were invented to express quantities with reference to a zero point.

> **EXAMPLES** A temperature of 23 degrees below zero is written as $-23°$.
>
> A depth of 235 feet below sea level is written as -235 feet.

Negative numbers are also used to indicate changes in quantities.

> **EXAMPLES** A weight loss of $7\frac{1}{2}$ pounds is recorded as $-7\frac{1}{2}$ pounds.
>
> A decrease in income of $1,500 is recorded as $-\$1,500$.

Place Value for Whole Numbers

Any number, no matter how large or small, can be written using one or more of the **digits** 0, 1, 2, 3, 4, 5, 6, 7, 8, and 9. A **place-value chart** is used to show how much each digit in a number is worth. The **place** for a digit is its position in the number. The **value** of a digit is how much it is worth according to its place in the number.

Study the place-value chart below. As you move from right to left in the chart, the value of each place is 10 times greater.

10,000s ten thousands	1,000s thousands	100s hundreds	10s tens	1s ones
9	4	8	0	5

EXAMPLE   The number 94,805 is shown in the place-value chart above.
The value of the 9 is 90,000 (9 * 10,000).
The value of the 4 is 4,000 (4 * 1,000).
The value of the 8 is 800 (8 * 100).
The value of the 0 is 0 (0 * 10).
The value of the 5 is 5 (5 * 1).
94,805 is read as "ninety-four thousand, eight hundred five."

In larger numbers, groups of 3 digits are separated by commas. Commas help identify the thousands, millions, billions, and trillions, as shown in the following place-value chart:

trillions				billions				millions				thousands				ones		
100	10	1	,	100	10	1	,	100	10	1	,	100	10	1	,	100	10	1
2	4	6	,	3	5	7	,	0	2	6	,	9	0	9	,	3	8	9

EXAMPLE   The number 246,357,026,909,389 is shown in the place-value chart above. This number is read as 246 **trillion,** 357 **billion,** 26 **million,** 909 **thousand,** 389.

The next group of 3 places to the left of trillions names **quadrillions,** then **quintillions, sextillions, septillions, octillions,** and so on.

CHECK YOUR UNDERSTANDING

Read each number to yourself. What is the value of the 6 in each number?

1. 36,798   **2.** 87,674,132   **3.** 597,361   **4.** 9,962,010

Check your answers on page 371.

Powers of 10

Numbers like 10, 100, and 1,000 are called **powers of 10.** They are numbers that can be written as products of 10s.

100 can be written as $10 * 10$ or 10^2.
1,000 can be written as $10 * 10 * 10$ or 10^3.

The raised number is called an **exponent.** The exponent tells how many times 10 is multiplied by itself. 10^2 is read "10 to the second power" or "10 squared." 10^6 is read "10 to the sixth power."

A number that is written with an exponent, like 10^3, is in **exponential notation.** The number 1,275 is written in **standard notation.**

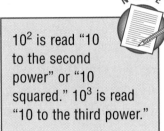

NOTE

10^2 is read "10 to the second power" or "10 squared." 10^3 is read "10 to the third power."

The chart below shows powers of 10 from ten through one billion.

Powers of 10

Standard Notation	Product of 10s	Exponential Notation
10	10	10^1
100	$10*10$	10^2
1,000 (1 thousand)	$10*10*10$	10^3
10,000	$10*10*10*10$	10^4
100,000	$10*10*10*10*10$	10^5
1,000,000 (1 million)	$10*10*10*10*10*10$	10^6
10,000,000	$10*10*10*10*10*10*10$	10^7
100,000,000	$10*10*10*10*10*10*10*10$	10^8
1,000,000,000 (1 billion)	$10*10*10*10*10*10*10*10*10$	10^9

EXAMPLE $1,000 * 1,000 = ?$

Use the table above to write 1,000 as $10 * 10 * 10$.
$$1,000 * 1,000 = (10 * 10 * 10) * (10 * 10 * 10)$$
$$= 10^6$$
$$= 1 \text{ million}$$

So, $1,000 * 1,000 = 1$ million.

EXAMPLE $1,000 \text{ millions} = ?$

Write $1,000 * 1,000,000$ as $(10 * 10 * 10) * (10 * 10 * 10 * 10 * 10 * 10)$.
This is a product of nine 10s, or 10^9.

1,000 millions = 1 billion

Exponential Notation

A **square array** consists of the same number of rows and columns. A whole number that can be represented by a square array is called a **square number.** Any square number can be written as the product of a number multiplied by itself.

EXAMPLE 16 is a square number. It can be represented by an array consisting of 4 rows and 4 columns. 16 = 4 * 4.

Here is a shorthand way to write square numbers: $16 = 4 * 4 = 4^2$. 4^2 is read as "4 times 4," "4 squared," or "4 to the second power." The raised 2 is called an **exponent.** It tells that 4 is used as a factor two times. The 4 is called the **base.** Numbers written with an exponent are said to be in **exponential notation.**

exponent
4^2
base

Exponents are also used to show that a factor is used more than twice.

EXAMPLES

$2^3 = 2 * 2 * 2$

The number 2 is used as a factor 3 times.
2^3 is read "2 cubed" or "2 to the third power."

$9^5 = 9 * 9 * 9 * 9 * 9$

The number 9 is used as a factor 5 times.
9^5 is read "9 to the fifth power."

Any number raised to the first power is equal to itself. For example, $5^1 = 5$.

Some calculators have special keys for changing numbers written in exponential notation to standard notation.

262

EXAMPLES Use a calculator. Find the value of 15^2 and 8^6.

To find the value of 15^2, key in: 15 $\boxed{\wedge}$ 2 $\boxed{\text{Enter}}$. Answer: 225

To find the value of 8^6, key in: 8 $\boxed{\wedge}$ 6 $\boxed{\text{Enter}}$. Answer: 262,144
You can verify this by keying in 8 $\boxed{\times}$ 8 $\boxed{\times}$ 8 $\boxed{\times}$ 8 $\boxed{\times}$ 8 $\boxed{\times}$ 8 $\boxed{\text{Enter}}$

CHECK YOUR UNDERSTANDING

Write each number in standard notation. Do not use a calculator to solve Problems 1–4.

1. 5^2 2. 3^3 3. 10^5 4. 8^1 5. 345^2 6. 12^4

Check your answers on page 371.

Scientific Notation

Scientific Notation for Big Numbers

In the statement "The population of the world is about $6 * 10^9$ people," $6 * 10^9$ is written in **scientific notation.** It is read "six times ten to the ninth power."

Scientific notation is a way to represent big and small numbers with only a few symbols. A number in scientific notation is written as the product of two factors. The first factor is at least 1 but less than 10. The second factor is a power of 10.

Earth weighs about $1.2 * 10^{24}$ pounds.

EXAMPLE   Write $6 * 10^9$ in standard notation.

First, look at the power of 10. It is 10 to the ninth power, so it is the product of 10 used as a factor 9 times:

$10^9 = 10 * 10 * 10 * 10 * 10 * 10 * 10 * 10 * 10$
$= 1,000,000,000$
$= 1 \text{ billion}$

So, $6 * 10^9 = 6 * 1,000,000,000$
$= 6,000,000,000$
$= 6 \text{ billion}$

Often the first factor of a number in scientific notation has digits to the right of the decimal point.

EXAMPLE   The nearest star beyond the sun is about $2.5 * 10^{13}$ miles away.

In standard notation, $2.5 * 10^{13} = 2.5 * 10,000,000,000,000 = 25,000,000,000,000$.
$2.5 * 10^{13}$ is best read "two and five-tenths times ten to the thirteenth power."
It can be read more briefly as "two point five times ten to the thirteenth."

Scientific Notation for Small Numbers

Small positive numbers less than 1 are written in scientific notation with **negative powers of 10.**

A number raised to a negative power is equal to the fraction 1 over the number raised to the positive power. For example, $10^{-5} = \frac{1}{10^5}$.

Converting from Scientific Notation to Standard Notation

> **EXAMPLES** Convert to standard notation.

$8.7 * 10^6$

- Note the exponent in the power of 10.

- If the exponent is positive, as in $8.7 * 10^6$, move the decimal point in the other factor that many places to the right. (Insert the decimal point if necessary, and attach 0s as you move it.)

$8.7 * 10^6$

8 . 7 0 0 0 0 0 ,

(6 places)

$8.7 * 10^6 = 8,700,000$

$5.6 * 10^{-4}$

- Note the exponent in the power of 10.

- If the exponent is negative, as in $5.6 * 10^{-4}$, move the decimal point in the other factor that many places to the left. (Insert the decimal point if necessary, and attach 0s as you move it.)

$5.6 * 10^{-4}$

0 . 0 0 0 5 . 6

(4 places)

$5.6 * 10^{-4} = 0.00056$

Converting from Standard Notation to Scientific Notation

> **EXAMPLES** Convert from standard notation to scientific notation.

1. Locate the decimal point. Write or imagine the decimal point if it isn't there.

   8,700,000.   0.00056

2. Move the decimal point so that you get a number with only one digit (not 0) to the left of the decimal point (in the ones place). Count the number of places you moved the decimal point.

   8 . 7 0 0 0 0 0 ,   0 . 0 0 0 5 . 6
   (6 places)   (4 places)

3. The number of places you moved the decimal point tells which power of 10 to use. If the original number was between 0 and 1, the power is negative.

   10^6 10^{-4}

4. Use the number you got in Step 2 and the power of 10 you got in Step 3 to write the number in scientific notation. Omit any 0s you don't need.

   $8,700,000 = 8.7 * 10^6$ $0.00056 = 5.6 * 10^{-4}$

CHECK YOUR UNDERSTANDING

Write in scientific notation.

1. 500,000   **2.** 10 billion   **3.** 750,000,000   **4.** 0.00008   **5.** 0.045

Write in standard notation.

6. $3 * 10^8$ **7.** $4.1 * 10^7$ **8.** $7.09 * 10^{10}$ **9.** $4 * 10^{-3}$ **10.** $9.06 * 10^{-2}$

Check your answers on page 371.

Comparing Numbers and Amounts

When two numbers or amounts are compared, there are two possible results: They are equal, or they are not equal because one is larger than the other.

Different symbols are used to show that numbers and amounts are equal or not equal.

- Use an **equal sign** (=) to show that the numbers or amounts *are equal*.
- Use a **not-equal sign** (≠) to show that they are *not equal*.
- Use a **greater-than symbol** (>) or a **less-than symbol** (<) to show which one is larger (or smaller).

EXAMPLES

Symbol	=	≠	>	<
Meaning	"equals" or "is the same as"	"is not equal to"	"is greater than"	"is less than"
	$\frac{1}{2} = 0.5$	$4 \neq 5$	$8 > 4$	$2 < 4$
	$45 = 9 * 5$	$4^2 \neq 8$	$1.34 > 1.3$	$789 < 1{,}110$
	$4^3 = 64$	$2\text{ m} \neq 200\text{ mm}$	$15\text{ ft }8\text{ in.} > 14\text{ ft }10\text{ in.}$	$97\text{ minutes} < 4\text{ hours}$
	$5\text{ cm} = 50\text{ mm}$		$7 + 9 > 9 + 6$	$4 * (5 + 5) < 6 * 7$
	$8 + 8 = 9 + 9 - 2$		$5 * 7 > 34 / 2$	$100 - 3 < 99 + 3$
	$2 * 6 = 11 + 1$		$10^4 > 100$	$\frac{1}{10^4} < 1$

When you compare amounts that include units, use the same unit for both amounts.

EXAMPLE Compare 30 yards and 60 feet.

The units are different—yards and feet. Change yards to feet, then compare.
1 yd = 3 ft
So, 30 yd = 30 * 3 ft, or 90 ft.
90 ft > 60 ft

Therefore, 30 yd > 60 ft.

CHECK YOUR UNDERSTANDING

True or false?

1. $7^2 < 15$ **2.** 37 in. > 3 ft   **3.** $8 * 5 \neq 120 / 3$ **4.** $16 + 1 > 18 - 1$

Check your answers on page 371.

Factors

A **rectangular array** is an arrangement of objects in rows and columns. Each row has the same number of objects, and each column has the same number of objects. A rectangular array can be represented by a multiplication **number model**.

> **EXAMPLE** This rectangular array has 14 red dots.
>
> It has 2 rows with 7 dots in each row.
> $2 * 7 = 14$ is a number model for this array.
> 2 and 7 are **factors** of 14.
> 14 is the **product** of 2 and 7.
> 2 and 7 are a **factor pair** for 14.
>
> $2 * 7 = 14$
> factors   product

Numbers can have more than one factor pair. 1 and 14 are another factor pair for 14 because $1 * 14 = 14$.

To test whether a number is a factor of another number, divide the larger number by the smaller number. If the result is a whole number and the remainder is 0, then the smaller number is a factor of the larger number.

> **EXAMPLES** 4 is a factor of 12 because 12 / 4 gives 3 with a remainder of 0.
> 6 is not a factor of 14 because 14 / 6 gives 2 with a remainder of 2.

One way to find all the factors of a whole number is to find all the factor pairs for that number.

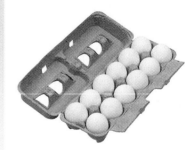

> **EXAMPLE** Find all the factors of the number 36.
>
> | Number Models | Factor Pairs |
> |---|---|
> | $36 = 1 * 36$ | 1, 36 |
> | $36 = 2 * 18$ | 2, 18 |
> | $36 = 3 * 12$ | 3, 12 |
> | $36 = 4 * 9$ | 4, 9 |
> | $36 = 6 * 6$ | 6, 6 |
>
> The factors of 36 are 1, 2, 3, 4, 6, 9, 12, 18, and 36.

CHECK YOUR UNDERSTANDING

List all the factors of each number.

1. 10   **2.** 81   **3.** 63   **4.** 48   **5.** 17   **6.** 100

Check your answers on page 371.

Divisibility

When a counting number is divided by a counting number and the quotient is a counting number with a remainder of 0, then the first number is **divisible by** the second number.

> **EXAMPLE** 128 / 4 → 32 R0. The remainder is 0, so 128 is divisible by 4.

When a counting number is divided by a counting number and the quotient is a whole number with a non-zero remainder, then the first number is *not divisible by* the second number.

> **EXAMPLE** 92 / 5 → 18 R2. The remainder is not 0, so 92 is *not divisible by* 5.

It is possible to test for divisibility without actually dividing.

Here are a few **divisibility tests** that make it unnecessary to divide:
- Counting numbers with a 0, 2, 4, 6, or 8 in the ones place are **divisible by 2.** They are the even numbers.
- Counting numbers with 0 in the ones place are **divisible by 10.**
- Counting numbers with 0 or 5 in the ones place are **divisible by 5.**
- If the sum of the digits in a counting number is divisible by 3, then the number is **divisible by 3.**
- If the sum of the digits in a counting number is divisible by 9, then the number is **divisible by 9.**
- If a counting number is divisible by both 2 and 3, it is **divisible by 6.**

> **EXAMPLE** Tell which numbers 324 is divisible by.
>
> 324 is divisible by
> - 2 because 4 in the ones place is an even number
> - 3 because the sum of its digits is 9, which is divisible by 3
> - 9 because the sum of its digits is divisible by 9
> - 6 because it is divisible both by 2 and by 3
>
> 324 is not divisible by 10 because it does not have a 0 in the ones place. It is not divisible by 5 because it does not have 5 in the ones place.

CHECK YOUR UNDERSTANDING

Which numbers are divisible by 2? By 3? By 5? By 6? By 9? By 10?

1. 240   **2.** 7,260   **3.** 427   **4.** 531   **5.** 14,850

Check your answers on page 371.

Prime and Composite Numbers

A **prime number** is a counting number greater than 1 that has exactly two factors: 1 and the number itself. A prime number is divisible only by 1 and itself.

A **composite number** is a counting number that has more than two factors. A composite number is divisible by at least three whole numbers.

> **NOTE**
> The number 1 is neither prime nor composite.

EXAMPLES   13 is a prime number because its only factors are 1 and 13.

18 is a composite number because it has more than two factors. Its factors are 1, 2, 3, 6, 9, and 18.

Every composite number can be renamed as a product of prime numbers. This is called the **prime factorization** of that number.

EXAMPLE   Find the prime factorization of 80.

The number 80 can be renamed as the product 2 * 2 * 2 * 2 * 5.

The prime factorization of 80 can be written as $2^4 * 5$.

One way to find the prime factorization of a number is to make a **factor tree.** First, write the number. Then, underneath, write any two factors whose product is that number. Repeat the process for these two factors. Continue until all the factors are prime numbers.

EXAMPLE   Find the prime factorization of 36.

No matter which two factors are used to start the tree, the tree will always end with the same prime factors.

36 = 3 * 3 * 2 * 2

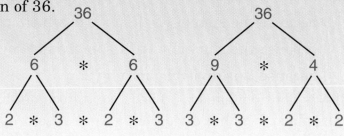

The prime factorization of 36 is 2 * 2 * 3 * 3.

CHECK YOUR UNDERSTANDING

Make a factor tree to find the prime factorization of each number.

1. 16   **2.** 32   **3.** 63   **4.** 40   **5.** 45   **6.** 100

Check your answers on page 371.

Addition Algorithms
Partial-Sums Method

The **partial-sums method** is used to find sums mentally or with paper and pencil.

To use the partial-sums method, add from left to right, one column at a time. Then add the partial sums.

EXAMPLE 679 + 345 = ?

		100s	10s	1s
		6	7	9
	+	3	4	5
Add the 100s.	600 + 300 →	9	0	0
Add the 10s.	70 + 40 →	1	1	0
Add the 1s.	9 + 5 →		1	4
Add the partial sums.	900 + 110 + 14 →	**10**	**2**	**4**

679 + 345 = 1,024

Column-Addition Method

The **column-addition method** may be used to find sums with paper and pencil, but it is not a good method for finding sums mentally.

To add numbers using the column-addition method:

• Draw lines to separate the 1s, 10s, 100s, and any other places.
• Add the numbers in each column. Write each sum in its column.
• If the sum of any column is a 2-digit number, adjust that column sum. Trade part of the sum into the column to its left.

EXAMPLE 467 + 764 = ?

	100s	10s	1s
	4	6	7
+	7	6	4
Add the numbers in each column.	11	12	11
Adjust the 1s and 10s:	11	13	1

   11 ones = 1 ten and 1 one
   Trade the 1 ten into the tens column.

	100s	10s	1s
Adjust the 10s and 100s:	**12**	**3**	**1**

   13 tens = 1 hundred and 3 tens.
   Trade the 1 hundred into the hundreds column.

467 + 764 = 1,231

A Short Algorithm

This is the method for adding that most adults in the United States were taught. Add from right to left. Add one column at a time, without displaying the partial sums.

EXAMPLE $359 + 298 = ?$

Step 1:	**Step 2:**	**Step 3:**
Add the ones.	Add the tens.	Add the hundreds.
1	1 1	1 1
3 5 9	3 5 9	3 5 9
+ 2 9 8	+ 2 9 8	+ 2 9 8
7	5 7	6 5 7
9 ones + 8 ones = 17 ones = 1 ten + 7 ones	1 ten + 5 tens + 9 tens = 15 tens = 1 hundred + 5 tens	1 hundred + 3 hundreds + 2 hundreds = 6 hundreds

$359 + 298 = 657$

The Opposite-Change Rule

Addends are numbers that are added. In $8 + 4 = 12$, the numbers 8 and 4 are addends.

Here is the **opposite-change rule:** If you subtract a number from one addend and add the same number to the other addend, the sum is the same.

Use this rule to make a problem easier by changing either of the addends to a number that has zero in the ones place.

EXAMPLE $69 + 36 = ?$

One way: Add and subtract 1.

69	(add 1)	70
+ 36	(subtract 1)	+ 35
		105

Another way: Subtract and add 4.

69	(subtract 4)	65
+ 36	(add 4)	+ 40
		105

$69 + 36 = 105$

CHECK YOUR UNDERSTANDING

Add.

1. $324 + 63$ **2.** $78 + 35$ **3.** $\begin{array}{r} 538 \\ + 427 \end{array}$ **4.** $769 + 348 + 692$ **5.** $\begin{array}{r} 3,942 \\ + 5,081 \end{array}$

Check your answers on page 371.

Subtraction Algorithms
Trade-First Subtraction Method

The **trade-first method** is similar to the method for subtracting that most adults in the United States were taught.

- If each digit in the top number is greater than or equal to the digit below it, subtract separately in each column.
- If any digit in the top number is less than the digit below it, adjust the top number before doing any subtracting. Adjust the top number by "trading."

EXAMPLE $574 - 386 = ?$

100s	10s	1s
5	7	4
− 3	8	6

Look at the 1s place.
You cannot remove 6 ones from 4 ones.

100s	10s	1s
	6	14
5	7̸	4̸
− 3	8	6

So trade 1 ten for 10 ones.
Look at the 10s place.
You cannot remove 8 tens from 6 tens.

100s	10s	1s
	16	
4	6̸	14
5̸	7̸	4̸
− 3	8	6
1	8	8

So trade 1 hundred for 10 tens.
Now subtract in each column.

$574 - 386 = 188$

CHECK YOUR UNDERSTANDING

Subtract.

1. $95 - 49$

2. $872 - 481$

3. $747 - 386$

4.   909
       − 838

5.   6,533
       − 3,088

Check your answers on page 371.

Counting-Up Method

You can subtract two numbers by counting up from the smaller number to the larger number. First, count up to the nearest multiple of 10. Next, count up by 10s and 100s. Then count up to the larger number.

EXAMPLE $525 - 58 = ?$

Write the smaller number, 58.

$$
\begin{array}{r}
5\ 8 \\
+\quad ② \\
\hline
6\ 0
\end{array}
$$
Count up to the nearest 10.

As you count from 58 up to 525, circle each number that you count up.

$$
\begin{array}{r}
+④\ 0 \\
\hline
1\ 0\ 0
\end{array}
$$
Count up to the nearest 100.

Add the numbers you circled:
$2 + 40 + 400 + 25 = 467$

$$
\begin{array}{r}
+④\ 0\ 0 \\
\hline
5\ 0\ 0
\end{array}
$$
Count up to the largest possible hundred.

You counted up by 467.

$$
\begin{array}{r}
+\quad ②\ ⑤ \\
\hline
5\ 2\ 5
\end{array}
$$
Count up to the larger number.

So, $525 - 58 = 467$.

Left-to-Right Subtraction Method

Starting at the left, subtract column by column.

EXAMPLES $932 - 356 = ?$ $673 - 286 = ?$

Subtract the 100s.

$$
\begin{array}{r}
9\ 3\ 2 \\
-\ 3\ 0\ 0 \\
\hline
6\ 3\ 2
\end{array}
\qquad
\begin{array}{r}
6\ 7\ 3 \\
-\ 2\ 0\ 0 \\
\hline
4\ 7\ 3
\end{array}
$$

Subtract the 10s.

$$
\begin{array}{r}
-\quad 5\ 0 \\
\hline
5\ 8\ 2
\end{array}
\qquad
\begin{array}{r}
-\quad 8\ 0 \\
\hline
3\ 9\ 3
\end{array}
$$

Subtract the 1s.

$$
\begin{array}{r}
-\qquad 6 \\
\hline
5\ 7\ 6
\end{array}
\qquad
\begin{array}{r}
-\qquad 6 \\
\hline
3\ 8\ 7
\end{array}
$$

$932 - 356 = 576$ $673 - 286 = 387$

CHECK YOUR UNDERSTANDING

Subtract.

1. $255 - 73$ **2.** $624 - 572$ **3.** $935 - 46$ **4.** $503 - 372$

Check your answers on page 371.

Partial-Differences Method

1. Subtract from left to right, one column at a time.
2. Always subtract the smaller number from the larger number.
   - If the smaller number is on the bottom, the difference is **added** to the answer.
   - If the smaller number is on the top, the difference is **subtracted** from the answer.

EXAMPLE 7,465 − 2,639 = ?

$$\begin{array}{r} 7,465 \\ -\ 2,639 \\ \hline \end{array}$$

Subtract the 1,000s.	7,000 − 2,000 →	+ 5000
Subtract the 100s.	600 − 400 →	− 200
Subtract the 10s.	60 − 30 →	+ 30
Subtract the 1s.	9 − 5 →	− 4
Find the total.	5,000 − 200 + 30 − 4 →	4,826

7,465 − 2,639 = 4,826

Same-Change Rule

Here is the **same-change rule** for subtraction problems:

- If you add the same number to both numbers in the problem before subtracting, the answer is the same.
- If you subtract the same number from both numbers in the problem, the answer is the same.

Use this rule to change the second number in the problem to a number that has 0 in the ones place.

EXAMPLE 93 − 46 = ?

One way: Add 4.

93	(add 4)	97
− 46	(add 4)	− 50
		47

Another way: Subtract 6.

93	(subtract 6)	87
− 46	(subtract 6)	− 40
		47

93 − 46 = 47

CHECK YOUR UNDERSTANDING

Subtract.

1. 539 − 43 **2.** 863 − 238 **3.** 548 − 373 **4.** 6,118 − 2,619

Check your answers on page 371.

Extended Multiplication Facts

Numbers such as 10, 100, and 1,000 are called **powers of 10.**

It is easy to multiply a whole number, *n,* by a power of 10. To the right of the number *n,* write as many zeros as there are zeros in the power of 10.

EXAMPLES

10 * 84 = 840	10 * 60 = 600	100 * 490 = 49,000
100 * 84 = 8,400	100 * 60 = 6,000	10,000 * 81 = 810,000
1,000 * 84 = 84,000	1,000 * 60 = 60,000	1,000,000 * 7 = 7,000,000

If you have memorized the basic multiplication facts, you can solve problems such as 8 * 80 and 6,000 * 3 mentally.

EXAMPLES

8 * 80 = ?	6,000 * 3 = ?
Think: 8 [8s] = 64	*Think:* 6 [3s] = 18
8 [80s] is 10 times as much.	6,000 [3s] is 1,000 times as much.
8 * 80 = 10 * 64 = 640	6,000 * 3 = 1,000 * 18 = 18,000

You can use a similar method to solve problems such as 50 * 50 and 400 * 90 mentally.

EXAMPLES

50 * 50 = ?	400 * 90 = ?
Think: 5 [50s] = 250	*Think:* 4 [90s] = 360
50 [50s] is 10 times as much.	400 [90s] is 100 times as much.
50 * 50 = 10 * 250 = 2,500	400 * 90 = 100 * 360 = 36,000

CHECK YOUR UNDERSTANDING

Solve these problems mentally.

1. 7 * 100
2. 1,000 * 98
3. 9 * 700
4. 9,000 * 9
5. 700 * 300
6. 600 * 80

Check your answers on page 371.

Multiplication Algorithms
Partial-Products Method

EXAMPLE	$73 * 46 = ?$

Think of 73 as $70 + 3$.
Think of 46 as $40 + 6$.
Multiply each part of 73 by each part of 46.

		100s	10s	1s
			7	3
	*		4	6
$40 * 70 \rightarrow$	2	8	0	0
$40 * 3 \rightarrow$		1	2	0
$6 * 70 \rightarrow$		4	2	0
$6 * 3 \rightarrow$			1	8
	3	**3**	**5**	**8**

Add the partial products.

$73 * 46 = 3,358$

A Short Algorithm

EXAMPLE	$73 * 46 = ?$

Multiply each part of the second factor by the first factor. Then add the partial products.

$$\begin{array}{r} 73 \\ *\ 46 \\ \hline \end{array}$$

$6 * 73 \rightarrow$ 438
$40 * 73 \rightarrow$ $+\,2920$
          3358

$73 * 46 = 3,358$

The Egyptian Method

EXAMPLE	$73 * 46 = ?$

Step 1: Make a column for each factor. Start with 1 in the first column and 46 in the second column. Double the numbers in each column until the first column is as close as possible to the first factor, 73, without going past it.

Step 2: Start with the largest number in the first column. Find the other numbers in the first column whose sum is 73 ($64 + 8 + 1 = 73$), and check them off. Cross out the numbers in the unchecked rows in both columns.

Step 3: Add the remaining numbers in the second column ($46 + 368 + 2,944 = 3,358$)

73	*	46
✓ 1		46
2̶		9̶2̶
4̶		1̶8̶4̶
✓ 8		368
1̶6̶		7̶3̶6̶
3̶2̶		1̶4̶7̶2̶
✓ 64		$+\,2944$
		3358

So, $73 * 46 = 3,358$.

CHECK YOUR UNDERSTANDING

Multiply. Try all three methods.

1. $7 * 461$ **2.** $9 * 3,795$ **3.** $54 * 97$ **4.** $88 * 53$ **5.** $23 * 217$

Check your answers on page 372.

Lattice Method

The **lattice method** for multiplying has been used for hundreds of years. It is very easy to use if you know the basic multiplication facts.

EXAMPLE 4 * 915 = ?

The box with cells and diagonals is called a **lattice.** Write 915 above the lattice. Write 4 on the right side of the lattice.

Multiply 4 * 5. Then multiply 4 * 1. Then multiply 4 * 9. Write the answers as shown.

Add the numbers along each diagonal.

Read the answer. 4 * 915 = 3,660

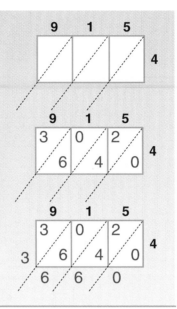

EXAMPLE 86 * 37 = ?

Write 37 above the lattice.
Write 86 on the right side.

Multiply 8 * 7. Then multiply 8 * 3.
Multiply 6 * 7. Then multiply 6 * 3.
Write the answers as shown.

Add the numbers along each diagonal.

When the numbers along a diagonal add up to 10 or more:

• record the ones digit in the sum
• add the tens digit to the sum in the next diagonal above.

Read the answer. 86 * 37 = 3,182

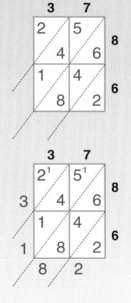

CHECK YOUR UNDERSTANDING

Draw a lattice for each problem. Then multiply.

1. 5 * 97   **2.** 88 * 47   **3.** 68 * 79   **4.** 9 * 537   **5.** 987 * 7

Check your answers on page 372.

Extended Division Facts

Numbers such as 10, 100, and 1,000 are called **powers of 10.**

In the examples below, use the following method to divide a whole number, n, by a power of 10:

- Cross out zeros in the number n, starting in the ones place.
- Cross out as many zeros as there are zeros in the power of 10.

EXAMPLES

80,000 / 10 = 80000	56,000 / 10 = 56000	930,000 / 10,000 = 930000
80,000 / 100 = 80000	56,000 / 100 = 56000	4,000,000 / 100,000 = 4000000
80,000 / 1,000 = 80000	56,000 / 1,000 = 56000	

If you know the basic division facts, you can solve problems such as 540 / 9 and $\frac{18,000}{3}$ mentally.

EXAMPLES

540 / 9 = ?
Think: 54 / 9 = 6
540 / 9 is 10 times as much.

540 / 9 = 10 * 6 = 60

18,000 / 3 = ?
Think: 18 / 3 = 6
18,000 / 3 is 1,000 times as much.

18,000 / 3 = 1,000 * 6 = 6,000

You can use a similar method to solve problems such as $\frac{18,000}{30}$ and 32,000 / 400 mentally.

EXAMPLES

18,000 / 30 = ?
Think: 18,000 / 3 = 6,000
18,000 / 30 is $\frac{1}{10}$ as much.

18,000 / 30 = $\frac{1}{10}$ of 6,000 = 600

32,000 / 400 = ?
Think: 32,000 / 4 = 8,000
32,000 / 400 is $\frac{1}{100}$ as much.

32,000 / 400 = $\frac{1}{100}$ of 8,000 = 80

CHECK YOUR UNDERSTANDING

Solve these problems mentally.

1. 97,000 / 1,000   **2.** 63,000 / 9   **3.** 5,400 / 60   **4.** $\frac{54,000}{600}$

Check your answers on page 372.

Division Algorithms

Different symbols may be used to indicate division. For example, "94 divided by 6" may be written as $94 \div 6$, $6\overline{)94}$, $94 / 6$, or $\frac{94}{6}$.

- The number that is being divided is called the **dividend.**
- The number by which the dividend is divided is called the **divisor.**
- The answer to a division problem is called the **quotient.**
- Some numbers cannot be divided evenly. When this happens, the answer includes a quotient and a **remainder.**

Partial-Quotients Method

In the **partial-quotients method,** it takes several steps to find the quotient. At each step, you find a partial answer (called a **partial quotient**). These partial answers are then added to find the quotient.

Study the example below. To find the number of 6s in 1,010, first find partial quotients, then add them. Record the partial quotients in a column to the right of the original problem.

EXAMPLE $1,010 / 6 = ?$

Write partial quotients in this column.

$6\overline{)1,010}$	↓	*Think:* How many [6s] are in 1,010? At least 100.
$-\ 600$	100	The first partial quotient is 100. 100 * 6 = 600
410		Subtract 600 from 1,010.
$-\ 300$	50	*Think:* How many [6s] are in 410? At least 50. The second partial quotient is 50. 50 * 6 = 300
110		Subtract.
$-\ 60$	10	*Think:* How many [6s] are in 110? At least 10. The third partial quotient is 10. 10 * 6 = 60
50		Subtract.
$-\ 48$	8	*Think:* How many [6s] are in 50? 8. The fourth partial quotient is 8. 8 * 6 = 48
2	168	Subtract. Add the partial quotients.
↑	↑	

Remainder   Quotient

The answer is 168 R2. Record the answer as $6\overline{)1,010}^{\ 168\ R2}$, or write $1,010 / 6 \rightarrow 168\ R2$.

The partial-quotients method works the same whether you divide by a 2-digit or a 1-digit divisor. It often helps to write down some easy facts for the divisor first.

EXAMPLE Divide 800 by 22.

Some facts for 22
(to help find partial quotients):

$$1 * 22 = 22$$
$$2 * 22 = 44$$
$$5 * 22 = 110$$
$$10 * 22 = 220$$

```
22)800
  -440 | 20   At least:
   360 |      (20 [22s] in 800)
  -220 | 10   (10 [22s] in 360)
   140 |
  -110 | 5    (5 [22s] in 140)
    30 |
   -22 | 1    (1 [22] in 30)
     8  36
```

Record the answer as 22)800 with 36 R8, or write 800 / 22 → 36 R8.

There are different ways to find partial quotients when you use the partial-quotients method. Study the example below. The answer is the same for each way.

EXAMPLE 391 / 4 = ?

One way:
```
4)391
-200 | 50
 191
-120 | 30
  71
- 40 | 10
  31
- 20 | 5
  11
-  8 | 2
  3   97
```

Another way:
```
4)391
-200 | 50
 191
-160 | 40
  31
- 20 | 5
  11
-  8 | 2
  3   97
```

Another way:
```
4)391
-360 | 90
  31
- 20 | 5
  11
-  8 | 2
  3   97
```

The answer, 97 R3, is the same for each way.

CHECK YOUR UNDERSTANDING

Divide.

1. 6)86   **2.** 855 / 5   **3.** 728 ÷ 8   **4.** 4)938

Check your answers on page 372.

Column-Division Method

The best way to understand column division is to think of a division problem as a money-sharing problem. In the example below, think of sharing $863 among 5 people.

EXAMPLE $5\overline{)863} = ?$

1. Draw lines to separate the digits in the dividend (the number being divided).
   Work left to right. Begin in the left column.

   $5\,)8\mid 6\mid 3$

2. Think of the 8 in the hundreds column as 8 $100 bills to be shared by 5 people. Each person gets 1 $100 bill. There are 3 $100 bills remaining.

   $$\begin{array}{c|c|c} 1 & & \\ 5\,)8 & 6 & 3 \\ -5 & & \\ \hline 3 & & \end{array}$$

3. Trade the 3 $100 bills for 30 $10 bills. Think of the 6 in the tens column as 6 $10 bills. That makes 30 + 6 = 36 $10 bills in all.

   $$\begin{array}{c|c|c} 1 & & \\ 5\,)8 & \not{6} & 3 \\ -5 & 36 & \\ \hline \not{3} & & \end{array}$$

4. If 5 people share 36 $10 bills, each person gets 7 $10 bills. There is 1 $10 bill remaining.

   $$\begin{array}{c|c|c} 1 & 7 & \\ 5\,)8 & \not{6} & 3 \\ -5 & 36 & \\ \hline \not{3} & -35 & \\ & 1 & \end{array}$$

5. Trade the 1 $10 bill for 10 $1 bills. Think of the 3 in the ones column as 3 $1 bills. That makes 10 + 3 = 13 $1 bills.

   $$\begin{array}{c|c|c} 1 & 7 & \\ 5\,)8 & \not{6} & \not{3} \\ -5 & 36 & 13 \\ \hline \not{3} & -35 & \\ & \not{1} & \end{array}$$

6. If 5 people share 13 $1 bills, each person gets 2 $1 bills. There are 3 $1 bills remaining.

   $$\begin{array}{c|c|c} 1 & 7 & 2 \\ 5\,)8 & \not{6} & \not{3} \\ -5 & 36 & 13 \\ \hline \not{3} & -35 & -10 \\ & \not{1} & 3 \end{array}$$

Record the answer as 172 R3.
Each person receives $172 and $3 are left over.

Decimals & Percents

Positive Rational Numbers Expressed as Decimals or Percents

Positive rational numbers can be written in any of three ways: as fractions, as decimals, and as percents.

When you share a pizza, you are more likely to use fractions than decimals. When you measure with metric units, it makes sense to express the measurements as decimals.

Four people will each get $\frac{1}{4}$ of the pizza.

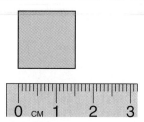

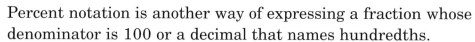

Each side of the square is 1.5 cm long.

Percents are used in many situations, such as sales, taxes, and statistics. Fractions are discussed elsewhere in this book; decimals and percents are discussed in this section.

97–98

Notation

Rational numbers are written in decimal form by extending the base-ten place-value system used for whole numbers. In the decimal base-ten place-value system, the value of each place is $\frac{1}{10}$ of the value of the place to its left.

27

Percent notation is another way of expressing a fraction whose denominator is 100 or a decimal that names hundredths.

55

Relations

The same rules for comparing whole numbers are used for comparing decimals: Start comparing the digits in the leftmost place and continue to the right until the digits in a place do not match.

Operations

When you do operations with decimals, you can use most of the same paper-and-pencil strategies that you use for doing operations with whole numbers. It is important to place the decimal point correctly in the answer to show the value of each digit.

Extending the Place-Value Chart to Decimals

Study the base-ten place-value chart.

1,000s thousands	100s hundreds	10s tens	1s ones	.	0.1s tenths	0.01s hundredths	0.001s thousandths
3	1	3	9	.	0	7	6
three thousand, one hundred thirty-nine				and	seventy-six thousandths		

Notice that the value of each place is $\frac{1}{10}$ of the value of the place to its left. This is true both for whole-number places and decimal places.

Whole Numbers	Decimals
$100 = \frac{1}{10}$ of 1,000	$0.1 = \frac{1}{10}$ of 1
$10 = \frac{1}{10}$ of 100	$0.01 = \frac{1}{10}$ of 0.1
$1 = \frac{1}{10}$ of 10	$0.001 = \frac{1}{10}$ of 0.01

A whole number that can be written using only 10s as factors is called a **power of 10.** A power of 10 can be written in exponential notation.

Powers of 10

100	10 * 10	10^2
1,000	10 * 10 * 10	10^3
10,000	10 * 10 * 10 * 10	10^4
100,000	10 * 10 * 10 * 10 * 10	10^5

Decimals that can be written using only 0.1s as factors are also powers of 10. They can be written in exponential notation with negative exponents.

Powers of 10 (less than 1)

0.01	0.1 * 0.1	10^{-2}
0.001	0.1 * 0.1 * 0.1	10^{-3}
0.0001	0.1 * 0.1 * 0.1 * 0.1	10^{-4}
0.00001	0.1 * 0.1 * 0.1 * 0.1 * 0.1	10^{-5}

The value of each place in a base-ten place-value chart is a power of 10.

100,000s	10,000s	1,000s	100s	10s	1s	.	0.1s	0.01s	0.001s	0.0001s	0.00001s
10^5	10^4	10^3	10^2	10^1	10^0	.	10^{-1}	10^{-2}	10^{-3}	10^{-4}	10^{-5}

Note the pattern in the exponents: Each exponent is 1 less than the exponent in the place to its left. According to this pattern:

$$10^1 = 10 \qquad 10^0 = 1 \qquad 10^{-1} = 0.1$$

Decimals

Each large square is worth 1.

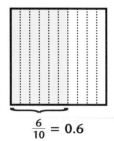

$\frac{6}{10} = 0.6$

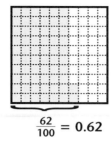

$\frac{62}{100} = 0.62$

Whole
large square

This square is divided into 10 equal parts. Each part is $\frac{1}{10}$ of the square. The decimal name for $\frac{1}{10}$ is 0.1.

$\frac{6}{10}$ of the square is shaded. The decimal name for $\frac{6}{10}$ is 0.6.

This square is divided into 100 equal parts. Each part is $\frac{1}{100}$ of the square. The decimal name for $\frac{1}{100}$ is 0.01.

$\frac{62}{100}$ of the square is shaded. The decimal name for $\frac{62}{100}$ is 0.62.

This number line shows tenths.

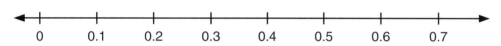

This number line shows hundredths. Each tenth is divided into 10 equal parts; each part is worth $\frac{1}{100}$, or 0.01.

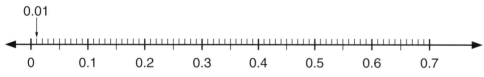

Reading Decimals

You can read a decimal as you would a fraction. For example, $8.7 = 8\frac{7}{10}$, so 8.7 can be read as "eight and seven-tenths."

$0.19 = \frac{19}{100}$, so 0.19 can be read as "nineteen-hundredths."

$2.061 = 2\frac{61}{1,000}$; it can be read as "two and sixty-one thousandths."

> **NOTE**
>
> In a decimal, the whole-number part is separated from the decimal part by a decimal point. Sometimes decimals are read by first saying the whole-number part, then saying "point," then finally saying the digits in the decimal part. For example, 8.7 can be read as "eight point seven." The decimal 0.15 can be read as "zero point one five." The decimal 0.001 can be read as "zero point zero zero one." This way of reading decimals is often used when there are many digits in the decimal.

CHECK YOUR UNDERSTANDING

Read each decimal to yourself.

1. 0.2   **2.** 1.36   **3.** 0.948   **4.** 19.07   **5.** 0.006   **6.** 74.082

Check your answers on page 372.

Fractions, Decimals, and Percents
Comparing Decimals

EXAMPLES

Compare 1.35 and 1.288.

1.35
1.288
 ↑ different
3 tenths > 2 tenths

So, 1.35 > 1.288.

Compare 0.5 and 0.102.

0.5
0.105
 ↑ different
5 tenths > 1 tenth

So, 0.5 > 0.102.

Fractions, decimals, and percents are different ways of naming numbers. Often, these numbers are used to name quantities that are less than 1 whole, or 100%. For example, $\frac{1}{2}$ cup is less than 1 cup, $0.25 is less than $1, and 75% of the capacity of a bus is less than 100% of the number of passengers allowed. But these numbers can also name numbers that are greater than 1 whole, or 100%. For example, $\frac{3}{2}$ cup is more than 1 cup, $2.75 is more than $1, and 110% of the capacity of a bus is more than 100% of the number of passengers allowed.

If fractions, decimals, and percents name the same number, they are **equivalent.** For example, each large square below represents 1 whole, or 100%. $\frac{3}{10}$, 0.3, $\frac{6}{20}$, $\frac{30}{100}$, 0.30, and 30% are all equivalent names for the shaded part of the squares.

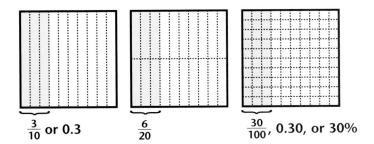

$\frac{3}{10}$ or 0.3 $\frac{6}{20}$ $\frac{30}{100}$, 0.30, or 30%

Percents can be shown on a number line. The Probability Meter, which you may remember from your work in fifth grade, is an example of a number line that shows percents. Fractions and decimals can also be shown on a number line.

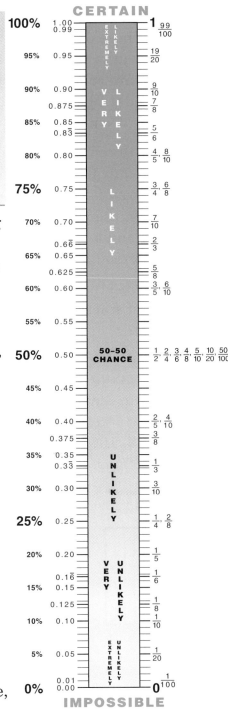

The Probability Meter

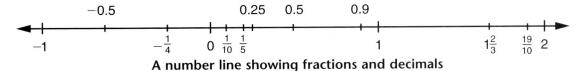

A number line showing fractions and decimals

Renaming Fractions as Decimals

A fraction that names a rational number can always be changed to a decimal. Sometimes all of the digits of a decimal can be written; these decimals are called **terminating.** Sometimes a decimal will repeat certain digits over and over forever; these decimals are called **repeating.** The fraction $\frac{1}{2}$ is equivalent to the terminating decimal 0.5. The fraction $\frac{1}{3}$ is equivalent to the repeating decimal 0.3333....

> **NOTE**
>
> All fractions in this book are assumed to be rational numbers unless otherwise stated.

One way to rename a fraction as a decimal is to remember the decimal equivalent: $\frac{1}{2} = 0.5$, $\frac{1}{4} = 0.25$, $\frac{1}{8} = 0.125$, and so on. Another way is to use logical thinking. For example, if $\frac{1}{8} = 0.125$, then $\frac{3}{8} = 0.125 + 0.125 + 0.125 = 0.375$. Logical thinking and a few memorized equivalents will help you rename many common fractions as decimals.

You can also find decimal equivalents for fractions by using equivalent fractions, the Fraction-Stick Chart, division, or a calculator.

Using Equivalent Fractions

One way to rename a fraction as a decimal is to find an equivalent fraction with a denominator that is a power of 10, that is, 10, 100, 1,000, and so on. This method only works for some fractions.

EXAMPLE

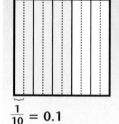

$\frac{1}{10} = 0.1$

The solid lines divide the square into 5 equal parts. Each part is $\frac{1}{5}$ of the square. $\frac{3}{5}$ of the square is shaded. The dashed lines divide each fifth into 2 equal parts. Each part is $\frac{1}{10}$, or 0.1, of the square. $\frac{6}{10}$, or 0.6, of the square is shaded.

$$\frac{3}{5} = \frac{6}{10} = 0.6$$

┌── **Whole** ──┐
│ large square │
└────────────────┘

CHECK YOUR UNDERSTANDING

Rename as decimals.

1. $\frac{1}{4}$ **2.** $\frac{4}{5}$ **3.** $\frac{5}{2}$ **4.** $\frac{13}{20}$ **5.** $\frac{4}{25}$

Check your answers on page 372.

Using the Fraction-Stick Chart

The Fraction-Stick Chart, along with a number line for decimals, can be used to rename fractions as decimals. Note that the result is usually only an approximation. You can use division or a calculator to obtain better approximations.

EXAMPLE Rename $\frac{2}{3}$ as a decimal.

1. Locate $\frac{2}{3}$ on the "thirds" stick.
2. Place one edge of a straightedge at $\frac{2}{3}$.
3. Find where the straightedge crosses the number line.

The straightedge crosses the number line between 0.66 and 0.67.

So, $\frac{2}{3}$ is equivalent to about 0.66 or 0.67.

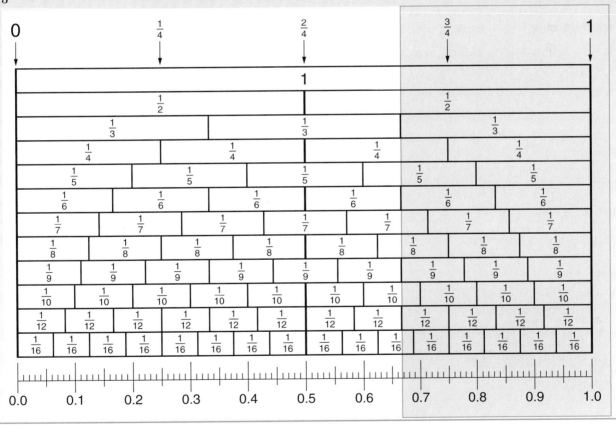

CHECK YOUR UNDERSTANDING

Use the Fraction-Stick Chart to find an approximate decimal name for each fraction or mixed number.

1. $\frac{3}{10}$ 2. $\frac{7}{8}$ 3. $4\frac{1}{3}$ 4. $\frac{12}{16}$ 5. $1\frac{7}{9}$ 6. $\frac{2}{7}$

Check your answers on page 372.

Using Division

The following examples illustrate how to rename a fraction as a decimal by dividing its numerator by its denominator.

EXAMPLE Use partial-quotients division to rename $\frac{7}{8}$ as a decimal.

Step 1: Estimate the quotient.
It will be less than 1 but greater than $\frac{1}{2}$.

Step 2: Decide how many decimal places you want.
For measuring or solving everyday problems, two or three decimal places are usually enough. In this case, rename $\frac{7}{8}$ as a decimal with three decimal places.

Step 3: Rewrite the numerator with a 0 for each decimal place you want.
Rewrite the numerator, 7, as 7.000.

Step 4: Use partial-quotients division to divide the numerator by the denominator.
Divide 7.000 by 8. When you ignore the decimal point in 7.000, this means you divide 7000 by 8.

```
  8)7000    |
  − 6400    | 800
    600     |
  −  560    |  70
     40     |
  −   40  |___5
      0     875
```

Step 5: Use the estimate from Step 1 to place the decimal point in the quotient.
Since $\frac{7}{8}$ is between $\frac{1}{2}$ and 1, the decimal point should be placed before the 8: 0.875.

So, $\frac{7}{8} = 0.875$.

In this case, the answer worked out to exactly three decimal places. Sometimes you will find a decimal name that is only approximately equal to the fraction.

EXAMPLE Use partial-quotients division to rename $\frac{2}{3}$ as a decimal.

Step 1: Estimate the quotient.
It will be less than 1 but greater than $\frac{1}{2}$.

Step 2: Decide how many decimal places you want.
In this example, find a decimal equivalent with four decimal places.

Step 3: Rewrite the numerator with a 0 for each decimal place you want.
You want four decimal places, so write the numerator, 2, as 2.0000.

Step 4: Use partial-quotients division to divide the numerator by the denominator.

Divide 2.0000 by 3. When you ignore the decimal point in 2.0000, this means you divide 20000 by 3.

```
3)20000
 − 18000    6000
    2000
   − 1800     600
     200
    − 180      60
      20
     − 18       6
       2     6666
```

The algorithm shows that $20000 / 3 = 6666\frac{2}{3}$, which rounds to 6667.

Step 5: Use the estimate from Step 1 to place the decimal point in the quotient.
Since $\frac{2}{3}$ is between $\frac{1}{2}$ and 1, the decimal point should be placed before the first 6: 0.6667.

So, $\frac{2}{3} \approx 0.6667$.

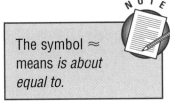

The symbol $\approx$ means *is about equal to*.

CHECK YOUR UNDERSTANDING

Use partial-quotients division to find decimal equivalents for these fractions.

1. $\frac{3}{8}$ (to 3 decimal places)   **2.** $\frac{1}{6}$ (to 3 decimal places)   **3.** $\frac{5}{9}$ (to 4 decimal places)

Check your answers on page 372.

EXAMPLE Use column division to rename $\frac{5}{8}$ as a decimal.

Step 1: Write $\frac{5}{8}$ as a division problem. Draw a line and make decimal points to show amounts smaller than 1. Write 0 in the first decimal place in the dividend to show there are 0 tenths.

Step 2: Since 5 ones cannot be shared 8 ways, trade the 5 ones for 50 tenths. Share the 50 tenths 8 ways. Each share is 6 tenths. There are 2 tenths left over.

```
       0 .  6
  8) 5 .  0
          50
         -48
           2
```

Step 3: Draw a line to show amounts smaller than 1 tenth. Write 0 to show there are no hundredths. Trade the 2 tenths for 20 hundredths. Share the 20 hundredths 8 ways. Each share is 2 hundredths. There are 4 hundredths left over.

```
       0 .  6    2
  8) 5 .  0    0
          50   20
         -48  -16
           2    4
```

Step 4: Draw another line and write another 0. Trade the 4 hundredths for 40 thousandths. Share the 40 thousandths 8 ways. Each share is 5 thousandths.

```
       0 .  6    2    5
  8) 5 .  0    0    0
          50   20   40
         -48  -16  -40
           2    4    0
```

The answer works out to exactly three decimal places.

$\frac{5}{8} = 0.625$

Sometimes a fraction's decimal equivalent repeats.

EXAMPLE Rename $\frac{2}{11}$ as a decimal.

The column-division algorithm keeps repeating. The digits 1 and 8 will repeat forever.

```
        0 .  1    8    1    8    1    8
  11) 2 .  0    0    0    0    0    0
          20   90   20   90   20   90
         -11  -88  -11  -88  -11  -88
           9    2    9    2    9    2
```

The decimal equivalent of $\frac{2}{11}$ can be written 0.18181818...

CHECK YOUR UNDERSTANDING

Use column division to find decimal equivalents for each fraction.

1. $\frac{1}{8}$ **2.** $\frac{5}{6}$ **3.** $\frac{8}{9}$

Check your answers on page 372.

Using a Calculator

You can also rename a fraction as a decimal by dividing the numerator by the denominator using a calculator.

EXAMPLES Rename $\frac{3}{4}$ and $\frac{7}{8}$ as decimals.

Key in: 3 ÷ 4 [Enter]	Key in: 7 ÷ 8 [Enter]
Answer: 0.75	Answer: 0.875
$\frac{3}{4} = 0.75$	$\frac{7}{8} = 0.875$

In some cases, the decimal takes up the entire calculator display. If one or more digits repeat, the decimal can be written by writing the repeating digit or digits just once and putting a bar over whatever digit or digits repeats.

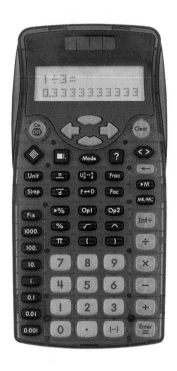

EXAMPLES

Fraction	Key in:	Calculator Display	Answer
$\frac{1}{3}$	1 ÷ 3 [Enter]	0.3333333333	$0.\overline{3}$
$\frac{2}{3}$	2 ÷ 3 [Enter]	0.6666666666 or 0.6666666667 (depending on the calculator)	$0.\overline{6}$
$\frac{1}{6}$	1 ÷ 6 [Enter]	0.1666666666 or 0.1666666667 (depending on the calculator)	$0.1\overline{6}$
$\frac{4}{9}$	4 ÷ 9 [Enter]	0.4444444444	$0.\overline{4}$
$\frac{6}{11}$	6 ÷ 11 [Enter]	0.5454545454 or 0.5454545455 (depending on the calculator)	$0.\overline{54}$
$\frac{7}{12}$	7 ÷ 12 [Enter]	0.5833333333	$0.58\overline{3}$

Some calculators have special keys for entering fractions and renaming them as decimals. For example, to rename $\frac{3}{5}$, you could key in 3 [n] 5 [d] [Enter] [F→D]. The result would be the same as if you had divided the numerator by the denominator.

CHECK YOUR UNDERSTANDING

Use a calculator to rename each fraction as a decimal.

1. $\frac{1}{8}$ **2.** $\frac{8}{12}$ **3.** $\frac{5}{12}$ **4.** $\frac{5}{6}$ **5.** $\frac{7}{9}$ **6.** $\frac{3}{16}$

Check your answers on page 372.

Renaming Fractions, Decimals, and Percents

Any rational number can be written as a fraction, a decimal, or a percent, but sometimes it's easier to work with a number written in one of these forms rather than another.

Renaming Decimals as Fractions

Every decimal equals some fraction whose denominator is a power of 10. To change a decimal to a fraction, use the place value of the rightmost digit as the denominator.

EXAMPLES

$0.4 = \frac{4}{10} = \frac{2}{5}$ $0.08 = \frac{8}{100} = \frac{4}{50} = \frac{2}{25}$ $0.25 = \frac{25}{100} = \frac{5}{20} = \frac{1}{4}$ $0.124 = \frac{124}{1,000} = \frac{62}{500} = \frac{31}{250}$

Some calculators have special keys for renaming decimals as fractions and for simplifying fractions.

EXAMPLE

To rename 0.48 as a fraction, key in: 0 ⊙ 48 (Enter) (F↔D). Answer: $\frac{48}{100}$

To simplify the fraction, key in: (Simp) (Enter) (Simp) (Enter). Answer: $\frac{12}{25}$

Renaming Fractions as Percents

One way to rename some fractions as percents is to first find an equivalent fraction with 100 as the denominator, and then write the fraction as a percent. For example, $\frac{3}{4} = \frac{75}{100} = 75\%$

Another way is to divide the numerator by the denominator of the fraction, then multiply the result by 100. You can do this with paper and pencil or with a calculator.

100%
large square

EXAMPLE Use a calculator to rename $\frac{3}{8}$ as a percent.

- Divide 3 by 8.
  Key in: 3 ÷ 8 (Enter) Answer: 0.375
- Multiply 0.375 by 100.
  Key in: 0 ⊙ 375 ✕ 100 (Enter) Answer: 37.5

So, $\frac{3}{8} = 37.5\%$.

256–257

Renaming Percents as Fractions

A percent can always be renamed as a fraction whose denominator is 100. The fraction can be renamed in simplest form if you want.

EXAMPLES

$40\% = \frac{40}{100} = \frac{2}{5}$ $85\% = \frac{85}{100} = \frac{17}{20}$ $150\% = \frac{150}{100} = \frac{3}{2} = 1\frac{1}{2}$

Renaming Percents as Decimals

A percent can be renamed as a decimal by first changing it to a fraction whose denominator is 100.

EXAMPLES

$75\% = \frac{75}{100} = 0.75$

$37.5\% = \frac{37.5}{100} = \frac{375}{1,000} = 0.375$

$300\% = \frac{300}{100} = 3$

Renaming Decimals as Percents

A decimal can be renamed as a percent by multiplying it by 100.

EXAMPLES

$0.35 = (0.35 * 100)\% = 35\%$
$1.2 = (1.2 * 100)\% = 120\%$
$0.0675 = (0.0675 * 100)\% = 6.75\%$

CHECK YOUR UNDERSTANDING

1. Rename each fraction as a percent.
   a. $\frac{1}{5}$ b. $\frac{7}{10}$ c. $\frac{5}{8}$ d. $1\frac{1}{4}$ e. $\frac{1}{3}$
2. Rename each percent as a fraction or mixed number.
   a. 60%   b. 35%   c. 250%
3. Rename each decimal as a fraction or mixed number. Check your answers on your calculator.
   a. 0.8   b. 0.25   c. 3.32   d. 0.028

Check your answers on page 372.

Addition and Subtraction of Decimals

Addition of Decimals

There are many ways to add and subtract decimals. One way is to use base-10 blocks. When working with decimals, use a flat as the ONE.

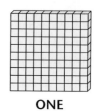

ONE

To add with base-10 blocks, count out blocks for each number, put all the blocks together, make any trades for larger blocks that you can, then count the blocks for the sum.

For example, to solve 2.34 + 1.27, you would first count out blocks for 2.34 and 1.27.

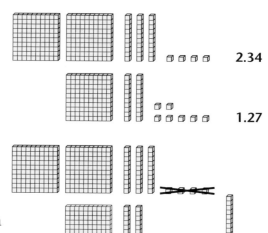

2.34

1.27

Since there are 11 cubes, you can trade 10 of them for 1 long.

By counting the blocks, you can see that 2.34 + 1.27 = 3.61.

Subtraction of Decimals

To subtract with base-10 blocks, count out blocks for the larger number, take away blocks for the smaller number, then count the remaining blocks.

For example, to solve 1.5 − 0.25, first count out blocks for 1.5.

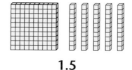

1.5

Since you need to take away 0.25, trade 1 long for 10 cubes.

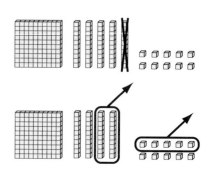

Next, take away 2 longs and 5 cubes (0.25).

The 1 flat, 2 longs, and 5 cubes that are left are worth 1.25.

So, 1.5 − 0.25 = 1.25.

Using the blocks is a good idea, especially at first, but they are not very efficient. Drawing pictures is usually easier and quicker.

EXAMPLE   1.61 + 4.7 = ?

First, draw pictures for each number.

Next, draw a ring around 10 longs to show that they can be traded for 1 flat.

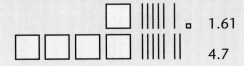

1.61

4.7

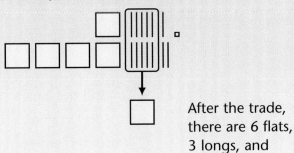

After the trade, there are 6 flats, 3 longs, and 1 cube.

This means that 1.61 + 4.7 = 6.31. This makes sense because 1.61 is near $1\frac{1}{2}$ and 4.7 is near $4\frac{1}{2}$, so the answer should be near 6, which it is.

So, 1.61 + 4.7 = 6.31.

Pictures of blocks are also useful for subtraction.

EXAMPLE   5.07 − 2.7 = ?

The picture at the right shows 5 flats and 7 cubes for 5.07. Then one of the flats was traded for 10 longs. Finally, 2 flats and 7 longs were taken away to show subtracting 2.7.

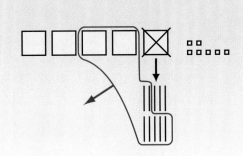

2 flats, 3 longs, and 7 cubes are left.

So, 5.07 − 2.7 = 2.37.

Decimals and Percents

Most paper-and-pencil methods for adding and subtracting whole numbers also work for decimals. The main difference is that you have to line up the places correctly, either by adding 0s to the end of the numbers or by lining up the ones place or the decimal points.

EXAMPLES $32.5 + 19.6 = ?$

Partial-Sums Method

	10s	1s		0.1s
	3	2	.	5
+	1	9	.	6

Add the tens.	$30 + 10 \rightarrow$	4 0 . 0
Add the ones.	$2 + 9 \rightarrow$	1 1 . 0
Add the tenths.	$0.5 + 0.6 \rightarrow$	1 . 1
Add the partial sums.	$40.0 + 11.0 + 1.1 \rightarrow$	5 2 . 1

Column-Addition Method

	10s	1s	0.1s
	3	2 .	5
+	1	9 .	6

Add each column. $\rightarrow$	4	11 .	11
Rename 11 ones and 11 tenths as 12 ones and 1 tenth. $\rightarrow$	4	12 .	1
Rename 4 tens and 12 ones as 5 tens and 2 ones. $\rightarrow$	5	2 .	1

$32.5 + 19.6 = 52.1$, using either method.

EXAMPLE $5.67 - 1.84 = ?$

Trade-First Method
First, write the problem in vertical format, being sure to line up the places correctly.

1s	0.1s	0.01s
5 .	6	7
− 1 .	8	4

Look at the 0.01s place. You can remove 4 hundredths from 7 hundredths. Look at the 0.1s place. You cannot remove 8 tenths from 6 tenths.

1s	0.1s	0.01s
4	16	
5̸ .	6̸	7
− 1 .	8	4

So, trade 1 one for 10 tenths.

1s	0.1s	0.01s
4	16	
5̸ .	6̸	7
− 1 .	8	4
3 .	8	3

Subtract in each column.

$5.67 - 1.84 = 3.83$

EXAMPLE   5.67 − 1.84 = ?

Left-to-Right Subtraction Method

There are no tens to subtract, so start with the ones.	5.67 − 1.00
	4.67
Then, subtract the tenths.	− 0.80
	3.87
Finally, subtract the hundredths.	− 0.04
	3.83

5.67 − 1.84 = 3.83

EXAMPLE   5.67 − 1.84 = ?

Counting-Up Method

There are many ways to count up from 1.84 to 5.67. Here is one.

		Add the numbers you circled.
1.84	Start with the smaller number.	
+⟨0.16⟩	Count to 2.00.	
2.00		
+⟨3.00⟩	Count to 5.00.	0.16
5.00		3.00
+⟨0.67⟩	Count to 5.67.	+ 0.67
5.67		3.83

You counted up by 3.83, so 5.67 − 1.84 = 3.83.

If you use a calculator, be sure to check your answer by first estimating, because it's easy to accidentally press a wrong key.

CHECK YOUR UNDERSTANDING

Add or subtract.

1. 3.78 + 5.24   **2.** 27.3 − 5.7   **3.** 9.6 + 2.06

Check your answers on page 372.

Units and Precision in Decimal Addition and Subtraction

Counts and measures always have units. For addition or subtraction, all the numbers must have the same unit. If they do not, before solving the problem you will have to convert at least one of the numbers so that all units are the same.

EXAMPLES Find the perimeter of the triangle.

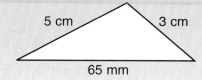

5 cm   3 cm
65 mm

Method 1
Convert the centimeter measures to millimeters, then add.
5 cm = 50 mm   3 cm = 30 mm
Perimeter = 50 mm + 30 mm + 65 mm = 145 mm

Method 2
Convert the millimeter measure to centimeters, then add.
65 mm = 6.5 cm
Perimeter = 5 cm + 3 cm + 6.5 cm = 14.5 cm

In most practical situations, all measures have the same degree of precision. If all the measures in a situation do not, convert them so that they all agree with the *least precise* measure.

EXAMPLE The *1994 Information Please Almanac* gives the winning times in the men's 100-meter dash in the 1936 and 1988 Olympic Games (shown at the right).

Year	Winner	Time
1936	Jesse Owens, U.S.A.	10.3 seconds
1988	Carl Lewis, U.S.A.	9.92 seconds

How much faster did Carl Lewis run than Jesse Owens?

Carl Lewis was timed to the nearest hundredth of a second; Jesse Owens was timed to the nearest tenth of a second.

Round the more precise measure, 9.92 seconds, to match the less precise measure, 10.3 seconds. 9.92 seconds rounded to the nearest tenth of a second is 9.9 seconds.

Since 10.3 − 9.9 = 0.4, Carl Lewis ran the 100-meter dash about 0.4 second faster than Jesse Owens.

CHECK YOUR UNDERSTANDING

1. Which measurement is less precise: 7.3 meters or 2.58 meters?

2. Solve. Use the degree of precision of the less precise measure.

   a. 7.3 m − 2.58 m   **b.** 9.867 sec − 9.85 sec

Check your answers on page 372.

Multiplying by Powers of 10

These are some powers of 10.

$10 * 10 * 10 * 10$	$10 * 10 * 10$	$10 * 10$	10	1	.	$\frac{1}{10}$	$\frac{1}{10} * \frac{1}{10}$	$\frac{1}{10} * \frac{1}{10} * \frac{1}{10}$	$\frac{1}{10} * \frac{1}{10} * \frac{1}{10} * \frac{1}{10}$
10,000	1,000	100	10	1	.	0.1	0.01	0.001	0.0001

Multiplying decimals by a positive power of 10 is easy. One way is to use partial-products multiplication.

EXAMPLE Solve $1,000 * 45.6$ by partial-products multiplication.

Step 1: Solve the problem as if there were no decimal point.

Step 2: Estimate the answer to $1,000 * 45.6$, and place the decimal point where it belongs.

$1,000 * 45 = 45,000$, so $1,000 * 45.6$, must be near 45,000.

So, the answer to $1,000 * 45.6$ is 45,600.

$$
\begin{array}{r}
1000 \\
* \quad 456 \\
\hline
\end{array}
$$

$400 * 1000 \rightarrow \quad 400000$
$50 * 1000 \rightarrow \quad 50000$
$6 * 1000 \rightarrow \quad + 6000$
$$\overline{456000}$$

Here is another method. This works for both positive and negative powers of 10.

EXAMPLES

	$1,000 * 45.6 = ?$	$0.001 * 45.6 = ?$
Step 1: Locate the decimal point in the power of 10.	$1,000 = 1000.$	0.001
Step 2: Move the decimal point to the LEFT or RIGHT until you get the number 1.	$1\,0\,0\,0.$	$0.0\,0\,1$
Step 3: Count the number of places you moved the decimal point.	3 places to the left	3 places to the right
† Step 4: Move the decimal point in the other factor the same number of places but in the OPPOSITE direction. Insert 0s as needed.	$45\,6\,0\,0.$	$0.0\,4\,5\,6$
	$1,000 * 45.6 = 45,600$	$0.001 * 45.6 = 0.0456$

---

† To help you decide whether to move the decimal point to the right or left, think: "Should the answer be *greater than* or *less than* the decimal I started with?" If the answer should be greater, move the decimal point to the right. If the answer should be less, move the decimal point to the left.

Powers of 10

10^4	10^3	10^2	10^1	10^0	.	10^{-1}	10^{-2}	10^{-3}	10^{-4}
10,000	1,000	100	10	1	.	0.1	0.01	0.001	0.0001

Here is another method for multiplying by a power of 10.

EXAMPLES $1,000 * 45.6 = ?$ $0.001 * 45.6 = ?$

Step 1: Think of the power of $1,000 = 10^3$ $0.001 = 10^{-3}$
10 in exponential notation.

Step 2: Note the number in $10^3_\uparrow$ $10^{-3}_\uparrow$
the exponent.

† **Step 3:** If the exponent is POSITIVE, $4\,5\,.\,6\,0\,0\,.$
move the decimal point in the other
factor that number of places to the
RIGHT. Insert 0s as needed.

If the exponent is NEGATIVE, $0\,.\,0\,4\,5\,.\,6$
move the decimal point in the other
factor that number of places to the
LEFT. Insert 0s as needed.

                                                 $1,000 * 45.6 = 45,600$ $0.001 * 45.6 = 0.0456$

---

† To help you decide whether to move the decimal point to the
right or left, think: "Should the answer be *greater than* or
less than the decimal I started with?" If the answer should be
greater, move the decimal point to the right. If the answer
should be less, move the decimal point to the left.

CHECK YOUR UNDERSTANDING

Multiply.

1. $100 * 3.45$ **2.** $0.01 * 3.45$ **3.** $0.16 * 10,000$ **4.** $5.09 * 0.1$

5. $0.55 * 0.001$ **6.** $1,000 * \$5.50$ **7.** $1.08 * 10$ **8.** $0.01 * 32.7$

Check your answers on page 372.

Multiplication of Decimals

You can use the same procedures for multiplying decimals as you use for whole numbers. The main difference is that with decimals you have to decide where to place the decimal point in the product.

Here is one way to multiply with decimals.

Step 1: Make a magnitude estimate of the product.

Step 2: Multiply the factors as if they were whole numbers, ignoring any decimal points. Use the multiplication algorithm you would use for whole numbers. The answer will be a whole number.

Step 3: Use your estimate of the product from Step 1 to place the decimal point accordingly.

> **N O T E**
>
> A *magnitude estimate* is a very rough estimate that answers questions like: *Is the solution in the ones? Tens? Hundreds? Thousands?* A magnitude estimate helps you judge whether the solution to a problem is "in the ballpark."

EXAMPLE $16.3 * 4.7 = ?$

Step 1: Estimate the product.

16.3 is a little more than 16 and 4.7 is between 4 and 5. Therefore, $16.3 * 4.7$ is between $4 * 16$, or 64, and $5 * 16$, or 80.

Step 2: Multiply. Ignore the decimal points.

$$
\begin{array}{rcr}
 & & 163 \\
 & & *\ 47 \\
\hline
40 * 100 & \rightarrow & 4000 \\
40 * 60 & \rightarrow & 2400 \\
40 * 3 & \rightarrow & 120 \\
7 * 100 & \rightarrow & 700 \\
7 * 60 & \rightarrow & 420 \\
7 * 3 & \rightarrow & +\ 21 \\
\hline
 & & 7661 \\
\end{array}
$$

Step 3: Use the estimate to place the decimal point in the product. Our estimate was that $16.3 * 4.7$ is between 64 and 80. Put a decimal point between the 6s in 7661.

So, $16.3 * 4.7 = 76.61$.

There is another way to find where to place the decimal point in the product. This method is especially useful when the factors are less than 1 and have many decimal places.

EXAMPLE   0.05 * 0.0062 = ?

Count the decimal places in each factor.	2 decimal places in 0.05 4 decimal places in 0.0062
Add the number of decimal places.	2 + 4 = 6
Multiply the factors as though they were whole numbers.	5 * 62 = 310
Start at the right of the product. Move left the necessary number of decimal places.	0.000310

Note that when these two numbers are multiplied as if they were whole numbers, there are only 3 digits in the product (5 * 62 = 310). It is necessary to insert 3 zeros in front of 310 in order to obtain 6 decimal places in the product, since the product of ten-thousandths times hundredths is millionths.

0.05 * 0.0062 = 0.000310

CHECK YOUR UNDERSTANDING

Multiply.

1. 3.9 * 5.7   **2.** 2.55 * 10.4   **3.** 0.63 * 4.04   **4.** 0.3 * 0.027

Check your answers on page 373.

Lattice Multiplication with Decimals

Lattice multiplication can be used to multiply decimals.

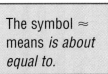

EXAMPLE Find 45.5 * 3.06 using lattice multiplication.

Step 1: Estimate the answer. $45.5 * 3.06 \approx 45 * 3 = 135$

Step 2: Draw the lattice and write the factors, including the decimal points, at the top and right side. In the factor above the grid, the decimal point should be above a column line. In the factor on the right side of the grid, the decimal point should be to the right of a row line.

Step 3: Find the products inside the lattice.

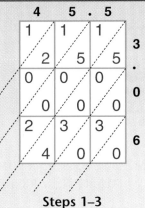

Steps 1–3

Step 4: Add along the diagonals, moving from right to left.

Step 5: Locate the decimal point in the answer as follows. Slide the decimal point in the factor above the grid down along the column line. Slide the decimal point in the factor on the right side of the grid across the row line until they meet on a diagonal line. Slide the decimal point down along the diagonal line to its end. Write a decimal point there in the answer area.

Step 6: Compare the result with the estimate from Step 1.

The product, 139.230, is very close to the estimate of 135.

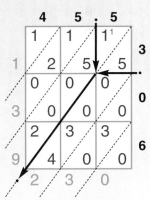

Steps 4–6

EXAMPLE Find 84.5 * 11.6 using lattice multiplication.

A good magnitude estimate is $84.5 * 11.6 \approx 85 * 10 = 850$. The answer to 84.5 * 11.6 should be in the hundreds. (*In the hundreds* means between 100 and 1,000.)

The product, 980.20, and the magnitude estimate, 850, are both in the hundreds.

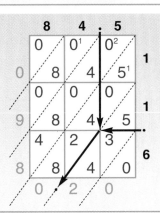

CHECK YOUR UNDERSTANDING

Draw a lattice for each problem and multiply.

1. 24.5 * 3.5   **2.** 3.02 * 19   **3.** 6.7 * 25.2

Check your answers on page 373.

Dividing by Powers of 10

Some Powers of 10

10^4	10^3	10^2	10^1	10^0	.	10^{-1}	10^{-2}	10^{-3}	10^{-4}
10,000	1,000	100	10	1	.	0.1	0.01	0.001	0.0001

Dividing by a power of 10 is easy. Here is one method.

EXAMPLES

45.6 / 1,000 = ?   45.6 / 0.001 = ?

Step 1: Locate the decimal point in the power of 10.

1,000 = 1000.   0.001

Step 2: Move the decimal point to the LEFT or RIGHT until you get the number 1.

1 0 0 0.   0 0 0 1.

Step 3: Count the number of places you moved the decimal point.

3 places to the left   3 places to the right

† Step 4: Move the decimal point in the other factor the same number of places and in the SAME direction. Insert 0s as needed.

0 0 4 5 6   4 5 6 0 0.

45.6 / 1,000 = 0.0456   45.6 / 0.001 = 45,600

† To help you decide whether to move the decimal point to the right or left, think: "Should the answer be *greater than* or *less than* the decimal I started with?" If the answer should be greater, move the decimal point to the right. If the answer should be less, move the decimal point to the left.

CHECK YOUR UNDERSTANDING

Divide.

1. 67.8 / 10

2. 67.8 / 0.1

3. 0.54 / 100

4. $290 / 1,000

5. 7.75 / 0.001

6. 40 / 10,000

7. 37.5 / 0.01

8. 0.02 / 0.001

Check your answers on page 373.

Here is another method for dividing by a power of 10.

EXAMPLES	45.6 / 1,000 = ?	45.6 / 0.001 = ?
Step 1: Think of the power of 10 in exponential notation.	$1,000 = 10^3$	$0.001 = 10^{-3}$
Step 2: Note the number in the exponent.	$10^{\overset{\uparrow}{3}}$	$10^{\overset{\uparrow}{-3}}$
† **Step 3:** If the exponent is POSITIVE, move the decimal point in the other factor that number of places to the LEFT. Insert 0s as needed.	0 . 0 4 5 . 6	
If the exponent is NEGATIVE, move the decimal point in the other factor that number of places to the RIGHT. Insert 0s as needed.		4 5 . 6 0 0 .
	45.6 / 1,000 = 0.0456	45.6 / 0.001 = 45,600

† To help you decide whether to move the decimal point to the right or left, think: "Should the answer be *greater than* or *less than* the decimal I started with?" If the answer should be greater, move the decimal point to the right. If the answer should be less, move the decimal point to the left.

CHECK YOUR UNDERSTANDING

Divide.

1. 67.8 / 10   **2.** 67.8 / 0.1   **3.** 0.54 / 100   **4.** $290 / 1,000

5. 7.75 / 0.001   **6.** 40 / 10,000   **7.** 37.5 / 0.01   **8.** 0.02 / 0.001

Check your answers on page 373.

Division of Decimals

One way to divide decimals uses the same basic procedure as for division of whole numbers.

$$\boxed{\text{dividend / divisor = quotient}}$$

Step 1: Estimate the quotient.

Step 2: Divide as if the divisor and dividend were whole numbers.

Step 3: Use your estimate from Step 1 to place the decimal point in the quotient correctly.

EXAMPLE 97.24 / 23 = ?

Step 1: Estimate the quotient.

97.24 is about 100, and 23 is about 25. 100 / 25 = 4, so 97.24 / 23 should be about 4.

Step 2: Divide, ignoring the decimal points.

If there is a remainder, round the answer to the nearest whole number.

```
23)9724
  − 9200   400
     524
   − 460    20
      64
    − 46     2
      18   422
```

$9724 / 23 = 422\frac{18}{23} \approx 423$

Step 3: Use the estimate from Step 1 to place the decimal point.

Since the estimate is that the quotient should be about 4, the decimal point should be placed between the 4 and the 2 in 423.

So, 97.24 / 23 = 4.23.

NOTE

People sometimes believe that "division makes numbers smaller" and "multiplication makes numbers larger." While this is true for numbers that are greater than 1, it is false for numbers that are less than 1.

• When a positive number is multiplied by a number that is less than 1, the product is smaller: $8 * 0.5 = 4$.

• When a positive number (the dividend) is divided by a number that is less than 1 (the divisor), the quotient will be greater than the dividend: $8 / 0.5 = 16$.

You can use the same method when dividing by a decimal.

EXAMPLE 8.25 / 0.3 = ?

Step 1: Estimate the quotient.

Since 8.25 is being divided by 0.3, which is less than 1, the answer must be greater than 8.25. 0.3 is about $\frac{1}{3}$ and 8.25 is about 8. If each of 8 pieces is divided into thirds, there will be 24 pieces, that is, $8 / \frac{1}{3} = 24$. So 8.25 / 0.3 should be about 24.

Step 2: Divide, ignoring the decimal points.

Step 3: Use the estimate from Step 1 to place the decimal point.

Since the estimate was about 24, place the decimal point between the 7 and the 5 in 275.

```
  3)825
  - 600      200
    225
  - 210       70
     15
  -  15        5
      0      275
   825 / 3 = 275
```

So, 8.25 / 0.3 = 27.5.

To rename a fraction as a decimal, you can divide the numerator by the denominator.

EXAMPLE Rename $\frac{3}{4}$ as a decimal.

Step 1: Estimate the quotient. It must be less than 1 but greater than $\frac{1}{2}$.

Step 2: Rewrite 3 as 3.00.

Step 3: Divide, ignoring the decimal point.

Step 4: Use the estimate from Step 1 to place the decimal point in the quotient.

0.75

```
  4)300
  - 200       50
    100
  - 100       25
      0       75
   300 / 4 = 75
```

So, $\frac{3}{4} = 0.75$.

CHECK YOUR UNDERSTANDING

Divide.

1. 9.6 / 3.2   **2.** 7.68 / 2.4   **3.** 56.8 / 0.1   **4.** 5 / 8

Check your answers on page 373.

Division with Many Decimal Places

Sometimes division problems involve decimals with many decimal places. Estimating the quotient is difficult. In such cases, find an equivalent division problem that is easier to solve.

Step 1: Think about the division problem as a fraction.

Step 2: Use the multiplication rule to find an equivalent fraction with no decimals.

Step 3: Think of this equivalent fraction as a division problem.

Step 4: Solve the equivalent problem using partial-quotients division or another method.

The answer to the original problem is the same as the answer to the equivalent problem.

EXAMPLE 2.05 / 0.004 = ?

Step 1: Think of the division problem as a fraction.

$$2.05 / 0.004 = \frac{2.05}{0.004}$$

Step 2: Find an equivalent fraction with no decimals.

$$\frac{2.05}{0.004} * \frac{1,000}{1,000} = \frac{2,050}{4}$$

Step 3: Think of this equivalent fraction as a division problem.

$$\frac{2,050}{4} = 2,050 / 4$$

Step 4: Solve the equivalent problem.

```
  4)2,050
  - 2,000  | 500
      50
    - 48   |  12
       2     512
```

$$2,050 / 4 = 512\frac{2}{4} = 512\frac{1}{2} = 512.5$$

Since the two fractions, $\frac{2.05}{0.004}$ and $\frac{2,050}{4}$, are equivalent, the answer to 2.05 / 0.004 is the same as the answer to 2,050 / 4.

So, 2.05 / 0.004 = 512.5.

Column Division with Decimal Quotients

Column division can be used to find quotients that have a decimal part. Think of sharing $50 among 8 people.

EXAMPLE   8)50 = ?

Step 1: Set the problem up. Draw a line to separate the digits in the dividend. Work left to right. Think of the 5 in the tens column as 5 $10 bills.

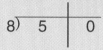

Step 2: The 5 $10 bills cannot be shared by 8 people. So trade them for 50 $1 bills. Think of the 0 in the ones column as 0 $1 bills. That makes 50 + 0, or 50 $1 bills in all.

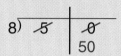

Step 3: If 8 people share 50 $1 bills, each person gets 6 $1 bills. There are 2 $1 bills left over.

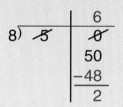

Step 4: Draw a line and make decimal points to show amounts smaller than $1. Write 0 in the first decimal place in the dividend to show there are 0 dimes. Then trade the 2 $1 bills for 20 dimes.

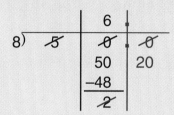

Step 5: If 8 people share 20 dimes, each person gets 2 dimes. There are 4 dimes left over. Draw another line and write another 0 in the dividend to show pennies.

```
          6 ┊   2  │
8) 5̶ │ 0̶ ┊ 0̶ │ 0
     │ 50 ┊ 20 │
     │-48 │-16 │
     │ 2̶ │  4 │
```

Step 6: Trade the 4 dimes for 40 pennies.

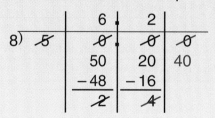

Step 7: If 8 people share 40 pennies, each person gets 5 pennies.

```
          6 ┊   2  │  5
8) 5̶ │ 0̶ ┊ 0̶ │ 0̶
     │ 50│ 20 │ 40
     │-48│-16 │-40
     │ 2̶ │  4̶ │  0
```

The column division shows that 50 / 8 = 6.25.
This means that $50 shared among 8 people is $6.25 each.

Rounding Decimals

Sometimes numbers have more digits than you need. Rounding is a way to get rid of unnecessary digits. Rounding also helps in making estimates since it makes numbers easier to use.

Here is one way to round decimals.

Step 1: Find the digit in the place to which you are rounding.

Step 2: Rewrite the number, replacing all digits to the right of this digit with zeros. This is the lower number.

Step 3: Add 1 to the digit in the place to which you are rounding. This is the higher number. If the sum is 10, write 0 and add 1 to the digit to its left.

Step 4: Ask, "Is the number I am rounding closer to the lower number or to the higher number?"

Step 5: Round to the closer of the two numbers. If it is halfway between the higher and the lower number, round to the higher number. Drop any trailing 0s on the right side.

EXAMPLES	Round the decimals to the nearest place.		
	2.851 (nearest tenth)	**8.35** (nearest tenth)	**2.851** (nearest hundredth)
Step 1: Find the place to which you are rounding.	2.851	8.35	2.851
Step 2: Find the lower number.	2.800	8.30	2.850
Step 3: Find the higher number.	2.900	8.40	2.860
Step 4: Is it closer to the lower or higher number?	higher	halfway	lower
Step 5: Round to the closer number.	2.900 = 2.9	8.40 = 8.4	2.850 = 2.85

CHECK YOUR UNDERSTANDING

Round the numbers below to the nearest tenth, hundredth, and thousandth.

1. 5.7946   2. 3.2079   3. 1.0298

Check your answers on page 373.

Percents

A percent is another way to name a fraction or decimal.
Percent means *per hundred* or *out of a hundred*. The word
percent comes from the Latin *per centum: per* means *for* and
centum means *one hundred.*

The statement "40% of students were absent" means that
40 out of 100 students were absent. This does *not* mean that
there were exactly 100 students and that 40 of them were
absent. It does mean that *for every* 100 students, 40 students
were absent.

A percent usually represents a percent of something. The
"something" is the whole (or ONE, or 100%). In the statement,
"40% of the students were absent," the whole is the total
number of students in the school.

Percents are used in many ways in everyday life:

• *Business:* "75% off" means that the price of an item
  will be reduced by 75 cents for every 100 cents the
  item usually costs.

> Sale—75% Off
> Everything Must Go

• *Statistics:* "45% voter turnout" means that
  45 out of every 100 registered voters
  actually voted.

> Voter Turnout Pegged at 45% of Registered Voters

• *School:* A 90% score on a spelling
  test means that a student scored
  90 out of 100 possible points for that
  test. One way to score 90% is to spell 90 words correctly out
  of 100. Another way to score 90% is to spell 9 words correctly
  out of 10.

• *Probability:* A "20% chance of snow" means that for every
  100 days that have similar weather conditions, you would
  expect it to snow on 20 of the days.

> For Tuesday, there is a 20%
> chance of snow.

Percents That Name Part of a Whole

Fractions, decimals, and percents are simply different ways to write numbers. Any number can be written in any of these three ways.

EXAMPLE

The amounts shown in the pictures below can be written as $\frac{3}{4}$, 75%, or 0.75.

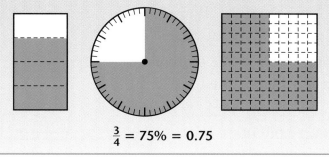

$$\frac{3}{4} = 75\% = 0.75$$

Percents are another way of naming fractions with a denominator of 100.

> You can think of the fraction $\frac{50}{100}$ as 50 parts per hundred, or 50 out of every 100, and write 50%.
>
> You can rename the fraction $\frac{1}{4}$ as $\frac{1*25}{4*25}$, or $\frac{25}{100}$, or 25%.
>
> 20% can be written as $\frac{20}{100}$, or $\frac{1}{5}$.

Percents are another way of naming decimals in terms of hundredths.

> Since 0.01 can be written as $\frac{1}{100}$, you could think of 0.62 as $\frac{62}{100}$, or 62%.
>
> 47% means 47 hundredths, or 0.47.

Percents can also be used to name the whole.

> 100 out of 100 can be written as the fraction $\frac{100}{100}$, or 100 hundredths. This is the same as 1 whole, or 100%.

Finding a Percent of a Number

Finding a percent of a number is a basic problem that comes up over and over again.

A backpack that regularly sells for $40 is on sale for 20% off. What is the sale price?

The sales tax on food is 5%. What is the tax on $60 worth of groceries?

A borrower pays 10% interest on a car loan. If the loan is $5,000, how much is the interest?

There are many ways to find the percent of a number.

Use a Fraction

Some percents are equivalent to "easy" fractions. For example, it is usually easier to find 25% of a number by thinking of 25% as $\frac{1}{4}$.

EXAMPLE   What is 25% of 64?

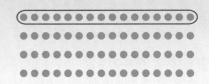

Think: 25% = $\frac{1}{4}$, so 25% of 64 is the same as $\frac{1}{4}$ of 64.
If you divide 64 into 4 equal groups, each group has 16.

So, 25% of 64 is 16.

Use Decimal Multiplication

Finding a percent of a number is the same as multiplying the number by the percent. Usually, it's easiest to change the percent to a decimal and use a calculator.

EXAMPLE   What is 35% of 65?

35% of 65 is the same as 0.35 ∗ 65.
Using a calculator, we find 0.35 ∗ 65 = 22.75.

So, 35% of 65 is 22.75.

CHECK YOUR UNDERSTANDING

Solve.

1. A backpack that regularly sells for $45 is on sale for 28% off. What is the sale price?

2. The sales tax on food is 3%. What is the tax on $65 worth of groceries?

Check your answers on page 373.

Unit Percents

Unit percent is another name for 1%.

Finding a Percent of a Number

> **EXAMPLE**   What is 7% of 400?
>
> $1\% = \frac{1}{100}$, so 1% of 400 is the same as $\frac{1}{100}$ of 400. If you divide
> 400 into 100 equal groups, there are 4 in each group.
> So, 1% of 400 is 4. Then 7% of 400 is 7 * 4, or 28.
>
> So, 7% of 400 = 28.

Sometimes it might be helpful to find 10% first.

> **EXAMPLE**   What is 30% of 70?
>
> 10% of 70 is $\frac{1}{10}$ of 70.
> If you divide 70 into 10 equal groups, each group has 7.
> So, 10% of 70 is 7. Then 30% of 70 is 3 * 7, or 21.
>
> So, 30% of 70 = 21.

Finding the Whole

Unit percents are used in solving problems in which the part of
the whole is given as a percent and you need to find the whole.

> **EXAMPLE**   Ms. Partee spends $1,000 a month. $1,000 is 80%
> of her monthly earnings. How much does she earn per month?
>
> **Step 1:** Find 1% of her monthly earnings.
>
> $1,000 is 80% of her monthly earnings. Therefore, to find 1%
> of her earnings, divide $1,000 by 80. $1,000 / 80 = $12.50
> So, $12.50 is 1% of her monthly earnings.
>
> **Step 2:** Find her total monthly earnings.
>
> To find her total monthly earnings (or 100% of her monthly
> earnings), multiply $12.50 by 100. $12.50 * 100 = $1,250
>
> So, Ms. Partee earns $1,250 per month.

```
           100%
  monthly earnings
```

CHECK YOUR UNDERSTANDING

All bicycles at Art's Cycle Shop are on sale at 75% of the regular price.
If the sale price of a bicycle is $150, how much did the bicycle cost before
it was put on sale?

Check your answer on page 373.

Using Proportions to Solve Percent Problems

Many percent problems can be solved using proportions. Using proportions is not always the best approach, but it almost always works.

To solve a percent problem with proportions, start with this number model:

$$\frac{\text{part}}{\text{whole}} = \frac{\text{percent}}{100}$$

Often you can find two of the three unknowns in this number model right away, usually just by reading the problem. Then you can use what you know about solving proportions to find the third unknown.

Finding the Percent

EXAMPLE   Jennifer Azzi made 30 of 58 3-point shots in the 1999 WNBA season. What was her 3-point shooting percentage?

Step 1: Write a proportion. Find two of the three unknowns by reading the problem.

$$\frac{\text{part}}{\text{whole}} = \frac{\text{percent}}{100}$$

$$\frac{\text{shots made}}{\text{shots attempted}} = \frac{\text{shooting percentage}}{100}$$

$$\frac{30}{58} = \frac{\text{shooting percentage}}{100}$$

Step 2: Find the cross products and set them equal.

shooting percentage $* 58 = 30 * 100$

Step 3: Solve the equation.

shooting percentage $* 58 / 58 = 30 * 100 / 58$

shooting percentage $= 30 * 100 / 58 = 51.7$

So, Azzi made 51.7% of her 3-point shots.

You can also use the three steps shown above to solve percent problems in which you have to find the whole or the part. You will find examples of these problems on the following page.

Finding the Whole

> **EXAMPLE**   Regina bought a CD on sale for $9. This was 25% off the everyday price. What was the everyday price for the CD?
>
> $$\frac{\text{part}}{\text{whole}} = \frac{\text{percent}}{100}$$
>
> $$\frac{\text{sale price}}{\text{everyday price}} = \frac{\text{percent paid}}{100}$$
>
> Since Regina got 25% off, she paid only 75% of the everyday price.
>
> $$\frac{\$9}{\text{everyday price}} = \frac{75}{100}$$
>
> $9 * 100 = $ everyday price $* 75$
>
> $9 * 100 / 75 = $ everyday price $* 75 / 75$
>
> $9 * 100 / 75 = $ everyday price
>
> $12 = $ everyday price
>
> So, the everyday price of the CD was $12.

Finding the Part

> **EXAMPLE**   Dana Barros made 40% of his 160 3-point attempts in the 1999–2000 NBA season. How many 3-point shots did he make?
>
> $$\frac{\text{part}}{\text{whole}} = \frac{\text{percent}}{100}$$
>
> $$\frac{\text{shots made}}{\text{shots attempted}} = \frac{\text{shooting percentage}}{100}$$
>
> $$\frac{\text{shots made}}{160} = \frac{40}{100}$$
>
> shots made $* 100 = 160 * 40$
>
> shots made $* 100 / 100 = 160 * 40 / 100$
>
> shots made $= 160 * 40 / 100 = 64$
>
> So, Barros made 64 3-point shots.

CHECK YOUR UNDERSTANDING

Use proportions to solve these problems.

1. A dress is on sale for 20% off. The everyday price is $45. What is the sale price?

2. Ukari Figgs's free-throw shooting percentage for the 1999 WNBA season was 87.5%. Figgs attempted 24 free throws. How many did she make?

Check your answers on page 373.

Fractions & Rational Numbers

Positive Rational Numbers

Whole numbers work fine for counting, but there are times when people need numbers that are between consecutive whole numbers. Thousands of years ago, this led to the invention of positive rational numbers such as $\frac{2}{3}$ and 47.5.

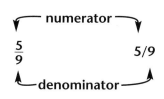

The stone must be exactly five and two-thirds cubits high.

Notation

Positive rational numbers can be written as fractions, as decimals, and as percents. Even though these three types of notation are interchangeable, each way of writing numbers has a different way of doing standard operations.

A fraction consists of a numerator and a denominator. In simple cases, the denominator indicates the number of equal divisions, or parts, of some ONE or whole, and the numerator indicates the number of parts named by the fraction. In these simple cases, the denominator may be any whole number except zero, and the numerator may be any whole number.

numerator

$\frac{5}{9}$ 5/9

denominator

A fraction may be used to indicate division of *any* two numbers (except division by zero), not just whole numbers. The numerator or denominator of a fraction might be a decimal, a fraction, or a mixed number.

$\frac{2.3}{6.5}$ $\frac{1\frac{4}{5}}{12}$ $\frac{\frac{3}{4}}{\frac{5}{8}}$

Divisions shown by fractions

If you look in any high school mathematics book, you will see numbers such as $\sqrt{2}$ or $\frac{4\pi}{3}$. These are **irrational numbers.** One way in which irrational numbers differ from rational numbers is that they cannot be written as decimals that terminate, such as 2.25, or as decimals that have one or more repeating digits, such as 0.66666.... Decimals that name irrational numbers go on without end, without any repeating pattern in the digits.

In *Everyday Mathematics,* all fractions represent rational numbers unless you are specifically told otherwise.

Relations

Fractions that name the same rational number are called **equivalent fractions.** Common denominators can be used to determine which of two fractions is greater or whether two fractions are equivalent. Simply rename one or both fractions as equivalent fractions with a common denominator and compare the numerators. Another way to compare two fractions is to convert both to decimal form.

Operations

The basic operations of arithmetic—addition, subtraction, multiplication, and division—apply to fractions as well as whole numbers.

Addition and Subtraction	Simply rename the fractions as fractions with a common denominator. Then add or subtract the numerators. Write the result over the common denominator.	$\frac{2}{3} + \frac{1}{4} = \frac{8}{12} + \frac{3}{12} = \frac{11}{12}$ $\frac{5}{8} - \frac{1}{2} = \frac{5}{8} - \frac{4}{8} = \frac{1}{8}$
Multiplication	Multiply the numerators, and multiply the denominators.	$\frac{2}{5} * \frac{1}{3} = \frac{2 * 1}{5 * 3} = \frac{2}{15}$
Reciprocals	For any rational number except 0, you can find another rational number so that the product of the two numbers is 1. The numbers whose product is 1 are called **multiplicative inverses,** or **reciprocals,** of each other. Reciprocals are useful when dividing fractions and in simplifying certain complicated fractions.	
	The reciprocal of any fraction, $\frac{a}{b}$, is the fraction $\frac{b}{a}$. For example, the reciprocal of $\frac{3}{4}$ is $\frac{4}{3}$ because $\frac{3}{4} * \frac{4}{3} = 1$.	If $a \neq 0$ and $b \neq 0$, then $\frac{a}{b} * \frac{b}{a} = 1$.
	Since any whole number can be written as a fraction with a denominator of 1, the reciprocal of any whole number (except 0) is a fraction with 1 in the numerator and the whole number in the denominator. For example, $5 = \frac{5}{1}$ and the reciprocal of $\frac{5}{1}$ is $\frac{1}{5}$. Similarly, the reciprocal of any fraction, $\frac{1}{a}$, is the number a. For example, the reciprocal of $\frac{1}{4}$ is $\frac{4}{1}$, or simply 4.	If $a \neq 0$, then $a * \frac{1}{a} = 1$ $2 * \frac{1}{2} = 1$ $\frac{1}{3} * 3 = 1$
Division	Multiply the first fraction by the reciprocal of the second fraction.	$\frac{3}{8} \div \frac{1}{4} = \frac{3}{8} * \frac{4}{1} = \frac{12}{8}$ $= 1\frac{4}{8} = 1\frac{1}{2}$
	Another way to divide two fractions is to rename the fractions as fractions with a common denominator and then divide the numerators.	$\frac{3}{8} \div \frac{1}{4} = \frac{3}{8} \div \frac{2}{8}$ $= 3 \div 2 = 1\frac{1}{2}$

Fractions

Notation

A fraction is a number $\frac{a}{b}$, where the **numerator** a can be any number at all and the **denominator** b is any number except zero.

$$\frac{a}{b} \quad \begin{array}{l} \leftarrow\text{numerator} \\ \leftarrow\text{denominator} \end{array} \qquad b \neq 0$$

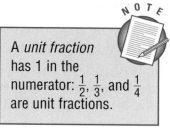

A *unit fraction* has 1 in the numerator: $\frac{1}{2}, \frac{1}{3},$ and $\frac{1}{4}$ are unit fractions.

Equivalent Names

A number can be written as a fraction in infinitely many ways by multiplying or dividing both the numerator and the denominator by the same (nonzero) number. Every fraction also has a decimal name and a percent name, which can be found by dividing the numerator by the denominator.

| $\frac{1}{2}$, | $\frac{2}{4}$, | $\frac{3}{6}$, | $\frac{4}{8}$, | $\frac{5}{10}$, | $\frac{6}{12}$, | $\frac{7}{14}$, | $\frac{8}{16}$, | $\frac{9}{18}$, | $\frac{10}{20}$, | $\frac{11}{22}$, | $\frac{12}{24}$, | $\frac{13}{26}$, | $\frac{14}{28}$, | $\frac{15}{30}$ | 0.5 | 50% |
| $\frac{1}{3}$, | $\frac{2}{6}$, | $\frac{3}{9}$, | $\frac{4}{12}$, | $\frac{5}{15}$, | $\frac{6}{18}$, | $\frac{7}{21}$, | $\frac{8}{24}$, | $\frac{9}{27}$, | $\frac{10}{30}$, | $\frac{11}{33}$, | $\frac{12}{36}$, | $\frac{13}{39}$, | $\frac{14}{42}$, | $\frac{15}{45}$ | $0.\overline{3}$ | $33\frac{1}{3}\%$ |

Using Equivalent Names

Two fractions can be compared, added, or subtracted by using fractions with the same denominator. You can also use the decimal names to decide which is larger or smaller and to add and subtract.

$\frac{2}{3} < \frac{3}{4}$ since $\frac{8}{12} < \frac{9}{12}$ and $0.\overline{6} < 0.75$.

$$\frac{2}{3} + \frac{1}{6} = \frac{4}{6} + \frac{1}{6} = \frac{5}{6} \qquad \frac{3}{4} - \frac{3}{5} = 0.75 - 0.60 = 0.15$$

Uses

Parts of Wholes

Fractions are used to name a part of a whole object or a part of a collection of objects.

$\frac{5}{6}$ of the hexagon is green.

$\frac{6}{10}$ of the dimes are circled.

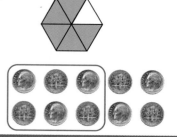

Points on Number Lines

Fractions can name points on a number line that are between whole numbers.

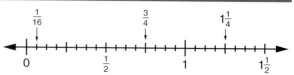

"In-Between" Measures

Fractions can name measures that are between whole measures.

Division Notation

A fraction $\frac{a}{b}$ is another way of saying a divided by b.

$$\frac{a}{b} \qquad a/b$$

$$a \div b \qquad b\overline{)a}$$

Ratios

Fractions are used to compare quantities with the same unit.

King won 14 out of 18 ($\frac{14}{18}$, or about 78%) games during last year's basketball season.

PUBLIC-RED CENTRAL		
	Conf.	Overall
Dunbar	4–0	9–6
King	4–1	14–4
Robeson	3–2	8–9
Gage Park	2–3	8–10
Harper	2–3	8–7
Curie	1–3	7–10
Hubbard	1–4	8–9

Rates

Fractions are used to compare quantities with different units.

Luke's car can travel about 36 miles on 1 gallon of gasoline. At this rate, it can travel about 324 miles on 9 gallons of gasoline.

$$\frac{36 \text{ mi}}{1 \text{ gal}} = \frac{324 \text{ mi}}{9 \text{ gal}}$$

Scales

Fractions are used to compare a drawing or a model to the actual size of the object.

A scale on a map given as 1:100,000 (another way of expressing $\frac{1}{100,000}$) means that each inch on the map represents 100,000 inches, or about $1\frac{1}{2}$ miles.

$$\frac{\text{map distance}}{\text{real distance}} = \frac{1 \text{ inch}}{100,000 \text{ inches}}$$

Probabilities

Fractions are a way to describe the chance that an event will happen.

In a well-shuffled deck of 52 playing cards, the chance of selecting the ace of spades on a given draw is $\frac{1}{52}$, or about 2%. The chance of drawing any ace is $\frac{4}{52}$, or about 8%.

Renaming a Mixed or Whole Number as a Fraction

A mixed number, such as $2\frac{3}{4}$, names a number of wholes and a part of a whole. A mixed number is the sum of its whole-number part and its fraction part: $2\frac{3}{4} = 2 + \frac{3}{4}$.

This shows the mixed number $2\frac{3}{4}$.

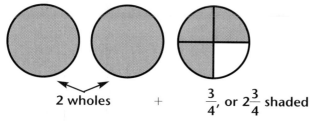

2 wholes $+$ $\frac{3}{4}$, or $2\frac{3}{4}$ shaded

A mixed number can be renamed as a fraction. Study the shortcut in the following example.

EXAMPLE Rename $2\frac{3}{4}$ as a fraction.

┌─Whole─┐

$$1 + 1 + \frac{3}{4} = \frac{4}{4} + \frac{4}{4} + \frac{3}{4}$$

$$2\frac{3}{4} = \frac{11}{4}$$

Shortcut:

Step 1: Multiply the whole-number part, 2, by the denominator of the fraction part, 4: $2 * 4 = 8$. This is the number of fourths in 2 wholes: $2 = \frac{8}{4}$.

Step 2: Add the numerator of the fraction part, 3, to the result, 8: $8 + 3 = 11$. This is the number of fourths in the mixed number $2\frac{3}{4}$.

So, $2\frac{3}{4} = \frac{8}{4} + \frac{3}{4} = \frac{11}{4}$.

CHECK YOUR UNDERSTANDING

Rename as a fraction.

1. $1\frac{2}{3}$ **2.** $4\frac{1}{2}$ **3.** $3\frac{3}{4}$ **4.** $2\frac{1}{2}$ **5.** $3\frac{2}{5}$ **6.** 4

Check your answers on page 373.

Renaming a Fraction as a Mixed or Whole Number

An **improper fraction** is a fraction that is greater than or equal to 1. Fractions like $\frac{4}{3}$, $\frac{5}{5}$, and $\frac{125}{10}$ are improper fractions. In an improper fraction, the numerator is greater than or equal to the denominator. In a **proper fraction,** the numerator is smaller than the denominator.

> **N O T E**
>
> For a mixed number to be in *simplest form,* the fraction part must be in simplest form.

Improper fractions can be renamed as mixed or whole numbers.

EXAMPLE Rename $\frac{23}{6}$ as a mixed number.

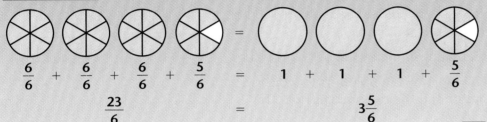

$$\frac{6}{6} + \frac{6}{6} + \frac{6}{6} + \frac{5}{6} = 1 + 1 + 1 + \frac{5}{6}$$

$$\frac{23}{6} = 3\frac{5}{6}$$

Shortcut: Divide the numerator, 23, by the denominator, 6.

- The quotient, 3, is the whole-number part of the mixed number. It tells how many wholes there are in $\frac{23}{6}$.

- The remainder, 5, is the numerator of the fraction part. It tells how many sixths there are left that cannot be made into wholes.

$$6\overline{)23} \quad \begin{array}{c} 3 \\ \end{array}$$
$$\underline{-18} \quad \begin{array}{|c} 3 \\ \end{array}$$
$$5 \quad 3$$

$\frac{23}{6}$ gives 3 R5.

$$\frac{23}{6} = 3\frac{5}{6}$$

Some calculators have a special key for renaming fractions as whole numbers or mixed numbers.

253

EXAMPLE Use a calculator to rename $\frac{23}{6}$ as a mixed number.

Key in: 23 ⓝ 6 ⓓ (Enter)   Answer: $3\frac{5}{6}$

$$\frac{23}{6} = 3\frac{5}{6}$$

CHECK YOUR UNDERSTANDING

Rename each improper fraction as a mixed number or a whole number.

1. $\frac{6}{5}$ **2.** $\frac{21}{8}$ **3.** $\frac{24}{6}$ **4.** $\frac{11}{2}$ **5.** $\frac{15}{4}$ **6.** $\frac{20}{3}$

Check your answers on page 373.

Equivalent Fractions

Two fractions that name the same number are called **equivalent fractions.**

One way to rename a fraction as an equivalent fraction is to *multiply* the numerator and the denominator of the fraction by the same number.

EXAMPLE Rename $\frac{3}{4}$ as an equivalent fraction using multiplication.

The rectangle is divided into 4 equal parts. 3 of the parts are blue. $\frac{3}{4}$ of the rectangle is blue.

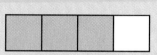

If each of the 4 parts is split into 2 equal parts, there are now 8 equal parts. 6 of them are blue. $\frac{6}{8}$ of the rectangle is blue.

$\frac{3}{4}$ and $\frac{6}{8}$ both name the same amount of the rectangle that is blue.

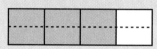

$\frac{3}{4} = \frac{6}{8}$

The number of parts in the rectangle was doubled. You can show this by multiplying the numerator and the denominator of $\frac{3}{4}$ by 2.

$\frac{3 * 2}{4 * 2} = \frac{6}{8}$

$\frac{3}{4}$ is equivalent to $\frac{6}{8}$.

If each part in the rectangle is divided into 3 equal parts, the number of parts is tripled. You can show this by multiplying the numerator and the denominator of $\frac{3}{4}$ by 3.

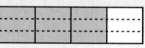

$\frac{9}{12}$ is equivalent to $\frac{3}{4}$.

$\frac{3 * 3}{4 * 3} = \frac{9}{12}$

Another way to rename a fraction as an equivalent fraction is to *divide* the numerator and the denominator of the fraction by the same number.

EXAMPLE Rename $\frac{6}{9}$ as an equivalent fraction using division.

$\frac{6}{9}$ of the region is green.   Divide the region into 3 equal parts. $\frac{2}{3}$ is green.

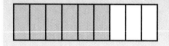

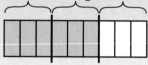

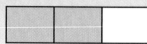

$\frac{6 \div 3}{9 \div 3} = \frac{2}{3}$

So $\frac{2}{3}$ is equivalent to $\frac{6}{9}$.

CHECK YOUR UNDERSTANDING

Rename each fraction as an equivalent fraction. Use multiplication for Problems 1–3 and division for Problems 4–6.

1. $\frac{1}{4}$ **2.** $\frac{4}{8}$ **3.** $\frac{3}{2}$ **4.** $\frac{9}{12}$ **5.** $\frac{8}{10}$ **6.** $\frac{12}{15}$

Check your answers on page 373.

Simplifying Fractions

When a fraction is renamed as an equivalent fraction with a smaller numerator and denominator, the new fraction is in **simpler form.** You can simplify a fraction by dividing its numerator and denominator by a common factor greater than 1.

EXAMPLE Rename $\frac{8}{12}$ in simpler form.

First, find common factors of the numerator and the denominator.
2 and 4 are common factors of 8 and 12.
Then, divide the numerator and the denominator of $\frac{8}{12}$ by either 2 or 4.

$\frac{8 \div 2}{12 \div 2} = \frac{4}{6}$ $\frac{4}{6}$ is equivalent to $\frac{8}{12}$ and is in simpler form.

or

$\frac{8 \div 4}{12 \div 4} = \frac{2}{3}$ $\frac{2}{3}$ is equivalent to $\frac{8}{12}$ and is in simpler form.

$\frac{4}{6}$ and $\frac{2}{3}$ are simpler forms of $\frac{8}{12}$.

A proper fraction is in **simplest form** if it cannot be renamed in simpler form. You can rename a fraction in simplest form by dividing its numerator and denominator by the **greatest common factor** of both the numerator and the denominator. A fraction is in simplest form when 1 is the only common factor of both the numerator and the denominator.

Some calculators have a special key for renaming fractions in simpler form.

EXAMPLE Rename $\frac{8}{12}$ in simplest form.

Key in: 8 ⓝ 12 ⓓ Ⓢⓘⓜⓟ Ⓔⓝⓣⓔⓡ

The display shows $\frac{4}{6}$. If, without clearing the display, you press Ⓢⓘⓜⓟ Ⓔⓝⓣⓔⓡ again, the display will show $\frac{2}{3}$. If you press Ⓢⓘⓜⓟ Ⓔⓝⓣⓔⓡ one more time, the display will show $\frac{2}{3}$ again.

Therefore, $\frac{2}{3}$ is in simplest form. Try it on your calculator.

CHECK YOUR UNDERSTANDING

Write the fractions in Problems 1–3 in simpler form and those in Problems 4–6 in simplest form.

1. $\frac{4}{8}$ **2.** $\frac{12}{16}$ **3.** $\frac{20}{24}$ **4.** $\frac{9}{12}$ **5.** $\frac{12}{18}$ **6.** $\frac{20}{24}$

Check your answers on page 373.

Comparing Fractions

There are several strategies that can help in comparing fractions.

Use a Common Numerator	$\frac{5}{7} > \frac{5}{8}$ because sevenths are larger than eighths and there are 5 of each.	$\frac{5}{7} > \frac{5}{8}$
Compare to $\frac{1}{2}$	$\frac{4}{9}$ is less than $\frac{1}{2}$, and $\frac{3}{5}$ is more than $\frac{1}{2}$. So, $\frac{3}{5} > \frac{4}{9}$.	 $\frac{3}{5} > \frac{4}{9}$
Compare to 1	Both $\frac{3}{4}$ and $\frac{2}{3}$ are less than 1. But $\frac{3}{4}$ is closer to 1 because $\frac{1}{4}$ is less than $\frac{1}{3}$. This means $\frac{3}{4} > \frac{2}{3}$.	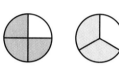 $\frac{3}{4} > \frac{2}{3}$
Use an Equivalent for One of the Fractions	To compare $\frac{2}{7}$ and $\frac{1}{4}$, change $\frac{1}{4}$ to $\frac{2}{8}$. Since $\frac{2}{8} < \frac{2}{7}$ (remember, the denominator names smaller pieces of the whole in fractions), you know that $\frac{1}{4} < \frac{2}{7}$.	$\frac{2}{7} > \frac{2}{8}$
Use a Common Denominator	To compare $\frac{3}{5}$ and $\frac{5}{8}$, rename both fractions with the **common denominator** 40. Since $\frac{24}{40} < \frac{25}{40}$, you know that $\frac{3}{5} < \frac{5}{8}$.	$\frac{3}{5} = \frac{3*8}{5*8} = \frac{24}{40}$ $\frac{5}{8} = \frac{5*5}{8*5} = \frac{25}{40}$
Convert to Decimals	To compare $\frac{13}{17}$ and $\frac{32}{41}$, use a calculator to convert both to decimals. Since $0.76... < 0.78...$, you know that $\frac{13}{17} < \frac{32}{41}$.	$\frac{13}{17} = 13 \div 17$ (Enter) 0.7647058824 $\frac{32}{41} = 32 \div 41$ (Enter) 0.7804878049

CHECK YOUR UNDERSTANDING

Compare. Use > or <.

1. $\frac{4}{7} \square \frac{2}{5}$ **2.** $\frac{10}{11} \square \frac{13}{14}$ **3.** $\frac{5}{9} \square \frac{3}{5}$ **4.** $\frac{17}{23} \square \frac{67}{93}$

Check your answers on page 373.

Fraction-Stick Chart

Each stick on the Fraction-Stick Chart represents 1 whole.
Each stick (except the 1-stick) is divided into equal pieces. Each
piece represents a fraction of 1 whole.

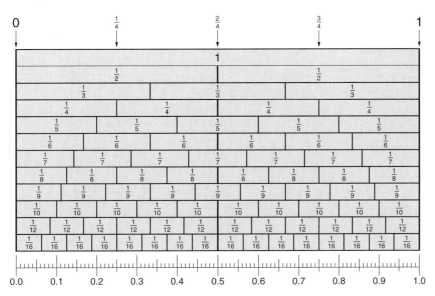

Locating a Fraction on the Fraction-Stick Chart

1. Select the stick shown by the denominator of the fraction.

2. Count the number of pieces shown by the numerator,
   starting at the left edge of the chart.

EXAMPLE Find $\frac{3}{4}$ on the Fraction-Stick Chart.

The "fourths" stick is divided into 4 pieces, each labeled $\frac{1}{4}$.
This stick can be used to locate fractions whose denominators are 4.
To locate the fraction $\frac{3}{4}$, count 3 pieces, starting at the left.

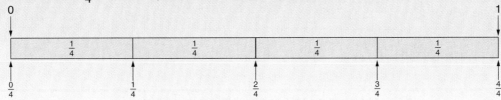

$\frac{3}{4}$ is located at the right edge of the third piece.

CHECK YOUR UNDERSTANDING

Locate each fraction on the Fraction-Stick Chart.

1. $\frac{1}{3}$ **2.** $\frac{5}{8}$ **3.** $\frac{5}{5}$ **4.** $\frac{10}{12}$ **5.** $\frac{0}{6}$ **6.** $\frac{4}{9}$

Finding Equivalent Fractions

EXAMPLE Find fractions that are equivalent to $\frac{2}{3}$.

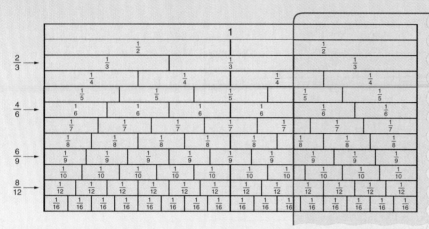

Step 1: Place one edge of a straightedge at $\frac{2}{3}$.

Step 2: Find all the pieces whose right edge touches the edge of the straightedge. The right edge of each of these pieces shows the location of a fraction that is equivalent to $\frac{2}{3}$.

$\frac{4}{6}$, $\frac{6}{9}$, and $\frac{8}{12}$ are equivalent to $\frac{2}{3}$.

Comparing Two Fractions

EXAMPLE Compare $\frac{4}{9}$ and $\frac{3}{8}$. Which is less?

Step 1: Place one edge of a straightedge at $\frac{4}{9}$.

Step 2: Locate $\frac{3}{8}$ on the "eighths" stick.

Step 3: $\frac{3}{8}$ is to the left of $\frac{4}{9}$.

$\frac{3}{8}$ is less than $\frac{4}{9}$.

CHECK YOUR UNDERSTANDING

Use the Fraction-Stick Chart to find an equivalent fraction for each fraction.

1. $\frac{2}{4}$ **2.** $\frac{4}{12}$ **3.** $\frac{3}{4}$ **4.** $\frac{10}{16}$ **5.** $\frac{4}{6}$

Which fraction is less? Use the Fraction-Stick Chart to decide.

6. $\frac{1}{10}$ or $\frac{1}{8}$ **7.** $\frac{3}{5}$ or $\frac{3}{7}$ **8.** $\frac{11}{12}$ or $\frac{15}{16}$ **9.** $\frac{5}{9}$ or $\frac{6}{10}$ **10.** $\frac{5}{8}$ or $\frac{2}{3}$

Check your answers on page 373.

Common Denominators

When solving problems that involve fractions with different denominators, rename the fractions so they have the same denominator. There are several methods for renaming fractions with a common denominator.

EXAMPLES Rename $\frac{3}{4}$ and $\frac{1}{6}$ with a common denominator.

Equivalent Fractions Method

List equivalent fractions for $\frac{3}{4}$ and $\frac{1}{6}$.

$\frac{3}{4} = \frac{6}{8} = \frac{9}{12} = \frac{12}{16} = \cdots$

$\frac{1}{6} = \frac{2}{12} = \frac{3}{18} = \frac{4}{24} = \cdots$

Both $\frac{3}{4}$ and $\frac{1}{6}$ can be renamed as fractions with the common denominator 12.

$\frac{3}{4} = \frac{9}{12}$ and $\frac{1}{6} = \frac{2}{12}$

The Multiplication Method

Multiply the numerator and the denominator of each fraction by the denominator of the other fraction.

$\frac{3}{4} = \frac{3*6}{4*6} = \frac{18}{24}$ $\frac{1}{6} = \frac{1*4}{6*4} = \frac{4}{24}$

Least Common Multiple Method

Find the least common multiple of the denominators.
Multiples of 4: 4, 8, **12**, 16, 20, ...
Multiples of 6: 6, **12**, 18, 24, ...
The least common multiple of 4 and 6 is 12.

Rename the fractions so that their denominator is the least common multiple.

$\frac{3}{4} = \frac{3*3}{4*3} = \frac{9}{12}$ and $\frac{1}{6} = \frac{1*2}{6*2} = \frac{2}{12}$

This method gives what is known as the **least common denominator.**

> **NOTE** The Multiplication Method gives what *Everyday Mathematics* calls the **quick common denominator.** The quick common denominator can be used with variables, so it is common in algebra.

> **NOTE** The least common denominator is usually easier to use in complicated calculations, though finding it can often take more time.

CHECK YOUR UNDERSTANDING

Rename each pair of fractions as fractions with a common denominator.

1. $\frac{2}{3}$ and $\frac{1}{6}$ **2.** $\frac{1}{4}$ and $\frac{2}{5}$ **3.** $\frac{3}{10}$ and $\frac{1}{2}$ **4.** $\frac{3}{4}$ and $\frac{7}{10}$ **5.** $\frac{3}{6}$ and $\frac{6}{8}$

Check your answers on page 374.

Least Common Multiples

A **multiple of a number _n_** is the product of any whole number and the number _n_. A multiple of _n_ is always divisible by _n_.

EXAMPLES

6 is a multiple of 3 because $3 * 2 = 6$; 6 is divisible by 3.

24 is a multiple of 4 because $4 * 6 = 24$; 24 is divisible by 4.

The **least common multiple** of two whole numbers is the smallest number that is a multiple of both numbers.

EXAMPLE   Find the least common multiple of 8 and 12.

Step 1: List multiples of 8: 8, 16, **24**, 32, 40, **48**, ...
Step 2: List multiples of 12: 12, **24**, 36, **48**, 60, ...

24 and 48 are common multiples of 8 and 12.

24 is smaller, so it is the least common multiple of 8 and 12.

Another way to find the least common multiple of two numbers is to use **prime factorization.**

EXAMPLE   Find the least common multiple of 8 and 12.

Step 1:	**Step 2:**	**Step 3:**	**Step 4:**
Write the prime factorization of each number.	Circle pairs of common factors.	Cross out one factor in each circled pair.	Multiply the factors that have not been crossed out.
$8 = 2 * 2 * 2$	$8 = \boxed{2} * \boxed{2} * 2$	$8 = \cancel{2} * \cancel{2} * 2$	$2 * 2 * 2 * 3 = 24$
$12 = 2 * 2 * 3$	$12 = \boxed{2} * \boxed{2} * 3$	$12 = \cancel{2} * \cancel{2} * 3$	

The least common multiple of 8 and 12 is 24.

The least common multiple of the denominators of two fractions is the **least common denominator** of the fractions. For example, 12 is the least common denominator of $\frac{3}{4}$ and $\frac{5}{6}$ because 12 is the least common multiple of 4 and 6.

CHECK YOUR UNDERSTANDING

Find the least common multiple of each pair of numbers.

1. 6 and 12   **2.** 4 and 10   **3.** 3 and 4   **4.** 6 and 8   **5.** 6 and 9   **6.** 9 and 15

Check your answers on page 374.

Using Unit Fractions

A **unit fraction** is a fraction with 1 in its numerator, such as $\frac{1}{2}$, $\frac{1}{10}$, and $\frac{1}{25}$. If you know the part of a whole represented by a unit fraction, you can find the whole by multiplying the part of the whole by the denominator of the unit fraction.

EXAMPLE   6 is $\frac{1}{4}$ of what number?

Since $\frac{1}{4}$ is 6, $\frac{2}{4}$ must be 2 ∗ 6, or 12;
$\frac{3}{4}$ must be 3 ∗ 6, or 18;
and $\frac{4}{4}$ must be 4 ∗ 6, or 24.

So, 6 is $\frac{1}{4}$ of 24.

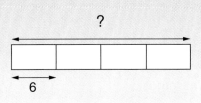

EXAMPLE   Mark owns 2 white shirts. This is $\frac{1}{4}$ of the total number of shirts he owns. How many shirts does he own?

If 2 shirts are $\frac{1}{4}$ of the total number of shirts, then the total number of shirts is 4 times that number.

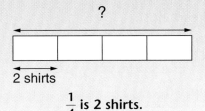

$\frac{1}{4}$ is 2 shirts.

Since 4 ∗ 2 = 8, Mark owns a total of 8 shirts.

Unit fractions can be used even when a part is given as a fraction that is not a unit fraction.

EXAMPLE   Sara lives 8 blocks from the library. This is $\frac{2}{3}$ of the distance from her home to school. How many blocks is it from Sara's home to school?

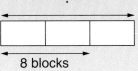

Step 1: Find $\frac{1}{3}$ of the distance to school.
8 blocks is $\frac{2}{3}$ of the distance to school.
Therefore, to find $\frac{1}{3}$ of the distance, divide 8 blocks by 2. 8 / 2 = 4

Step 2: Find the total distance to school.
4 blocks is $\frac{1}{3}$ of the distance to school.
Therefore, to find the total distance to school (or $\frac{3}{3}$ of the distance), multiply 4 blocks by 3.
4 ∗ 3 = 12

Sara lives 12 blocks from school.

EXAMPLE Ms. Partee spends $1,000 a month. This amount is $\frac{4}{5}$ of her monthly earnings. How much does she earn per month?

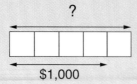

?

$1,000

Step 1: Find $\frac{1}{5}$ of her monthly earnings.

$1,000 is $\frac{4}{5}$ of her monthly earnings.
Therefore, to find $\frac{1}{5}$ of her earnings,
divide $1,000 by 4.
$1,000 / 4 = $250

Step 2: Find her total monthly earnings.

$250 is $\frac{1}{5}$ of her monthly earnings.
Therefore, to find her total earnings
(or $\frac{5}{5}$ of her earnings), multiply $250 by 5.
$250 * 5 = $1,250

Ms. Partee earns $1,250 each month.

If you can enter a fraction on your calculator, you can use your calculator to solve the problem in the example. Divide the amount that Ms. Partee spends by the fraction.

Key in: 1000 ÷ 4 (n) 5 (d) (Enter)

Answer: 1,250

CHECK YOUR UNDERSTANDING

Solve each problem.

1. Natalie collects movie posters. Her 3 posters from *Titanic* are $\frac{1}{5}$ of her collection. How many posters does Natalie have in her whole collection?

2. If 9 counters are $\frac{3}{4}$ of a set, how many counters are in the whole set?

Check your answers on page 374.

Greatest Common Factors

The **greatest common factor** of two whole numbers is the largest number that is a factor of both numbers.

> **EXAMPLE**   Find the greatest common factor of 20 and 24.
>
> **Step 1:** List all the factors of 20: **1**, **2**, **4**, 5, 10, and 20.
> **Step 2:** List all the factors of 24: **1**, **2**, 3, **4**, 6, 8, 12, and 24.
> 1, 2, and 4 are common factors of 20 and 24.
>
> 4 is the **greatest common factor** of 20 and 24.

Another way to find the greatest common factor of two numbers is to use prime factorization.

> **EXAMPLE**   Find the greatest common factor of 20 and 24.
>
> | **Step 1:** | **Step 2:** | **Step 3:** | **Step 4:** |
> |---|---|---|---|
> | Write the prime factorization of each. | Circle pairs of common prime factors. | Cross out the factors that are not circled. | Multiply one factor from each pair of circled factors. |
> | $20 = 2 * 2 * 5$ | $20 = (2) * (2) * 5$ | $20 = (2) * (2) * \cancel{5}$ | $2 * 2 = 4$ |
> | $24 = 2 * 2 * 2 * 3$ | $24 = (2) * (2) * 2 * 3$ | $24 = (2) * (2) * \cancel{2} * \cancel{3}$ | |
>
> The greatest common factor of 20 and 24 is 4.

An Interesting Fact

The product of the least common multiple and the greatest common factor of two numbers is the same as the product of the two numbers themselves.

> **EXAMPLE**
>
> The least common multiple of 4 and 6 is 12.
>
> The greatest common factor of 4 and 6 is 2.
>
> The product of the least common multiple and the greatest common factor of 4 and 6 is 12 * 2, or 24, and the product of 4 and 6 is also 24.

CHECK YOUR UNDERSTANDING

Find the greatest common factor of each pair of numbers.

1. 3 and 5   **2.** 4 and 10   **3.** 8 and 24   **4.** 35 and 28   **5.** 18 and 12   **6.** 9 and 15

Check your answers on page 374.

Addition and Subtraction of Fractions

To find the sum of fractions that have the same denominator, you add just the numerators. The denominator does not change. Subtraction of fractions with like denominators is done in the same way.

EXAMPLES

Find $\frac{1}{4} + \frac{2}{4}$.

$$\frac{1}{4} + \frac{2}{4} = \frac{1+2}{4} = \frac{3}{4}$$

Find $\frac{4}{5} - \frac{3}{5}$.

$$\frac{4}{5} - \frac{3}{5} = \frac{4-3}{5} = \frac{1}{5}$$

To find the sum of fractions that do not have the same denominator, first rename the fractions as fractions with a common denominator. Then proceed as above. Subtraction of fractions with unlike denominators is done in the same way.

EXAMPLES

Find $\frac{3}{4} + \frac{1}{8}$.

$$\frac{3}{4} + \frac{1}{8} = \frac{6}{8} + \frac{1}{8} = \frac{7}{8} \qquad \left(\frac{3}{4} = \frac{6}{8}\right)$$

So, $\frac{3}{4} + \frac{1}{8} = \frac{7}{8}$.

Find $\frac{5}{6} - \frac{1}{4}$.

$$\frac{5}{6} - \frac{1}{4} = \frac{10}{12} - \frac{3}{12} = \frac{7}{12} \qquad \left(\frac{5}{6} = \frac{10}{12}, \frac{1}{4} = \frac{2}{8} = \frac{3}{12}\right)$$

So, $\frac{5}{6} - \frac{1}{4} = \frac{7}{12}$.

It is possible to add and subtract fractions on some calculators. See if you can do this on your calculator.

EXAMPLES

Find $\frac{3}{8} + \frac{1}{3}$.

Key in: 3 $\boxed{n}$ 8 $\boxed{d}$ $\boxed{+}$ 1 $\boxed{n}$ 3 $\boxed{d}$ $\boxed{\text{Enter}}$

Answer: $\frac{17}{24}$

Find $\frac{7}{8} - \frac{3}{5}$.

Key in: 7 $\boxed{n}$ 8 $\boxed{d}$ $\boxed{-}$ 3 $\boxed{n}$ 5 $\boxed{d}$ $\boxed{\text{Enter}}$

Answer: $\frac{11}{40}$

CHECK YOUR UNDERSTANDING

Solve each problem. Check the answers on a calculator.

1. $\frac{2}{9} + \frac{4}{9}$
2. $\frac{3}{2} - \frac{3}{4}$
3. $\frac{1}{4} + \frac{1}{3}$
4. $\frac{5}{4} - \frac{7}{6}$
5. $\frac{5}{8} + \frac{1}{6}$

Check your answers on page 374.

Zeno's Paradox

Zeno (c. 490 B.C.–425 B.C.) was an ancient Greek philosopher who wrote a book of puzzles. These puzzles are called *paradoxes*. One of Zeno's paradoxes is a proof that it is impossible to move from one place to another. (This is a paradox because, of course, you can do so.)

In his proof, Zeno began by saying that when you move, you must go from a starting point to an ending point.

START ●————————————————————● END

Now, to move from START to END, you must first go halfway.

$$\frac{1}{2}$$
——————————→
START ●————————————————————● END

After you have gone halfway, you still have to go half the remaining distance.

$$\frac{1}{2}$$ $$\frac{1}{4}$$
————————→ ————→
START ●————————————————————● END

There is still some distance left, and you have to go half of it before you can go all of it.

$$\frac{1}{2}$$ $$\frac{1}{4}$$ $$\frac{1}{8}$$
————————→ ——→ →
START ●————————————————————● END

This pattern repeats over and over: No matter how little distance is left, you still have to go halfway first. Since there will always be half of some distance left, you can never get anywhere.

This paradox is like trying to add $\frac{1}{2} + \frac{1}{4} + \frac{1}{8} + \dots$, with the fractions continuing forever. Zeno would say that $\frac{1}{2} + \frac{1}{4} + \frac{1}{8} + \dots$ is always less than 1. But mathematicians today can prove that $\frac{1}{2} + \frac{1}{4} + \frac{1}{8} + \dots = 1$, which seems to say that you can move from one point to another. Even if you believe the mathematicians, Zeno's paradox is still puzzling.

Addition of Mixed Numbers

One way to add mixed numbers is to first add the fractions that are part of the mixed numbers and then add the whole-number parts. This may require renaming the sum.

EXAMPLE Find $4\frac{5}{8} + 2\frac{7}{8}$.

Step 1: Add the fractions.

$$\begin{array}{r} 4\frac{5}{8} \\ + 2\frac{7}{8} \\ \hline \frac{12}{8} \end{array}$$

$$4\frac{5}{8} + 2\frac{7}{8} = 7\frac{1}{2}$$

Step 2: Add the whole numbers.

$$\begin{array}{r} 4\frac{5}{8} \\ + 2\frac{7}{8} \\ \hline 6\frac{12}{8} \end{array}$$

Step 3: Rename the sum.

$$6\frac{12}{8} = 6 + \frac{8}{8} + \frac{4}{8}$$
$$= 6 + 1 + \frac{4}{8}$$
$$= 7\frac{4}{8}$$
$$= 7\frac{1}{2}$$

If the fractions in the mixed numbers do not have the same denominator, first rename the fractions so that they have a common denominator.

EXAMPLE Find $3\frac{3}{4} + 5\frac{2}{3}$.

Step 1: Rename the fractions.

$$\begin{array}{rcl} 3\frac{3}{4} & = & 3\frac{9}{12} \\ + 5\frac{2}{3} & = & + 5\frac{8}{12} \\ \hline & & \frac{17}{12} \end{array}$$

$$3\frac{3}{4} + 5\frac{2}{3} = 9\frac{5}{12}$$

Step 2: Add the whole numbers.

$$\begin{array}{r} 3\frac{9}{12} \\ + 5\frac{8}{12} \\ \hline 8\frac{17}{12} \end{array}$$

Step 3: Rename the sum.

$$8\frac{17}{12} = 8 + \frac{12}{12} + \frac{5}{12}$$
$$= 8 + 1 + \frac{5}{12}$$
$$= 9\frac{5}{12}$$

Some calculators have special keys for entering and renaming mixed numbers.

EXAMPLE Solve $3\frac{3}{4} + 5\frac{2}{3}$ on a calculator.

Key in: 3 (Unit) 3 (n) 4 (d) (+) 5 (Unit) 2 (n) 3 (d) (Enter)   Answer: $9\frac{5}{12}$

CHECK YOUR UNDERSTANDING

Solve Problems 1–3 without a calculator. Solve Problem 4 with a calculator.

1. $6\frac{1}{8} + 4\frac{7}{8}$ **2.** $1\frac{1}{2} + 4\frac{2}{5}$ **3.** $7\frac{5}{6} + 2\frac{1}{4}$ **4.** $12\frac{4}{7} + 9\frac{7}{9}$

Check your answers on page 374.

Subtraction of Mixed Numbers

If the fraction parts do not have the same denominator, first
rename the fractions as fractions with a common denominator.

EXAMPLE Find $3\frac{7}{8} - 1\frac{3}{4}$.

Step 1: Rename the fractions. | **Step 2:** Subtract the fractions. | **Step 3:** Subtract the whole numbers.

$$3\frac{7}{8} = 3\frac{7}{8}$$
$$-1\frac{3}{4} = -1\frac{6}{8}$$

$$3\frac{7}{8} - 1\frac{3}{4} = 2\frac{1}{8}$$

$$\begin{array}{r} 3\frac{7}{8} \\ -1\frac{6}{8} \\ \hline \frac{1}{8} \end{array}$$

$$\begin{array}{r} 3\frac{7}{8} \\ -1\frac{6}{8} \\ \hline 2\frac{1}{8} \end{array}$$

To subtract a mixed number from a whole number, first rename
the whole number as the sum of a whole number and a fraction
that is equivalent to 1.

EXAMPLE Find $5 - 2\frac{2}{3}$.

Step 1: Rename the whole number. | **Step 2:** Subtract the fractions. | **Step 3:** Subtract the whole numbers.

$$5 = 4\frac{3}{3}$$
$$-2\frac{2}{3} = -2\frac{2}{3}$$

$$5 - 2\frac{2}{3} = 2\frac{1}{3}$$

$$\begin{array}{r} 4\frac{3}{3} \\ -2\frac{2}{3} \\ \hline \frac{1}{3} \end{array}$$

$$\begin{array}{r} 4\frac{3}{3} \\ -2\frac{2}{3} \\ \hline 2\frac{1}{3} \end{array}$$

When subtracting mixed numbers, rename the larger mixed
number if it contains a fraction that is less than the fraction in
the smaller mixed number.

EXAMPLE Find $7\frac{1}{5} - 3\frac{3}{5}$.

Step 1: Rename the larger mixed number. | **Step 2:** Subtract the fractions. | **Step 3:** Subtract the whole numbers.

$$7\frac{1}{5} = 6\frac{6}{5}$$
$$-3\frac{3}{5} = -3\frac{3}{5}$$

$$7\frac{1}{5} - 3\frac{3}{5} = 3\frac{3}{5}$$

$$\begin{array}{r} 6\frac{6}{5} \\ -3\frac{3}{5} \\ \hline \frac{3}{5} \end{array}$$

$$\begin{array}{r} 6\frac{6}{5} \\ -3\frac{3}{5} \\ \hline 3\frac{3}{5} \end{array}$$

The example below shows three methods of solving $4\frac{1}{6} - 2\frac{2}{3}$.

EXAMPLE Find $4\frac{1}{6} - 2\frac{2}{3}$.

Method 1: This is the method shown on page 81.

Step 1: Rename the fractions.

$$4\frac{1}{6} = 4\frac{1}{6}$$
$$-2\frac{2}{3} = -2\frac{4}{6}$$

Step 2: Rename the larger mixed number.

$$4\frac{1}{6} = 3\frac{7}{6}$$
$$-2\frac{4}{6} = -2\frac{4}{6}$$

Step 3: Subtract.

$$3\frac{7}{6}$$
$$-2\frac{4}{6}$$
$$\overline{1\frac{3}{6} = 1\frac{1}{2}}$$

Method 2: Work with the fraction names for the mixed numbers.

Step 1: Rename the mixed numbers.

$$4\frac{1}{6} = \frac{25}{6}$$
$$-2\frac{2}{3} = -\frac{8}{3}$$

Step 2: Rename the fractions. Subtract.

$$\frac{25}{6} = \frac{25}{6}$$
$$-\frac{8}{3} = -\frac{16}{6}$$
$$\overline{\frac{9}{6}}$$

Step 3: Rename the result as a mixed number.

$$\frac{9}{6} = 1\frac{3}{6} = 1\frac{1}{2}$$

Method 3: Use the partial-differences method.

$$4\frac{1}{6}$$
$$-2\frac{2}{3}$$

$$4 - 2 \rightarrow +2$$

$$\frac{2}{3} - \frac{1}{6} = \frac{4}{6} - \frac{1}{6} \rightarrow -\frac{3}{6} \qquad \left(\frac{2}{3} > \frac{1}{6}, \text{ so subtract } \frac{2}{3} - \frac{1}{6}.\right)$$

$$2 - \frac{3}{6} \rightarrow 1\frac{3}{6} = 1\frac{1}{2}$$

$$4\frac{1}{6} - 2\frac{2}{3} = 1\frac{1}{2}$$

You can also subtract mixed numbers on calculators that have the
$\boxed{n}$, $\boxed{d}$, and $\boxed{\text{Unit}}$ keys for entering mixed numbers. Try it.

253

CHECK YOUR UNDERSTANDING

Subtract. Check your answers on a calculator.

1. $4\frac{3}{5} - 2\frac{1}{3}$
2. $7 - 3\frac{5}{8}$
3. $3\frac{2}{9} - \frac{8}{9}$
4. $6\frac{1}{2} - 2\frac{5}{6}$

Check your answers on page 374.

Finding a Fraction of a Number

Many problems with fractions involve finding a fraction of a number.

EXAMPLE Find $\frac{2}{3}$ of 24.

Model the problem by using 24 pennies. Divide the pennies into 3 equal groups.

Each group has $\frac{1}{3}$ of the pennies. So, $\frac{1}{3}$ of 24 pennies is 8 pennies.

Since $\frac{1}{3}$ of 24 is 8, $\frac{2}{3}$ of 24 must be twice as much: $2 * 8 = 16$.

$\frac{1}{3}$ of $24 = 8$, so $\frac{2}{3}$ of $24 = 16$.

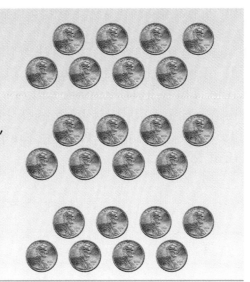

> **NOTE**
>
> "$\frac{2}{3}$ of 24" can also be written "$\frac{2}{3} * 24$." The word *of* often, though not always, means multiplication.

EXAMPLE A jacket that sells for $45 is on sale for $\frac{2}{3}$ of the regular price. What is the sale price?

To find the sale price, you have to find $\frac{2}{3}$ of $45.

Step 1: Find $\frac{1}{3}$ of 45. $45 \div 3 = 15$, so $\frac{1}{3}$ of 45 is 15.

Step 2: Use the answer from Step 1 to find $\frac{2}{3}$ of 45.

Since $\frac{1}{3}$ of 45 is 15, then $\frac{2}{3}$ of 45 is $2 * 15 = 30$.

The sale price is $30.

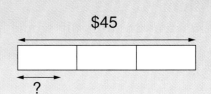

CHECK YOUR UNDERSTANDING

Solve each problem.

1. $\frac{1}{4}$ of 36

2. $\frac{3}{4}$ of 36

3. $\frac{4}{5}$ of 20

4. Gina and Robert earned $15 raking lawns, but Gina did most of the work. They decided that Gina should get $\frac{2}{3}$ of the money. How much does each person get?

Check your answers on page 374.

Multiplying Fractions and Whole Numbers

People usually think that "multiplication makes things bigger." But multiplication involving fractions can lead to products that are smaller than at least one of the factors. For example, $10 * \frac{1}{2} = 5$.

Number-Line Model

One way to multiply a whole number and a fraction is to think about "hops" on a number line. The whole number tells how many hops to make, and the fraction tells how long each hop should be. For example, to find $5 * \frac{2}{3}$, imagine taking 5 hops on a number line, each $\frac{2}{3}$ of a unit long.

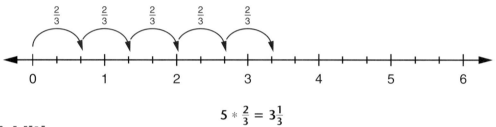

$$5 * \frac{2}{3} = 3\frac{1}{3}$$

Addition

Another way to multiply whole numbers and fractions is to use addition. For example, to find $4 * \frac{2}{3}$, draw 4 models of $\frac{2}{3}$:

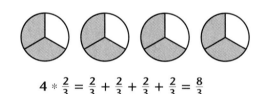

$$4 * \frac{2}{3} = \frac{2}{3} + \frac{2}{3} + \frac{2}{3} + \frac{2}{3} = \frac{8}{3}$$

Area Model

EXAMPLE Find $\frac{2}{3} * 2$.

Notice that the number of large rectangles equals the whole number.

Both rectangles are divided into thirds.

In each rectangle, there are 3 parts; 2 of which are shaded.

In the 2 rectangles, there are 4 shaded thirds altogether.

So, $\frac{2}{3} * 2 = \frac{4}{3}$, or $1\frac{1}{3}$.

CHECK YOUR UNDERSTANDING

Multiply.

1. $5 * \frac{1}{2}$

2. $6 * \frac{3}{4}$

3. $\frac{4}{5} * 3$

Check your answers on page 374.

Multiplying Fractions

When both numbers to be multiplied are fractions, addition and number-line hopping are not helpful in finding the answer. Fortunately, the **area model** does help.

EXAMPLE $\frac{3}{4} * \frac{2}{3} = ?$

$\frac{2}{3}$ of the rectangular region is shaded this way:

$\frac{3}{4}$ of the region is shaded this way:

$\frac{3}{4}$ of $\frac{2}{3}$ of the region is shaded both ways:

That's $\frac{6}{12}$ or $\frac{1}{2}$ of the whole region.

$\frac{3}{4} * \frac{2}{3} = \frac{6}{12} = \frac{1}{2}$

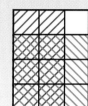

Multiplication of Fractions Property

The problem above is an example of the following general pattern: To multiply fractions, simply multiply the numerators, and multiply the denominators.

This pattern can be expressed as follows:

$\frac{a}{b} * \frac{c}{d} = \frac{a * c}{b * d}$ (b and d may not be 0)

EXAMPLE $\frac{3}{4} * \frac{2}{3} = \frac{3 * 2}{4 * 3} = \frac{6}{12} = \frac{1}{2}$

The Multiplication of Fractions Property can be used to multiply a whole number and a fraction. First, rename the whole number as a fraction with 1 in the denominator.

> **NOTE**
> Check page 253 to see how a calculator can be used to multiply fractions.

EXAMPLE Find $5 * \frac{2}{3}$.

$5 * \frac{2}{3} = \frac{5}{1} * \frac{2}{3} = \frac{5 * 2}{1 * 3} = \frac{10}{3} = 3\frac{1}{3}$

CHECK YOUR UNDERSTANDING

Multiply.

1. $\frac{1}{3} * \frac{1}{2}$ **2.** $\frac{3}{5} * \frac{1}{4}$ **3.** $\frac{5}{6} * \frac{3}{10}$ **4.** $\frac{5}{8} * \frac{0}{8}$ **5.** $\frac{9}{4} * \frac{2}{3}$

Check your answers on page 374.

Multiplying Mixed Numbers

One way to multiply two mixed numbers is to rename each
mixed number as an improper fraction, multiply the fractions,
and rename the product as a mixed number.

EXAMPLE Find $3\frac{1}{4} * 1\frac{5}{6}$.

Rename the mixed numbers as
fractions and multiply.

$$3\frac{1}{4} * 1\frac{5}{6} = \frac{13}{4} * \frac{11}{6}$$

$$= \frac{13 * 11}{4 * 6} = \frac{143}{24}$$

Rename the product as a mixed
number.

$$\begin{array}{r} 24)\overline{143} \\ -120 \\ \hline 23 \end{array} \begin{array}{l} 5 \\ \hline 5 \end{array} \qquad \frac{143}{24} = 5\frac{23}{24}$$

So, $3\frac{1}{4} * 1\frac{5}{6} = 5\frac{23}{24}$.

Another way to multiply mixed numbers is to find partial
products and add them.

EXAMPLE Find $6\frac{1}{2} * 3\frac{3}{5}$.

Step 1: Find all the partial products.

$6 * 3 = 18$

$6 * \frac{3}{5} = \frac{6}{1} * \frac{3}{5} = \frac{18}{5} = 3\frac{3}{5}$

$\frac{1}{2} * 3 = \frac{1}{2} * \frac{3}{1} = \frac{3}{2} = 1\frac{1}{2}$

$\frac{1}{2} * \frac{3}{5} = \frac{3}{10}$

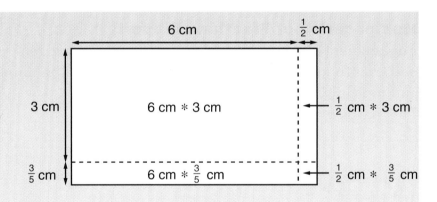

Step 2: Add the partial products.

$$18 + 3\frac{3}{5} + 1\frac{1}{2} + \frac{3}{10}$$

$$= 22 + \frac{3}{5} + \frac{1}{2} + \frac{3}{10}$$

$$= 22 + \frac{6}{10} + \frac{5}{10} + \frac{3}{10}$$

$$= 22 + \frac{14}{10}$$

$$= 23\frac{4}{10} = 23\frac{2}{5}$$

So, $6\frac{1}{2} * 3\frac{3}{5} = 23\frac{3}{5}$.

CHECK YOUR UNDERSTANDING

Multiply.

1. $6 * \frac{1}{4}$

2. $2\frac{2}{3} * 9$

3. $3\frac{3}{5} * 4\frac{1}{2}$

Check your answers on page 374.

Division of Fractions

Dividing a number by a fraction often gives a quotient that is larger than the dividend. For example, $4 \div \frac{1}{2} = 8$. To understand why this is, it's helpful to think about what division means.

Equal Groups

A division problem like $a \div b = ?$ is asking "How many b's are there in a?" For example, the problem $6 \div 3 = ?$ asks, "How many 3s are there in 6?" The figure at the right shows that there are two 3s in 6, so $6 \div 3 = 2$.

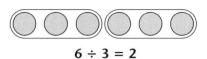

$6 \div 3 = 2$

A division problem like $6 \div \frac{1}{3} = ?$ is asking, "How many $\frac{1}{3}$s are there in 6?" The figure at the right shows that there are 18 thirds in 6, so $6 \div \frac{1}{3} = 18$.

$6 \div \frac{1}{3} = 18$

EXAMPLE Scott has 5 pounds of rice. A cup of rice is about $\frac{1}{2}$ pound. How many cups of rice does Scott have?

This problem is solved by finding how many $\frac{1}{2}$s are in 5, which is the same as $5 \div \frac{1}{2}$.

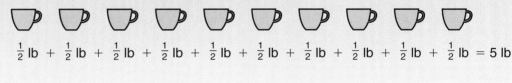

$\frac{1}{2}$ lb $+$ $\frac{1}{2}$ lb $+$ $\frac{1}{2}$ lb $+$ $\frac{1}{2}$ lb $+$ $\frac{1}{2}$ lb $+$ $\frac{1}{2}$ lb $+$ $\frac{1}{2}$ lb $+$ $\frac{1}{2}$ lb $+$ $\frac{1}{2}$ lb $+$ $\frac{1}{2}$ lb $= 5$ lb

So, Scott has about 10 cups of rice.

Missing Factors

A division problem is equivalent to a multiplication problem with a missing factor.

A problem like $6 \div \frac{1}{2} = \square$ is equivalent to $\frac{1}{2} * \square = 6$.

$\frac{1}{2} * \square = 6$ is the same as asking "$\frac{1}{2}$ of what number equals 6?"

Since $\frac{1}{2} * 12 = 6$, you know that $6 \div \frac{1}{2} = 12$.

EXAMPLE Find $6 \div \frac{2}{3}$.

This problem is equivalent to $\frac{2}{3} * \square = 6$, which means "$\frac{2}{3}$ of what number is 6?"

The diagram shows that $\frac{2}{3}$ of the missing number is 6.
Since $\frac{2}{3}$ of the missing number is 6, $\frac{1}{3}$ must be 3.
Since $\frac{1}{3}$ of the missing number is 3, the missing number must be 9.

So, $\frac{2}{3}$ of 9 = 6, which is equivalent to $\frac{2}{3} * 9 = 6$.

$6 \div \frac{2}{3} = 9$

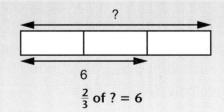

$\frac{2}{3}$ of ? = 6

Common Denominators

One way to solve a fraction division problem is to rename both the dividend and the divisor as fractions with a common denominator. Then divide the numerators and the denominators.

EXAMPLE Find $6 \div \frac{2}{3}$.

Rename 6 as $\frac{18}{3}$.
Divide the numerators and the denominators.

$$6 \div \frac{2}{3} = \frac{18}{3} \div \frac{2}{3}$$
$$= \frac{18 \div 2}{3 \div 3}$$
$$= \frac{9}{1}, \text{ or } 9$$

So, $6 \div \frac{2}{3} = 9$.

To see why this method works, imagine putting the 18 thirds in groups of $\frac{2}{3}$s each. There would be 9 groups.

EXAMPLE Julia has 8 pounds of sugar. She wants to put it in packages that hold $\frac{2}{3}$ of a pound each. How many packages can she make?

To solve $8 \div \frac{2}{3}$, rename 8 as $\frac{24}{3}$.
Then divide.
The 24 thirds can be put into 12 groups of $\frac{2}{3}$s each.

$$8 \div \frac{2}{3} = \frac{24}{3} \div \frac{2}{3}$$
$$= \frac{24 \div 2}{3 \div 3}$$
$$= \frac{12}{1}, \text{ or } 12$$

So, Julia can make 12 packages of sugar.

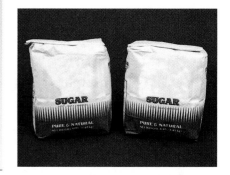

CHECK YOUR UNDERSTANDING

Solve. Then write a division number model for each problem.

1. Regina has 6 pizzas. If each person can eat $\frac{1}{2}$ of a pizza, how many people can Regina serve?

2. Selena has 8 yards of plastic strips for making bracelets. She needs $\frac{1}{2}$ yard for each bracelet. How many bracelets can she make?

3. 5 is $\frac{1}{2}$ of a number. What is the number?

Check your answers on page 374.

Division of Fractions and Mixed Numbers

Division of Fractions Property

To find the quotient of two fractions, multiply the first fraction by the reciprocal of the second fraction.

> Division of Fractions Property
> $$\frac{a}{b} \div \frac{c}{d} = \frac{a}{b} * \frac{d}{c}$$

EXAMPLES

$$\frac{4}{5} \div \frac{2}{3} = \frac{4}{5} * \frac{3}{2}$$
$$= \frac{12}{10}$$
$$= 1\frac{2}{10}, \text{ or } 1\frac{1}{5}$$

$$2\frac{3}{4} \div 1\frac{1}{3} = \frac{11}{4} \div \frac{4}{3}$$
$$= \frac{11}{4} * \frac{3}{4}$$
$$= \frac{33}{16}, \text{ or } 2\frac{1}{16}$$

The Division of Fractions Property is based on the following rules.

Rule 1: A fraction can have any number in its numerator and any number except 0 in its denominator.

EXAMPLES

$27 \div 55$ can be written as the fraction $\frac{27}{55}$.

$\frac{2}{3} \div \frac{3}{4}$ can be written as $\dfrac{\frac{2}{3}}{\frac{3}{4}}$.

Rule 2: $\frac{a}{b} * \frac{c}{d} = \frac{a * c}{b * d}$; a and c may be any numbers; b and d may be any numbers except 0.

EXAMPLES

$$\frac{5}{8} * \frac{3}{2} = \frac{5 * 3}{8 * 2} = \frac{15}{16}$$

$$\frac{3}{5} * 7 = \frac{3}{5} * \frac{7}{1} = \frac{3 * 7}{5 * 1} = \frac{21}{5}, \text{ or } 4\frac{1}{5}$$

Rule 3: If the product of two numbers is 1, then the numbers are called **reciprocals** of each other. If a number is written as a fraction, then its reciprocal is the fraction written "upside down."

EXAMPLES

5 and $\frac{1}{5}$ are reciprocals because $5 * \frac{1}{5} = 1$.

$\frac{3}{4}$ and $\frac{4}{3}$ are reciprocals because $\frac{3}{4} * \frac{4}{3} = 1$.

$2\frac{3}{5}$ and $\frac{5}{13}$ are reciprocals because $2\frac{3}{5} = \frac{13}{5}$ and $\frac{13}{5} * \frac{5}{13} = 1$.

Rule 4: If the numerator and the denominator of a fraction are multiplied by the same number, then the result is equivalent to the original fraction.

EXAMPLE $\frac{3}{5} = \frac{3 * 4}{5 * 4} = \frac{12}{20}$

Rule 5: Any number, *a*, divided by 1 is equal to *a*; that is,
$a \div 1 = \frac{a}{1} = a.$

EXAMPLES

$23 \div 1 = \frac{23}{1} = 23$

$46.3 \div 1 = \frac{46.3}{1} = 46.3$

$\frac{3}{8} \div 1 = \frac{\frac{3}{8}}{1} = \frac{3}{8}$

The following example shows why the Division of Fractions Property works.

EXAMPLE Divide $\frac{3}{4}$ by $\frac{2}{5}$.

Step 1: Write the problem as a fraction. (Rule 1)

$\frac{3}{4} \div \frac{2}{5} = \dfrac{\frac{3}{4}}{\frac{2}{5}}$ ← numerator
← denominator

Step 2: Multiply the numerator and the denominator of the fraction by the reciprocal of the denominator. (Rules 3 and 4)

$\dfrac{\frac{3}{4}}{\frac{2}{5}} = \dfrac{\frac{3}{4} * \frac{5}{2}}{\frac{2}{5} * \frac{5}{2}}$

Step 3: Simplify the denominator. (Rule 3)

$\dfrac{\frac{3}{4} * \frac{5}{2}}{\frac{2}{5} * \frac{5}{2}} = \dfrac{\frac{3}{4} * \frac{5}{2}}{1}$

Step 4: Divide by 1. (Rule 5)

$\dfrac{\frac{3}{4} * \frac{5}{2}}{1} = \frac{3}{4} * \frac{5}{2}$

Step 5: Multiply. (Rule 2)

$\frac{3}{4} * \frac{5}{2} = \frac{3 * 5}{4 * 2} = \frac{15}{8}$, or $1\frac{7}{8}$

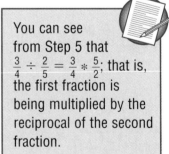

N O T E

You can see from Step 5 that $\frac{3}{4} \div \frac{2}{5} = \frac{3}{4} * \frac{5}{2}$; that is, the first fraction is being multiplied by the reciprocal of the second fraction.

CHECK YOUR UNDERSTANDING

Divide.

1. $\frac{3}{5} \div \frac{1}{4}$ **2.** $5 \div \frac{5}{3}$ **3.** $\frac{1}{7} \div \frac{3}{7}$ **4.** $2\frac{2}{3} \div 4$ **5.** $3\frac{1}{2} \div 1\frac{1}{4}$

Check your answers on page 374.

Positive and Negative Rational Numbers

You have seen positive and negative numbers on temperature scales and thermometers. They express temperatures with reference to a zero point (0 degrees). There are many other situations in which positive and negative numbers are used.

Situation	Negative (−)	Zero (0)	Positive (+)
bank account	withdrawal	no transaction	deposit
weight	loss	no change	gain
time	past	present	future
games	behind	even	ahead
business	loss	break even	profit
elevation	below sea level	at sea level	above sea level

Just as withdrawal/deposit, loss/gain, past/future, behind/ahead, profit/loss, and below/above are opposites, a negative number is the opposite of a positive number, and a positive number is the opposite of a negative number.

Notation

The symbol "−" is written before a numeral to show that it represents a negative number. For example, −5 is read as "negative 5," −12.3 as "negative 12.3," and $-\frac{5}{8}$ as "negative $\frac{5}{8}$."

Relations

When two rational numbers are shown on a number line, the number that is farther to the right is the larger number. This rule applies to both positive and negative rational numbers. Thus, $4 > -7$, and $-2.435 > -3.627$.

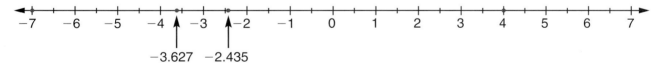

Absolute Value

The **absolute value** of a number is the distance of the number from 0. The absolute value of any number is either positive or 0. The absolute value of a positive number is the number itself; for example, the absolute value of 15 is 15. The absolute value of a negative number is the opposite of the number; for example, the absolute value of −8 is 8. The absolute value of 0 is 0.

Addition and Subtraction of Positive and Negative Rational Numbers

Addition of Positive and Negative Numbers

One way to add positive and negative numbers is to imagine walking along a number line.

- The first number tells you where to start.
- The operation sign + tells you to face the positive end of the number line.
- If the second number is negative (has a − sign), you will walk backward; otherwise, walk forward.
- The second number tells you how many steps to take.
- The number where you end is the answer.

> N O T E
> When a negative number follows an operation symbol, the negative number appears in parentheses.
> For example,
> $8 + (-7)$

EXAMPLE   Find $-3 + 5$.

Start at −3.
The operation sign is + so face in the positive direction.
The second number is positive so walk forward 5 steps.
You will end at 2.
So, $-3 + 5 = 2$.

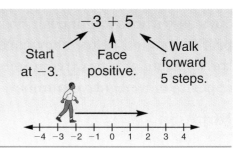

$-3 + 5$

Start at −3.   Face positive.   Walk forward 5 steps.

EXAMPLE   Find $4 + (-2)$.

Start at 4.
The operation sign is +, so face in the positive direction.
The second number is negative, so walk backward 2 steps.
You will end at 2.
So, $4 + (-2) = 2$.

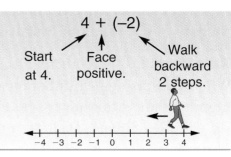

$4 + (-2)$

Start at 4.   Face positive.   Walk backward 2 steps.

EXAMPLE   Find $-1 + (-4)$.

Start at −1.
The operation sign is +, so face in the positive direction.
The second number is negative, so walk backward 4 steps.
You will end at −5.
So, $-1 + (-4) = -5$.

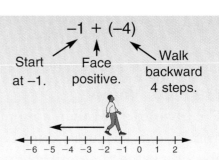

$-1 + (-4)$

Start at −1.   Face positive.   Walk backward 4 steps.

CHECK YOUR UNDERSTANDING

Add.

1. $3 + (-5)$ **2.** $-3 + (-5)$ **3.** $-4 + 7$ **4.** $-6 + 2$

Check your answers on page 374.

Subtraction of Positive and Negative Numbers

You can use the same idea you used for addition to subtract positive and negative numbers. The only difference is that for subtraction, you must face in the negative direction. Everything else is the same.

Operation	Direction
addition	positive
subtraction	negative

EXAMPLE Find $1 - 4$.

Start at 1.
The operation sign is $-$, so face in the negative direction.
The second number is positive, so walk forward 4 steps.
You will end at -3.

So, $1 - 4 = -3$.

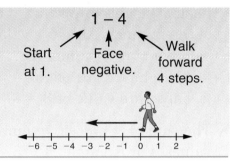

EXAMPLE Find $-2 - (-4)$.

Start at -2.
The operation sign is $-$, so face in the negative direction.
The second number is negative, so walk backward 4 steps.
You will end at 2.

So, $-2 - (-4) = 2$.

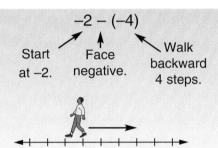

Changing Subtraction to Addition

Another way to think about subtraction of rational numbers is to change the subtraction problem into an addition problem.

For any numbers a and b, $a - b = a +$ (the opposite of b), or $a - b = a + (-b)$.

EXAMPLES

$1 - 4 = 1 + (-4) = -3$ $2 - (-3) = 2 + 3 = 5$

$-2 - (-4) = -2 + 4 = 2$ $-2 - 3 = -2 + (-3) = -5$

CHECK YOUR UNDERSTANDING

Subtract.

1. $-4 - 2$ **2.** $-5 - (-8)$ **3.** $4 - (-3)$ **4.** $2 - 6$

Check your answers on page 374.

Using Absolute Value to Add Positive and Negative Numbers

Here is another way to think about addition of positive and negative rational numbers.

- The **absolute value** of a positive number is the number itself. The absolute value of a negative number is the opposite of the number. Absolute value is shown by vertical lines before and after a number.

  $$\text{absolute value of } -6 = |-6| = (OPP)(-6) = 6$$
  $$\text{absolute value of } 3 = |3| = 3$$

- The sum of two positive numbers is the sum of their absolute values. For example, $3 + 5 = |3| + |5| = 8$.

- To find the sum of two negative numbers, add the absolute values of the addends. The sum is the opposite of the result.
  $$-3 + (-5) = (OPP)(|-3| + |-5|)$$
  $$= (OPP)(3 + 5)$$
  $$= (OPP)8$$
  $$= -8$$

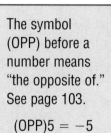

> **NOTE**
>
> The symbol (OPP) before a number means "the opposite of." See page 103.
>
> $(OPP)5 = -5$
>
> $(OPP)(-7) = 7$

- To find the sum of a positive number and a negative number, subtract the smaller absolute value from the larger absolute value. The sum takes the sign of the addend with the larger absolute value.
  $$-7 + 3 = -(|-7| - |3|)$$
  $$= -(7 - 3)$$
  $$= -4 \quad \text{The sum takes the sign of } -7.$$
  $$-2 + 8 = (|8| - |-2|)$$
  $$= 8 - 2$$
  $$= 6 \quad \text{The sum takes the sign of } 8.$$

- The sum of two opposites is zero. For example, $-5 + 5 = 0$.

CHECK YOUR UNDERSTANDING

Add or subtract.

1. $-9 + (-6)$ **2.** $-14 + 38$ **3.** $5.2 + (-5.6)$ **4.** $9 + (-27)$

5. $3 - 7$ **6.** $-5 - (-2)$ **7.** $-6 - 4$ **8.** $8 - (-9)$

Check your answers on page 374.

Multiplication and Division of Positive and Negative Rational Numbers

To multiply or divide two rational numbers, calculate the answer as if both numbers were positive. Then use one of the following rules to decide whether the answer is a positive or a negative rational number.

- If the signs on both numbers match, the result is a positive number.
- If the signs on both numbers do not match, the result is a negative number.

EXAMPLE

	Multiplication	Division	Result
Signs match • both positive • both negative	$8 * 3 = 24$ $-2 * (-3) = 6$	$51 \div 17 = 3$ $-81 \div (-3) = 27$	positive
Signs don't match • one positive and one negative	$12 * (-6) = -72$ $-25 * 8 = -200$	$-75 \div 25 = -3$ $10 \div (-2) = -5$	negative

Why $(-) * (-) = (+)$

One way to understand why the product of two negative numbers is positive is to look at patterns in products of positive and negative numbers.

Notice how the pattern in the first table at the right shows that the product of a positive number and a negative number is negative.

The second table begins with a negative number times a positive number. As the second factor gets smaller, the product gets closer to 0. When both factors are negative, the product must be positive to keep the pattern going.

a	b	$a * b$
5	2	10
5	1	5
5	0	0
5	-1	-5
5	-2	-10

a	b	$a * b$
-5	2	-10
-5	1	-5
-5	0	0
-5	-1	5
-5	-2	10

CHECK YOUR UNDERSTANDING

Multiply or divide.

1. $-5 * 6$
2. $10 * (-27)$
3. $9 * (-8)$
4. $42 \div (-6)$
5. $-54 \div 9$
6. $-100 \div (-20)$

Check your answers on page 374.

Multiplication and Division with Zero

Multiplication with Zero: a * 0 = 0

If one (or more) of the factors in a multiplication problem is 0, the product is 0.

> **EXAMPLES** $-38 * 0 = 0$ $5 * 12 * 0 * 4 = 0$ $0 * 0 = 0$

Division of Zero: 0 / a = 0

When 0 is divided by any number (except 0), the answer is 0.

To understand this, think about multiplication. Any division problem can be rewritten as a multiplication problem with a missing factor. The missing factor in every such multiplication problem is 0.

Division Problem	Multiplication Problem	Missing Factor
0 / 8 = ☐	8 * ☐ = 0	0
0 / 75 = ☐	75 * ☐ = 0	0
0 / a = ☐ (if $a \neq 0$)	a * ☐ = 0	0

Division by Zero: a / 0 = ?

Division by 0 is not allowed.

Again, thinking about multiplication can help you understand this fact. Any division problem can be rewritten as a multiplication problem with a missing factor.

Division Problem	Multiplication Problem	Missing Factor
8 / 0 = ☐	0 * ☐ = 8	no solution
75 / 0 = ☐	0 * ☐ = 75	no solution
a / 0 = ☐ (if $a \neq 0$)	0 * ☐ = a	no solution

Any number multiplied by 0 is 0, so there are no solutions to the multiplication problems above. This means *none* of the division problems have answers either. This is why we say division by 0 is not allowed: There is no answer.

> **NOTE**
>
> The problem $0 / 0 = $ ☐ is interesting. It is equivalent to the multiplication problem $0 * $ ☐ $ = 0$. Since any number at all (5, 73, -245, $\frac{1}{2}$, and so on) will make $0 * $ ☐ $ = 0$ true, there are too many answers. So, people usually say $0 / 0$ is not allowed. (If you study calculus in high school or college, you may learn about special cases when $0 / 0$ is allowed, but for elementary mathematics, division of 0 by 0 is not allowed.)

CHECK YOUR UNDERSTANDING

Multiply or divide.

1. $0 * (-1{,}234)$ **2.** $5 * 15 * 3 * 0$ **3.** $0 / 75$ **4.** $27 / 0$

Check your answers on page 374.

Rational and Irrational Numbers

Counting is almost as old as the human race and has been used in some form by every human society. Long ago, however, people found that the counting numbers did not meet all their mathematical needs.

- Counting numbers could not be used to express measures between two consecutive whole numbers, such as $4\frac{1}{2}$ inches and 1.6 kilometers.

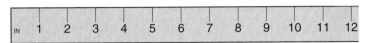

- With just the counting numbers, division problems such as 9 / 2 and 2 / 7 could not be answered.

Positive rational numbers were invented to meet these needs. Positive rational numbers can be expressed as fractions, decimals, and percents. With the invention of positive rational numbers, it became possible to express rates and ratios, to name many more points on the number line, and to solve any division problem involving whole numbers (except division by 0).

The positive rational numbers still did not meet every need. For example, problems such as $4 - 7$ and $3\frac{1}{4} - 6\frac{3}{4}$ could not be answered. This led to the invention of **negative rational numbers.** Negative numbers serve several purposes in mathematics and everyday life.

- Negative numbers can be used to express locations such as temperatures below 0 on a thermometer and depths below sea level.

- Negative numbers can be used to express changes such as yards lost in a football game and decreases in weight.

- Negative numbers allow the number line to be extended to less than 0.

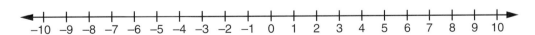

- Negative numbers allow answers to many subtraction problems.

Rational numbers are made up of all the positive and negative rational numbers and zero.

Integers are a special kind of rational number. The set of integers consists of all the counting numbers, all the opposites of counting numbers, and zero. Rational numbers are called *rational* because they can be written as ratios of integers. This means that every rational number can be written as a fraction using only integers in the numerator and the denominator. You can find a summary of the Properties of Rational Numbers, beginning on page 102.

There are other kinds of numbers called **irrational numbers.** Some of these, like the number π, you have used before. Others with which you are not familiar, such as $\sqrt{2}$ and tan 30°, are shown on The Real Number Line on page 100. Irrational numbers cannot be written as ratios of integers, which is why they are called *irrational.* You will learn more about irrational numbers when you study algebra.

The rational and irrational numbers together make up the **real numbers.** The real numbers complete the number line. Every point on the number line corresponds to a real number, and every real number has a point on the number line.

There are infinitely many rational numbers. You could count them and not miss any, but it would take forever. The number of rational numbers is represented by the symbol $\aleph_0$, which is read *aleph null.* In 1873, the mathematician Georg Cantor proved there are even more irrational numbers than rational numbers. He showed that you could never count all the irrational numbers, even if you counted forever.

Counting Numbers:
1, 2, 3, 4, 5, ...

Positive Rational Numbers:
5, $\frac{1}{2}$, 2, 7.08, 40%

Negative Rational Numbers:
-6, $-\left(\frac{3}{8}\right)$, -0.006, $-1\frac{1}{2}$

Integers:
12, 0, -37

Irrational Numbers:
$\sqrt{2}$, tan 30°

Real Numbers:
All of the examples above.

Notation

A rational number is any number that can be written in the form $\frac{a}{b}$, where a and b are integers and b is not 0. A rational number can also be written either as a **terminating decimal,** for which all the digits can be written, or as a **repeating decimal,** in which a pattern of one or more digits is repeated endlessly.

EXAMPLES $\frac{5}{8} = 0.625$ $\frac{1}{3} = 0.\overline{3} = 0.3333...$

$\frac{1}{7} = 0.\overline{142857} = 0.142857142857142857142857142857142857...$

An irrational number can be written as a decimal, but not as a terminating or repeating decimal; a decimal for an irrational number would be infinitely long. An irrational number cannot be written in the form $a \div b$, where a and b are integers.

EXAMPLES

$\pi = 3.141592653...$	The decimal continues without a repeating pattern.
$\sqrt{2} = 1.414213562...$	The decimal continues without a repeating pattern.
$1.010010001...$	There is a pattern in the decimal, but it does not repeat.

CHECK YOUR UNDERSTANDING

Refer to The Real Number Line on page 100 to answer these questions.

1. Which counting numbers are labeled on The Real Number Line?

2. Which integers are labeled on the number line?

3. Can 0.2 be written as a fraction?

4. Can 1.1666... be written as a fraction?

5. Is 10^{-1} a positive rational number?

6. Is 1.333... a rational number?

7. Which rational numbers between 1 and 2 are labeled?

8. Is $\sqrt{16}$ a rational number?

9. Which numbers labeled on The Real Number Line cannot be written as either terminating or repeating decimals?

Check your answers on page 374.

The Real Number Line

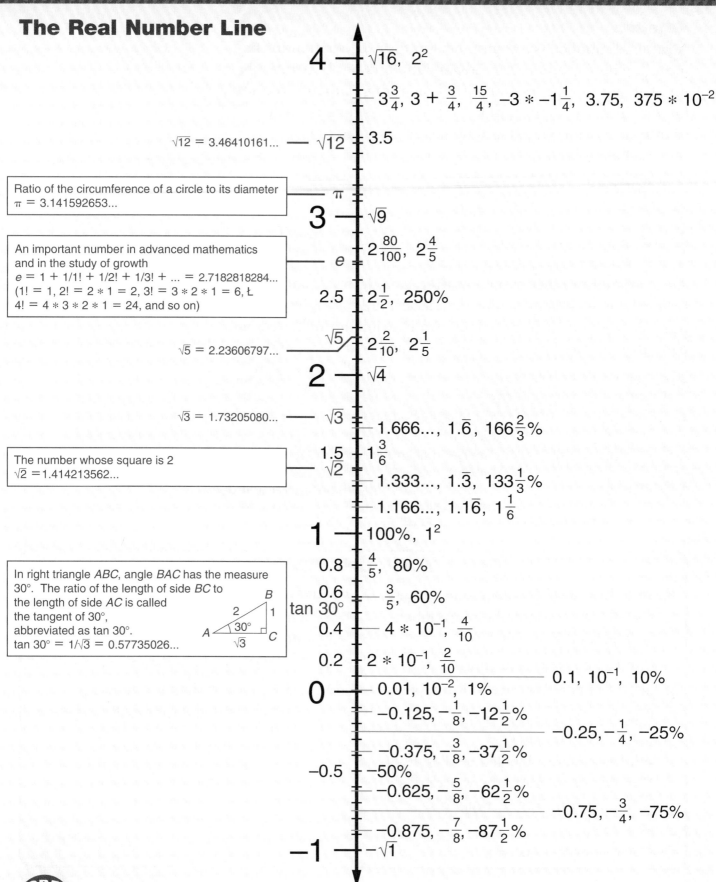

4 — $\sqrt{16},\ 2^2$

$3\frac{3}{4},\ 3 + \frac{3}{4},\ \frac{15}{4},\ -3 * -1\frac{1}{4},\ 3.75,\ 375 * 10^{-2}$

$\sqrt{12} = 3.46410161...$ — $\sqrt{12}$ 3.5

Ratio of the circumference of a circle to its diameter
$\pi = 3.141592653...$

π

3 — $\sqrt{9}$

An important number in advanced mathematics and in the study of growth
$e = 1 + 1/1! + 1/2! + 1/3! + ... = 2.7182818284...$
$(1! = 1, 2! = 2 * 1 = 2, 3! = 3 * 2 * 1 = 6, Ł$
$4! = 4 * 3 * 2 * 1 = 24,$ and so on)

e

$2\frac{80}{100},\ 2\frac{4}{5}$

2.5 $2\frac{1}{2},\ 250\%$

$\sqrt{5} = 2.23606797...$ — $\sqrt{5}$ $2\frac{2}{10},\ 2\frac{1}{5}$

2 — $\sqrt{4}$

$\sqrt{3} = 1.73205080...$ — $\sqrt{3}$

$1.666...,\ 1.\overline{6},\ 166\frac{2}{3}\%$

1.5 $1\frac{3}{6}$

The number whose square is 2
$\sqrt{2} = 1.414213562...$

$\sqrt{2}$

$1.333...,\ 1.\overline{3},\ 133\frac{1}{3}\%$

$1.166...,\ 1.1\overline{6},\ 1\frac{1}{6}$

1 — $100\%,\ 1^2$

In right triangle ABC, angle BAC has the measure $30°$. The ratio of the length of side BC to the length of side AC is called the tangent of $30°$, abbreviated as tan $30°$.
$\tan 30° = 1/\sqrt{3} = 0.57735026...$

0.8 $\frac{4}{5},\ 80\%$

0.6 $\frac{3}{5},\ 60\%$

tan $30°$

0.4 $4 * 10^{-1},\ \frac{4}{10}$

0.2 $2 * 10^{-1},\ \frac{2}{10}$

$0.1,\ 10^{-1},\ 10\%$

0 — $0.01,\ 10^{-2},\ 1\%$

$-0.125,\ -\frac{1}{8},\ -12\frac{1}{2}\%$

$-0.25,\ -\frac{1}{4},\ -25\%$

$-0.375,\ -\frac{3}{8},\ -37\frac{1}{2}\%$

−0.5 — -50%

$-0.625,\ -\frac{5}{8},\ -62\frac{1}{2}\%$

$-0.75,\ -\frac{3}{4},\ -75\%$

$-0.875,\ -\frac{7}{8},\ -87\frac{1}{2}\%$

−1 — $-\sqrt{1}$

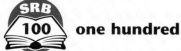

General Patterns and Special Cases

Many rules involving numbers can be described with the help of variables, such as n or $\square$. For example, the rule "The sum of a number and its opposite is 0" can be expressed as $a + (-a) = 0$, where a stands for any number. This is sometimes called a **general pattern.** A **special case** of this general pattern can be given by replacing the variable a with any number. For example, $5 + (-5) = 0$ and $27\frac{1}{2} + (-27\frac{1}{2}) = 0$ are special cases of the general pattern $a + (-a) = 0$.

EXAMPLE   Express the following rule with variables: "The square of a number is the number multiplied by itself." Give three special cases of the general pattern.

General pattern: $n^2 = n * n$

Special cases: For $n = 3$: $3^2 = 3 * 3$

For $n = -7$: $(-7)^2 = -7 * (-7)$

For $n = \frac{2}{3}$: $(\frac{2}{3})^2 = \frac{2}{3} * \frac{2}{3}$

EXAMPLE   Use variables to describe the general pattern for the following special cases.

Special cases: $8 / 8 = 1$ $0.5 / 0.5 = 1$ $2\frac{3}{4} / 2\frac{3}{4} = 1$

Step 1:
Write everything that is the same for all the special cases, and use blanks for the parts that change.

_____ / _____ = 1

Step 2:
Fill in the blanks. Use a variable for the number that varies.

$\underline{x} / \underline{x} = 1$

Remember, x may not be 0.

CHECK YOUR UNDERSTANDING

Write three special cases for each general pattern.

1. $2 * r + r = 3 * r$

2. $b + (b + 1) + (b + 2) = 3 * (b + 1)$

Use variables to express the general pattern for these special cases.

3. $4 + 8 = 8 + 4$

$0.25 + 0.75 = 0.75 + 0.25$

$\frac{3}{5} + \frac{1}{5} = \frac{1}{5} + \frac{3}{5}$

4. $\frac{3}{4} * \frac{4}{3} = 1$

$\frac{2}{1} * \frac{1}{2} = 1$

$\frac{3}{8} * \frac{8}{3} = 1$

Check your answers on page 374.

Properties of Rational Numbers

The following properties are true for all rational numbers. The variables a, b, c, and d stand for any rational numbers (except 0, if the variable stands for a divisor).

Properties	Examples
Binary Operations Property When any two numbers are added, subtracted, multiplied, or divided, the result is a single number. $a + b$, $a - b$, $a * b$, and $a \div b$ are equal to single numbers.	$5 + 7 = 12$ $-3 - \frac{8}{3} = -5\frac{2}{3}$ $0.5 * (-4) = -2$ $2\frac{3}{5} \div \frac{8}{3} = \frac{39}{40}$
Commutative Property The sum or product of two numbers is the same, regardless of the order of the numbers. $a + b = b + a$ $a * b = b * a$	$7 + 8 = 8 + 7 = 15$ $-5 * (-6) = -6 * (-5) = 30$ $\frac{3}{4} * (-\frac{4}{5}) = -\frac{4}{5} * \frac{3}{4}$ $= -\frac{12}{20}$, or $-\frac{3}{5}$
Associative Property The sum or product of three or more numbers is the same, regardless of how the numbers are grouped. $a + (b + c) = (a + b) + c$ $a * (b * c) = (a * b) * c$	$(7 + 5) + 8 = 7 + (5 + 8)$ $12 \quad + 8 = 7 + \quad 13$ $20 = 20$ $2\frac{1}{2} * (2 * 3) = (2\frac{1}{2} * 2) * 3$ $2\frac{1}{2} * \quad 6 \quad = \quad 5 \quad * 3$ $15 = 15$
Distributive Property When a number is multiplied by the sum or difference of two or more numbers, the number is "distributed" over the numbers that are added or subtracted. $a * (b + c) = (a * b) + (a * c)$ $a * (b - c) = (a * b) - (a * c)$	$5 * (8 + 2) = (5 * 8) + (5 * 2)$ $5 * 10 = 40 + 10$ $50 = 50$ $-2 * (8 - 3) = (-2 * 8) - (-2 * 3)$ $-2 * \quad 5 \quad = \quad -16 \quad - \quad (-6)$ $-10 = -10$
Addition Property of Zero The sum of any number and 0 is equal to the original number. $a + 0 = 0 + a = a$	$5.37 + 0 = 5.37$ $0 + (-6) = -6$
Multiplication Property of One The product of any number and 1 is equal to the original number. $a * 1 = 1 * a = a$	$\frac{2}{3} * 1 = \frac{2}{3}$ $1 * 19 = 19$

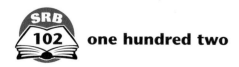

Properties	**Examples**
Opposites Property The opposite of a number, a, is normally written $-a$ or (OPP)a. Sometimes in *Everyday Mathematics,* we write (OPP)a for the opposite of a. If a is a positive number, then (OPP)a is a negative number. If a is a negative number, then (OPP)a is a positive number. If $a = 0$, then (OPP)$a = 0$. Zero is the only number that is its own opposite.	(OPP)$8 = -8$ (OPP)$-\frac{3}{4} = \frac{3}{4}$ (OPP)$-7 = 7$ (OPP)$0 = 0$ $-(x + 2) = -1 * (x + 2)$ $= (-1 * x) + (-1 * 2)$ $= -x + (-2)$ $= -x - 2$
Opposite of Opposites Property The opposite of the opposite of a number is equal to the original number. (OPP)(OPP)$a = $ (OPP)$(-a) = a$	(OPP)(OPP)$\frac{2}{3} = $ (OPP)$-\frac{2}{3} = \frac{2}{3}$ (OPP)(OPP) $-9 = $ (OPP)$9 = -9$
Sum of Opposites Property The sum of any number and its opposite is 0. $a + (-a) = (-a) + a = 0$	$15 + (-15) = 0$ $-2 + 2 = 0$
Multiplication of Reciprocals Property The product of any number and its reciprocal is 1. $a * \frac{1}{a} = \frac{1}{a} * a = 1$	$20 * \frac{1}{20} = 1$ $-\frac{2}{5} * \left(-\frac{5}{2}\right) = 1$
Addition Property of Positive and Negative Numbers The sum of two positive numbers is a positive number. The sum of two negative numbers is the opposite of the sum of the "number parts" of the addends. To find the sum of a positive number and a negative number, subtract the smaller from the larger "number part." The sum takes on the sign of the addend with the larger "number part."	$7 + 8 = 15$ $-7 + (-8) = $ (OPP)$(7 + 8) = -15$ $-2.5 + 1.5 = -(2.5 - 1.5) = -1$ $\frac{3}{4} + \left(-\frac{1}{4}\right) = \frac{3}{4} - \frac{1}{4} = \frac{2}{4},$ or $\frac{1}{2}$
Multiplication Property of Positive and Negative Numbers The product of two positive numbers or two negative numbers is a positive number. The product of a positive number and a negative number is a negative number.	$6 * 3 = 18$ $-6 * (-3) = 18$ $\frac{1}{3} * \left(-\frac{4}{5}\right) = -\frac{4}{15}$
Subtraction and Division Properties All subtraction problems can be solved by addition, and all division problems can be solved by multiplication. $a - b = a + (-b)$ $\frac{a}{b} = a * \frac{1}{b}$ $a \div b = a * \frac{1}{b}$	$15 - 7 = 15 + (-7) = 8$ $-9 - (-6) = -9 + $ (OPP)-6 $= -9 + 6$ $= -3$ $\frac{12}{4} = 12 * \frac{1}{4} = 3$ $25 \div (-5) = 25 * \left(-\frac{1}{5}\right) = -\frac{25}{5} = -5$

Properties	Examples
Equivalent Fractions Property If the numerator and denominator of a fraction are multiplied or divided by the same number, the resulting fraction is equivalent to the original fraction. $\dfrac{a}{b} = \dfrac{a*c}{b*c}$ $\qquad$ $\dfrac{a}{b} = \dfrac{a \div c}{b \div c}$	$\dfrac{2}{3} = \dfrac{2*5}{3*5} = \dfrac{10}{15}$ $\dfrac{6}{8} = \dfrac{6 \div 2}{8 \div 2} = \dfrac{3}{4}$
Addition and Subtraction of Fractions Properties The sum or difference of fractions with like denominators is the sum or difference of the numerators over the denominator. $\dfrac{a}{c} + \dfrac{b}{c} = \dfrac{a+b}{c}$ $\dfrac{a}{c} - \dfrac{b}{c} = \dfrac{a-b}{c}$ To add or subtract fractions with unlike denominators, rename the fractions so that they have a common denominator. $\dfrac{a}{b} + \dfrac{c}{d} = \dfrac{ad+bc}{bd}$ $\dfrac{a}{b} - \dfrac{c}{d} = \dfrac{ad-bc}{bd}$	$\dfrac{3}{5} + \dfrac{1}{5} = \dfrac{3+1}{5} = \dfrac{4}{5}$ $\dfrac{5}{6} - \dfrac{1}{6} = \dfrac{5-1}{6} = \dfrac{4}{6} = \dfrac{2}{3}$ $\dfrac{2}{3} + \dfrac{1}{5} = \dfrac{10}{15} + \dfrac{3}{15} = \dfrac{10+3}{15} = \dfrac{13}{15}$ $\dfrac{2}{3} - \dfrac{1}{4} = \dfrac{8}{12} - \dfrac{3}{12} = \dfrac{8-3}{12} = \dfrac{5}{12}$
Multiplication of Fractions Property The product of two fractions is the product of the numerators over the product of the denominators. $\dfrac{a}{b} * \dfrac{c}{d} = \dfrac{a*c}{b*d}$	$\dfrac{5}{8} * \dfrac{3}{4} = \dfrac{5*3}{8*4} = \dfrac{15}{32}$
Division of Fractions Property The quotient of two fractions is the product of the dividend and the reciprocal of the divisor. $\dfrac{a}{b} \div \dfrac{c}{d} = \dfrac{a}{b} * \dfrac{d}{c} = \dfrac{a*d}{b*c}$	$9 \div \dfrac{2}{3} = 9 * \dfrac{3}{2} = \dfrac{27}{2}$, or $13\dfrac{1}{2}$ $\dfrac{5}{6} \div \dfrac{1}{4} = \dfrac{5}{6} * \dfrac{4}{1} = \dfrac{20}{6}$, or $3\dfrac{1}{3}$
Powers of a Number Property If a is any number and b is a positive whole number, then a^b is the product of a used as a factor b times. $a^b = \underbrace{a*a*a*\ldots*a}_{b\ \text{factors}}$	$5^2 = 5 * 5 = 25$ $\left(\dfrac{2}{3}\right)^4 = \dfrac{2}{3} * \dfrac{2}{3} * \dfrac{2}{3} * \dfrac{2}{3} = \dfrac{16}{81}$
a^0 is equal to 1.	$4^0 = 1$
If a is any nonzero number and b is a positive whole number, then a^{-b} is 1 divided by the product of a used as a factor b times. $a^{-b} = \dfrac{1}{a^b} = \dfrac{1}{\underbrace{a*a*a*\ldots*a}_{b\ \text{factors}}}$	$3^{-2} = \dfrac{1}{3^2} = \dfrac{1}{3*3} = \dfrac{1}{9}$

Rates, Ratios, & Proportions

Rates, Ratios, and Proportions

Many fractions, such as $\frac{3}{8}$ of a pizza, name parts of wholes. Other fractions, such as $\frac{1}{2}$ inch, are used in measurement. In working with such fractions, it's important to keep in mind what the ONE, or whole, is: $\frac{3}{4}$ of a mile is much longer than $\frac{3}{4}$ of an inch.

Not all fractions name parts of wholes. Some fractions compare two different amounts, where one amount is not part of the other. For example, a store might sell apples at 3 apples for 89 cents, or a car's gas mileage might be 143 miles per 7 gallons. These can be written as fractions: $\frac{3 \text{ apples}}{89¢}$, $\frac{143 \text{ miles}}{7 \text{ gallons}}$. These fractions do not name parts of wholes: The apples are *not* part of the money; the miles are *not* part of the gallons.

Fractions like $\frac{143 \text{ miles}}{7 \text{ gallons}}$ show rates. A **rate** tells how many of one thing there are for a certain number of another thing. Rates often contain the word **per,** meaning *for each* or *for every*.

> **EXAMPLE**   Alan rode his bicycle 12 miles in 1 hour. His rate was 12 miles per hour. This rate describes the distance he traveled and the time it took. The rate *12 miles per hour* is written as "12 mph." The fraction for this rate is $\frac{12 \text{ miles}}{1 \text{ hour}}$.

Ratios are like rates, but they compare two amounts that have the same unit.

> **EXAMPLES**   The ratio of the length of the side of a square to the perimeter of the square is 1 to 4, or $\frac{1}{4}$. A square with a side 1 inch long has a perimeter of 4 inches. A square with a side 1 yard long has a perimeter of 4 yards.

Proportions are number models that state that two fractions are equivalent.

> **EXAMPLES**   Write a proportion for each situation.
>
> 1. Alan's speed is 12 miles per hour. At the same speed, he can travel 36 miles in 3 hours.
>
> $\frac{12 \text{ miles}}{1 \text{ hour}} = \frac{36 \text{ miles}}{3 \text{ hours}}$
>
> 2. Since the ratio of the length of a side of a square to the perimeter is 1 to 4, a square with a side 6 inches long has a perimeter of 24 inches.
>
> $\frac{1 \text{ inch}}{4 \text{ inches}} = \frac{6 \text{ inches}}{24 \text{ inches}}$

Many of the fractions you will work with in high school and beyond are rates and ratios. Many of these rates and ratios are used in proportions. The pages in this section discuss rates, ratios, and proportions.

Rates and Rate Tables

A **rate** tells how many of one thing there are for a certain number of another thing. Rates often contain the word **per** meaning *for each, for every,* or a similar phrase.

Some rates use special abbreviations. For example, *miles per hour* can be written as "mph" and *miles per gallon* can be written as "mpg."

EXAMPLE Alan rode his bicycle 12 miles in 1 hour. He traveled at a rate of 12 *miles per hour,* or 12 *mph.* This rate describes the distance Alan traveled and the time it took him.

Here are other examples of rates.

typing speed	50 words per minute	$\frac{50 \text{ words}}{1 \text{ minute}}$
price	$14\frac{1}{2}$ cents per ounce	$\frac{14\frac{1}{2}¢}{1 \text{ ounce}}$
scoring average	17 points per game	$\frac{17 \text{ points}}{1 \text{ game}}$
exchange rate	5.4 French francs for each U.S. dollar	$\frac{5.4 \text{ French francs}}{1 \text{ U.S. dollar}}$

Rate information can be organized in **rate tables.**

EXAMPLE Make a rate table for the statement, "A computer printer prints 4 pages per minute."

The table shows that if a printer prints 4 pages per minute, it will print 8 pages in 2 minutes, 12 pages in 3 minutes, and so on.

pages	4	8	12	16	20	24	28
minutes	1	2	3	4	5	6	7

Rates are often written with a slash (/) or as a fraction. The slash and fraction bar can be read as "per" or "for each."

Rate	Slash	Fraction
per-hour rate: 65 miles per hour	65 miles/hour	$\frac{65 \text{ miles}}{1 \text{ hour}}$
per-candy rate: $\frac{1}{2}$ cent per candy	$\frac{1}{2}$ cent/candy	$\frac{\frac{1}{2} \text{ cent}}{1 \text{ candy}}$

CHECK YOUR UNDERSTANDING

Write each rate with a slash and as a fraction. Make a rate table for each rate.

1. Rebecca earns $4 per hour helping her neighbor in the garden.

2. Todd can type 35 words per minute.

Check your answers on page 375.

Solving Rate Problems

Each rate in a rate table is **equivalent** to each of the other rates in the table. In many rate problems, one rate is given and you need to find an equivalent rate. Such problems can be solved in several ways.

Using Rate Tables

EXAMPLE Beth's car can travel 35 miles on 1 gallon of gasoline. How far can it travel on 7 gallons?

First, set up a rate table and enter what you know and what you want to find.

miles	35					?
gallons	1					7

Next, work from what you know to what you need to find. In this case, by doubling, you can find how far the car could travel on 2 gallons, 4 gallons, and 8 gallons of gasoline.

miles	35	70	140	280			?
gallons	1	2	4	8			7

There are two different ways to use the rate table.

- By adding the distances for 1 gallon, 2 gallons, and 4 gallons (a total of 7 gallons):
  35 miles + 70 miles + 140 miles = 245 miles
- By subtracting the distance for 1 gallon from the distance for 8 gallons:
  280 miles − 35 miles = 245 miles

So, Beth's car can travel 245 miles on 7 gallons of gas.

EXAMPLE Krystal receives an allowance of $20 for 4 weeks. At this rate, how much does she receive for 10 weeks?

First, set up a table and enter what you know, and what you want to find.

allowance	$20				?
weeks	4				10

Next, work from what you know to what you want. By halving $20, you can find how much Krystal gets for 2 weeks; by halving again you can find what she gets for 1 week. Then, by doubling $20 for 4 weeks, you find that Krystal will get $40 for 8 weeks.

allowance	$20	$10	$5	$40		?
weeks	4	2	1	8		10

Since 10 weeks is 8 weeks plus 2 weeks, Krystal would get $40 + $10, or $50, for 10 weeks.

Using Per-Unit Rates

A **per-unit rate** is a rate that tells how many of something there are for a single one of another thing. Per-unit rates can be useful for solving certain rate problems.

EXAMPLES $\frac{\$2.00}{1 \text{ gallon}}$ $\frac{50 \text{ miles}}{1 \text{ hour}}$ $\frac{36 \text{ inches}}{1 \text{ yard}}$

A rate problem may be easier to solve if you can find a per-unit rate that is equivalent to the rate given in the problem. The multiplication and division rules for finding equivalent fractions can be helpful in finding equivalent rates.

EXAMPLES Find equivalent per-unit rates.

$$\frac{60 \text{ pages}}{3 \text{ hours}} = \frac{60 \text{ pages} \div 3}{3 \text{ hours} \div 3}$$

$$= \frac{20 \text{ pages}}{1 \text{ hour}}$$

$$\frac{300 \text{ miles}}{5 \text{ hours}} = \frac{300 \text{ miles} \div 5}{5 \text{ hours} \div 5}$$

$$= \frac{60 \text{ miles}}{1 \text{ hour}}$$

A rate problem can be solved in two steps using a per-unit rate:

Step 1: Find a per-unit rate equivalent to the rate given in the problem.

Step 2: Use the per-unit rate to solve the problem.

The following example was also solved using a rate table on page 109. Here it is solved using a per-unit rate.

EXAMPLE   Krystal receives an allowance of $20 for 4 weeks. At this rate, how much does she receive for 10 weeks?

Step 1: Find a per-unit rate equivalent to the given rate.

$$\frac{\$20}{4 \text{ weeks}} = \frac{\$20 \div 4}{4 \text{ weeks} \div 4} = \frac{\$5}{1 \text{ week}}$$

Step 2: Use the per-unit rate to solve the problem.
If Krystal gets $5 for 1 week, then she gets 10 * $5, or $50, for 10 weeks.

Krystal receives $50 for 10 weeks.

EXAMPLE   A carton of 12 eggs costs 84¢. At this rate, how much do 8 eggs cost?

Step 1: Find a per-unit rate equivalent to the given rate.

$$\frac{84¢}{12 \text{ eggs}} = \frac{84¢ \div 12}{12 \div 12} = \frac{7¢}{1 \text{ egg}}$$

Step 2: Use the per-unit rate to solve the problem.
If 1 egg costs 7 cents, then 8 eggs cost 8 * 7 cents, or 56 cents.

So, 8 eggs cost 56 cents.

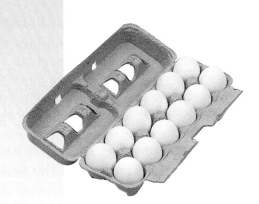

CHECK YOUR UNDERSTANDING

Solve.

1. There are 3 feet in 1 yard. How many feet are there in 6 yards?

2. Andy baby-sat for 6 hours. He was paid $30. How much did he earn per hour?

3. Judy saved $360 last year. How much did she save per month?

4. Jean swam 15 laps in 9 minutes. At this rate, how many laps would she swim in 15 minutes?

Check your answers on page 375.

Proportions

A **proportion** is a number sentence which states that two fractions are equivalent.

> **EXAMPLES** $\frac{1}{2} = \frac{3}{6}$ $\frac{3}{4} = \frac{9}{12}$ $\frac{5}{8} = \frac{10}{16}$

If you know any three numbers in a proportion, you can find the fourth number. Finding a missing number in a proportion is called **solving the proportion.**

Solving Proportions Using Rules for Equivalent Fractions

One way to solve a proportion is to use the multiplication and division rules for equivalent fractions.

> **EXAMPLE** Solve $\frac{2}{3} = \frac{n}{15}$
>
> $\frac{2}{3} = \frac{2 * 5}{3 * 5} = \frac{10}{15}$ The multiplication rule for equivalent fractions tells you that the numerator and denominator must be multiplied by the same number.
>
> $\frac{2}{3} = \frac{10}{15}$
>
> So, $n = 10$.

> **EXAMPLE** Solve $\frac{6}{15} = \frac{x}{5}$
>
> $\frac{6}{15} = \frac{6 \div 3}{15 \div 3} = \frac{2}{5}$ The division rule for equivalent fractions tells you the numerator and denominator must be divided by the same number.
>
> $\frac{6}{15} = \frac{2}{5}$
>
> So, $x = 2$.

You may find diagrams like those below helpful when you solve proportions using rules for equivalent fractions.

$$* 5$$
$$\frac{2}{3} = \frac{n}{15}$$
$$* 5$$

$$\div 3$$
$$\frac{6}{15} = \frac{x}{5}$$
$$\div 3$$

Rates, Ratios, and Proportions

Solving Proportions by Cross Multiplication

Another way to solve proportions is by using cross multiplication. **Cross multiplication** is the process of finding **cross products.** The cross products of two fractions are found by multiplying the numerator of each fraction by the denominator of the other fraction.

Using cross multiplication to solve proportions depends on the following fact:

If the cross products of two fractions are equal, then the fractions are equivalent. If the cross products of two fractions are not equal, then the fractions are not equivalent.

EXAMPLE Use cross products to decide whether $\frac{2}{3}$ and $\frac{1}{4}$ are equivalent.

The cross products are $2 * 4 = 8$ and $3 * 1 = 3$.

The cross products of $\frac{2}{3}$ and $\frac{1}{4}$ are not equal.

So, $\frac{2}{3}$ and $\frac{1}{4}$ are not equivalent.

$$\frac{2}{3} \times \frac{1}{4}$$

$$3 * 1 = 3$$
$$2 * 4 = 8$$
$$3 \neq 8$$

EXAMPLE Use cross products to decide whether $\frac{5}{6}$ and $\frac{10}{12}$ are equivalent.

The cross products are $5 * 12 = 60$ and $6 * 10 = 60$.

The cross products of $\frac{5}{6}$ and $\frac{10}{12}$ are equal.

So, $\frac{5}{6}$ and $\frac{10}{12}$ are equivalent.

$$\frac{5}{6} \times \frac{10}{12}$$

$$6 * 10 = 60$$
$$5 * 12 = 60$$
$$60 = 60$$

Solving a proportion by using cross multiplication involves several steps.

Step 1: Find the cross products of the two fractions in the proportion.

Step 2: Write an equation for the two cross products.

Step 3: Solve the equation from Step 2.

EXAMPLE Solve $\frac{3}{4} = \frac{z}{20}$ by cross multiplication.

Step 1: Cross multiply. Note that the cross product of 4 and z is $4 * z$.

$$\frac{3}{4} = \frac{z}{20}$$

$4 * z$

$3 * 20 = 60$

Step 2: Since the two fractions in the proportion, $\frac{3}{4}$ and $\frac{z}{20}$, are equivalent, the two cross products must be equal.
Write this as an equation.
$60 = 4 * z$

Step 3: Solve the equation from Step 2 by dividing both sides by 4.
$60 / 4 = (4 * z) / 4$
$15 = z$

So, $\frac{3}{4} = \frac{15}{20}$.

CHECK YOUR UNDERSTANDING

Solve.

1. $\frac{2}{3} = \frac{t}{60}$

2. $\frac{18}{24} = \frac{6}{x}$

3. $\frac{3}{10} = \frac{m}{5}$

Check your answers on page 375.

Using Proportions to Solve Rate Problems

Proportions can be used to solve many rate problems. The first step is to write a proportion that fits the problem you want to solve. The second step is to solve the proportion.

EXAMPLES Bill's new car can travel 35 miles on 1 gallon of gasoline. At this rate, how far can the car travel on 7 gallons?

Organizing the information from the problem in a simple rate table can help you write a correct proportion.

miles	35	n
gallons	1	7

From this table, you can write the following proportion.

$$\frac{35 \text{ miles}}{1 \text{ gallon}} = \frac{n \text{ miles}}{7 \text{ gallons}}$$

One way to solve this proportion is to notice that 7 gallons is 7 * 1 gallon, so n miles must be 7 * 35 miles, or 245 miles.

$$\frac{35}{1} = \frac{n}{7}$$

* 7

* 7

Another way is to use cross multiplication.
First, calculate the cross products.

$$\frac{35}{1} = \frac{n}{7}$$

$$1 * n = n$$

$$35 * 7 = 245$$

Second, write an equation for the cross product.
$n = 245$ miles

Bill's car can travel 245 miles on 7 gallons.

EXAMPLE   A gray whale's heart beats 24 times in 3 minutes. At this rate, how many times does it beat in 2 minutes?

Set up a simple rate table.

beats	24	x
minutes	3	2

From this table, you can write the following proportion.

$\dfrac{24\ \text{beats}}{3\ \text{minutes}} = \dfrac{x\ \text{beats}}{2\ \text{minutes}}$

To solve this proportion, first find the cross products.

$\dfrac{24}{3} = \dfrac{x}{2}$ $3 * x$ $24 * 2 = 48$

Next, set the cross products equal. $3 * x = 48$

Finally, solve the equation by dividing both sides by 3.

$(3 * x) / 3 = 48 / 3$ $x = 16$

The gray whale's heart beats 16 times in 2 minutes.

EXAMPLE   Henry typed 192 words in 4 minutes. At this rate, how long would it take him to type 288 words?

Step 1: Write a proportion.

$\dfrac{192\ \text{words}}{4\ \text{minutes}} = \dfrac{288\ \text{words}}{n\ \text{minutes}}$

Step 2: Find the cross products.

$\dfrac{192}{4} = \dfrac{288}{n}$ $4 * 288 = 1{,}152$ $192 * n$

Step 3: Set the cross products equal.

$1{,}152 = 192 * n$

Step 4: Solve the equation.

$1{,}152 / 192 = (192 * n) / 192$ $n = 6$

Henry typed 288 words in 6 minutes.

CHECK YOUR UNDERSTANDING

Solve.

1. Erica is making syrup. She uses 2 parts sugar to 5 parts water. How much water should she use for 5 cups of sugar?

2. Of Sarah's cousins, $\frac{2}{5}$ are girls. Sarah has 8 girl cousins. How many cousins does Sarah have in all?

Check your answers on page 375.

Ratios

In her monthly report, the manager of a grocery store wrote: "We sold three times as many quarts of ice cream as quarts of frozen yogurt." This statement is an example of a comparison of two like quantities called a **ratio.** You can say that the ratio of quarts of ice cream to quarts of frozen yogurt is 3 to 1. This means that for every 3 quarts of ice cream the store sold, it sold 1 quart of frozen yogurt.

All of the following are statements of ratios:

- It is estimated that by 2020, there will be *5 times as many* people at least 100 years old as there were in 1990.

- Elementary school students make up about *14%* of the United States population.

- On an average evening, about $\frac{1}{3}$ of the United States population watches TV.

- The chances of winning a prize in a lottery can be less than *1 in 1 million*.

- A common scale for dollhouses is *1 inch to 12 inches*.

> **NOTE**
>
> **Like quantities** are numbers with the same unit. For example, 5 inches and 8 inches are like quantities since they have the same unit, inches.

Percent notation is especially useful for comparing ratios. When ratios are renamed as percents, they are given the number 100 as their common denominator. For example, if Cindy got 14 out of 25 votes in the fifth grade class election, this is the same as getting 56 out of 100 votes, or 56% of the votes. If Bruce got 18 out of 30 votes in the sixth grade class election, this is the same as getting 60 out of 100 votes, or 60% of the votes. Once each ratio is renamed in percent form, it is easy to see that Bruce got a larger portion of votes than Cindy did.

Cindy got 14 out of 25 votes in the fifth grade class election.	Bruce got 18 out of 30 votes in the sixth grade class election.
$\frac{14}{25} = \frac{56}{100} = 56\%$	$\frac{18}{30} = \frac{60}{100} = 60\%$

Some ratios compare quantities that involve a whole and its parts.

EXAMPLES In a class of 20 students, there are 12 girls and 8 boys.

You can think of the 20 students as the **whole** and the 12 girls and 8 boys as **parts of the whole.**

A **part-to-whole** ratio compares a part of the whole to the whole. The statements, "8 out of 20 students are boys" and "12 out of 20 students are girls," each express a part-to-whole ratio.

A **part-to-part** ratio compares a part of the whole to another part of the whole. The statement, "There are 8 boys for every 12 girls," expresses a part-to-part ratio.

Ratios can be expressed in a number of ways. For the above example, the ratio of girls to the total number of students can be expressed—

In *words*: Twelve out of 20 students are girls.
Twelve in 20 students are girls.
There are 12 girls for every 20 students.
The ratio of girls to all students is 12 to 20.

With a *fraction*: $\frac{12}{20}$, or $\frac{3}{5}$, of the students are girls.

With a *percent*: 60% of the students are girls.

With a *colon* between the two numbers being compared:
The ratio of girls to all students is 12:20 (12 to 20).

In a *proportion*: $\frac{\text{number of girls}}{\text{number of students}} = \frac{12 \text{ girls}}{20 \text{ students}}.$

> **NOTE**
>
> When ratios are made up of smaller numbers, such as the ratio 3 to 2, they are usually easier to understand.

Equivalent Ratios

Ratios that can be named by equivalent fractions are called **equivalent ratios.** The ratios 12 to 20, 6 to 10, and 3 to 5 are equivalent, because $\frac{12}{20}$, $\frac{6}{10}$, and $\frac{3}{5}$ are equivalent fractions. If 12 out of 20 students are girls, then you can also say that 6 out of 10 students are girls, or 3 out of 5 students are girls. Similarly, the ratios 12 girls to 8 boys, 6 girls to 4 boys, and 3 girls to 2 boys are equivalent, because $\frac{12}{8}$, $\frac{6}{4}$, and $\frac{3}{2}$ are equivalent fractions.

: girl
: boy

The ratio of girls to boys is 3 to 2.

Every ratio can be converted to a ratio of some number to 1. These are called ***n*-to-1 ratios.** One way to convert a ratio to an *n*-to-1 ratio is to divide the first number in the ratio by the second number. For example, to convert the ratio of 3 girls to 2 boys to an *n*-to-1 ratio, divide 3 by 2. The answer is 1.5. This means that the ratio of girls to boys is 1.5 to 1; that is, there are 1.5 girls for every boy. Another way to state this is to say that there are 1.5 times as many girls as boys. When comparing ratios, *n*-to-1 ratios are useful.

Some ratios compare two quantities that are not part of the same whole.

EXAMPLE A book appears in both a hardcover version and a paperback version. The hardcover version costs $25, and the paperback version costs $10. Compare the costs.

The ratio of the cost of the hardcover version to the cost of the paperback version is 25 to 10, or, in simplest form, 5 to 2.

To find the *n*-to-1 ratio, divide. 5 / 2 = 2.5

$$\frac{\text{hardcover cost}}{\text{paperback cost}} = \frac{25}{10} = \frac{5}{2} = \frac{2.5}{1}$$

The hardcover version costs 2.5 times as much as the paperback version.

CHECK YOUR UNDERSTANDING

Last month, Ellen received an allowance of $20. She spent $12 and saved the rest.

1. What is the ratio of the money she spent to her total allowance?

2. What is the ratio of the money she saved to the money she spent?

3. The money she spent is how many times the money she saved?

4. What percent of her allowance did she save?

Check your answers on page 375.

Using Ratios to Describe Size Changes

Many situations produce a **size change.** For example, a magnifying glass, a microscope, and an overhead projector all produce size changes that enlarge the original image. Most copying machines can create a variety of size changes—both enlargements and reductions of the original document.

Similar figures are figures that have the same shape but not necessarily the same size. In the examples of size changes above, the enlargement or reduction is **similar** to the original; that is, they have the same shape.

The **size-change factor** is a number that tells the amount of enlargement or reduction that takes place. For example, if you use a copy machine to make a 2X change in size, then every length in the copy is twice the size of the original. The size-change factor is 2. If you make a 0.5X change in size, then every length in the copy is half the size of the original. The size-change factor is $\frac{1}{2}$, or 0.5.

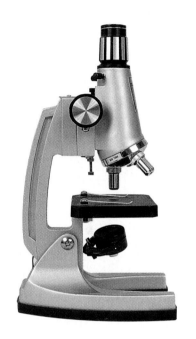

You can think of the size-change factor as a ratio. For a 2X size change, the ratio of a length in the copy to the corresponding length in the original is 2 to 1.

$$\text{size-change factor 2: } \frac{\text{copy size}}{\text{original size}} = \frac{2}{1}$$

For a 0.5X size change, the ratio of a length in the copy to a corresponding length in the original is 0.5 to 1.

$$\text{size-change factor 0.5: } \frac{\text{copy size}}{\text{original size}} = \frac{0.5}{1}$$

If the size-change factor is greater than 1, then the copy is an **enlargement** of the original; if it is less than 1, then the copy is a **reduction** of the original.

Devices That Magnify and Reduce

A photographer uses an enlarger to make prints from negatives. If the size of the image on the negative is 2" by 2" and the size of the image on the print is 4" by 4", then the size-change factor is 2. Binoculars that are 8X, or "8 power," magnify all the lengths you see with the naked eye to 8 times their actual size.

Scale Models

A model that is a careful, reduced copy of an actual object is called a **scale model.** You have probably seen scale models of cars, trains, and airplanes. The size-change factor in scale models is usually called the **scale factor.**

Dollhouses often have a scale factor of $\frac{1}{12}$. You can write this as "$\frac{1}{12}$ of actual size," "scale 1:12," "$\frac{1}{12}$ scale," or as a proportion:

"$\dfrac{\text{dollhouse length}}{\text{real house length}} = \dfrac{1"}{12"}$."

All the dimensions of an E-scale model railroad are $\frac{1}{96}$ of the actual size. We can write this as "scale 1:96," or "scale: $\frac{1}{8}$ inch represents 1 foot," "scale: 0.125 inch represents 1 foot," or

"$\dfrac{\text{model railroad length}}{\text{real railroad length}} = \dfrac{1"}{96"}$."

Note: The scale is 1:96 since "$\frac{1}{8}$ inch:12 inches" is the same as "1 inch:96 inches."

Maps

The size-change factor for maps is usually called the **scale.** If a map scale is 1:25,000, then every length on the map is $\frac{1}{25,000}$ of the actual length, and any real distance is 25,000 times the distance shown on the map.

$$\frac{\text{map distance}}{\text{real distance}} = \frac{1}{25,000}$$

Scale Drawings

The size-change factor for scale drawings is also usually called the **scale.** If an architect's scale drawing shows "scale $\frac{1}{4}$ inch:1 foot" or "scale $\frac{1}{4}$ inch represents 1 foot," then the drawing is $\frac{1}{48}$ of the actual size.

$$\frac{\text{drawing length}}{\text{real length}} = \frac{\frac{1}{4}\text{ inch}}{1\text{ foot}}$$

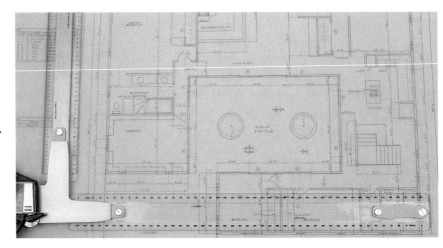

You may see scales written with an equal sign, such as "$\frac{1}{4}$ inch = 1 foot." But $\frac{1}{4}$ inch is certainly not equal to 1 foot, so "$\frac{1}{4}$ inch = 1 foot" is not mathematically correct. What is meant is that $\frac{1}{4}$ inch on the map or scale drawing stands for 1 foot in the real world.

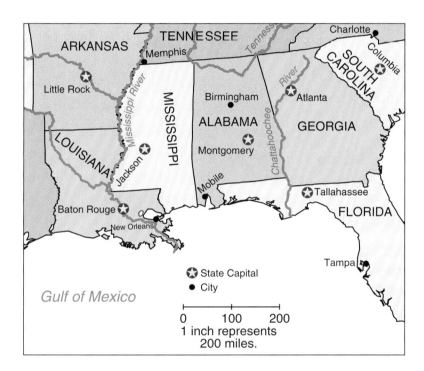

CHECK YOUR UNDERSTANDING

Solve.

1. The side of a square is 2.5 cm. A copier is used to make an enlargement of the square. The scale factor is 3.

   a. What is the side of the enlarged square?

   b. What is the perimeter of the enlarged square?

Check your answers on page 375.

2. Look at the map above. Two cities are 3 inches apart. The map scale is

$$\frac{\text{map distance}}{\text{real distance}} = \frac{1 \text{ inch}}{200 \text{ miles}}.$$

What is the actual distance between the two cities?

Map Scales

Cartographers (mapmakers) show large areas of land and water in small areas on paper. Using a map and a **map scale,** you can estimate actual distances. Different maps use different scales.

On the map scale at the right, the length of the bar stands for 10 actual miles. Half the length of the bar stands for 5 actual miles.

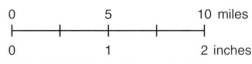

Since the bar is 2 inches long and stands for 10 actual miles, the map scale can also be written:

$$\frac{\text{real distance}}{\text{map distance}} = \frac{10\ \text{miles}}{2\ \text{inches}}.$$

Finding Distances Using a Map Scale

There are many ways to find distances on a map.

Method 1 Use a ruler if the distance you want to measure is in a straight line.

Step 1: Use a ruler to measure the distance on the map.

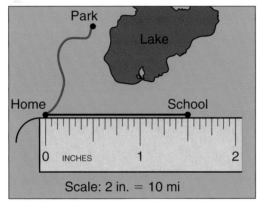

Scale: 2 in. = 10 mi

Step 2: Use the map scale to find the real distance for the map distance you measured. The map distance is 1.5 inches and the scale is 10 miles to 2 inches. To find the real distance we can solve this number model:

$$\frac{\text{real distance}}{1.5\ \text{inches}} = \frac{10\ \text{miles}}{2\ \text{inches}}.$$

One way to solve this number model is to change $\frac{10\ \text{miles}}{2\ \text{inches}}$ to the equivalent n-to-1 ratio $\frac{5\ \text{miles}}{1\ \text{inch}}$.

$$\frac{\text{real distance}}{1.5\ \text{inches}} = \frac{5\ \text{miles}}{1\ \text{inch}}$$

1 inch on the map stands for 5 miles, so 1.5 inches must stand for 7.5 miles.

Method 2 Use a piece of paper.

You can find distances on a map that has a scale using only paper and pencil.

Step 1: Lay an edge of a piece of paper along the path from the starting point to the ending point of the distance you want to find.

If the path is straight: Mark the starting point and the endpoint on the paper.

If the path is curved: Mark the starting point on the paper. Then pick another point along the path you want to measure. If the path is very curved, pick a point close to the start. If the path is not so curved, the point can be farther away. Mark this second point on your paper. Since you are using straight segments to fit a curved path, shorter segments will fit better. Pivot the paper to follow the path, marking distances as you go. Make a heavy mark when you reach the endpoint.

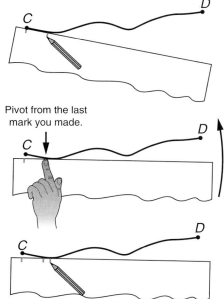

Pivot from the last mark you made.

Step 2: Compare the distance, as marked on your paper, from the starting point to the endpoint with the map scale.

Method 3 Use a compass if you are measuring a curved path.

Step 1: Adjust the compass so that the distance between the anchor point and the pencil point is the same as a distance on the map scale.

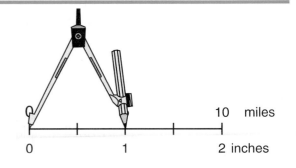

10 miles

0   1   2 inches

Step 2: Imagine a path connecting the starting point and ending point of the distance you want to measure. Put the anchor point of the compass at the starting point. Use the pencil point to make an arc on the path. Move the anchor point to the spot where the arc and the path meet. Continue walking the compass along the path until you reach or pass the ending point. Be careful to keep the same compass opening.

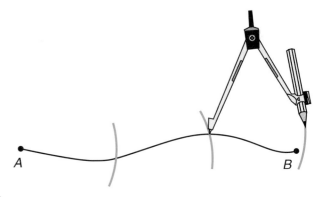

A   B

Step 3: Keep track of how many times you move the compass. Each move stands for the distance on the map scale. To estimate the total distance, multiply the number of moves by the distance each move stands for.

CHECK YOUR UNDERSTANDING

Use the map scale to estimate the distance along the path from point X to point Y.

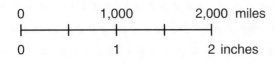

0   1,000   2,000 miles

0   1   2 inches

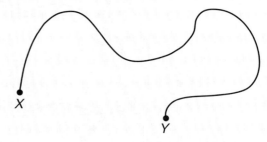

X

Y

Check your answers on page 375.

Data & Probability

Collecting Data

There are different ways to collect information about something. You can count, measure, ask questions, or observe and describe what you see. The information you collect is called **data.**

Surveys

Much of the information used to make decisions comes from **surveys.** Many surveys collect data about people. Stores survey their customers to find out which products they should carry. Television stations survey viewers to learn which programs are popular. Politicians survey people to learn how they plan to vote in elections.

The survey data about people is collected in several ways. These include face-to-face interviews, telephone interviews, printed questionnaires that are returned by mail, and group discussions (often called *focus groups*).

However, not all surveys gather information about people. For example, there are surveys of cars, buildings, and animal groups.

EXAMPLE A bird survey is conducted during December and January each year in the Chicago area. Bird watchers list the different bird species observed. Then, they count the number of each species they see. The lists are combined to create a final data set.

From the 1999–2000 Chicago Bird Survey

Species	Number of Birds Seen
Canada goose	3,768
house finch	304
snowy owl	1
starling	1,573

Some surveys collect data in ways other than through interviews or questionnaires.

EXAMPLE Highway engineers sometimes make videotapes of vehicles and drivers along a street or highway. They use the video data to analyze vehicle speeds and driving patterns.

Samples

The **population** is a group of people or things that is being studied. Because the population may be very large, it may not be possible to collect data from every member. Therefore, data are collected only from a sample group to provide information that is probably valid for the population. A **sample** is a part of the population that is chosen to represent the whole population.

Large samples give more dependable estimates than small ones. For example, if you want to estimate the percentage of adults who drive to work, a sample of 100 persons provides a better estimate than a sample of 10.

EXAMPLE A survey of teenagers needs data on people aged 13 to 19. There are about 27 million teenagers in the United States. So, it is not possible to collect data from every teenager. Instead, data are collected from a large sample of teenagers.

The results from a recent survey of teens are shown in the table.

How Teens Divide Their Media Time

Watching TV/videos/movies	56%
Listening to music	22%
Reading	12%
Playing video games	3%
Using computers	3%

Source: Henry J. Kaiser Foundation, as reported in 12/6/99 *N.Y. Times.*

The decennial (every 10 years) census is an example of a survey that includes *all* the people in the United States. Every household is required to fill out a census form, but certain questions are asked only in a sample of 1 in 6 households.

A **random sample** is a sample that gives all members of the population the same chance of being selected. Random samples give more dependable information than those that are not random.

EXAMPLE Suppose you want to estimate what percentage of the population will vote for Mr. Jenkins.

- If you use a sample of 100 best friends of Mr. Jenkins, the sample is *not* a random sample. People who do not know Mr. Jenkins have no chance of being selected.
- A sample of best friends will not fairly represent the entire population. It will not furnish a dependable estimate of how the entire population will vote.

Organizing Data

Once the data have been collected, it helps to organize them in order to make them easier to understand. **Line plots** and **tally charts** are two methods of organizing data.

EXAMPLE Mrs. Halko's class got the following scores on a 20-word vocabulary test. Make a line plot and a tally chart to show the data below.

20 15 18 17 20 12 15 17 19 18 20 16 16

17 14 15 19 18 18 15 10 20 19 18 15 18

Scores on a 20-Word Vocabulary Test

Number of Students

				X			X			
				X			X			X
				X		X	X	X	X	X
				X	X	X	X	X	X	X
X		X		X	X	X	X	X	X	X

10 11 12 13 14 15 16 17 18 19 20

Number Correct

Scores on a 20-Word Vocabulary Test

Number Correct	Number of Students
10	/
11	
12	/
13	
14	/
15	####
16	//
17	///
18	#### /
19	///
20	////

In the line plot, there are 5 Xs above 15.
In the tally chart, there are 5 tallies to the right of 15.

Both the line plot and the tally chart help to organize the data. They make it easier to describe the data. For example,

- 4 students had 20 correct (a perfect score).
- 18 correct is the score that came up most often.
- 10, 12, and 14 correct are scores that came up least often.
- 0–9, 11, and 13 correct are scores that did not occur at all.

CHECK YOUR UNDERSTANDING

Here are the numbers of hits made by 12 players in a baseball game: 1 0 4 2 1 0 2 3 0 2 1 0

Organize the data.

1. Make a tally chart.   **2.** Make a line plot.

Check your answers on page 375.

Sometimes the data are spread over a wide range of numbers. This makes a tally chart and a line plot difficult to draw. In such cases, you can make a tally chart in which the results are grouped, or, you may organize the data by making a **stem-and-leaf plot.**

For a health project, the students in Mr. Preston's class took each other's pulse rates. (A *pulse rate* is the number of heartbeats per minute.) These were the results:

92	72	90	86	102	78	88	75	72	82
90	94	70	94	78	75	90	102	65	94
70	94	85	88	105	86	78	75	86	108
94	75	88	86	99	78	86			

Tally Chart of Grouped Data

The data have been sorted or grouped into intervals of 10.

The chart shows that most of the students had a pulse rate from 70 to 99. More students had a pulse rate in the 70s than in any other interval.

Pulse Rates of Students

Number of Heartbeats	Number of Students
60–69	/
70–79	#### #### //
80–89	#### ####
90–99	#### ####
100–109	////

Stem-and-Leaf Plot

In a stem-and-leaf plot, the digit or digits in the left column (the **stem**) are combined with a single digit in the right column (the **leaf**) to form a numeral.

Each row has as many entries as there are digits in the right column. For example, the row with 9 in the left column has 10 entries: 92, 90, 90, 94, 94, 90, 94, 94, 94, and 99.

Pulse Rates of Students

Stems (10s)	Leaves (1s)
6	5
7	2 8 5 2 0 8 5 0 8 5 5 8
8	6 8 2 5 8 6 6 8 6 6
9	2 0 0 4 4 0 4 4 4 9
10	2 2 5 8

CHECK YOUR UNDERSTANDING

The first manned spaceflight occurred during the early 1960s. The ages of the first 10 space travelers were
27 25 43 37 32 31 39 36 28 26.

Organize the data.

1. Make a tally chart of grouped data.

2. Make a stem-and-leaf plot.

Check your answers on page 375.

Statistical Landmarks

The **landmarks** for a set of data are used to describe the data.

- The **minimum** is the smallest value.
- The **maximum** is the largest value.
- The **range** is the difference between the maximum and the minimum.
- The **mode** is the value (or values) that occurs most often.
- The **median** is the middle value.

EXAMPLE Here is a record of one week's absences at Medgar Evers School. Find the landmarks for the data.

Day	Number Absent
Monday	24
Tuesday	21
Wednesday	9
Thursday	13
Friday	13

Minimum (lowest) number: 9
Maximum (highest) number: 24
Range of numbers: 24 − 9 = 15
Mode (most frequent number): 13

To find the median (middle value), list the numbers in sequential order. Then, find the middle number.

9̷ 1̷3̷ 13 2̷1̷ 2̷4̷
median

EXAMPLE The **line plot** shows students' scores on a 20-word spelling test. Find the landmarks for the data.

Minimum: 10
Maximum: 20
Range: 20 − 10 = 10
Mode: 18

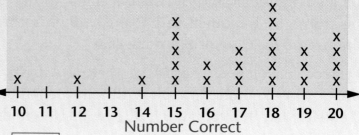

Scores on a 20-Word Spelling Test

Number of Students

Number Correct

10 12 14 15 15 15 15 15 16 16 17 17 [17 18] 18 18 18 18 18 19 19 19 20 20 20 20

middle scores

There are two middle scores, 17 and 18. The median is 17.5, which is the number halfway between 17 and 18.

CHECK YOUR UNDERSTANDING

Here are science quiz scores (number correct): 1 3 2 1 0 2 1 0 2 0 2 4

Find the minimum, maximum, range, mode, and median for this set of data.

Check your answers on page 375.

The Mean (or Average)

The **mean** of a set of numbers is often called the *average*. To find the mean, do the following:

Step 1: Add the numbers.
Step 2: Divide the sum by the number of addends.

> **NOTE**
> The mean and the median are often the same or almost the same. Both the mean and the median can be thought of as a "typical" number for the data set.

EXAMPLE On a 4-day trip, Kenny's family drove 200, 120, 160, and 260 miles. What is the mean number of miles they drove per day?

Step 1: Add the numbers: 200 + 120 + 160 + 260 = 740.
Step 2: Divide the sum by the number of addends: 740 ÷ 4 = 185.

The mean is 185 miles. They drove an average of 185 miles per day.

If you use a calculator, key in: 200 ⊕ 120 ⊕ 160 ⊕ 260 (Enter)
Divide the sum by 4. Key in: 740 ⊕ 4 (Enter) Answer: 185

When calculating the mean of a large set of numbers, it often helps to first organize the data in a tally chart or line plot.

EXAMPLE The students in Mrs. Dillard's class measured each other's height in inches. What is the mean height?

The students organized the measurements in a tally chart (the first two columns on the right).

On their calculators, they multiplied each height by the number of students of that height and kept a running total. Then, they divided the final total by the number of students.

The mean, rounded to the nearest inch, is 54 inches.

Height (inches)	Number of Students	Key in:	Calculator Answer
49	//	2 ⊗ 49 (Enter)	98
50	//	⊕ 2 ⊗ 50 (Enter)	198
51	/	⊕ 51 (Enter)	249
52	////	⊕ 4 ⊗ 52 (Enter)	457
53	/	⊕ 53 (Enter)	510
54	//	⊕ 2 ⊗ 54 (Enter)	618
55	///	⊕ 3 ⊗ 55 (Enter)	783
56	##//	⊕ 5 ⊗ 56 (Enter)	1063
57			
58	//	⊕ 2 ⊗ 58 (Enter)	1179
Total	22	⊕ 22 (Enter)	53.59090909

CHECK YOUR UNDERSTANDING

Megan received these scores on math tests: 90 75 75 75 80 90 80 85 80 80 80
Use your calculator to find Megan's mean score.

Check your answer on page 375.

Bar Graphs

A **bar graph** is a drawing that uses bars to represent numbers. Bar graphs display information in a way that makes it easy to show comparisons.

The title of a bar graph describes the information in the graph. Each bar has a label. Units are given to show how something was counted or measured. When possible, the graph gives the source of the information.

EXAMPLE This is a **vertical bar graph.**

- Each bar represents the mean (average) weight of the primate named beneath the bar.
- It is easy to compare primate weights by comparing the bars. A gorilla is about 3 times as heavy as a human. Humans and orangutans have approximately the same weight.

Heaviest Primates

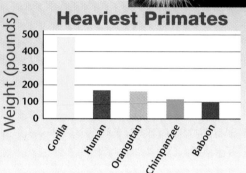

EXAMPLE This is a **horizontal bar graph.**

- Each bar represents the percent of adults in an age group who live alone.
- The bars show a clear trend. As the age for a group increases, the percent of adults in that group who live alone increases. Only 3% of 15- to 24-year-olds live alone. But 41% of those 75 and older live alone.

Adults Living Alone

75 years and over
65 to 74 years
45 to 64 years
25 to 44 years
15 to 24 years

Age

0 10 20 30 40 50
Percent

CHECK YOUR UNDERSTANDING

The table at the right shows the percent of U.S. households that own popular pets. Make a bar graph to show this information.

Popular Pets in the United States

Pet	Percent of U.S. Households
dog	37%
cat	31%
bird	6%
fish	3%
horse	3%

Check your answers on page 375.

Side-by-Side and Stacked Bar Graphs

Sometimes there are two or more bar graphs that are related to the same situation. Related bar graphs are often combined into a single graph. The combined graph saves space and makes it easier to compare the data. The examples below show two different ways to draw combined bar graphs.

EXAMPLE The first bar graph shows road miles from Boston to different cities. The second bar graph shows air miles.

The graphs are combined into a **side-by-side bar graph** by drawing the related bars side-by-side in different colors. It is easy to compare road miles and air miles on the side-by-side graph.

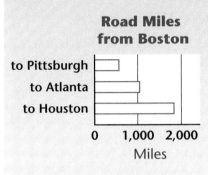

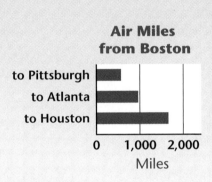

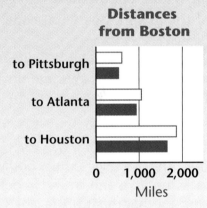

Source: The World Almanac

EXAMPLE The bar graphs below show the number of sports teams that boys and girls joined during a 1-year period.

The bars within each graph can be stacked on top of one another, as shown at the right. The **stacked bar graph** includes each of the stacked bars.

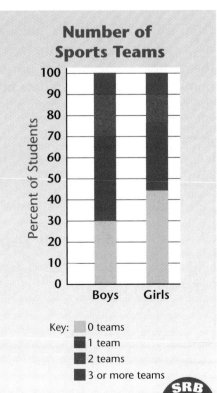

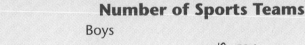

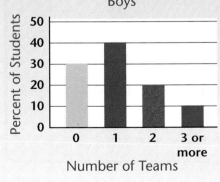

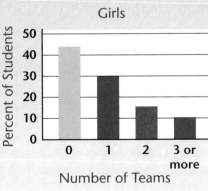

Line Graphs

Line graphs are used to display information that shows trends. They often show how something has changed over a period of time.

Line graphs are often called **broken-line graphs.** Line segments connect the points on the graph. The segments joined end-to-end look like a broken line.

Line graphs have a horizontal and a vertical scale. Each of these scales is called an **axis** (plural: **axes**). Each axis is labeled to show what is being measured and what the unit of measure is. When looking at a line graph, try to determine the purpose of the graph. See what conclusions you can draw from it.

Broken-Line Graph

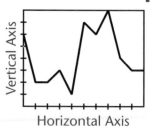

Joined end-to-end, the segments look like a broken line.

EXAMPLE The broken-line graph to the right shows the average number of thunderstorm days for each month in Chicago, Illinois.

The horizontal axis shows each month of the year. The average number of thunderstorm days for a month is shown with a dot above the label for that month. The labels on the vertical axis are used to estimate the number of days represented by that dot.

From January to June, the number of thunderstorm days increases each month. From June to January, the number decreases. The greatest change in number of thunderstorm days from one month to the next occurs from September to October.

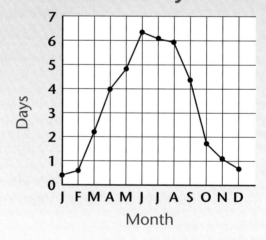

Average Number of Thunderstorm Days in Chicago

CHECK YOUR UNDERSTANDING

The following table shows average temperatures for Boston, Massachusetts. Make a line graph to show this information.

Average Temperatures for Boston, Massachusetts

Month	Jan	Feb	Mar	Apr	May	Jun	Jul	Aug	Sep	Oct	Nov	Dec
Temp (°F)	29	30	39	48	58	68	74	72	65	55	45	34

Check your answers on page 375.

Step Graphs

Step graphs are used to describe situations in which changes in values are not gradual but occur in jumps.

EXAMPLE The step graph at the right shows the cost of renting a bicycle from B & H Rentals.

According to the graph, it costs $10 to rent a bike for 1 hour or less and $2.50 for each additional half-hour or fraction thereof. For example, it costs $10 whether you rent a bike for $\frac{1}{2}$ hour, 45 minutes, or 1 hour. It costs $12.50 whether you rent a bike for $1\frac{1}{2}$ hours or just 1 hour and 1 minute. Note the dot at the end of the segment for the first hour. It indicates that the cost is $10 for 1 hour. There is no dot at the beginning of the segment for the second hour. This indicates that $12.50 is not the cost for 1 hour. The other dots in the graph are interpreted in the same way.

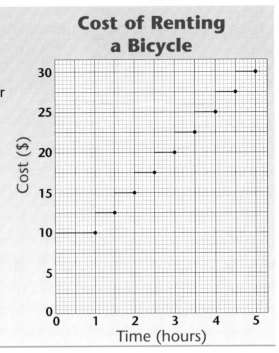

Cost of Renting a Bicycle

Telephone and parking lot rates are other examples of situations that can be shown by step graphs. Such rates do not change gradually over time but change at the end of intervals of time, such as minutes or hours.

CHECK YOUR UNDERSTANDING

The step graph at the right shows the cost of taking a cab for various distances.

1. Find the cost of taking a cab for each distance.
   a. 1 mile   b. 1.2 miles   c. 2 miles
   d. 4 miles   e. 3.5 miles

2. a. What is the cost of taking a cab for a distance of 1 mile or less?

   b. What is the cost for each additional mile or fraction of a mile?

Check your answers on page 376.

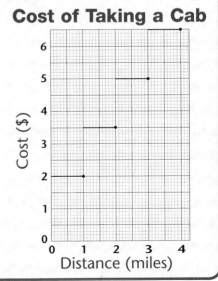

Cost of Taking a Cab

History and Uses of Spreadsheets

Everyday Rentals–Debit Statement for May, 1964

Company	Type	Invoice #	Invoice Amount	Amount Paid	Balance Due
Electric	Utility	2704-3364	342.12	100.00	242.12
Gas	Utility	44506-309	129.43	50.00	79.43
Phone	Utility	989-2209	78.56	78.56	0.00
Water	Utility	554-2-1018	13.12		13.12
NW Bank	Mortgage	May 1964	1,264.00	1,264.00	0.00
Waste Removal	Garbage	387-219	23.00		23.00
NW Lumber	Supplies	e-318	239.47	50.00	189.47
Total			2,089.70	1,542.56	547.14

Above is a copy of a financial record for Everyday Rentals Corporation for May, 1964. Often a financial record had more columns of figures than would fit on one sheet of paper, so accountants taped several sheets together. They folded the sheets for storage and spread them out to read or make entries. Such sheets came to be called **spreadsheets.**

Note that the "Balance Due" **column** and the "Total" **row** are calculated from other numbers in the spreadsheet. Before they had computers, accountants wrote spreadsheets by hand. If an accountant changed a number in one row or column, several other numbers would have to be erased, recalculated, and reentered.

For example, when Everyday Rentals Corporation pays the $23 owed to Waste Removal, the accountant must enter that amount in the "Amount Paid" column. That means the total of the "Amount Paid" column must be changed as well. That's not all—making a payment changes the amount in the "Balance Due" column and the total of the "Balance Due" column. One entry requires three other changes to **update** (revise) the spreadsheet.

When personal computers were developed, spreadsheet programs were among the first applications. Spreadsheet programs save time by making changes automatically. Suppose the record at the top of this page is on a computer spreadsheet. When the accountant enters the payment of $23, the computer automatically recalculates all of the numbers that are affected by that payment.

> **N O T E**
>
> In mathematics and science, computer spreadsheets are used to store large amounts of data and to perform complicated calculations. People use spreadsheets at home to keep track of budgets, payments, and taxes.

Spreadsheets and Computers

A **spreadsheet program** enables you to use a computer to evaluate formulas quickly and efficiently. On a computer screen, a spreadsheet looks like a table. Each **cell** in the table has an **address** made up of a letter and a number. The letter identifies the column, and the number identifies the row in which the cell is found. For example, cell B3 is in column B, row 3.

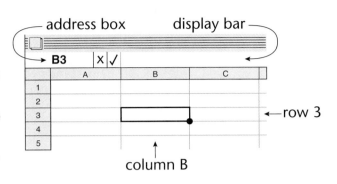

To enter information in a cell, you can use a computer mouse to click on the cell; the address of the cell will appear in the **address box.** Then, you type the information you want to enter in the cell; the information will appear in the **display bar.**

There are three kinds of information that may be entered in a spreadsheet.

- **Labels** (may consist of words, numbers, or both) These are used to display information about the spreadsheet, such as the headings for the columns and rows. Numbers in labels are never used in calculations. When a label is entered from the keyboard, it is stored in its address and shown in its cell on the screen.
- **Numbers** (those not included in labels) These are used in calculations. When a number is entered from the keyboard, it is stored in its address and appears in its cell on the screen.
- **Formulas** These tell the computer what calculations to make on the numbers in other cells. When a formula is entered from the keyboard, it is stored in its address but is *not* shown in its cell on the screen. Instead, a number is shown in the cell. This number is the result of applying the formula to numbers in other cells.

EXAMPLE   Study the spreadsheet at the right.

All the entries in row 1 and column A are *labels.*

The entries in cells B3 through B6 and cells C3 through C6 are *numbers* that are not labels. They have been entered from the keyboard and are used in calculations.

Cells D3 through D10 also display numbers, but they have not been entered from the keyboard. Instead, a *formula* was entered in each of these cells. The formulas were used by the computer program to calculate the numbers that appear in column D.

The numbers in column D are the results of calculations.

D3 |X|√ =B3*C3

	A	B	C	D
1	item name	unit price	quantity	totals
2				
3	pencils	0.29	6	1.74
4	graph paper	1.19	2	2.38
5	ruler	0.50	1	0.50
6	book	5.95	1	5.95
7				
8	Subtotal			10.57
9	tax 7%			.74
10	Total			$11.31

EXAMPLE Study the spreadsheet at the right.

The *address box* shows that cell D3 has been selected; the *display bar* shows " = B3 * C3." This stands for the formula D3 = B3 * C3. It is not necessary to enter D3, since D3 is already identified as the address of the cell. This formula is stored in the computer; it is not shown in cell D3.

D3	X ✓ =B3*C3		
	A	B	C	D
1	item name	unit price	quantity	totals
2				
3	pencils	0.29	6	1.74
4	graph paper	1.19	2	2.38
5	ruler	0.50	1	0.50
6	book	5.95	1	5.95
7				
8	Subtotal			10.57
9	tax 7%			.74
10	Total			$11.31

When the formula is entered, the program multiplies the number in cell B3 (0.29) by the number in cell C3 (6) and displays the product (1.74) in cell D3.

Suppose that you clicked on cell C3 and changed the 6 to an 8. The entry in cell D3 would change automatically to 2.32 (= 0.29 * 8). At the same time, the entries in cells D8, D9, and D10 would also change automatically. The entry in cell D8 is the result of a calculation involving the entry in cell D3, the entry in cell D8 is used to calculate the entry in cell D9, and the entries in cells D8 and D9 are used to calculate the entry in cell D10.

CHECK YOUR UNDERSTANDING

The following spreadsheet gives budget information for a class picnic.

Class Picnic ($$)

	A	B	C	D
1		budget for class picnic		
2				
3	quantity	food items	unit price	cost
4	6	packages of hamburgers	2.79	16.74
5	5	packages of hamburger buns	1.29	6.45
6	3	bags of potato chips	3.12	9.36
7	3	quarts of macaroni salad	4.50	13.50
8	4	bottles of soft drinks	1.69	6.76
9			subtotal	52.81
10			8% tax	4.23
11			total	57.04

Use the spreadsheet to answer the following questions.

1. What kind of information is shown in column B?

2. What information is shown in cell C7?

3. Which cell shows the title of the spreadsheet?

4. What information is shown in cell A5?

5. Which occupied cells do not hold labels or formulas?

6. Which column holds formulas?

Check your answers on page 376.

How to Use the Percent Circle

A **compass** is a device for drawing circles. You can also use some of the shapes on your **Geometry Template** to draw circles.

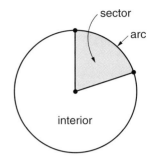

An **arc** is a piece of a circle. If you mark two points on a circle, these points and the part of the circle between them form an arc.

The region inside a circle is called its **interior.**

A **sector** is a wedge-shaped piece of a circle and its interior. A sector consists of two radii (singular: radius), the arc determined by their endpoints, and the part of the interior of the circle bounded by the radii and the arc.

A **circle graph** is sometimes called a **pie graph** because it looks like a pie that has been cut into several pieces. Each "piece" is a sector of the circle.

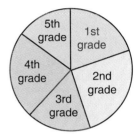

The circle graph shows the distribution of students in grades 1 to 5 at Elm Place School.

You can use the **Percent Circle** on your Geometry Template to find what percent of the circle graph each sector represents. Here are two methods for using the Percent Circle.

Method 1: Direct Measure

- Place the center of the Percent Circle over the center of the circle graph.
- Rotate the template so that the 0% mark is aligned with one side (line segment) of the sector you are measuring.
- Read the percent at the mark on the Percent Circle located over the other side of the sector. This tells what percent the sector represents.

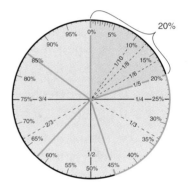

For example, the sector for first grade represents 20%.

Method 2: Difference Comparison

- Place the center of the Percent Circle over the center of the circle graph.
- Note the percent reading for one side of the sector you are measuring.
- Find the percent reading for the other side of the sector.
- Find the difference between these readings.

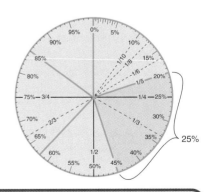

The sector for second grade represents 45% – 20%, or 25%.

CHECK YOUR UNDERSTANDING

What percents are represented by the other three sectors in the above circle graph?

Check your answers on page 376.

How to Draw a Circle Graph Using a Percent Circle

EXAMPLE Draw a circle graph to show the following information. The students in Mr. Zajac's class were asked to name their favorite colors: 9 students chose blue, 7 students chose green, 4 students chose yellow, and 5 chose red.

Step 1: Find what percent of the total each part represents. The total number of students who voted is $9 + 7 + 4 + 5 = 25$.

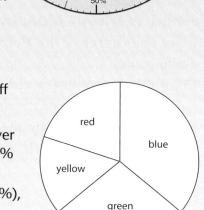

- 9 out of 25 chose blue.

    $\frac{9}{25} = \frac{36}{100} = 36\%$, so 36% chose blue.

- 7 out of 25 chose green.

    $\frac{7}{25} = \frac{28}{100} = 28\%$, so 28% chose green.

- 4 out of 25 chose yellow.

    $\frac{4}{25} = \frac{16}{100} = 16\%$, so 16% chose yellow.

- 5 out of 25 chose red.

    $\frac{5}{25} = \frac{20}{100} = 20\%$, so 20% chose red.

Step 2: Check that the sum of the percents is 100%.
$36\% + 28\% + 16\% + 20\% = 100\%$

Step 3: Use the Percent Circle on the Geometry Template to mark off the sectors.

- To mark off 36%, place the center of the Percent Circle over the center of the circle graph. Make a mark at 0% and 36% on the circle.
- To mark off 28%, make a mark at 64% ($36\% + 28\% = 64\%$), without moving the Percent Circle.
- To mark off 16%, make a mark at 80% ($64\% + 16\% = 80\%$).
- Check that the final sector represents 20%.

Step 4: Label each sector of the circle.

CHECK YOUR UNDERSTANDING

Draw a circle graph to display the following information:
- The Hot Shots basketball team scored 30 points in one game.
- Frank scored 3 points.
- Leah and Jill each scored 6 points.
- Dave scored 15 points.

Check your answers on page 376.

How to Draw a Circle Graph Using a Protractor

EXAMPLE Draw a circle graph to show the following information: In the month of June, there were 5 cloudy days, 6 sunny days, and 19 partly cloudy days.

Step 1: Find out what fraction or percent of the total each part represents. June has 30 days.

- 5 out of 30 were cloudy days.
  $\frac{5}{30} = \frac{1}{6}$, so $\frac{1}{6}$ of the days were cloudy.
- 6 out of 30 were sunny days.
  $\frac{6}{30} = \frac{1}{5}$, so $\frac{1}{5}$ of the days were sunny.
- 19 out of 30 were partly cloudy days.
  $\frac{19}{30} = 0.633... \approx 63.3\%$, so about 63.3% of the days were partly cloudy.

Step 2: Calculate the degree measure of the sector for each piece of data.

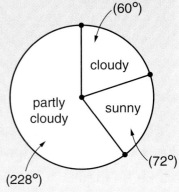

- The number of cloudy days in June was $\frac{1}{6}$ of the total number of days. Therefore, the degree measure of the sector for cloudy days is $\frac{1}{6}$ of 360°. $\frac{1}{6}$ of 360° = 60°.
- The number of sunny days in June was $\frac{1}{5}$ of the total number of days. Therefore, the degree measure of the sector for sunny days is $\frac{1}{5}$ of 360°. $\frac{1}{5}$ of 360° = 72°.
- The number of partly cloudy days in June was 63.3% of the total number of days. Therefore, the degree measure of the sector for partly cloudy days is 63.3% of 360°. 0.633 * 360° = 228°, rounded to the nearest degree.

Step 3: Check that the sum of the degree measures of the sectors is 360°.
60° + 72° + 228° = 360°

Step 4: Measure each sector with a protractor. Draw and label the sector.

CHECK YOUR UNDERSTANDING

Use your protractor to make a circle graph to display the following information. What is the degree measure of each sector, rounded to the nearest degree?

Favorite Subjects

Subject	Number of Students
Reading	3
Art	1
Math	6
Music	3
Social Studies	2
Science	5

Check your answers on page 376.

Probability

A **probability** is a number from 0 to 1 that indicates the likelihood that something will happen. The closer a probability is to 1, the more likely it is that an event will occur.

- A probability of 0 means that it is *impossible* for an event to happen. The probability is 0 that you will live to the age of 150.
- A probability of 1 means that an event is certain to occur. The probability is 1 that the sun will rise tomorrow.
- A probability of $\frac{1}{2}$ means that in the long run, an event is expected to occur about 1 in 2 times (half of the time, or 50% of the time). The probability that a tossed coin will land heads up is $\frac{1}{2}$. A tossed coin has a "50-50 chance" of landing heads up.

Probabilities can be expressed with fractions, percents, or decimals.

> **EXAMPLE**   The weather bureau predicts that there is an 80% chance of snow today and a 2 in 3 chance of snow tomorrow. On which day is it more likely to snow?
>
> A 2 in 3 chance means that the probability is $\frac{2}{3}$ (or about 67%).
>
> Since 80% is greater than 67%, it is more likely to snow today.

Calculating a Probability

Four common ways for finding probabilities are shown below.

Make a Guess	Nick guesses that he has a 75% chance (a 3 in 4 chance) of returning home by 9 o'clock.
Conduct an Experiment	Genevieve dropped 100 tacks: 60 landed point up and 40 landed point down. The chance of a tack landing point up is $\frac{60}{100}$, or 60%.
Use a Data Table	Pat got 48 hits in his last 100 times at bat. He estimates the probability that he will get a hit the next time at bat is $\frac{48}{100}$, or 48%.
Assume Equally Likely Outcomes	A die has 6 faces. Each face has the same chance of coming up. The probability of rolling a 5 is $\frac{1}{6}$. The probability of rolling a 4 or a 5 is double this—$\frac{2}{6}$, or $\frac{1}{3}$.

Hits	48
Walks	11
Outs	41
Total	100

Tree Diagrams

The diagram at the right represents a maze. Without retracing their steps, people walk through the maze, taking paths at random without any pattern or preference. Some people end up in Room A; some end up in Room B.

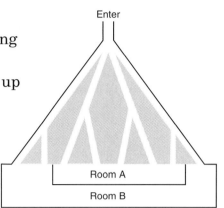

The diagrams in the example below represent this maze. Notice that they look like upside-down trees.

Tree diagrams like the ones below can help in analyzing probability situations. Tree diagrams are especially useful when some events follow or are affected by other events. In a tree diagram, the branches represent different paths, possibilities, or cases.

Tree diagrams can help answer questions about a maze.

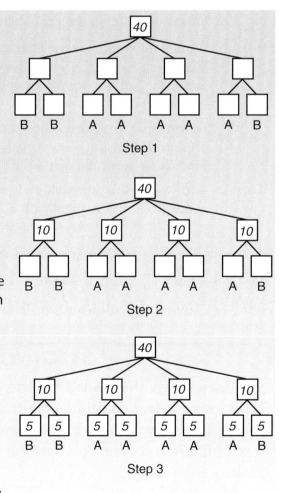

EXAMPLE Suppose 40 people walk through the maze shown at the top of the page. How many can be expected to end up in Room A? in Room B?

Step 1: In the top box of the tree diagram, record the number of people (40) who reach the first intersection where the path divides.

Step 2: The path divides. Since there is an equal chance of selecting any one of the next paths, an equal number of people will select each path. Write 10 in each box in the second row of boxes. $\frac{1}{4}$ of 40 is 10.

Step 3: Each path divides at the next intersection. Again, an equal number of people will select each of the next paths. Write 5 in the next set of boxes. Each path divides into two paths.

$\frac{1}{2}$ of 10 is 5.

Step 4: Add to find how many people reach each room. Five boxes are labeled A, representing exits into Room A. 25 people end up in Room A. Three boxes are labeled B, representing exits into Room B. 15 people end up in Room B.

So, 25 people can be expected to end up in Room A, and 15 people can be expected to end up in Room B.

A different kind of tree diagram can help find probabilities.

The tree diagram at the right represents the maze on page 143. The branching paths are shown, but there are no boxes. You can use this kind of tree diagram to calculate probabilities.

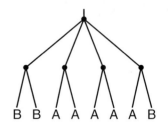

EXAMPLE Find the probability of ending up in Room A and Room B.

Step 1: At the first place where the path divides, there is an equal chance of selecting any one of the paths. Write this probability next to each path. There are four paths, so the probability of taking any one path is $\frac{1}{4}$.

Step 2: Each of these paths divides at the next intersection. Again, an equal number of people will select each of the next paths. Write the appropriate probability next to each path. Each path divides into two paths, so the probability of taking any one path is $\frac{1}{2}$.

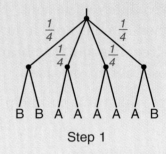

Step 1

Step 3: Continue to write probabilities on the diagram until all the exits have been reached. To find the probability of reaching a particular exit, multiply the probabilities of taking the paths leading to it.

For any exit, the probability of taking the first path to it is $\frac{1}{4}$. The probability of the next path is $\frac{1}{2}$. So, the probability of reaching a particular exit is $\frac{1}{2}$ of $\frac{1}{4}$, which is $\frac{1}{8}$.

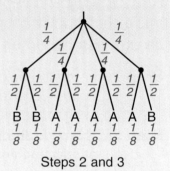

Steps 2 and 3

Step 4: Add to find the probability of entering each room. There are 5 exits to Room A, each with a probability of $\frac{1}{8}$. There are 3 exits to Room B, each with a probability of $\frac{1}{8}$.

So, the probability of entering Room A is $\frac{1}{8} + \frac{1}{8} + \frac{1}{8} + \frac{1}{8} + \frac{1}{8}$, or $\frac{5}{8}$.

The probability of entering Room B is $\frac{1}{8} + \frac{1}{8} + \frac{1}{8}$, or $\frac{3}{8}$.

Note that the sum of all the final probabilities is 1 since $\frac{5}{8} + \frac{3}{8} = 1$.

CHECK YOUR UNDERSTANDING

The map shows the roads from the town of Alpha. Suppose you start in Alpha and drive south. When the road divides, you choose the next road at random. Draw a tree diagram to help you find the probability of getting from Alpha:

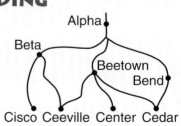

1. to Cisco   **2.** to Ceeville   **3.** to Center   **4.** to Cedar

Check your answers on page 376.

Geometry &
Constructions

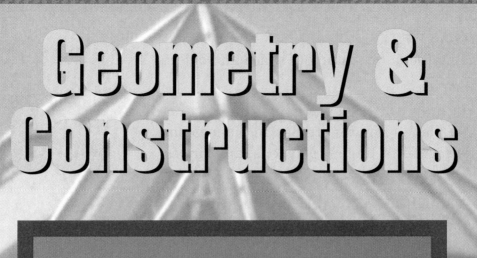

What Is Geometry?

Geometry is the mathematical study of space and objects in space.

Plane geometry concerns 2-dimensional objects (figures) on a flat surface (a plane). Figures studied in plane geometry include lines, line segments, angles, polygons, and circles.

Solid geometry is the study of 3-dimensional objects. These objects are often simplified versions of familiar everyday things. For example, *cylinders* are suggested by food cans, *spheres* by balls, and *prisms* by boxes.

Graphs, coordinates, and coordinate grids have also been part of *Everyday Mathematics*. The branch of geometry dealing with figures on a coordinate grid is called **coordinate geometry**, or **analytic geometry.** Analytic geometry combines algebra with geometry.

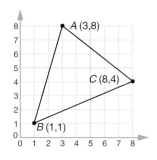

Transformation geometry is the study of geometric properties under motion. **Translations** (slides), **reflections** (flips), and **rotations** (turns) are familiar operations in transformation geometry.

168–169

Geometry originated in ancient Egypt and Mesopotamia as a practical tool for surveying land and constructing buildings. (The word *geometry* comes from the Greek words *ge*, meaning *the Earth*, and *metron*, meaning *to measure*.) About 300 B.C., the Greek mathematician Euclid gathered the geometric knowledge of his time into a book known as the *Elements*. Euclid's *Elements* is one of the great achievements of human thought. It begins with ten unproved statements, called postulates, and common notions. In modern wording, one of the postulates reads, "Through a given point not on a given line, there is exactly one line parallel to the given line."

Euclid used logic to deduce several hundred propositions (theorems) from the postulates and common notions—for example, "In any triangle, the side opposite the greater angle is greater."

Mathematicians began to develop other forms of geometry in the seventeenth century, beginning with René Descartes' analytic geometry (1637). The problem of perspective in paintings led to **projective geometry.** In the nineteenth century, mathematicians explored the results of changing Euclid's postulate about parallel lines quoted above. In **non-Euclidean geometry,** there are either no lines parallel to the given line or at least two lines parallel to the given line. **Topology,** a modern branch of geometry, deals with properties of geometric objects that do not change when their shapes are changed. You can read more about how to decide if two objects are topologically equivalent on pages 172 and 173.

There is exactly one line through point F parallel to $\overleftrightarrow{DE}$.

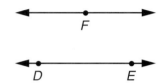

A coffee mug and a doughnut are topologically equivalent because they both have one hole.

A lidless teapot with a handle and a trophy cup with two handles are topologically equivalent because they both have two holes.

Angles

An **angle** is formed by 2 rays or 2 line segments that share the same endpoint. The symbol for an angle is ∠.

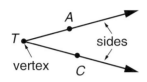

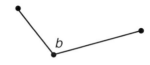

angle formed by 2 rays
names: ∠T, or ∠ATC, or ∠CTA

angle formed by 2 segments
name: ∠b

Measuring Angles

The **protractor** is a tool used to measure angles. Angles are measured in **degrees.** A degree is the unit of measure for the size of an angle.

The **degree symbol** (°) is often used in place of the word *degrees*. The measure of ∠T above is 30 degrees, or 30°.

Sometimes there is confusion about which angle should be measured. The small curved arrow in each picture shows which angle opening should be measured.

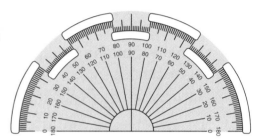

half-circle protractor

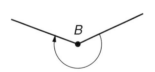

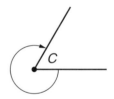

Measure of ∠A is 60°.

Measure of ∠B is 225°.

Measure of ∠C is 300°.

Classifying Angles

Angles may be classified according to their size.

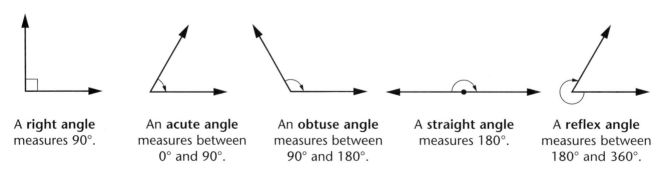

A **right angle**
measures 90°.

An **acute angle**
measures between
0° and 90°.

An **obtuse angle**
measures between
90° and 180°.

A **straight angle**
measures 180°.

A **reflex angle**
measures between
180° and 360°.

Parallel Lines and Segments

Parallel lines are lines on a flat surface that never meet. Think of a railroad track that goes on forever. The two rails are parallel lines. They never meet or cross and are always the same distance apart.

Parallel line segments are segments that are always the same distance apart. The top and bottom edges of this page are parallel segments because they are always about 11 inches apart.

The symbol for *parallel* is a pair of vertical lines ‖. If $\overline{BF}$ and $\overline{TG}$ are parallel, write $\overline{BF} \parallel \overline{TG}$.

If lines or segments cross each other, they **intersect**. Lines or segments that intersect and form right angles are called **perpendicular** lines or segments.

The symbol for *perpendicular* is ⊥, which looks like an upside-down letter T. If $\overleftrightarrow{SU}$ and $\overleftrightarrow{XY}$ are perpendicular, write $\overleftrightarrow{SU} \perp \overleftrightarrow{XY}$.

EXAMPLES

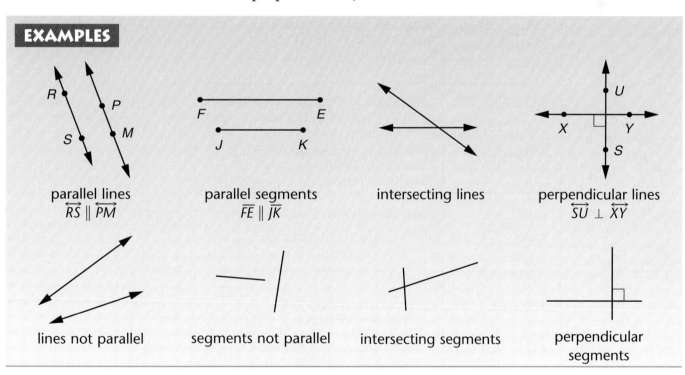

parallel lines
$\overleftrightarrow{RS} \parallel \overleftrightarrow{PM}$

parallel segments
$\overline{FE} \parallel \overline{JK}$

intersecting lines

perpendicular lines
$\overleftrightarrow{SU} \perp \overleftrightarrow{XY}$

lines not parallel

segments not parallel

intersecting segments

perpendicular segments

CHECK YOUR UNDERSTANDING

Draw and label the following.

1. Parallel line segments *AB* and *JK*

2. A line segment that is perpendicular to both $\overline{EF}$ and $\overline{CD}$

Check your answers on page 376.

Line Segments, Rays, Lines, and Angles

Figure	Name or Symbol	Description
• A	point A	**point:** A location in space
F C endpoints	$\overline{CF}$, or $\overline{FC}$	**line segment:** A straight path between two points, called its endpoints
K L endpoint	$\overrightarrow{LK}$	**ray:** A straight path that goes on forever in one direction from an endpoint
R P	$\overleftrightarrow{PR}$, or $\overleftrightarrow{RP}$	**line:** A straight path that goes on forever in both directions
vertex S P R	$\angle R$, or $\angle SRP$, or $\angle PRS$	**angle:** Two rays or line segments with a common endpoint, called the vertex
D C S R	$\overleftrightarrow{CD} \parallel \overleftrightarrow{RS}$	**parallel lines:** Lines that never meet and are everywhere the same distance apart
	$\overline{CD} \parallel \overline{RS}$	**parallel line segments:** Segments that are everywhere the same distance apart
R E D S	none	**intersecting lines:** Lines that meet
	none	**intersecting line segments:** Segments that meet
B D E C	$\overleftrightarrow{BC} \perp \overleftrightarrow{DE}$	**perpendicular lines:** Lines that intersect at right angles
	$\overline{BC} \perp \overline{DE}$	**perpendicular line segments:** Segments that intersect at right angles

CHECK YOUR UNDERSTANDING

Draw and label each of the following.

1. point J **2.** $\overleftrightarrow{MN}$ **3.** $\angle ABC$ **4.** $\overline{PQ}$ **5.** $\overleftrightarrow{ST} \parallel \overleftrightarrow{JK}$ **6.** $\overrightarrow{TU}$

Check your answers on page 376.

Parallel Lines and Angle Relationships

Two angles that have a common side and whose interiors do not overlap are called **adjacent angles.**

Figure 1

Angles a and b in Figure 1 are adjacent angles.

When two lines intersect, the angles opposite each other are called **vertical angles**, or **opposite angles.** The measures of any pair of vertical angles are equal.

The sum of the measures of adjacent angles, formed by two intersecting lines, is 180°. Pairs of angles whose measures total 180° are called **supplementary angles.**

> **EXAMPLES** The intersecting lines in Figure 2 form four angles, numbered 1, 2, 3, and 4.
> ∠1 and ∠3 are vertical angles and have the same measure.
> ∠1 and ∠2 are supplementary angles. The sum of their measures is 180°.

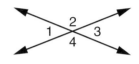

Figure 2

A line that crosses two lines is called a **transversal.** Any two angles formed by one of the lines and the transversal are either vertical or supplementary angles.

> **EXAMPLES** ∠b and ∠d in Figure 3 are vertical angles; they have the same measure.
> ∠a and ∠b are supplementary angles; the sum of their measures is 180°.

Pairs of angles between two parallel lines that are on the same side of the transversal are supplementary angles.

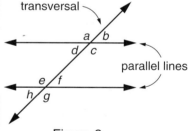

> **EXAMPLE** ∠c and ∠f in Figure 3 are supplementary angles. The sum of their measures is 180°.

Figure 3

CHECK YOUR UNDERSTANDING

1. In Figure 3 above, which of the following pairs of angles have the same measure? Which are supplementary angles?

   a. ∠e and ∠g   **b.** ∠d and ∠e   **c.** ∠b and ∠g

   d. ∠d and ∠c   **e.** ∠c and ∠e   **f.** ∠h and ∠b

2. In the parallelogram at the right, what is the measure of

   a. ∠1?   **b.** ∠2?   **c.** ∠3?

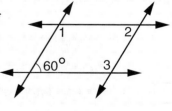

Check your answers on page 377.

Polygons

A **polygon** is a flat, **2-dimensional** figure made up of line segments called **sides**. A polygon can have any number of sides, as long as it has at least three. The **interior** (inside) of the polygon is not a part of the polygon. A polygon can enclose only one interior.

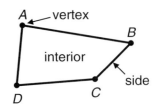

- The sides of a polygon are connected end to end and make a closed path.

- The sides of a polygon do not intersect (cross).

Each endpoint where two sides meet is called a **vertex.** The plural of vertex is **vertices.**

Figures That Are Polygons

4 sides, 4 vertices   3 sides, 3 vertices   7 sides, 7 vertices

Figures That Are NOT Polygons

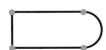

All sides of a polygon must be line segments. Curved lines are not line segments.

The sides of a polygon must form a closed path.

A polygon must have at least 3 sides.

The sides of a polygon must not cross.

Polygons are named after the number of their sides. The prefix for a polygon's name tells the number of sides it has.

Prefixes

tri-	3
quad-	4
penta-	5
hexa-	6
hepta-	7
octa-	8
nona-	9
deca-	10
dodeca-	12

Convex Polygons

A **convex** polygon is a polygon in which all the sides are pushed outward. The polygons below are convex.

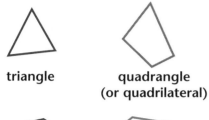

triangle   quadrangle   pentagon   hexagon
(or quadrilateral)

heptagon   octagon   nonagon   decagon

Nonconvex (Concave) Polygons

A **nonconvex,** or **concave,** polygon is a polygon in which at least two sides are pushed in. The four polygons at the right are nonconvex.

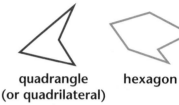

quadrangle   hexagon
(or quadrilateral)

Regular Polygons

A **regular polygon** is a polygon whose sides all have the same length and whose angles are all the same size. A regular polygon is always convex. The polygons below are regular.

pentagon   octagon

equilateral triangle   square   pentagon

hexagon   octagon   nonagon

CHECK YOUR UNDERSTANDING

1. What is the name of a polygon that has
   a. 8 sides?   **b.** 4 sides?   **c.** 6 sides?

2. **a.** Draw a convex heptagon.   **b.** Draw a concave decagon.

3. Explain why a sheet of notebook paper is not a regular polygon.

Check your answers on page 377.

Triangles

Triangles are the simplest type of polygon. The prefix *tri-* means *three*. All triangles have 3 vertices, 3 sides, and 3 angles.

For the triangle shown here:

side

vertex

Angle *A* is formed by sides that meet at vertex *A*.

- The vertices are the points *B*, *C*, and *A*.

- The sides are $\overline{BC}$, $\overline{BA}$, and $\overline{CA}$.

- The angles are ∠*B*, ∠*C*, and ∠*A*.

Triangles have 3-letter names. You name a triangle by listing the letter names for the vertices. The triangle above has 6 possible names: triangle *BCA, BAC, CAB, CBA, ABC,* or *ACB*.

Triangles may be classified according to the length of their sides.

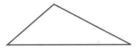

A scalene triangle is a triangle whose sides all have different lengths.

An **isosceles triangle** is a triangle that has two sides of the same length.

An **equilateral triangle** is a triangle whose sides are all the same length.

Triangles may be classified according to the size of their angles.

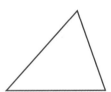   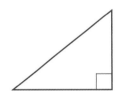   

An **acute triangle** is a triangle whose angles all are acute.

A **right triangle** is a triangle with one right angle.

An **obtuse triangle** is a triangle with one obtuse angle.

CHECK YOUR UNDERSTANDING

1. Draw and label an equilateral triangle named *JKL*. Write the five other possible names for this triangle.

2. Draw an isosceles triangle.

3. Draw a right scalene triangle.

Check your answers on page 377.

The Theorem of Pythagoras

A right triangle is a triangle that has a right angle (90°). In a right triangle, the side opposite the right angle is called the **hypotenuse.** The other two sides are called **legs.**

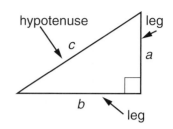

In the diagram at the right, a and b represent the lengths of the legs, and c represents the length of the hypotenuse.

There is a surprising connection between the lengths of the three sides of any right triangle. It is probably the most useful property in all of geometry and is known as the Pythagorean Theorem. It is stated at the right.

Pythagorean Theorem
If the legs of a right triangle have lengths a and b, and the hypotenuse has length c, then $a^2 + b^2 = c^2$.

Nobody knows when this relationship was first discovered. The Babylonians, Egyptians, and Chinese knew of it before the Greeks. But Pythagoras, a Greek philosopher born about 572 B.C., was the first person to prove that the relationship is true for any right triangle. It is called a **theorem** because it is a statement that has been proved.

A Chinese proof of the Pythagorean Theorem (written about A.D. 40) is shown below. Two identical squares, each with sides of length $a + b$, are partitioned in different ways.

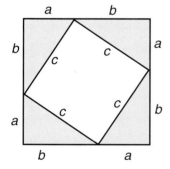

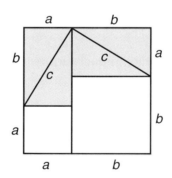

This square contains four identical right triangles and one square whose area is $c * c = c^2$.

This square contains four identical right triangles and two squares whose areas are a^2 and b^2.

The four right triangles inside each square all have the same area. Therefore, the area of the large square (c^2) inside the first square must be equal to the total area of the two smaller squares ($a^2 + b^2$) that are inside the second square; that is, c^2 must equal $a^2 + b^2$.

Quadrangles

A **quadrangle** is a polygon that has 4 sides. Another name for quadrangle is **quadrilateral.** The prefix *quad-* means *four.* All quadrangles have 4 vertices, 4 sides, and 4 angles.

For the quadrangle shown here:

- The sides are $\overline{RS}$, $\overline{ST}$, $\overline{TU}$, and $\overline{UR}$.

- The vertices are *R*, *S*, *T*, and *U*.

- The angles are $\angle R$, $\angle S$, $\angle T$, and $\angle U$.

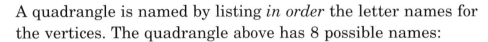

A quadrangle is named by listing *in order* the letter names for the vertices. The quadrangle above has 8 possible names:

RSTU, RUTS, STUR, SRUT, TURS, TSRU, URST, UTSR

Some quadrangles have two pairs of parallel sides. These quadrangles are called **parallelograms.**

Reminder: Two sides are parallel if they are the same distance apart everywhere.

Figures That Are Parallelograms

Opposite sides are parallel in each figure.

Figures That Are NOT Parallelograms

No parallel sides

Only 1 pair of parallel sides

3 pairs of parallel sides

A parallelogram must have exactly 2 pairs of parallel sides.

CHECK YOUR UNDERSTANDING

1. Draw and label a quadrangle named *QUAD* that has exactly one pair of parallel sides.

2. Is *QUAD* a parallelogram?

3. Write the seven other possible names for this quadrangle.

Check your answers on page 377.

Special types of quadrangles have been given names. Some of these are parallelograms, others are not.

The tree diagram at the right shows how the different types of quadrangles are related. For example, quadrangles are divided into two major groups—"parallelograms" and "not parallelograms." The special types of parallelograms include rectangles, rhombuses, and squares.

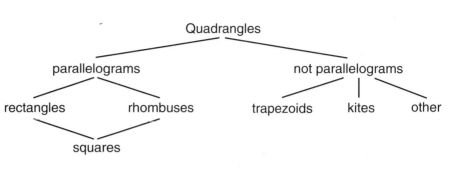

Quadrangles That Are Parallelograms

rectangle		**Rectangles** are parallelograms. A rectangle has 4 right angles (square corners). The sides do not all have to be the same length.
rhombus		**Rhombuses** are parallelograms. A rhombus has 4 sides that are all the same length. The angles of a rhombus are usually not right angles, but they may be.
square		**Squares** are parallelograms. A square has 4 right angles (square corners). Its 4 sides are all the same length. *All* squares are rectangles. *All* squares are also rhombuses.

Quadrangles That Are NOT Parallelograms

trapezoid		**Trapezoids** have exactly 1 pair of parallel sides. The 4 sides of a trapezoid can all have different lengths.
kite		A **kite** is a quadrangle with 2 pairs of equal sides. The equal sides are next to each other. The 4 sides cannot all have the same length. (A rhombus is not a kite.)
other		Any closed figure with 4 sides that is not a parallelogram, a trapezoid, or a kite

CHECK YOUR UNDERSTANDING

What is the difference between the quadrangles in each pair below?

1. a rhombus and a rectangle **2.** a trapezoid and a square **3.** a kite and a parallelogram

Check your answers on page 377.

Geometric Solids

Polygons and circles are flat, **2-dimensional** figures. The surfaces they enclose take up a certain amount of area, but they do not have any thickness and do not take up any volume.

Three-dimensional shapes have length, width, *and* thickness. They take up volume. Boxes, pails, books, cans, and balls are all examples of 3-dimensional shapes.

A **geometric solid** is the surface or surfaces that surround a 3-dimensional shape. The surfaces of a geometric solid may be flat, curved, or both. Despite its name, a geometric solid is hollow. It does not include the points within its interior.

- A **flat surface** of a solid is called a **face.**

- A **curved surface** of a solid does not have any special name.

EXAMPLES Describe the surface of each geometric solid.

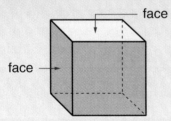

A cube has 6 square faces that are the same size.

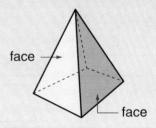

A rectangular pyramid has 4 triangular faces and 1 four-sided face.

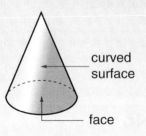

A cone has 1 circular face and 1 curved surface. The circular face is called its **base.**

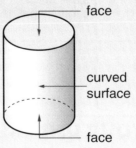

A cylinder has 1 curved surface. It has 2 circular faces that are the same size and are parallel. These two faces are called its **bases.**

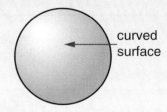

A sphere has 1 curved surface.

The **edges** of a geometric solid are the line segments or curves where surfaces meet.

A corner of a geometric solid is called a **vertex** (plural, *vertices*).

A vertex is a point at which edges meet. The vertex of a cone is an isolated corner completely separated from the edge of the cone.

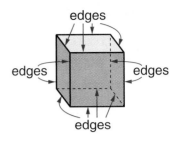

A cone has 1 edge and 1 vertex. This vertex is opposite the circular base and is called the **apex.**

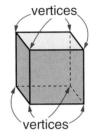

A cube has 12 edges and 8 vertices.

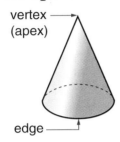

The pyramid shown below has 8 edges and 5 vertices. The vertex opposite the rectangular base is called the **apex.**

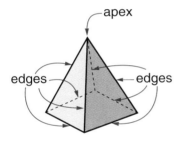

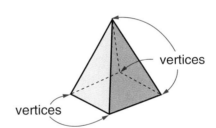

A cylinder has 2 edges. It has no vertices.

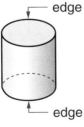

A sphere has no edges and no vertices.

CHECK YOUR UNDERSTANDING

1. a. How are cylinders and spheres alike?   **b.** How are they different?

2. a. How are pyramids and cones alike?   **b.** How are they different?

Check your answers on page 377.

Polyhedrons

A **polyhedron** is a geometric solid whose surfaces are all formed by polygons. These surfaces are the faces of the polyhedron. A polyhedron does not have any curved surfaces.

Two important groups of polyhedrons are shown below. These are **pyramids** and **prisms.**

Pyramids

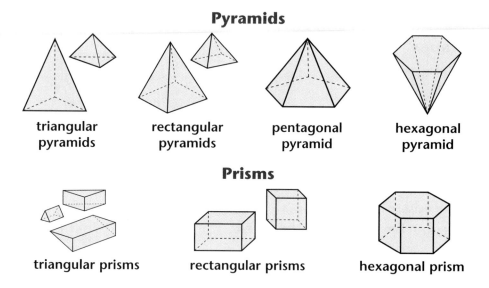

triangular
pyramids

rectangular
pyramids

pentagonal
pyramid

hexagonal
pyramid

Prisms

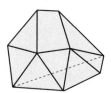 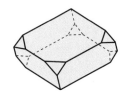

triangular prisms   rectangular prisms   hexagonal prism

Many polyhedrons are not pyramids or prisms. Some examples are shown below.

Polyhedrons That Are NOT Pyramids or Prisms

To find out why these are neither pyramids nor prisms, read pages 161 and 162.

CHECK YOUR UNDERSTANDING

1. a. How many faces does a hexagonal pyramid have?

   b. How many faces have a hexagonal shape?

2. a. How many faces does a hexagonal prism have?

   b. How many faces have a hexagonal shape?

3. Which solid has more faces, a rectangular pyramid or a rectangular prism?

Check your answers on page 377.

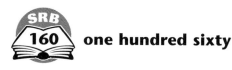

Prisms

All of the geometric solids below are **prisms.**

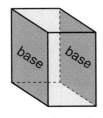
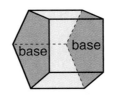
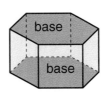
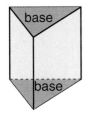

triangular prism   rectangular prism   pentagonal prism   hexagonal prism

The two shaded faces of each prism are called **bases.**

• The bases have the same size and shape.

• The bases are parallel. This means that they are the same distance apart everywhere.

• All edges that connect the bases are parallel to each other.

The shape of its bases is used to name a prism. If the bases are triangular shapes, it is called a **triangular prism.** If the bases are rectangular shapes, it is called a **rectangular prism.** Rectangular prisms have three possible pairs of bases.

The number of faces, edges, and vertices that a prism has depends on the shape of the base.

EXAMPLE   The triangular prism shown here has 5 faces—3 rectangular faces and 2 triangular bases. It has 6 vertices and 9 edges.

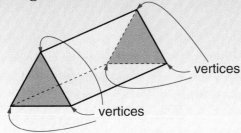
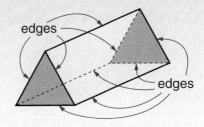

CHECK YOUR UNDERSTANDING

1. a. How many faces does a pentagonal prism have?

　b. How many edges?

　c. How many vertices?

2. What is the name of a prism that has 10 faces?

Check your answers on page 377.

Pyramids

All of the geometric solids below are **pyramids.**

triangular pyramid

square pyramid

pentagonal pyramid

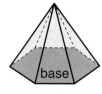
hexagonal pyramid

The shaded face of each of these pyramids is called the **base** of the pyramid.

• The polygon that forms the base can have any number of sides.

• The faces that are not a base all have a triangular shape.

• The faces that are not a base all meet at the same vertex.

The shape of its base is used to name a pyramid. If the base is a triangle shape, it is called a **triangular pyramid.** If the base is a square shape, it is called a **square pyramid.**

The pyramids of Egypt have square bases. They are square pyramids.

The number of faces, edges, and vertices that a pyramid has depends on the shape of the base.

EXAMPLE   The hexagonal pyramid shown here has 7 faces—6 triangular faces and a hexagonal base.

It has 12 edges. Six edges surround the hexagonal base. The other 6 edges meet at the apex (tip) of the pyramid.

It has 7 vertices. Six vertices are on the hexagonal base. The remaining vertex is the apex of the pyramid.

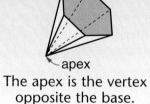
apex
The apex is the vertex opposite the base.

CHECK YOUR UNDERSTANDING

1. a. How many faces does a square pyramid have?

 b. How many edges?

 c. How many vertices?

2. What is the name of a pyramid that has 6 edges?

3. a. How are prisms and pyramids alike?

 b. How are they different?

Check your answers on page 377.

Regular Polyhedrons

A polyhedron is **regular** if:

• Each face is formed by a regular polygon.

• The faces all have the same size and shape.

• Every vertex looks exactly the same as every other vertex.

There are only five kinds of regular polyhedrons.

Regular Polyhedrons

| tetrahedron (pyramid) (4 faces) | cube (prism) (6 faces) | octahedron (8 faces) | dodecahedron (12 faces) | icosahedron (20 faces) |

The pictures below show each regular polyhedron with its faces unfolded. There is more than one way to unfold each polyhedron.

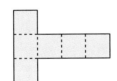

tetrahedron
(4 equilateral triangles)

cube
(6 squares)

octahedron
(8 equilateral triangles)

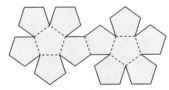

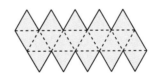

dodecahedron
(12 regular pentagons)

icosahedron
(20 equilateral triangles)

CHECK YOUR UNDERSTANDING

1. a. How many edges does a tetrahedron have?   **b.** How many vertices?

2. a. How are tetrahedrons and icosahedrons alike?   **b.** How are they different?

Check your answers on page 378.

Circles

A **circle** is a curved line that forms a closed path on a flat surface. All of the points on a circle are the same distance from the **center of the circle.**

The center is not part of the circle. The interior is not part of the circle.

The **compass** is a tool used to draw circles.

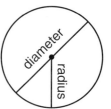

- The point of a compass (called the **anchor**) is placed at the center of the circle.

- The pencil in a compass traces out a circle. Every point on the circle is the same distance from the anchor.

The **radius** (plural, *radii*) of a circle is any line segment that connects the center of the circle with any point on the circle. The word *radius* can also refer to the length of this segment.

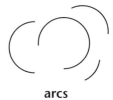

The **diameter** of a circle is any line segment that passes through the center of the circle and has its endpoints on the circle. The word *diameter* can also refer to the length of this segment.

An **arc** is part of a circle, from one point on the circle to another. For example, a **semicircle** is an arc. Its endpoints are the endpoints of the diameter of the circle.

arcs

All circles are similar because they have the same shape, but all circles do not have the same size.

EXAMPLE   Many pizzas have a circular shape. You can order a pizza by saying the diameter that you want.

A "12-inch pizza" means a pizza with a 12-inch diameter.

A "16-inch pizza" means a pizza with a 16-inch diameter.

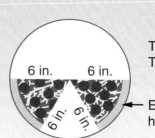

A 12-inch pizza

The pizza is 12 inches wide. The diameter is 12 inches.

Each slice is a wedge that has 6-inch-long sides.

Spheres

A **sphere** is a geometric solid that has a single curved surface shaped like a ball, a marble, or a globe. All of the points on the surface of the sphere are the same distance from the **center of the sphere.**

All spheres have the same shape. But spheres do not all have the same size. The size of a sphere is the distance across its center.

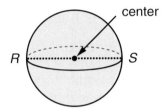

- The line segment *RS* passes through the center of the sphere. This line segment is called a **diameter of the sphere.**

- The length of line segment *RS* is also called the diameter of the sphere.

Globes and basketballs are examples of spheres that are hollow. The interior of each is empty. The hollow interior is not part of the sphere. The sphere includes only the points on the curved surface.

Marbles and baseballs are examples of spheres that have solid interiors. In cases like these, think of the solid interior as part of the sphere.

EXAMPLE The Earth is shaped very nearly like a sphere.

The diameter of the Earth is about 8,000 miles.

The distance from the Earth's surface to the center of the Earth is about 4,000 miles.

Every point on the Earth's surface is about 4,000 miles from the center of the Earth.

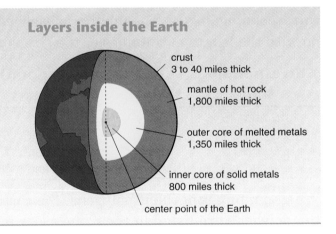

Layers inside the Earth

crust
3 to 40 miles thick

mantle of hot rock
1,800 miles thick

outer core of melted metals
1,350 miles thick

inner core of solid metals
800 miles thick

center point of the Earth

Congruent Figures

Two figures that are the same size and have the same shape are **congruent.**

- All line segments have the same shape. Two line segments are congruent if they have the same length.

- All circles have the same shape. Two circles are congruent if their diameters have the same length.

- All squares have the same shape. Two squares are congruent if their sides have the same length.

- Two angles are congruent if they have the same degree measure.

Two figures are congruent if they match exactly when one figure is placed on top of the other. The matching sides of congruent polygons are called **corresponding sides,** and their matching angles are called **corresponding angles.** Each pair of corresponding sides of congruent polygons is the same length, and each pair of corresponding angles has the same degree measure.

The slash marks and arcs are used to identify pairs of corresponding sides and angles. Sides with the same number of slash marks are corresponding sides, and angles with the same number of arcs are corresponding angles. The number of slashes or arcs has nothing to do with the length of the sides or the size of the angles.

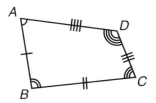

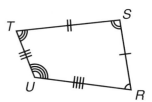

Quadrangles *ABCD* and *RSTU* are congruent.

Corresponding Sides	Length	Corresponding Angles	Degree Measure
$\overline{AB}$ and $\overline{RS}$	1.9 cm	∠A and ∠R	75°
$\overline{BC}$ and $\overline{ST}$	2.8 cm	∠B and ∠S	95°
$\overline{CD}$ and $\overline{TU}$	1.3 cm	∠C and ∠T	70°
$\overline{DA}$ and $\overline{UR}$	2.6 cm	∠D and ∠U	120°

When naming congruent polygons, the corresponding vertices of the polygons are listed in the same order for both polygons.

CHECK YOUR UNDERSTANDING

Which of the triangles at the right is not congruent to the other three?

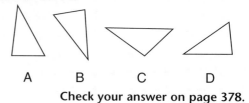

A   B   C   D

Check your answer on page 378.

Similar Figures

Figures that have exactly the same shape are called **similar figures**. They may also be the same size, but do not have to be. If two figures are similar, one figure is an enlargement of the other. The **size-change factor** tells the amount of enlargement or reduction.

In similar polygons, the size of the angles does not change. But if one polygon is an enlargement of another polygon, each of the sides of the smaller polygon is enlarged by the same size-change factor. Each side and its enlargement form a pair of sides called **corresponding sides**.

EXAMPLE   Triangles *BAT* and *HOG* are similar.

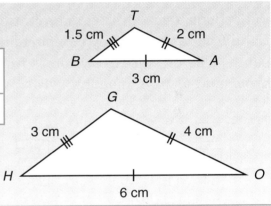

Length of Corresponding Sides	$\overline{HO}$: 6 cm $\overline{BA}$: 3 cm	$\overline{OG}$: 4 cm $\overline{AT}$: 2 cm	$\overline{GH}$: 3 cm $\overline{TB}$: 1.5 cm
Ratio of Lengths	$\frac{6}{3} = \frac{2}{1}$	$\frac{4}{2} = \frac{2}{1}$	$\frac{3}{1.5} = \frac{2}{1}$

The size-change factor is 2X. Each side in the larger triangle is twice the size of the corresponding side in the smaller triangle.

EXAMPLE   Quadrangles *ABCD* and *MNOP* are similar. What is the length of $\overline{AB}$?

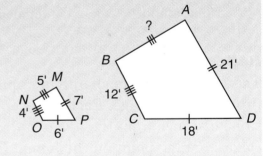

Since the quadrangles are similar, the ratio of the lengths of the corresponding sides are equal. Find the ratio of the length of a longer side to the length of the corresponding shorter side. Choose any pair of corresponding sides.

$$\frac{(\text{length of } \overline{BC})}{(\text{length of } \overline{NO})} = \frac{12}{4} = \frac{3}{1}$$

To find the length of side *AB*, solve $\frac{3}{1} = \frac{x}{5} \begin{matrix} \leftarrow (\text{length of } \overline{AB}) \\ \leftarrow (\text{length of } \overline{MN}) \end{matrix}$.

$$\frac{3 * 5}{1 * 5} = \frac{15}{5}$$

The length of side *AB* is 15 feet.

CHECK YOUR UNDERSTANDING

Polygons *RUDI* and *JOAN* are similar.

Find the length of these sides.

1. side *JO*   **2.** side *ID*

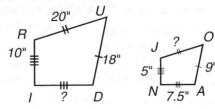

Check your answers on page 378.

SRB

Isometry Transformations

In geometry, a **transformation** is an operation on a figure that produces another figure. Transformations are sometimes thought of as motions that take a figure from one place to another. **Reflections** (flips), **rotations** (turns), and **translations** (slides) are familiar operations in **transformation geometry.**

These three types of transformations produce a new figure called the **image.** It has the same size and shape as the original figure, which is called the **preimage.** The image and preimage are congruent figures.

Reflections, translations, and rotations are called **isometry transformations.** They do not change the distances between points. The term *isometry* comes from the Greek *iso*, meaning *same*, and *metron*, meaning *measure*.

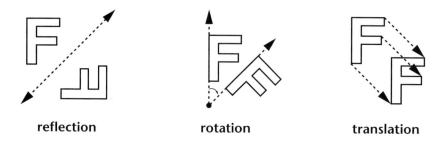

reflection   rotation   translation

Reflections

The reflection image of a figure appears to be a reversal, or flip, of the preimage. Each point on the preimage is the same distance from the *line of reflection* as the corresponding point on the image. The preimage and image are on opposite sides of the line of reflection.

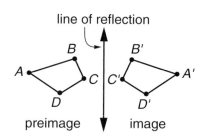

Rotations

When a figure is rotated, it is turned a specific number of degrees in a specific direction around a specific point. A figure can be rotated *clockwise* (the direction in which clock hands move) or *counterclockwise* (the opposite direction). A figure may be rotated around a point outside, on, or inside the figure. See page 171.

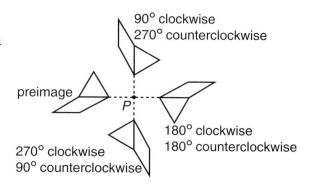

Translations

When a figure is translated, each point on the preimage slides a certain distance in the same direction to create the image.

Imagine a figure on a coordinate grid. If the same number (for example, 5) is added to the *x*-coordinates of all the points in the figure and the *y*-coordinates are not changed, the result is a **horizontal translation**.

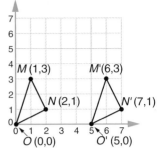

horizontal translation

If the same number (for example, 4) is added to all the *y*-coordinates and the *x*-coordinates are not changed, the result is a **vertical translation**.

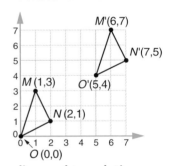

vertical translation

Suppose that the same number (for example, 5) is added to all the *x*-coordinates and another number (for example, 4) is added to all the *y*-coordinates. The result is a **diagonal translation**.

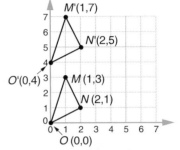

diagonal translation

CHECK YOUR UNDERSTANDING

1. Name the word that results when the figure at the right is reflected over $\overleftrightarrow{AB}$.

2. Triangle *C'A'T'* is the image of triangle *CAT* after a slide. Point *C* is at (1,1), point *A* at (3,9), point *T* at (8,5), and point *C'* at (4,7). What are the coordinates of points *A'* and *T'*?

3. Which figure is a 90° clockwise rotation of the given figure?

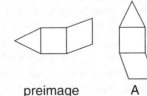

preimage   A   B   C

Check your answers on page 378.

Symmetry

Line Symmetry

A figure is **symmetric about a line** if the line divides the figure into two parts so that both parts look exactly alike but are facing in opposite directions. In a symmetric figure, each point in one of the halves of the figure is the same distance from the **line of symmetry** as the corresponding point in the other half.

EXAMPLE The figure at the right is symmetric about the dashed line. The dashed line is its line of symmetry.

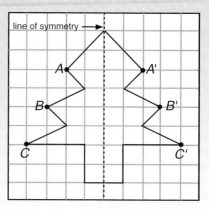

Points A and A' (read as "A prime") are corresponding points.

The shortest distance from point A to the line of symmetry is equal to the shortest distance from point A' to the line of symmetry. The same is true of points B and B', points C and C', and any other pairs of corresponding points.

The line of symmetry is the **perpendicular bisector** of line segments connecting corresponding points such as points A and A'. It bisects each line segment and is perpendicular to each line segment.

An easy way to check whether a figure has **line symmetry** is to fold it in half. If the two halves match exactly, the figure is symmetric about the fold.

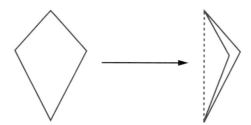

Some figures have more than one line of symmetry.	Some figures have no lines of symmetry.

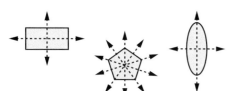

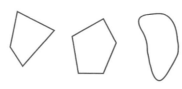

CHECK YOUR UNDERSTANDING

1. Trace each pattern-block (*PB*) shape on the Geometry Template onto a sheet of paper. Draw the lines of symmetry for each shape.

2. How many lines of symmetry does a circle have?

Check your answers on page 378.

Rotation Symmetry

A figure has **rotation symmetry** if it can be rotated around a point in such a way that the resulting figure exactly matches the original figure. The rotation must be more than 0 degrees but less than 360 degrees. The figure isn't flipped over.

In other words, a figure has rotation symmetry if it can be rotated so that the image and preimage match exactly without flipping the figure over.

If a figure has rotation symmetry, its **order of rotation symmetry** is the number of different ways it can be rotated to match itself exactly. "No rotation" is counted as one of the ways.

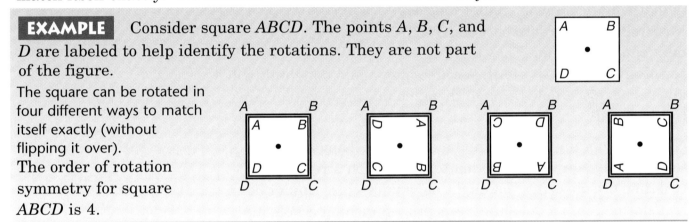

EXAMPLE Consider square *ABCD*. The points *A*, *B*, *C*, and *D* are labeled to help identify the rotations. They are not part of the figure.

The square can be rotated in four different ways to match itself exactly (without flipping it over). The order of rotation symmetry for square *ABCD* is 4.

Point Symmetry

A figure has **point symmetry** if it can be rotated 180° around a point to match the original figure exactly. Point symmetry is a special kind of rotation symmetry. A figure with point symmetry has rotation symmetry of at least order 2.

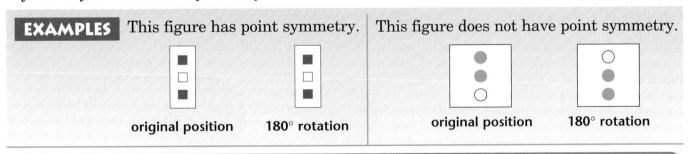

EXAMPLES This figure has point symmetry.   This figure does not have point symmetry.

original position   180° rotation   original position   180° rotation

CHECK YOUR UNDERSTANDING

1. Draw a square. Color or shade the interior of the square so that the resulting figure still has rotation symmetry of order 4.

2. Draw a rectangle. Color or shade the interior of the rectangle so that the figure has point symmetry.

Check your answers on page 378.

Topology

Topology is a branch of mathematics that has many
connections with geometry. In topology, two geometric shapes
are equivalent if one shape can be stretched, squeezed,
crumpled, twisted, or turned inside out (but not torn or broken)
until it looks like the other shape. These changes are called
topological transformations.

Topology studies the properties of geometric shapes that are not
changed by topological transformations. The number of holes in
an object is one of these properties. For this reason, it is
sometimes said that a topologist
(a mathematician who studies topology)
can't tell the difference between a coffee
mug and a doughnut. They are
topologically equivalent. A coffee mug and a doughnut will
always have one hole through them, no matter how they are
transformed.

Now, consider a juice glass and a doughnut. They are *not*
topologically equivalent. No matter how much stretching,
twisting, or squeezing you might do, a juice glass cannot be
transformed into a doughnut, except by punching a hole in it.
This is because a juice glass has no holes through it, whereas a
doughnut has one.

In topology, geometric shapes are sorted by the number of holes
they have. This property is called the **genus** (pronounced
"GEE-nuss") of the shape. Objects with the same genus are
topologically equivalent.

The objects below have genus 0.

The objects below have genus 1.

The objects below have genus 2.

  B 8

Topology is sometimes called **rubber-sheet geometry.** If you think of a figure as if it were drawn on a rubber sheet or a shape as if it were made from rubber, it may help you to see which properties remain the same after a topological transformation.

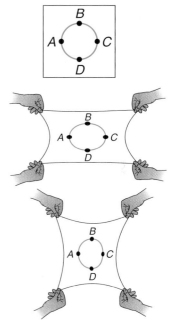

For example, the first diagram at the right shows a circle drawn on a rubber sheet. When the rubber sheet is stretched, the circle is transformed into other figures, as shown in the other diagrams.

No matter how the circle is transformed, the resulting figure is still a closed curve. Points that were originally inside remain inside, and points that were originally outside remain outside. Points on the circle stay in the same position relative to each other—for example, point *B* stays between points *A* and *C*.

Properties that do not change when a figure is distorted are called **topological properties.**

CHECK YOUR UNDERSTANDING

1. Triangle *ABC* is drawn on a rubber sheet. The sheet is stretched to represent a topological transformation. Which of the following must be true?

    a. The distance from point *A* to point *B* remains the same.

    b. The measure of angle *A* remains the same.

    c. The image of side *AB* might not be a line segment.

    d. The image of triangle *ABC* is a triangle.

    e. Figure *ABC* remains closed.

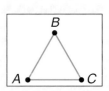

2. **Challenge** Imagine that this shape is made of clay. It may not seem possible, but the loops can be separated—without cutting or tearing them—by a series of topological transformations.

    Draw a series of diagrams to show how this might be done.

Check your answers on page 378.

The Geometry Template

The **Geometry Template** has many uses.

The template has two rulers. The inch scale measures in inches and fractions of an inch. The centimeter scale measures in centimeters or millimeters. Use either side of the template as a straightedge for drawing line segments.

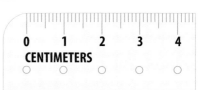

There are 17 different geometric figures on the template. The figures labeled "PB" are **pattern-block shapes.** These are half the size of real pattern blocks. There is a hexagon, a trapezoid, two different rhombuses, an equilateral triangle, and a square. These will come in handy for some of the activities you do this year.

Each triangle on the template is labeled with a T and a number. Triangle "T1" is an equilateral triangle whose sides all have the same length. Triangles "T2" and "T5" are right triangles. Triangle "T3" has sides that all have different lengths. Triangle "T4" has two sides of the same length.

The remaining shapes are circles, squares, a regular octagon, a regular pentagon, a kite, a rectangle, a parallelogram, and an ellipse.

The two circles near the inch scale can be used as ring-binder holes so you can store your template in your notebook.

Use the **half-circle** and **full-circle protractors** at the bottom of the template to measure and draw angles. Use the **Percent Circle** at the top of the template to construct and measure circle graphs. The Percent Circle is divided into 1% intervals, and some common fractions of the circle are marked.

Notice the tiny holes near the 0-, $\frac{1}{4}$-, $\frac{2}{4}$-, and $\frac{3}{4}$-inch marks of the inch scale and at each inch mark from 1 to 7. On the centimeter side, the holes are placed at each centimeter mark from 0 to 10. These holes can be used to draw circles.

EXAMPLE   Draw a circle with a 4-inch radius.

Place one pencil point in the hole at 0. Place another pencil point in the hole at 4 inches. Hold the pencil at 0 inches steady while rotating the pencil at 4 inches (along with the template) to draw the circle.

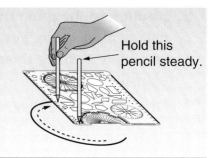

Hold this pencil steady.

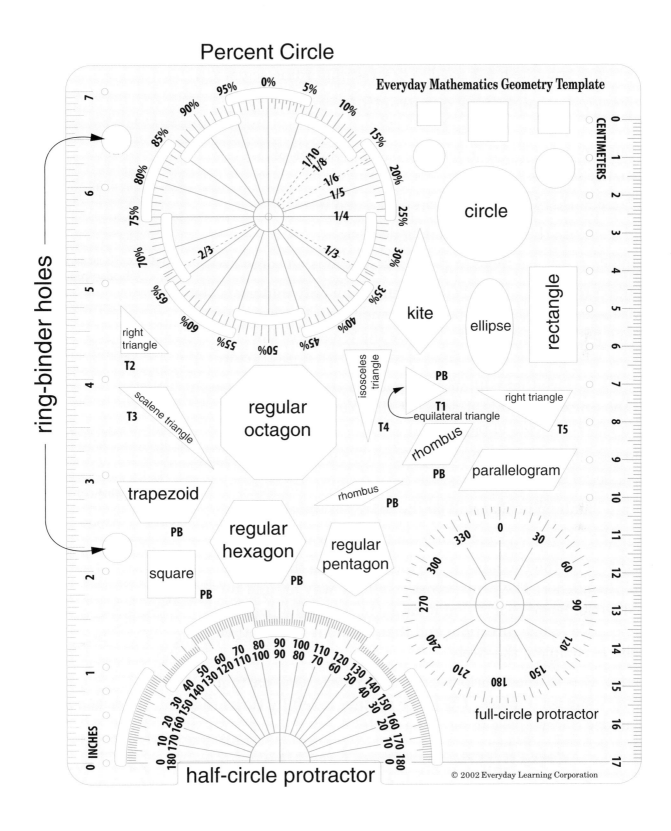

Percent Circle

Everyday Mathematics Geometry Template

circle

rectangle

kite

ellipse

right triangle
T2

isosceles triangle
T4

PB
T1
equilateral triangle

right triangle
T5

scalene triangle
T3

regular octagon

rhombus
PB

parallelogram

trapezoid

PB

regular hexagon

rhombus
PB

square
PB

PB

regular pentagon

PB

330 0 30

300   60

270   90

240   120

210   150

180

full-circle protractor

half-circle protractor

ring-binder holes

© 2002 Everyday Learning Corporation

Compass-and-Straightedge Constructions

Many geometric figures can be drawn using only a compass and straightedge. The compass is used to draw circles and mark off lengths. The straightedge is used to draw straight line segments.

Compass-and-straightedge constructions serve many purposes.

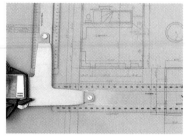

- Mathematicians use them for studying properties of geometric figures.

- Architects use them to make blueprints and drawings.

- Engineers use them for developing designs.

- Graphic artists use them to create illustrations on computers.

Architect's drawing of a house plan

In addition to a compass and straightedge, the only materials you need are a drawing tool (the best is a pencil with a sharp point) and some paper. You may not measure the lengths of line segments with a ruler or the sizes of angles with a protractor.

Draw on a surface that will hold the point of the compass (also called the **anchor**) so that it does not slip. You can draw on a stack of several sheets of paper.

The directions below describe two ways to draw circles. For each method, begin in the same way.

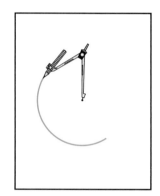

Method 1

- Draw a small point that will be the center of the circle.

- Press the compass anchor firmly on the center of the circle.

Method 1 Hold the compass at the top and rotate the pencil around the anchor. The pencil must go all the way around to make a circle. Some people find it easier to rotate the pencil as far as possible in one direction, and then rotate it in the other direction to complete the circle.

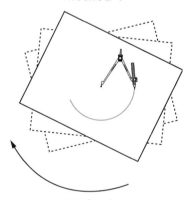

Method 2 This method works best with partners. One partner holds the compass in place. The other partner carefully turns the paper under the compass to form the circle.

Method 2

CHECK YOUR UNDERSTANDING

Concentric circles are circles that have the same center.

Use a compass to draw 3 concentric circles.

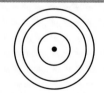

concentric circles

Copying a Line Segment

Follow each step carefully. Use a clean sheet of paper.

Step 1: Draw line segment *AB*.

Step 2: Draw a second line segment. It should be longer than segment *AB*. Label one of its endpoints point *A'* (read "*A* prime").

Step 3: Place the compass anchor at point *A* and the pencil point at point *B*.

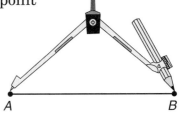

Step 4: Without changing your compass opening, place the compass anchor on point *A'* and draw a small arc that crosses the line segment. Label the point where the arc crosses the line segment point *B'*.

The segments *A'B'* and *AB* have the same length.

Line segment *A'B'* is **congruent** to line segment *AB*.

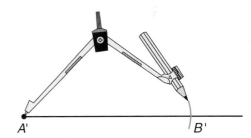

CHECK YOUR UNDERSTANDING

1. Draw a line segment. Using a compass and straightedge only, copy the line segment.

2. After you make your copy, measure the segments with a ruler to see how accurately you copied the original line segment.

Copying a Triangle

Follow each step carefully. Use a clean sheet of paper.

Step 1: Draw a triangle *ABC*. Draw a line segment that is longer than line segment *AB*. Copy line segment *AB* onto the segment you just drew. (See page 177.) Label the endpoints of the copy point *A'* and point *B'* (read as "A prime" and "B prime").

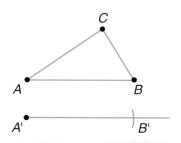

Step 2: Place the compass anchor at point *A* and the pencil point at point *C*. Without changing your compass opening, place the compass anchor on point *A'* and draw an arc.

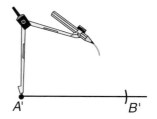

Step 3: Place the compass anchor at point *B* and the pencil point at point *C*. Without changing your compass opening, place the compass anchor on point *B'* and draw another arc. Label the point where the arcs intersect point *C'*.

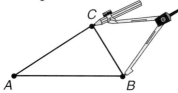
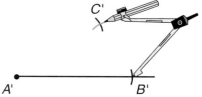

Step 4: Draw line segments *A'C'* and *B'C'*.

Triangles *ABC* and *A'B'C'* are congruent. That is, they are the same size and shape.

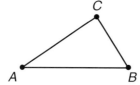
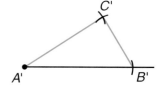

CHECK YOUR UNDERSTANDING

Draw a triangle. Using a compass and straightedge, copy the triangle. Cut out the copy and place it on top of the original triangle to check that the triangles are congruent.

Constructing a Parallelogram

Follow each step carefully. Use a clean sheet of paper.

Step 1: Draw an angle *ABC*.

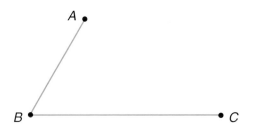

Step 2: Place the compass anchor at point *B* and the pencil point at point *C*. Without changing your compass opening, place the compass anchor on point *A* and draw an arc.

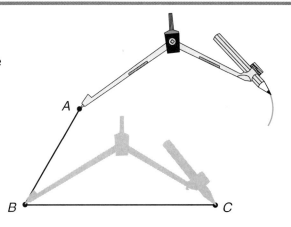

Step 3: Place the compass anchor at point *B* and the pencil point at point *A*. Without changing your compass opening, place the compass anchor on point *C* and draw another arc that crosses the first arc. Label the point where the two arcs cross point *D*.

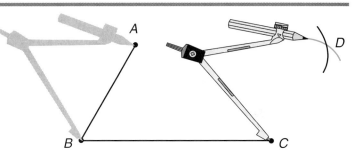

Step 4: Draw line segments *AD* and *CD*.

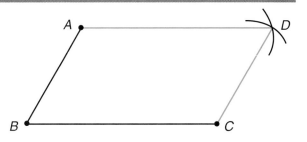

CHECK YOUR UNDERSTANDING

1. Use a compass and straightedge to construct a parallelogram.

2. Use a compass and straightedge to construct a rhombus. (*Hint:* A rhombus is a parallelogram whose sides are all the same length.)

Constructing a Regular Inscribed Hexagon

Follow each step carefully. Use a clean sheet of paper.

Step 1: Draw a circle and keep the same compass opening. Make a dot on the circle. Place the compass anchor on the dot and make a mark with the pencil point on the circle. Keep the same compass opening for Steps 2 and 3.

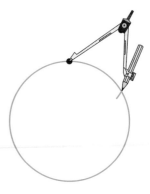

Step 2: Place the compass anchor on the mark you just made. Make another mark with the pencil point on the circle.

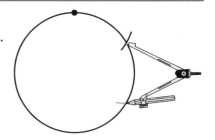

Step 3: Do this four more times to divide the circle into 6 equal parts. The 6th mark should be on the dot you started with or very close to it.

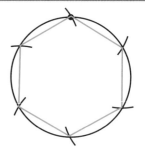

Step 4: With your straightedge, connect the 6 marks on the circle to form a regular hexagon.

Use your compass to check that the sides of the hexagon are the same length.

The hexagon is **inscribed** in the circle because each vertex of the hexagon is on the circle.

CHECK YOUR UNDERSTANDING

1. Draw a circle. Using a compass and straightedge, construct a regular hexagon that is inscribed in the circle.

2. Draw a line segment from the center of the circle to each vertex of the hexagon to form 6 triangles. Use your compass to check that the sides of each triangle are the same length.

Constructing an Inscribed Square

Follow each step carefully. Use a clean sheet of paper.

Step 1: Draw a circle with a compass.

Step 2: Draw a line segment through the center of the circle with endpoints on the circle. Label the endpoints point *A* and point *B*.

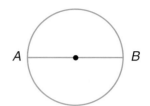

Step 3: Increase the compass opening. Place the compass anchor on point *A*. Draw an arc below the center of the circle and another arc above the center of the circle.

Step 4: Without changing the compass opening, place the compass anchor on point *B*. Draw arcs that cross the arcs you drew in Step 3. Label the points where the arcs intersect point *C* and point *D*.

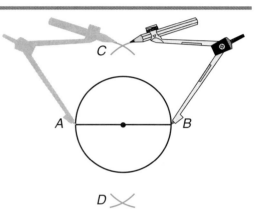

Step 5: Draw a line through points *C* and *D*.

Label the points where line *CD* intersects the circle point *E* and point *F*.

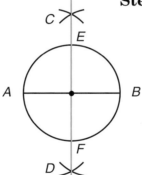

Step 6: Draw line segments *AE*, *EB*, *BF*, and *FA*.

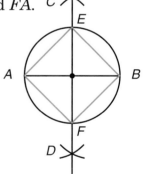

After you have completed Step 6, use your compass to check that all four line segments are the same length. Use the corner of your straightedge or some other square corner to check that all four angles are right angles.

The square is **inscribed** in the circle because all vertices of the square are on the circle.

CHECK YOUR UNDERSTANDING

Use a compass and straightedge to construct an inscribed square.

Constructing a Perpendicular Bisector of a Line Segment

Follow each step carefully. Use a clean sheet of paper.

Step 1: Draw line segment AB.

A   B

Step 2: Open your compass so that the compass opening is greater than half the distance between point A and point B. Place the anchor on point A. Draw a small arc below $\overline{AB}$ and another small arc above $\overline{AB}$.

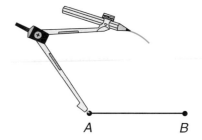

A   B

Step 3: Without changing the compass opening, place the anchor on point B. Draw an arc below $\overline{AB}$ and another arc above $\overline{AB}$ so that the arcs cross the first arcs you drew. Where pairs of arcs intersect, label the points point M and point N.

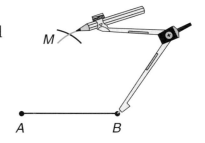

Step 4: Draw a line through point M and point N. Label the point where $\overleftrightarrow{MN}$ intersects $\overline{AB}$ point O.

Line segment MN **bisects** line segment AB at point O. The distance from point A to point O is the same as the distance from point B to point O.

Line segments MN and AB are perpendicular because the angles formed where they intersect are right angles. Line segment MN is a **perpendicular bisector** of line segment AB.

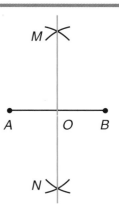

CHECK YOUR UNDERSTANDING

Draw a line segment. Use a compass and straightedge to bisect it. Then, measure to check that the line segment has been divided into two equal parts. Use a protractor to check that the segments are perpendicular.

Constructing a Perpendicular Line Segment (Part 1)

You can construct a line segment that is perpendicular to another line segment through a point *on* the line segment.

Follow each step carefully. Use a clean sheet of paper.

Step 1: Draw line segment AB. Make a dot on $\overline{AB}$ and label it point P.

Step 2: Place the compass anchor on point P, and draw an arc that crosses $\overline{AB}$. Label the point where the arc crosses the segment point C.

Keeping the compass anchor on point P and the same compass opening, draw another arc that crosses $\overline{AB}$. Label the point where the arc crosses the segment point D.

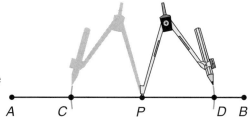

Step 3: Make sure the compass opening is greater than the length of $\overline{CP}$. Place the compass anchor on point C and draw an arc above $\overline{AB}$.

Keeping the same compass opening, place the compass anchor on point D and draw another arc above $\overline{AB}$ that crosses the first arc.

Label the point where the two arcs cross point Q.

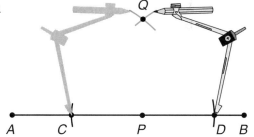

Step 4: Draw $\overline{QP}$.

$\overline{QP}$ is **perpendicular** to $\overline{AB}$.

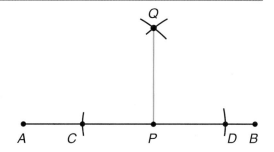

CHECK YOUR UNDERSTANDING

Draw a line segment. Draw a point on the segment and label it point R.

Use a compass and straightedge. Construct a line segment through point R that is perpendicular to the segment you drew.

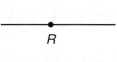

Use a protractor to check that the segments are perpendicular.

Constructing a Perpendicular Line Segment (Part 2)

You can construct a line segment perpendicular to another line segment from a point *not on* the line segment.

Follow each step carefully. Use a clean sheet of paper.

Step 1: Draw line segment *PQ*.
Draw a point *M* not on $\overline{PQ}$.

Step 2: Place the compass anchor on point *M* and draw an arc that crosses $\overline{PQ}$ at two points.

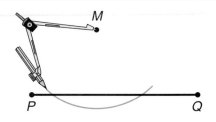

Step 3: Place the compass anchor on one of the points and draw an arc below $\overline{PQ}$.

Step 4: Keeping the same compass opening, place the compass anchor on the other point and draw another arc that crosses the first arc.

Label the point where the two arcs cross point *N*. Then draw the line segment *MN*.

$\overline{MN}$ is **perpendicular** to $\overline{PQ}$.

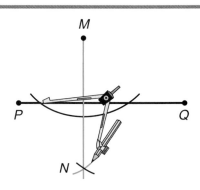

CHECK YOUR UNDERSTANDING

1. Draw a line segment *HI* and a point *G* above the line segment. Using a compass and straightedge, construct a line segment from point *G* that is perpendicular to $\overline{HI}$.

2. Use the Geometry Template to draw a parallelogram. Then construct a line segment to show the height of the parallelogram.

Bisecting an Angle

Follow each step carefully. Use a clean sheet of paper.

Step 1: Draw angle *ABC*.

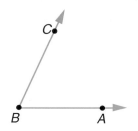

Step 2: Place the compass anchor on point *B*, and draw an arc that intersects both $\overrightarrow{BA}$ and $\overrightarrow{BC}$. Label the points where the arcs cross $\overrightarrow{BA}$ and $\overrightarrow{BC}$ point *M* and point *N*.

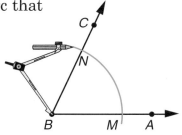

Step 3: Place the compass anchor on point *M*, and draw a small arc inside ∠*ABC*.

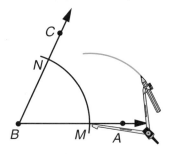

Step 4: Without changing the compass opening, place the compass anchor on point *N*, and draw a small arc that intersects the one you drew in Step 3. Label the point where the two arcs meet point *P*.

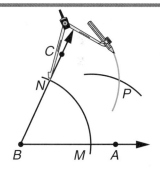

Step 5: Draw a ray from point *B* through point *P*.

Ray *BP* **bisects** ∠*ABC*. The measure of ∠*ABP* is equal to the measure of ∠*CBP*.

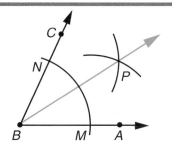

CHECK YOUR UNDERSTANDING

Draw an obtuse angle. Use a compass and straightedge to bisect it.

Copying an Angle

Follow each step carefully. Use a clean sheet of paper.

Step 1: Draw an angle B.

Step 2: To start copying the angle, draw a ray. Label the endpoint of the ray point B'.

Step 3: Place the compass anchor on point B. Draw an arc that crosses both sides of angle B. Label the point where the arc crosses one side point A. Label the point where the arc crosses the other side point C.

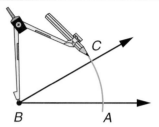

Step 4: Without changing the compass opening, place the compass anchor on point B'. Draw an arc about the same size as the one you drew in Step 3. Label the point where the arc crosses the ray point A'.

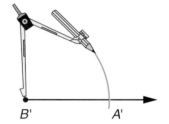

Step 5: Place the compass anchor on point A and the pencil point on point C.

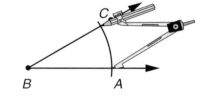

Step 6: Without changing the compass opening, place the compass anchor on point A'. Draw a small arc where the pencil point crosses the larger arc and label it point C'.

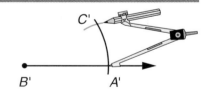

Step 7: Draw a ray from point B' through point C'. ∠A'B'C' is **congruent** to ∠ABC; that is, the two angles have the same degree measure.

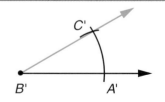

CHECK YOUR UNDERSTANDING

Draw an angle. Use a compass and straightedge to copy the angle. Then measure the two angles with a protractor to check that they are the same size.

Copying a Quadrangle

Follow each step carefully. Use a clean sheet of paper.

Before you can copy a quadrangle with a compass and straightedge, you need to know how to copy line segments and angles. Those constructions are described on pages 177 and 186.

Step 1: Draw a quadrangle *ABCD*. Copy ∠*BAD*. Label the vertex of the new angle point *A'*. The sides of your new angle should be longer than $\overline{AB}$ and $\overline{AD}$.

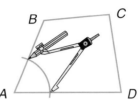

Step 2: Mark off the distance from point *A* to point *D* on the horizontal side of your new angle. Label the endpoint point *D'*.

Mark off the distance from point *A* to point *B* on the other side of your new angle. Label the endpoint point *B'*.

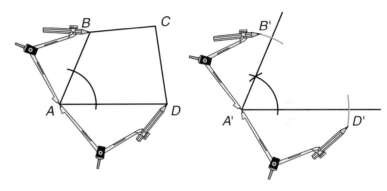

Step 3: Place the compass anchor on point *B* and the pencil point on point *C*. Without changing the compass opening, place the compass anchor on point *B'* and make an arc.

Step 4: Place the compass anchor on point *D* and the pencil point on point *C*. Without changing the compass opening, place the compass anchor on point *D'* and make an arc that crosses the arc you made in Step 3. Label the point where the two arcs meet point *C'*.

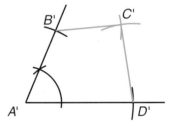

Step 5: Draw $\overline{B'C'}$ and $\overline{D'C'}$.

Quadrangle *A'B'C'D'* is **congruent** to quadrangle *ABCD*. The two quadrangles are the same size and shape.

CHECK YOUR UNDERSTANDING

Draw a quadrangle. Use a compass and straightedge to copy the quadrangle.

Constructing Parallel Lines

Follow each step carefully. Use a clean sheet of paper.

Step 1: Draw line AB and ray AC.

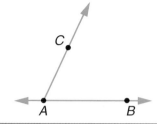

Step 2: Place the compass anchor on point A. Draw an arc that crosses both $\overrightarrow{AB}$ and $\overrightarrow{AC}$. Label the point where the arc crosses $\overrightarrow{AB}$ point D. Label the point where the arc crosses $\overrightarrow{AC}$ point E.

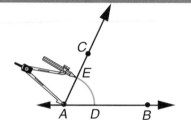

Step 3: Without changing the compass opening, place the compass anchor on point C. Draw an arc the same size as the one you drew in Step 2. Label the point where the arc crosses $\overrightarrow{AC}$ point F.

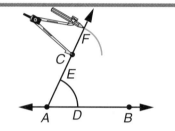

Step 4: Place the compass anchor on point E and the pencil point on point D.

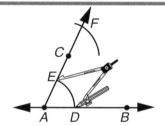

Step 5: Without changing the compass opening, place the compass anchor on point F. Draw a small arc where the pencil point crosses the larger arc. Label the point where the small arc crosses the larger arc point G.

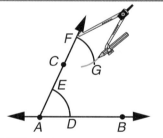

Step 6: Draw a line through points C and G.

Line CG is **parallel** to line AB. $\angle CAB$ is **congruent** to $\angle FCG$.

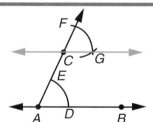

CHECK YOUR UNDERSTANDING

Draw a line. Use a compass and straightedge to draw a line that is parallel to it.

Measurement

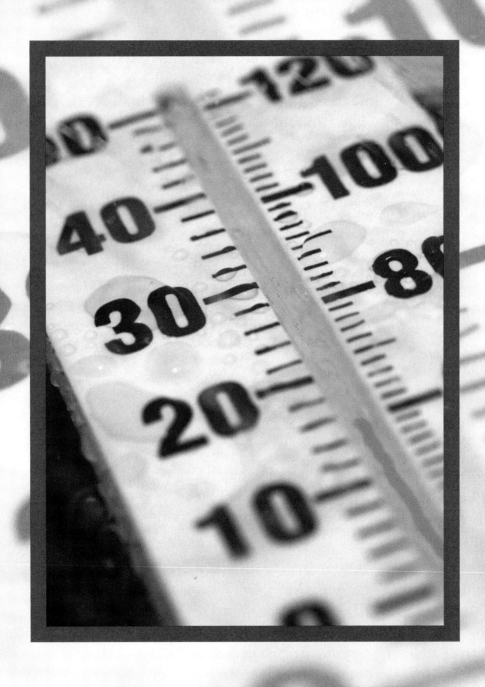

Natural Measures and Standard Units

Systems of weights and measures have been used in many parts of the world since ancient times. People measured lengths and weights for centuries before they had rulers and scales.

Ancient Measures of Weight

Shells and grains such as wheat or rice were often used as units of weight. For example, a small item might be said to weigh 300 grains. Large weights were often compared to the load that could be carried by a man or a pack animal.

Ancient Measures of Length

People used **natural measures** based on body parts to measure length and distance. Some of these units are shown below.

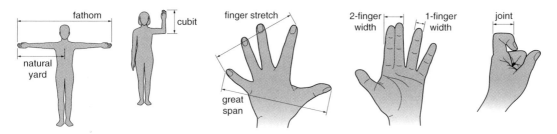

Standard Units of Length and Weight

Using shells and grains to measure weight is not exact. Even if the shells and grains are of the same type, they vary in size and weight.

Using body lengths to measure length is not exact. The body measures used depend upon the person who is doing the measuring. The problem is that different persons have hands and arms of different lengths.

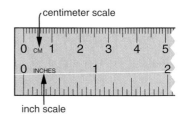

One way to solve this problem is to make **standard units** of length and weight. Most rulers are marked off using inches and centimeters as standard units. Bath scales are marked off using pounds and kilograms as standard units. Standard units never change and are the same for everyone. If two people measure the same object using standard units, their measurements will be the same or almost the same.

The Metric System and the U.S. Customary System

About 200 years ago, a system of weights and measures called the **metric system** was developed. The metric system has standard units for length, weight, and temperature. In the metric system:

- The **meter** is the standard unit for length. The symbol for a meter is **m.** A meter is about the width of a front door.
- The **gram** is the standard unit for weight. The symbol for a gram is **g.** A paper clip weighs about $\frac{1}{2}$ gram.
- The **Celsius degree,** or **°C,** is the standard unit for temperature. Water freezes at 0°C and boils at 100°C. Room temperature is about 20°C.

Scientists almost always measure with metric units. The metric system is easy to use because it is a base-ten system. Larger and smaller units are defined by multiplying or dividing the units above by powers of 10: 10, 100, 1,000, and so on.

> **EXAMPLES** All metric units of length are based on the meter. Each unit is defined by multiplying or dividing the meter by a power of 10.

Units of Length Based on the Meter	Prefix	Meaning
1 millimeter (mm) = $\frac{1}{1,000}$ meter	milli-	$\frac{1}{1,000}$
1 centimeter (cm) = $\frac{1}{100}$ meter	centi-	$\frac{1}{100}$
1 decimeter (dm) = $\frac{1}{10}$ meter	deci-	$\frac{1}{10}$
1 kilometer (km) = 1,000 meters	kilo-	1,000

NOTE

The U.S. customary system is not based on powers of 10. This makes it more difficult to use than the metric system. For example, to change inches to yards, you must know that 36 inches equals 1 yard.

The metric system is used in most countries around the world. In the United States, the **U.S. customary system** is used for everyday purposes. This system uses standard units like the **inch, foot, yard, mile, ounce, pound,** and **ton.**

CHECK YOUR UNDERSTANDING

1. Which of these units are in the metric system?

   ton   millimeter   pound   mile   gram   kilometer   decimeter   ounce

2. a. What does the prefix *kilo-* mean?   **b.** 2 grams = ? kilograms

Check your answers on page 378.

Converting Units of Length

The table below shows how different units of length in the metric system compare. You can use this table to rewrite a length using a different unit.

Comparing Metric Units of Length				Symbols for Units of Length	
1 cm = 10 mm	1 m = 1,000 mm	1 m = 100 cm	1 km = 1,000 m	mm = millimeter	cm = centimeter
1 mm = $\frac{1}{10}$ cm	1 mm = $\frac{1}{1,000}$ m	1 cm = $\frac{1}{100}$ m	1 m = $\frac{1}{1,000}$ km	m = meter	km = kilometer

EXAMPLES Use the table to rewrite each length using a different unit. Replace the unit given first with an equal length that uses the new unit.

Problem	Solution
56 centimeters = ? millimeters	56 cm = 56 * 10 mm = 560 mm
56 centimeters = ? meter	56 cm = 56 * $\frac{1}{100}$ m = 0.56 m
9.3 kilometers = ? meters	9.3 km = 9.3 * 1,000 m = 9,300 m
6.9 meters = ? centimeters	6.9 m = 6.9 * 100 cm = 690 cm

The table below shows how different units of length in the U.S. customary system compare. You can use this table to rewrite a length using a different unit.

Comparing U.S. Customary Units of Length				Symbols for Units of Length	
1 ft = 12 in.	1 yd = 36 in.	1 yd = 3 ft	1 mi = 5,280 ft	in. = inch	ft = foot
1 in. = $\frac{1}{12}$ ft	1 in. = $\frac{1}{36}$ yd	1 ft = $\frac{1}{3}$ yd	1 ft = $\frac{1}{5,280}$ mi	yd = yard	mi = mile

EXAMPLES Use the table to rewrite each length using a different unit. Replace the unit given first with an equal length that uses the new unit.

Problem	Solution
12 feet = ? inches	12 ft = 12 * 12 in. = 144 in.
18 feet = ? yards	18 ft = 18 * $\frac{1}{3}$ yd = $\frac{18}{3}$ yd = 6 yd
5 miles = ? feet	5 mi = 5 * 5,280 ft = 26,400 ft
144 inches = ? yards	144 in. = 144 * $\frac{1}{36}$ yd = $\frac{144}{36}$ yd = 4 yd

Personal References for Units of Length

Sometimes it is difficult to remember exactly how long a centimeter or a yard is or how a kilometer and a mile compare. You may not have a ruler, yardstick, or tape measure handy. When this happens, you can estimate lengths by using the lengths of common objects and distances that you know.

Some examples of **personal references** for length are given below. A good personal reference is something that you see or use often, so you don't forget it. A good personal reference doesn't change size. For example, a wooden pencil is not a good personal reference for length because it gets shorter as it is sharpened.

Personal References for Metric Units of Length

About 1 millimeter	About 1 centimeter
Thickness of a dime	Thickness of a crayon
Thickness of the point of a thumbtack	Width of the head of a thumbtack
Thickness of the thin edge of a paper match	Thickness of a pattern block
About 1 meter	**About 1 kilometer**
One big step (for an adult)	1,000 big steps (for an adult)
Width of a front door	Length of 10 football fields
Tip of the nose to tip of the thumb, with arm extended (for an adult)	

Personal References for U.S. Customary Units of Length

About 1 inch	About 1 foot
Length of a paper clip	A man's shoe length
Width (diameter) of a quarter	Length of a license plate
Width of a man's thumb	Length of this book
About 1 yard	**About 1 mile**
One big step (for an adult)	2,000 average-size steps (for an adult)
Width of a front door	
Tip of the nose to tip of the thumb, with arm extended (for an adult)	Length of 15 football fields (including the end zones)

NOTE

The personal references for 1 meter can also be used for 1 yard.
1 yard = 36 inches, while 1 meter is about 39.37 inches. One meter is often called a "fat yard," which means one yard plus one hand width.

Perimeter

The distance around a polygon is called its **perimeter**. To find the perimeter of any polygon, add the lengths of its sides.

> **EXAMPLE** Find the perimeter of polygon *ABCDE*.
>
> 2 cm + 2 cm + 1.5 cm + 2 cm + 2.5 cm
> =10 cm
>
>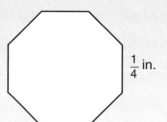
>
> The perimeter is 10 centimeters.

Perimeter Formulas

Rectangles	Squares	Regular Polygons
$p = 2 * (l + w)$	$p = 4 * s$	$p = n * s$
p is the perimeter,	p is the perimeter,	p is the perimeter,
l is the length,	s is the length of one side	n is the number of sides,
w is the width of the rectangle.	of the square.	s is the length of a side.

> **EXAMPLES** Find the perimeter of each polygon.
>
> **Rectangle**
> Use the formula $p = 2 * (l + w)$.
> • length (l) = 4 cm
> • width (w) = 3 cm
> • perimeter (p) = 2 * (4 cm + 3 cm)
>   = 2 * 7 cm = 14 cm
>
> The perimeter is 14 centimeters.
>
> **Square**
> Use the formula $p = 4 * s$.
> • length of side (s) = 9 ft
> • perimeter (p) = 4 * 9 ft = 36 ft
>
> The perimeter is 36 feet.
>
> **Regular Octagon**
> Use the formula $p = n * s$.
> • number of sides (n) = 8
> • length of side (s) = $\frac{1}{4}$ in.
> • perimeter (p) = 8 * $\frac{1}{4}$ in. = 2 in.
>
> The perimeter is 2 inches.

CHECK YOUR UNDERSTANDING

Solve. Be sure to include the unit in your answers.

1. Find the perimeter of a rectangle whose dimensions are 8 feet and 5 feet.

2. Find the perimeter of a regular hexagon whose sides are 12 yards long.

Check your answers on page 378.

Circumference

The perimeter of a circle is the **distance around** the circle. The perimeter of a circle has a special name. It is called the **circumference** of the circle.

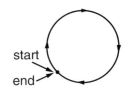

EXAMPLE Most food cans are cylinders. Their tops and bottoms have circular shapes. The circumference of a circular can top is how far a can opener turns in opening the can.

The **diameter** of a circle is any line segment that passes through the center of the circle and has both endpoints on the circle.

The length of a diameter segment is also called the diameter.

If you know the diameter of a circle, there is a simple formula for finding its circumference.

Formula for the Circumference of Circles

circumference = pi $*$ diameter or $c = \pi * d$

c is the circumference, and d is the diameter of the circle.

EXAMPLE Find the circumference of the circle.

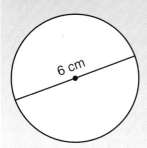

6 cm

Use the formula $c = \pi * d$.
- diameter (d) = 6 cm
- circumference $(c) = \pi * 6$ cm

Use the π key on the calculator, or use 3.14 as an approximate value for π.

circumference (c) = 18.8 cm, rounded to the nearest tenth of a centimeter

NOTE

The Greek letter π is called **pi**. It is approximately equal to 3.14. In your work with the number π, you can use 3.14 or $3\frac{1}{7}$ as the approximate value for π. You can also use a calculator with a π key.

CHECK YOUR UNDERSTANDING

1. Measure the diameter of the dollar coin in millimeters.
2. Find the circumference of the dollar coin in millimeters.
3. What is the circumference of a pizza whose diameter is 14 inches?

Check your answers on page 378.

Area

Area is a measure of the amount of surface inside a closed boundary. You can find the area of a figure by counting the number of squares of a certain size that cover the region inside the boundary. The squares must cover the entire region. They must not overlap, have any gaps, or cover any surface outside the boundary.

Sometimes a region cannot be covered by an exact number of squares. In that case, first count the number of whole squares, then the fractions of squares that cover the region.

Area is reported in square units. Units of area for small regions are square inches (in.^{2}), square feet (ft^2), square yards (yd^2), square centimeters (cm^2), and square meters (m^2). For large areas, square miles (mi^2) are used in the United States, while square kilometers (km^2) are used in most other countries.

You may report area using any of the square units, but you should choose a square unit that makes sense for the region being measured.

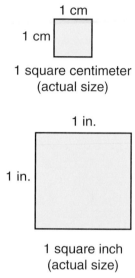

1 cm
1 cm
1 square centimeter
(actual size)

1 in.
1 in.
1 square inch
(actual size)

EXAMPLES The area of a field-hockey field is reported below in three different ways.

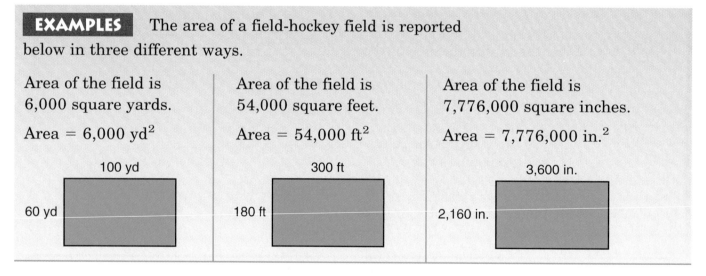

Area of the field is 6,000 square yards.

Area = 6,000 yd^2

100 yd
60 yd

Area of the field is 54,000 square feet.

Area = 54,000 ft^2

300 ft
180 ft

Area of the field is 7,776,000 square inches.

Area = 7,776,000 in.^{2}

3,600 in.
2,160 in.

Although each of these measurements is correct, giving the area in square inches really doesn't give a good idea about the size of the field. It is hard to imagine 7,776,000 of anything!

Area of Rectangles

When you cover a rectangular shape with unit squares, the squares can be arranged into rows. Each row contains the same number of squares and fractions of squares.

EXAMPLE Find the area of the rectangle.

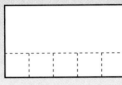
5 squares in a row

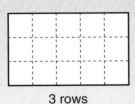
3 rows

3 rows with 5 squares in each row for a total of 15 squares
Area = 15 square units

To find the area of a rectangle, use either formula below:

Area = (the number of squares in 1 row) * (the number of rows)
Area = length of a base * height

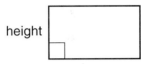

Either pair of parallel sides in a rectangle can be chosen as its **bases.** The **height** of a rectangle is the shortest distance between its bases.

Area Formulas

Rectangles	Squares
$A = b * h$	$A = s^2$
A is the area, b is the length of a base, h is the height of the rectangle.	A is the area, s is the length of a side of the square.

EXAMPLES Find the area of the rectangle.

Use the formula $A = b * h$.
• length of base (b) = 4 in.
• height (h) = 3 in.
• area (A) = 4 in. * 3 in. = 12 in.^{2}
The area of the rectangle is 12 in.^{2}.

3 in.

4 in.

Find the area of the square.

Use the formula $A = s^2$.
• length of a side (s) = 6 ft
• area (A) = 6 ft * 6 ft = 36 ft^2
The area of the square is 36 ft^2.

6 ft

CHECK YOUR UNDERSTANDING

Find the area of the following figures. Include the unit in your answers.

1. 3 units
2 units

2. 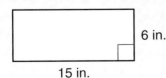 6 in.
15 in.

3. 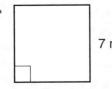 7 m
7 m

Check your answers on page 378.

Area of Parallelograms

In a parallelogram, either pair of opposite sides can be chosen as its **bases.** The **height** of the parallelogram is the shortest distance between the two bases.

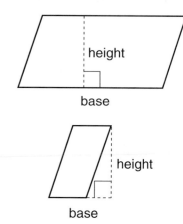

In the parallelograms at the right, the height is shown by a dashed line that is **perpendicular** (at a right angle) to the base. In the second parallelogram, the base has been extended, and the dashed height falls outside the parallelogram.

Any parallelogram can be cut into two pieces and the pieces rearranged to form a rectangle whose base and height are the same as the base and height of the parallelogram. The rectangle has the same area as the parallelogram. So, you can find the area of the parallelogram in the same way you find the area of the rectangle—by multiplying the length of the base by the height.

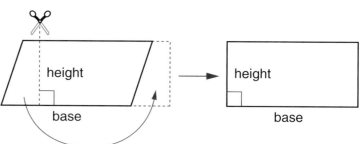

Formula for the Area of Parallelograms

$$A = b * h$$

A is the area, *b* is the length of the base, *h* is the height of the parallelogram.

EXAMPLE Find the area of the parallelogram.

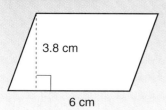
3.8 cm
6 cm

Use the formula $A = b * h$.
- length of base (*b*) = 6 cm
- height (*h*) = 3.8 cm
- area (*A*) = 6 cm * 3.8 cm
      = 22.8 cm²

So, the area of the parallelogram is 22.8 cm².

CHECK YOUR UNDERSTANDING

Find the area of each parallelogram. Include the unit in your answers.

1.
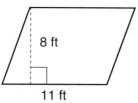
8 ft
11 ft

2.
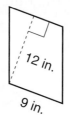
12 in.
9 in.

3.
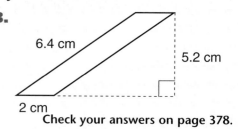
6.4 cm
5.2 cm
2 cm

Check your answers on page 378.

Area of Triangles

Any of the sides of a triangle can be chosen as its **base.** The **height** of the triangle (for that base) is the shortest distance between the base and the **vertex** opposite the base. The height is always perpendicular to the base.

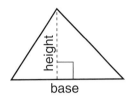
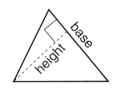

In the triangles at the right, the height is shown by a dashed line that is **perpendicular** (at a right angle) to the base. In one of the triangles, the base has been extended and the dashed height falls outside the triangle.

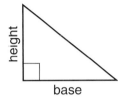
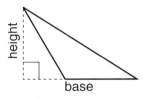

Any triangle can be combined with a second triangle of the same size and shape to form a parallelogram. Each triangle at the right has the same size base and height as the parallelogram. The area of each triangle is half the area of the parallelogram. Therefore, the area of a triangle is half the product of the base multiplied by the height.

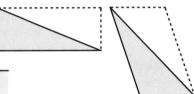
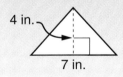

Area Formulas

Parallelograms	Triangles
$A = b * h$	$A = \frac{1}{2} * (b * h)$
A is the area, b is the length of a base, h is the height.	A is the area, b is the length of a base, h is the height.

EXAMPLE Find the area of the triangle.

4 in.
7 in.

Use the formula $A = \frac{1}{2} * (b * h)$.
- length of base (b) = 7 in.
- height (h) = 4 in.
- area (A) = $\frac{1}{2} * (7 \text{ in.} * 4 \text{ in.})$

$$= \frac{1}{2} * 28 \text{ in.}^2 = 14 \text{ in.}^2$$

So, the area of the triangle is 14 in.^{2}.

CHECK YOUR UNDERSTANDING

Find the area of each triangle. Include the unit in your answers.

1.
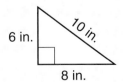
6 in. 10 in. 8 in.

2.
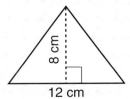
8 cm 12 cm

3.
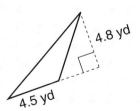
4.8 yd 4.5 yd

Check your answers on page 378.

Area of Circles

The **radius** of a circle is any line segment that connects the center of the circle with any point on the circle. The length of a radius segment is also called the radius.

The **diameter** of a circle is any segment that passes through the center of the circle and has both endpoints on the circle. The length of a diameter segment is also called the diameter.

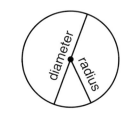

If you know either the radius or the diameter of a circle, you can find the other length using the following formulas:

$$\text{diameter} = 2 * \text{radius} \qquad \text{radius} = \frac{1}{2} * \text{diameter}$$

If you know the radius, there is a simple formula for finding the area of a circle.

Formula for the Area of Circles

Area = pi * (radius squared)   or $A = \pi * r^2$
A is the area, and *r* is the radius of the circle.

EXAMPLE Find the area of the circle.

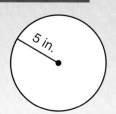

Use the formula $A = \pi * r^2$.
- radius (*r*) = 5 in.
- area (*A*) = π * 5 in. * 5 in.

Use the π key on the calculator, or use 3.14 as an approximate value for π.
- area (*A*) = 78.5 in.², rounded to the nearest tenth of a square inch.

The area of the circle is 78.5 in.².

> **NOTE**
> The Greek letter π is called **pi**, and it is approximately equal to 3.14. When you work with the number π, use 3.14 or $3\frac{1}{7}$ as the approximate value for π, or use a calculator with a π key.

CHECK YOUR UNDERSTANDING

1. Measure the diameter of the nickel in millimeters.
2. What is the radius of the nickel in millimeters?
3. Find the area of the nickel in square millimeters.

Check your answers on page 378.

Volume and Capacity

Volume

The **volume** of a solid object such as a brick or a ball is a measure of how much *space the object takes up*. The volume of a container such as a freezer is a measure of *how much the container will hold*.

Volume is measured in **cubic units,** such as cubic inches (in.^{3}), cubic feet (ft^3), and cubic centimeters (cm^3). It is easy to find the volume of objects that are shaped like cubes or other rectangular prisms. For example, picture a container in the shape of a 10-centimeter cube (that is, a cube that is 10 cm by 10 cm by 10 cm). It can be filled with exactly 1,000 centimeter cubes. Therefore, the volume of a 10-centimeter cube is 1,000 cubic centimeters (1,000 cm^3).

All you need to know to find the volume of a rectangular prism are the length and width of its base and its height. The length, width, and height are called the **dimensions** of the prism.

You can also find the volume of other solids (such as triangular prisms, pyramids, cones, and spheres) by measuring their dimensions. It is even possible to find the volume of irregular objects, such as rocks or your own body.

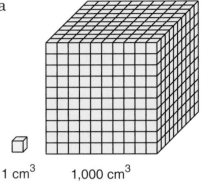

1 cm^3 1,000 cm^3

The Dimensions of a Rectangular Prism

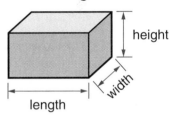

Capacity

We often measure things that can be poured into or out of containers, such as liquids, grains, salt, and so on. The volume of a container that is filled with a liquid or a solid that can be poured is often called its **capacity.**

Capacity is usually measured in units such as **gallons, quarts, pints, cups, fluid ounces, liters,** and **milliliters.**

The tables at the right show how equivalencies between units of capacity compare. These units of capacity are not cubic units, but liters and milliliters are easily converted to cubic units.

1 milliliter = 1 cm^3 1 liter = 1,000 cm^3

Metric Units

1 liter (L) = 1,000 milliliters (mL)
1 milliliter = $\frac{1}{1,000}$ liter
1 liter = 1,000 cubic centimeters
1 milliliter = 1 cubic centimeter

U.S. Customary Units

1 gallon (gal) = 4 quarts (qt)
1 gallon = 2 half-gallons
1 half-gallon = 2 quarts
1 quart = 2 pints (pt)
1 pint = 2 cups (c)
1 cup = 8 fluid ounces (fl oz)
1 pint = 16 fluid ounces
1 quart = 32 fluid ounces
1 half-gallon = 64 fluid ounces
1 gallon = 128 fluid ounces

Volume of Geometric Solids

You can think of the volume of a geometric solid as the total number of unit cubes and fractions of unit cubes that are needed to fill the interior of the solid without gaps or overlaps.

Prisms and Cylinders

In a prism or cylinder, the cubes can be arranged in layers, each containing the same number of cubes or fractions of cubes.

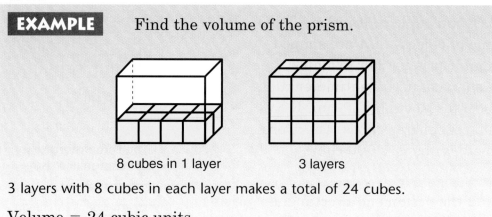

> **EXAMPLE** Find the volume of the prism.
>
> 8 cubes in 1 layer   3 layers
>
> 3 layers with 8 cubes in each layer makes a total of 24 cubes.
>
> Volume = 24 cubic units

The **height** of a prism or cylinder is the shortest distance between its **bases.** The volume of a prism or cylinder is the product of the area of the base (the number of cubes in one layer) multiplied by its height (the number of layers).

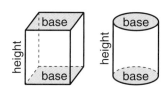

Pyramids and Cones

The height of a pyramid or cone is the shortest distance between its base and the vertex opposite its base.

If a prism and a pyramid have the same size base and height, then the volume of the pyramid is one-third the volume of the prism. If a cylinder and a cone have the same size base and height, then the volume of the cone is one-third the volume of the cylinder.

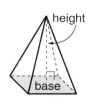

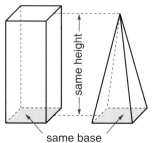
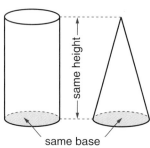

same base   same base

Volume of Rectangular and Triangular Prisms

Volume of Prisms	Area of Rectangles	Area of Triangles
$V = B * h$	$A = b * h$	$A = \frac{1}{2} * (b * h)$
V is the volume, B is the area of the base, h is the height of the prism.	A is the area, b is the length of the base, h is the height of the rectangle.	A is the area, b is the length of the base, h is the height of the triangle.

EXAMPLE   Find the volume of the rectangular prism.

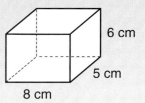

Step 1: Find the area of the base (B). Use the formula $A = b * h$.
  • length of the rectangular base (b) = 8 cm
  • height of the rectangular base (h) = 5 cm
  • area of base (B) = 8 cm * 5 cm = 40 cm²

Step 2: Multiply the area of the base by the height of the rectangular prism. Use the formula $V = B * h$.
  • area of base (B) = 40 cm²
  • height of prism (h) = 6 cm
  • volume (V) = 40 cm² * 6 cm = 240 cm³

So, the volume of the rectangular prism is 240 cm³.

EXAMPLE   Find the volume of the triangular prism.

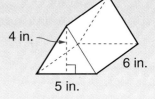

Step 1: Find the area of the base (B). Use the formula $A = \frac{1}{2} * (b * h)$.
  • length of the triangular base (b) = 5 in.
  • height of the triangular base (h) = 4 in.
  • area of base (B) = $\frac{1}{2}$ * (5 in. * 4 in.) = 10 in.²

Step 2: Multiply the area of the base by the height of the triangular prism. Use the formula $V = B * h$.
  • area of base (B) = 10 in.²
  • height of prism (h) = 6 in.
  • volume (V) = 10 in.² * 6 in. = 60 in.³

So, the volume of the triangular prism is 60 in.³.

CHECK YOUR UNDERSTANDING

Find the volume of each prism. Be sure to include the unit in your answers.

1.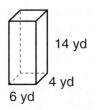
14 yd
4 yd
6 yd

2.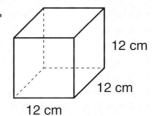
12 cm
12 cm
12 cm

3.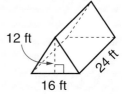
12 ft
24 ft
16 ft

Check your answers on page 378.

Volume of Cylinders and Cones

Volume of Cylinders	Volume of Cones	Area of Circles
$V = B * h$	$V = \frac{1}{3} * (B * h)$	$A = \pi * r^2$
V is the volume, B is the area of the base, h is the height of the cylinder.	V is the volume, B is the area of the base, h is the height of the cone.	A is the area, r is the radius of the base.

EXAMPLE   Find the volume of the cylinder.

Step 1: Find the area of the base (B).
Use the formula $A = \pi * r^2$.
- radius of base (r) = 5 cm
- area of base (B) = $\pi * 5$ cm $* 5$ cm

Use the π key on a calculator or 3.14 as an approximate value for π.
- area of base (B) = 78.5 cm^2, rounded to the nearest tenth of a square centimeter

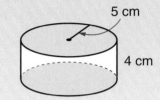
5 cm
4 cm

Step 2: Multiply the area of the base by the height of the cylinder.
Use the formula $V = B * h$.
- area of base (B) = 78.5 cm^2
- height of cylinder (h) = 4 cm
- volume (V) = 78.5 cm$^2 * 4$ cm = 314.0 cm^3

The volume of the cylinder is 314.0 cm^3.

EXAMPLE   Find the volume of the cone.

Step 1: Find the area of the base (B).
Use the formula $A = \pi * r^2$.
- radius of base (r) = 3 in.
- area of base (B) = $\pi * 3$ in. $* 3$ in.

Use the π key on a calculator or 3.14 as an approximate value for π.
- area of base (B) = 28.3 in.^{2}, rounded to the nearest tenth of a square inch

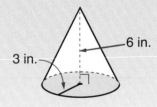
6 in.
3 in.

Step 2: Find $\frac{1}{3}$ of the product of the area of the base multiplied by the height of the cone.
Use the formula $V = \frac{1}{3} * (B * h)$.
- area of base (B) = 28.3 in.^{2}
- height of cone (h) = 6 in.
- volume (V) = $\frac{1}{3} * 28.3$ in.$^2 * 6$ in. = 56.6 in.^{3}

The volume of the cone is 56.6 in.^{3}.

Volume of Rectangular and Triangular Pyramids

Volume of Pyramids	Area of Rectangles	Area of Triangles
$V = \frac{1}{3} * (B * h)$	$A = b * h$	$A = \frac{1}{2} * (b * h)$
V is the volume, B is the area of the base, h is the height of the pyramid.	A is the area, b is the length of the base, h is the height of the rectangle.	A is the area, b is the length of the base, h is the height of the triangle.

EXAMPLE Find the volume of the rectangular pyramid.

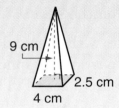

Step 1: Find the area of the base (B). Use the formula $A = b * h$.
- length of base (b) = 4 cm
- height of base (h) = 2.5 cm
- area of base (B) = 4 cm * 2.5 cm = 10 cm²

Step 2: Find $\frac{1}{3}$ of the product of the area of the base multiplied by the height of the rectangular pyramid.
Use the formula $V = \frac{1}{3} * (B * h)$.
- area of base (B) = 10 cm²
- height of pyramid (h) = 9 cm
- volume (V) = $\frac{1}{3}$ * 10 cm² * 9 cm = 30 cm³

The volume of the rectangular pyramid is 30 cm³.

EXAMPLE Find the volume of the triangular pyramid.

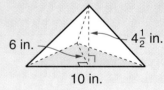

Step 1: Find the area of the base (B). Use the formula $A = \frac{1}{2} * (b * h)$.
- length of base (b) = 10 in.
- height of base (h) = 6 in.
- area of base (B) = $\frac{1}{2}$ * (10 in. * 6 in.) = 30 in.²

Step 2: Find $\frac{1}{3}$ of the product of the area of the base multiplied by the height of the triangular pyramid.
Use the formula $V = \frac{1}{3} * (B * h)$.
- area of base (B) = 30 in.²
- height of pyramid (h) = $4\frac{1}{2}$ in.
- volume (V) = $\frac{1}{3}$ * 30 in.² * $4\frac{1}{2}$ in. = 45 in.³

The volume of the triangular pyramid is 45 in.³.

CHECK YOUR UNDERSTANDING

Find the volume of each pyramid. Be sure to include the unit in your answers.

1.
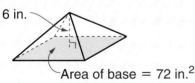
6 in.
Area of base = 72 in.²

2.
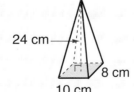
24 cm
8 cm
10 cm

3.
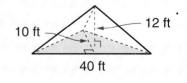
10 ft
12 ft
40 ft

Check your answers on page 378.

Volume of Spheres

Suppose you drew point A on a sheet of paper. Now, imagine that you could draw every point that is 2 inches from point A. You would get a circle whose **center** is point A and whose **radius** is 2 inches long. Any points inside the circle are not a part of the circle; they form the **interior** of the circle.

Now, imagine all of the points in space that are 2 inches from point A in every direction. You would get a figure that looks like the surface of a ball. This figure is called a **sphere.** Point A is the center of the **sphere.** The distance from point A to any point on the sphere is the **radius of the sphere.**

Just as with the circle, the points inside the sphere are not a part of the sphere. A good way to think of a sphere is to picture a soap bubble. Another way is to imagine a circle with a rod passing through its center. If the circle is rotated around the rod, the path of the circle will form a sphere.

If a sphere is cut in half, each half is a figure called a **half-sphere.** The rim of the half-sphere is a circle whose center is the center of the sphere.

Formula for the Volume of Spheres

$$V = \frac{4}{3} * \pi * r^3$$

V is the volume, r is the radius of the sphere.

EXAMPLE   Find the volume of the sphere.

Use the formula $V = \frac{4}{3} * \pi * r^3$.
- radius $(r) = 5$ cm
- volume $(V) = \frac{4}{3} * \pi * 5 * 5 * 5$

Use the π key on the calculator or 3.14 as an approximate value for π.
- volume $= 523.6$ cm^3, rounded to the nearest tenth of a cubic centimeter

The volume of the sphere is 523.6 cm^3.

CHECK YOUR UNDERSTANDING

Find the volume of each sphere to the nearest tenth of a cubic unit.
Be sure to include the unit in your answers.

1. radius of sphere = 2 inches   **2.** diameter of sphere = 8 centimeters

Check your answers on page 378.

Surface Area of Rectangular Prisms

A rectangular prism has six flat surfaces called **faces.** The **surface area** of a rectangular prism is the sum of the areas of its faces. One way to find the surface area of a rectangular prism is to think of the six faces as three pairs of opposite, parallel faces. Since opposite faces have the same area, you can find the area of one face in each pair of opposite faces, then find the sum of these three areas and double the result.

The dimensions of a rectangular prism are its length (l), width (w), and height (h), as shown in the prism at the right. You can find the surface area of rectangular prisms as follows:

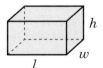

Step 1: Find the area of one face in each pair of opposite faces.

area of	area of front	area of side
base = $l * w$	face = $l * h$	face = $w * h$

Step 2: Find the sum of the areas of the three faces.
- sum of areas = $(l * w) + (l * h) + (w * h)$

Step 3: Multiply the sum of the three areas by 2.
- surface area of prism = $2 * ((l * w) + (l * h) + (w * h))$

Surface Area of Rectangular Prisms

$$S = 2 * ((l * w) + (l * h) + (w * h))$$

S is the surface area, l the length of the base, w the width of the base, h the height of the prism.

EXAMPLE Find the surface area of the rectangular prism.

Use the formula $S = 2 * ((l * w) + (l * h) + (w * h))$.
- length (l) = 8 in.   width (w) = 6 in.   height (h) = 4 in.
- surface area (S) = $2 * ((8 \text{ in.} * 6 \text{ in.}) + (8 \text{ in.} * 4 \text{ in.}) + (6 \text{ in.} * 4 \text{ in.}))$
  $= 2 * (48 \text{ in.}^2 + 32 \text{ in.}^2 + 24 \text{ in.}^2) = 2 * 104 \text{ in.}^2 = 208 \text{ in.}^2$

The surface area of the rectangular prism is 208 in.^{2}.

CHECK YOUR UNDERSTANDING

Find the surface area of each prism. Be sure to include the unit in your answer.

1. 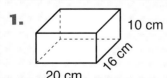 10 cm
20 cm
16 cm

2. 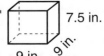 7.5 in.
9 in.
9 in.

3. $\frac{1}{4}$ ft
$\frac{1}{4}$ ft
$\frac{1}{4}$ ft

Check your answers on page 378.

Surface Area of Cylinders

A cylinder has two circular faces called **bases** that are connected by a curved surface. The bases are parallel and have the same area.

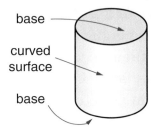

base
curved surface
base

right cylinder

To find the area of the curved surface of a cylinder, imagine a soup can with a label. If you cut the label perpendicular to the top and bottom of the can, peel it off, and lay it flat on a surface, you will have a rectangle. The length of the rectangle is the same as the circumference of the base of the cylinder. The width of the rectangle is the same as the height of the can. Therefore, the area of the curved surface is the product of the circumference of the base and the height of the can.

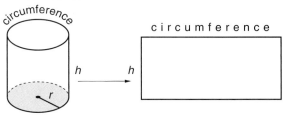

circumference of base = 2 * π * r
area of curved surface = (2 * π * r) * h

The surface area of a cylinder is the sum of the areas of the two bases $(2 * \pi * r^2)$ and the curved surface.

Surface Area of Cylinders

$$S = (2 * \pi * r^2) + ((2 * \pi * r) * h)$$

S is the surface area, r is the radius of the base, h is the height of the cylinder.

EXAMPLE   Find the surface area of the cylinder.

Use the formula $S = (2 * \pi * r^2) + ((2 * \pi * r) * h)$.
• radius of base (r) = 3 cm
• height (h) = 5 cm
Use the π key on the calculator or 3.14 as an approximate value for π.
• surface area (S) = (2 * π * 3 cm * 3 cm) + ((2 * π * 3 cm) * 5 cm)
$\qquad = (\pi * 18 \text{ cm}^2) + (\pi * 30 \text{ cm}^2)$
$\qquad = 150.8 \text{ cm}^2$, rounded to the nearest tenth of a square centimeter
The surface area of the cylinder is 150.8 cm².

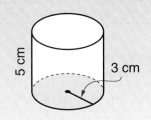

5 cm
3 cm

CHECK YOUR UNDERSTANDING

Find the surface area of the cylinder to the nearest tenth of a square inch. Be sure to include the unit in your answer.

4 in.
6 in.

Check your answers on page 379.

Temperature

Temperature is a measure of the hotness or coldness of something. To read a temperature in degrees, you need a reference frame that begins with a zero point and has an interval for the scale. The two most commonly used temperature scales, Fahrenheit and Celsius, have different zero points.

Fahrenheit

This scale was invented in the early 1700s by the German physicist G.D. Fahrenheit. Pure water freezes at 32°F and boils at 212°F. A saltwater solution freezes at 0°F (the zero point) at sea level. The normal temperature for the human body is 98.6°F. The Fahrenheit scale is used primarily in the United States.

Celsius

This scale was developed in 1742 by the Swedish astronomer Anders Celsius. The zero point (0 degrees Celsius, or 0°C) is the freezing point of pure water. Pure water boils at 100°C. The Celsius scale divides the interval between these two points into 100 equal parts. For this reason, it is sometimes called the *centigrade* scale. The normal temperature for the human body is 37°C. The Celsius scale is the standard for most people outside of the United States and for scientists everywhere.

A **thermometer** measures temperature. The common thermometer is a glass tube that contains a liquid. When the temperature goes up, the liquid expands and moves up the tube. When the temperature goes down, the liquid shrinks and moves down the tube.

Here are formulas for converting between degrees Fahrenheit (°F) and degrees Celsius (°C):

$$C = \frac{5}{9} * (F - 32) \quad \text{and} \quad F = \frac{9}{5} * C + 32$$

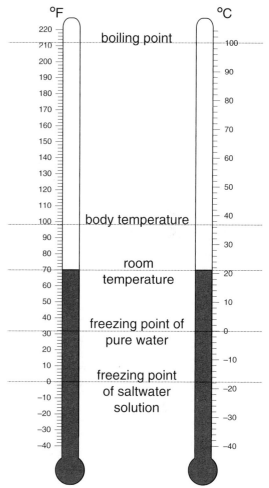

The thermometers show both the Fahrenheit and Celsius scales. Key reference temperatures, such as the boiling and freezing points of water, are indicated. A thermometer reading of 70°F (or about 21°C) is normal room temperature.

EXAMPLE Find the Celsius equivalent of 82°F.

Use the formula $C = \frac{5}{9} * (F - 32)$, and replace F with 82:

$C = \frac{5}{9} * (82 - 32)$

So, $C = \frac{5}{9} * (50) = 27.77...$, or about 28°C.

Weight

Today, in the United States, two different sets of standard units are used to measure weight.

- The standard unit for weight in the metric system is the **gram.** A small, plastic base-10 cube weighs about 1 gram. Heavier weights are measured in **kilograms.** One kilogram equals 1,000 grams.

- Two standard units for weight in the U.S. customary system are the **ounce** and the **pound.** Heavier weights are measured in pounds. One pound equals 16 ounces. Some weights are reported in both pounds and ounces. For example, we might say that "the suitcase weighs 14 pounds 6 ounces."

Metric Units	U.S. Customary Units
1 gram (g) = 1,000 milligrams (mg)	1 pound (lb) = 16 ounces (oz)
1 milligram = $\frac{1}{1,000}$ gram	1 ounce = $\frac{1}{16}$ pound
1 kilogram (kg) = 1,000 grams	1 ton (t) = 2,000 pounds
1 gram = $\frac{1}{1,000}$ kilogram	1 pound = $\frac{1}{2,000}$ ton
1 metric ton (t) = 1,000 kilograms	
1 kilogram = $\frac{1}{1,000}$ metric ton	

Rules of Thumb	Exact Equivalents
1 ounce equals about 30 grams.	1 ounce = 28.35 grams
1 kilogram weighs about 2 pounds.	1 kilogram = 2.205 pounds

EXAMPLE A bicycle weighs 14 kilograms. How many pounds is that?

Rough Solution: Use the Rule of Thumb. Since 1 kg equals about 2 lb, 14 kg equals about 14 * 2 = 28 lb.

Exact Solution: Use the exact equivalent. Since 1 kg = 2.205 lb, 14 kg = 14 * 2.205 = 30.870 lb.

NOTE

The Rules of Thumb Table shows how units of weight in the metric system relate to units in the U.S. customary system. You can use this table to convert ounces to grams and kilograms to pounds. You need only remember the simple Rules of Thumb for most everyday purposes.

CHECK YOUR UNDERSTANDING

Solve each problem.

1. A softball weighs 6 ounces. How many grams is that? Use both a Rule of Thumb and an exact equivalent.

2. Ella's brother weighs 22 pounds 14 ounces. How many ounces is that?

Check your answers on page 379.

Capacity and Precision

Samples of different kinds of scales are shown here. The **capacity** and **precision** are given for each scale.

The **capacity** of a scale is the greatest weight that the scale can hold. For example, most infant scales have a capacity of about 25 pounds. Bath scales are used to weigh older children and adults and usually have a capacity of about 300 pounds.

infant scale
capacity: 25 lb
precision: 1 oz

The **precision** of a scale is its accuracy. If you can read a weight on a bath scale to the nearest pound, then the precision for that scale is 1 pound. On most infant scales, you can read a weight to the nearest ounce, so the precision is 1 ounce.

bath scale
capacity: 300 lb or 136 kg
precision: 1 lb or 454 g

With a balance scale, you can measure weight to the nearest gram. A balance scale is much more precise than an infant scale because a gram is lighter than an ounce.

balance scale
capacity: 2 kg
precision: 1 g

weight set for balance scale

1g 1g 2g 2g   5g   10g   20g   50g

Some scales are extremely precise. They can weigh things that cannot be seen with the naked eye. Other scales are very large. They can be used to weigh objects that weigh as much as 900 tons (1,800,000 pounds). Most scales display weight in both metric and U.S. customary units.

platform scale
capacity: 1 T to 900 T
precision: 0.5 lb

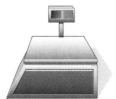

market scale
capacity: 30 lb or 15 kg
precision: 0.01 lb or 0.005 kg

diet/food scale
capacity: 11 lb or 5 kg
precision: 1 oz or 25 g

spring scale
capacity: 18 oz or 500 g
precision: $\frac{1}{2}$ oz or 20 g

Measuring and Drawing Angles

Angles are measured in **degrees.** When writing the measure of an angle, a small raised circle (°) is used as a symbol for the word *degree*.

Angles are measured with a tool called a **protractor.** You will find both a full-circle and a half-circle protractor on your Geometry Template. Since there are 360 degrees in a circle, a 1° angle marks off $\frac{1}{360}$ of a circle.

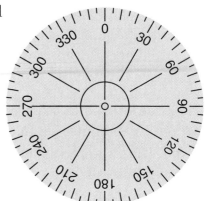

The **full-circle protractor** on the Geometry Template is marked off in 5° intervals from 0° to 360°. Although it can be used to measure angles, it cannot be used to draw angles of a given measure.

Sometimes you will use a full-circle protractor that is a paper cutout. This *can* be used to draw angles.

The **half-circle protractor** on the Geometry Template is marked off in 1° intervals from 0° to 180°.

It has two scales. Each scale starts at 0°. One scale is read clockwise, the other is read counterclockwise.

The half-circle protractor can be used both to measure angles and to draw angles of a given measure.

Two rays starting from the same endpoint form two angles. The smaller angle measures between 0° and 180°. The larger angle measures between 180° and 360°. It is called a **reflex angle.** The sum of the measures of the smaller angle and the reflex angle is 360°.

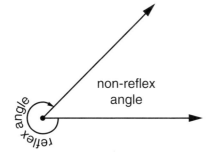

non-reflex angle

reflex angle

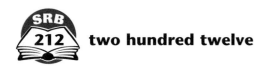

Measuring an Angle with a Full-Circle Protractor

Think of the angle as a rotation of the minute hand on a clock.
One side of the angle represents the minute hand at the
beginning of a time interval. The other side of the angle
represents the minute hand some time later.

EXAMPLE Measure angle *IJK* with a full-circle
protractor.

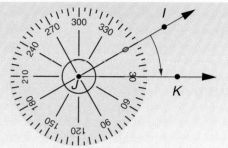

Step 1: Place the center of the protractor over the vertex
of the angle, point *J*.

Step 2: Line up the 0° mark on the protractor with $\overrightarrow{JI}$.

Step 3: Read the degree measure where $\overrightarrow{JK}$ crosses the
edge of the protractor.

The measure of angle *IJK* = 30°.

EXAMPLE Measure reflex angle *EFG*.

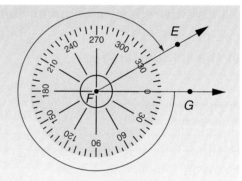

Step 1: Place the center of the protractor over point *F*.

Step 2: Line up the 0° mark on the protractor with $\overrightarrow{FG}$.

Step 3: Read the degree measure where $\overrightarrow{FE}$ crosses the
edge of the protractor.

The measure of angle *EFG* = 330°.

Measuring an Angle with a Half-Circle Protractor

EXAMPLE Measure angle *PQR* with a half-circle protractor.

Step 1: Lay the baseline of the protractor on $\overrightarrow{QR}$.

Step 2: Slide the protractor so that the
center of the baseline is over the
vertex of the angle, point *Q*.

Step 3: Read the degree measure where
$\overrightarrow{QP}$ crosses the edge of the
protractor. There are two scales
on the protractor. Use the scale
that makes sense for the size of
the angle you are measuring.

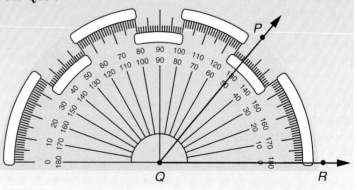

The measure of angle *PQR* = 50°.

Drawing an Angle with a Half-Circle Protractor

EXAMPLE   Draw a 40° angle.

Step 1: Draw a ray from point *A*.

Step 2: Lay the baseline of the protractor on the ray.

Step 3: Slide the protractor so that the center of the baseline is over point *A*.

Step 4: Make a mark at 40° on the protractor. There are two scales on the protractor. Use the scale that makes sense for the size of the angle you are drawing.

Step 5: Draw a ray from point *A* through the mark.

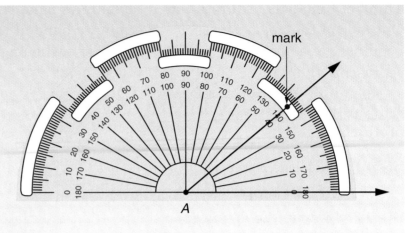

To draw a reflex angle using the half-circle protractor, subtract the measure of the reflex angle from 360°. This is the measure of the smaller angle.

EXAMPLE   Draw a 240° angle.

Step 1: Subtract: 360° − 240° = 120°.

Step 2: Draw a 120° angle.

The larger angle is a 240° reflex angle.

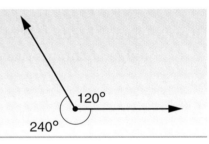

CHECK YOUR UNDERSTANDING

Measure each angle to the nearest degree.

1.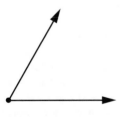

2.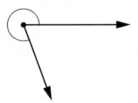

3.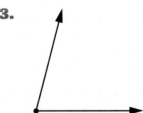

Draw each angle.

4. a 70° angle

5. a 280° angle

6. a 55° angle

Check your answers on page 379.

The Measures of the Angles of Polygons

Any polygon can be divided into triangles.

- The measures of the three angles of each triangle add up to 180°.
- To find the sum of the measures of all the angles of a polygon, multiply the number of triangles in the polygon by 180°.

EXAMPLE What is the sum of the measures of the angles of a hexagon?

Step 1: Draw any hexagon; then divide it into triangles.
This hexagon can be divided into four triangles.

Step 2: Multiply the number of triangles by 180°.

Since the measures of the angles of each triangle add up to 180°, the sum of the measures of the angles is 4 * 180° = 720°.

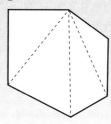

Hexagon

Finding the Measure of an Angle of a Regular Polygon

All the angles of a regular polygon have the same measure. So, the measure of an angle is equal to the sum of the measures of the angles of the polygon divided by the number of angles.

EXAMPLE What is the measure of an angle of a regular hexagon?

The sum of the measures of the angles of any hexagon is 720°. A regular hexagon has six congruent angles.

The measure of an angle of a regular hexagon is 720° / 6 = 120°.

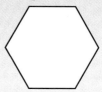

Regular Hexagon
(6 congruent sides and 6 congruent angles)

CHECK YOUR UNDERSTANDING

1. Into how many triangles can you divide each polygon?

   a. a quadrilateral   **b.** a pentagon   **c.** an octagon   **d.** a 12-sided polygon

2. What is the sum of the measures of the angles of a pentagon?

3. What is the measure of an angle of a regular octagon?

4. Suppose that you know the number of sides of a polygon. How can you calculate the number of triangles into which it can be divided without drawing a picture?

Check your answers on page 379.

Plotting Ordered Number Pairs

A **rectangular coordinate grid** is used to name points in the plane. It is made up of two number lines, called **axes,** that meet at right angles at their zero points. The point where the two lines meet is called the **origin.**

Every point on a coordinate grid can be named by an **ordered number pair.** The two numbers that make up an ordered pair are called the **coordinates** of the point. The first coordinate is always the *horizontal* distance of the point from the vertical axis. The second coordinate is always the *vertical* distance of the point from the horizontal axis. For example, the ordered pair (2,4) names point *A* on the grid at the right. The numbers 2 and 4 are the coordinates of point *A*.

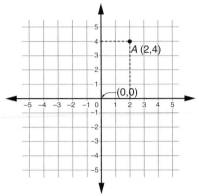

The ordered pair (0,0) names the origin.

EXAMPLE   Plot the ordered pair (4,2).

Step 1: Locate 4 on the horizontal axis.

Step 2: Locate 2 on the vertical axis.

Step 3: Draw a vertical line from point 4 on the horizontal axis and a horizontal line from point 2 on the vertical axis. The point (4,2) is located at the intersection of the two lines. The order of the numbers in an ordered pair is important. The ordered pair (4,2) does not name the same point as the ordered pair (2,4).

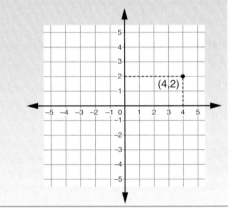

EXAMPLE   Locate (−4,3), (−4,−3), and (2,0).

For each ordered pair, locate the first coordinate on the horizontal axis and the second coordinate on the vertical axis. Draw intersecting lines from these two points.

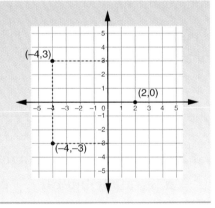

CHECK YOUR UNDERSTANDING

Draw a coordinate grid on graph paper, and plot the following points.

1. (1,5)   **2.** (−4,−4)   **3.** (0,−3)   **4.** (3,−2)

Check your answers on page 379.

Latitude and Longitude

The Earth is almost a perfect **sphere.** All points on Earth are about the same distance from its center. The Earth rotates on an **axis,** an imaginary line that connects the **North Pole** and the **South Pole.**

Reference lines are drawn on globes and maps to make places easier to locate. Lines that go east and west around the Earth are called **lines of latitude.** The lines of latitude are often called **parallels** because each one is a circle that is parallel to the equator. The **equator** is a special line of latitude. Every point on the equator is the same distance from both the North Pole and the South Pole.

Lines of latitude are measured in **degrees.** The symbol for degrees is (°). Lines north of the equator are labeled °N (degrees north); lines south of the equator are labeled °S (degrees south). The number of degrees tells how far north or south of the equator a place is located. The area north of the equator is called the **Northern Hemisphere.** The area south of the equator is called the **Southern Hemisphere.**

EXAMPLES The latitude of the North Pole is 90°N. The latitude of the South Pole is 90°S. The Poles are the points farthest north and farthest south on Earth.

The latitude of Cairo, Egypt, is 30°N. We say that Cairo is 30 degrees north of the equator.

The latitude of Durban, South Africa, is 30°S. Durban is in the Southern Hemisphere.

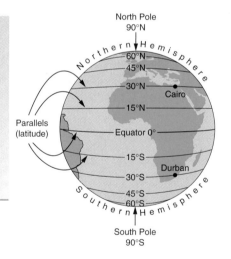

A second set of lines runs north to south. These are semicircles (half circles) that connect the two Poles. They are called **lines of longitude** or **meridians.** Meridians are not parallel since they meet at the Poles.

The **prime meridian** is a special meridian that is labeled 0°. The prime meridian passes through Greenwich near London, England. Another special meridian is the **International Date Line.** This meridian is labeled 180° and is exactly opposite the prime meridian on the other side of the world.

Longitude is measured in degrees. Lines west of the prime meridian are labeled °W. Lines east of the prime meridian are labeled °E. The number of degrees tells how far west or east of the prime meridian a place is located. The area west of the prime meridian is called the **Western Hemisphere.** The area east of the prime meridian is called the **Eastern Hemisphere.**

EXAMPLE   The longitude of Greenwich, England, is 0° because Greenwich lies on the prime meridian.

The longitude of Durban, South Africa, is 30°E. Durban is in the Eastern Hemisphere.

The longitude of Gambia (a small country in Africa) is about 15°W. We say that Gambia is 15 degrees west of the prime meridian.

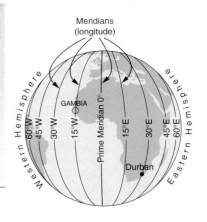

When lines of latitude and longitude are both shown on a globe or a map, they form a pattern of crossing lines called a **grid.** The grid can help you locate any place on the map by simply naming its latitude and longitude.

EXAMPLE   The map may be used to find the approximate latitude and longitude for the cities shown. For example, Denver, Colorado, is about 40° North and 105° West.

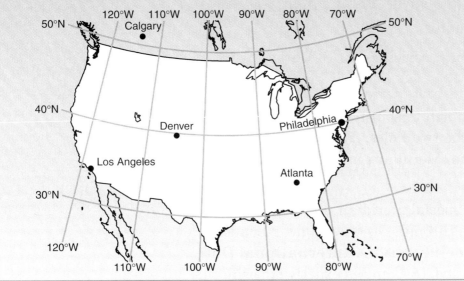

Algebra

Algebra

The origins of algebra can be traced back thousands of years to ancient Egypt and Babylon. Algebra got its name from the Arab world, where it was known as the "science of restoration and balancing." (Our word *algebra* comes from the Arabic word *al–jabru*, which means "restoration.")

The Rhind Papyrus,
written almost 4,000 years ago

In early times, algebra involved solving equations with "unknowns"; that is, finding the value of a missing number in an equation. Words were used for these unknowns: "Five plus *some number* equals eight." Then, in the late 1500s, François Viète began using letters to stand for unknown quantities, as in: $5 + x = 8$. Viète's invention made solving equations much easier and led to an explosion of discoveries in mathematics and science that has continued into modern times.

Most people think of algebra as a subject for high school, mostly involving symbols and equations. But you studied algebra as early as first grade when you had to find the missing number in simple equations such as $5 + \square = 9$. As you studied more mathematics, the equations became more complicated, but the basic problem remained the same: to find the missing number in an equation.

Letters, blanks, or other symbols that stand for unknown numbers are called **variables.** Variables are also used in several other ways.

Variables Can Be Used in the Study of the Properties of Number Systems

Properties of a number system are things that are true for all numbers. For example, the commutative property of addition states that for all numbers a and b, $a + b = b + a$. You were introduced to this property in first grade as the "turn-around" shortcut to help you memorize addition facts.

Variables Can Be Used in the Expression of General Relations or Functions

These may appear as "What's My Rule?" tables in which the relationship between the "in" numbers and the "out" numbers is given by a rule, such as "double and add 1," or by using variables, $y = 2x + 1$. Such relationships can also be graphed on a coordinate grid, as shown at the right.

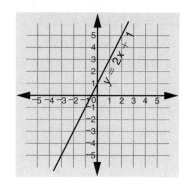

Variables Can Be Used in Formulas

Formulas are used in everyday life, in science, in business, and in many other situations as a compact way to express relationships. For example, the formula $d = r * t$ expresses the relationship between a distance, the rate at which one covers the distance, and the time it takes to cover the distance.

miles	50	100	150	?
hours	1	2	3	4

Variables Can Be Used in Computers and Calculators

Variables are used in computer spreadsheets, making it possible to evaluate formulas quickly and efficiently. Spreadsheets are very useful for making predictions based on trends. Variables are also used in writing computer programs. Computer programs are made up of a series of "commands" containing variables, much like the variables in equations.

Some calculators, especially graphing calculators, use variables to name calculator key functions and when specifying calculator procedures.

CHECK YOUR UNDERSTANDING

For each problem, write a number sentence using a letter for the unknown.

1. Twice some number equals 30.

2. Some number, decreased by 8, equals 12.

Solve each problem. Use the formula $d = r * t$.

3. How far will a car travel in $3\frac{1}{2}$ hours if its average speed is 45 miles per hour?

4. Joan swims 5 lengths of the pool in 2 minutes. How long will it take her to swim $7\frac{1}{2}$ lengths?

Check your answers on page 379.

Algebraic Expressions

Consider the following statement: "Marcia read four more books last year than Gina." You can't tell how many books Marcia read unless you know the number of books Gina read. There are many possibilities:

• If Gina read 8 books, then Marcia read 12 books.
• If Gina read 27 books, then Marcia read 31 books, and so on.

One way to represent the number of books Marcia read is to write an **algebraic expression,** in which a variable is used to represent the number of books Gina read. For example, if G represents the number of books Gina read, then $G + 4$ represents the number of books Marcia read.

EXAMPLES Write an algebraic expression to answer each question.

Statement	Algebraic Expression
Mary is 5 years older than her sister Carla. How old is Mary?	If Carla is C years old, then Mary is $C + 5$ years old.
Mrs. Roth weighs 30 pounds less than Mr. Roth. How much does Mrs. Roth weigh?	If Mr. Roth weighs R pounds, then Mrs. Roth weighs $R - 30$ pounds.
Mrs. Martinez bought a box of crayons with 8 crayons per box for each of her grandchildren. How many crayons did she buy altogether?	If Mrs. Martinez has G grandchildren, then she bought a total of $8 * G$ crayons.
Claude earned $6 an hour and was paid an additional $3.50 for his lunch. How much did Claude get paid?	If Claude worked H hours, he got paid $(6 * H) + 3.50$ dollars.

CHECK YOUR UNDERSTANDING

Write an algebraic expression for each situation using the suggested variable.

1. Mark is m inches tall. If Audrey is 2 inches shorter than Mark, what is Audrey's height?

2. It takes Herman H minutes to do his homework. If it takes Sue twice as long, how long does it take her?

3. Dawn went on R rides at the amusement park. If the park charges a $2 admission fee and $0.50 per ride, how much did Dawn spend?

Check your answers on page 379.

Number Sentences

Number sentences are made up of **mathematical symbols.**

Mathematical Symbols

Digits	Operation Symbols		Relation Symbols		Grouping Symbols	
0, 1, 2,	+	plus	=	is equal to	( )	parentheses
3, 4, 5,	−	minus	≠	is not equal to	[ ]	brackets
6, 7, 8,	× or *	times	<	is less than		
9	/ or ÷	divided by	>	is greater than		
			≤	is less than or equal to		
			≥	is greater than or equal to		

A number sentence must contain **numbers** and a **relation symbol.** It may or may not contain **operation symbols** and **grouping symbols.**

Number sentences that contain the = symbol are called **equations.** Number sentences that contain the symbols ≠, <, >, ≤, or ≥, are called **inequalities.**

If a number sentence is made up only of numbers, operation, symbols, and a relation symbol, then it is always possible to tell whether it is **true** or **false.**

EXAMPLES

Equations

$3 + 3 = 8$ False $3 + 3 = 6$, not 8

$(24 + 3) / 9 = 3$ True $27 / 9 = 3$

$100 = 9^2 + 9$ False $9^2 + 9 = 90$

Inequalities

$-27 * 4 > 42$ False $-27 * 4 = -108$, and -108 is not greater than 42.

$\frac{4}{5} - \frac{2}{3} < \frac{1}{2}$ True $\frac{4}{5} - \frac{2}{3} = \frac{2}{15}$, and $\frac{2}{15}$ is less than $\frac{1}{2}$.

$27 \neq 72$ True   27 is not equal to 72.

$19 < 19$ False   19 is not less than itself.

$16 \times 4 \geq 80 \div 3$ True   64 is greater than or equal to $26\frac{2}{3}$.

CHECK YOUR UNDERSTANDING

True or false?

1. $28 - 16 = 12$

2. $3 * 8 < 30$

3. $0 = \frac{4}{4}$

4. $27 + 3 \leq 5 * 6$

5. $60 = 9 + (6 * 2^2)$

6. $96 \neq 96$

Check your answers on page 379.

Parentheses

When there is more than one operation in a number sentence, parentheses can be used to tell which operation to do first. The parentheses in the following examples tell you which operation to do first.

EXAMPLE Evaluate. $(24 - 6) * 2 = ?$

The parentheses tell you to subtract $(24 - 6) * 2 = ?$
24 − 6 first, and then multiply by 2. $18 * 2 = 36$

So, $(24 - 6) * 2 = 36$.

EXAMPLE Evaluate. $24 - (6 * 2) = ?$

The parentheses tell you to multiply $24 - (6 * 2) = ?$
6 * 2 first, and then subtract. $24 - 12 = 12$

So, $24 - (6 * 2) = 12$.

Open Sentences

There are number sentences in which one or more of the numbers are missing. Symbols such as □, ?, a blank line, or a letter are written in place of a missing number. Such sentences are called **open sentences.** The number sentence $3 + x = 5$, for example, is open. Open sentences are neither true nor false.

A symbol used in place of a missing number is called a **variable.** For example, $5 + x = 12$ is an open sentence in which the variable x stands for some number. If the letter x is replaced by a number, then the number sentence is either true or false.

220-222

- If you replace x with 3 in $5 + x = 12$, you get the number sentence $5 + 3 = 12$, which is false.
- If you replace x with 7 in $5 + x = 12$, you get the number sentence $5 + 7 = 12$, which is true.

If the number used in place of the variable makes the number sentence true, this number is called a **solution** of the open sentence. For example, the number 7 is a solution of the open sentence $5 + x = 12$ because the number sentence $5 + 7 = 12$ is true. Finding a solution for an open number sentence is called **solving** the number sentence.

Many simple equations have just one solution, but inequalities may have many solutions. For example, 9, 3.5, $2\frac{1}{2}$, and -8 are all solutions of the inequality $x < 10$. In fact, $x < 10$ has infinitely many solutions—any number that is less than 10.

Number Models

In *Everyday Mathematics,* a number sentence that fits or describes some situation is called a **number model.** Suppose, for example, that you had $20, spent $8.50, and ended up with $11.50. The number model $20 - \$8.50 = \$11.50$ fits this situation. The number model $20 = \$8.50 + \$11.50$ also fits.

Number models can be useful in solving problems. For example, the problem "Juan is saving for a bicycle that costs $119. He has $55. How much more does he need?" can be modeled by "$119 = \$55 + x$" or by "$119 - \$55 = x$." The first of these number models suggests counting up to find how much more Juan needs; the second suggests subtracting to find the answer.

Other kinds of mathematical models are discussed in the section on problem solving.

238

CHECK YOUR UNDERSTANDING

Find the solution of each equation.

1. $8 + c = 20$ **2.** $35 = 5 * z$ **3.** $(2 * f) + 7 = 28$

Write a number model that fits each problem.

4. Hunter used a $20 bill to pay for a CD that cost $11.49. How much change did he get?

5. Eve earns $10 a week baby-sitting. How many weeks will it take her to earn $70?

Check your answers on page 379.

Inequalities

An **inequality** is a number sentence that contains one of these symbols: ≠, <, >, ≥, or ≤. An inequality that contains a variable is open. Any number that changes the inequality into a true number sentence when it is substituted for the variable is called a solution of the inequality.

Many open inequalities have an infinite number of solutions; therefore it is usually impossible to list all the solutions. Instead, the set of solutions, called the **solution set,** is described or the solutions are shown on a number-line graph.

223–225

EXAMPLE   Describe and graph the solution set of $x + 3 > 10$.

The inequality $x + 3 > 10$ is an open sentence.
100 is a solution of $x + 3 > 10$ because $100 + 3 > 10$ is true.
2 is not a solution of $x + 3 > 10$ because $2 + 3 > 10$ is not true.

Any number that is less than 7 is clearly not a solution of $x + 3 > 10$.
For example, 6 is not a solution of $x + 3 > 10$ because $6 + 3$ is not greater than 10.

Any number greater than 7 is a solution of $x + 3 > 10$.

The graph of the solution set of $x + 3 > 10$ looks like this:

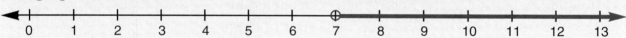

The shaded part of the number line tells you that any number greater than 7 is a solution (for example, 7.1, 8, 10.25). Notice the unshaded circle at 7. This tells you that 7 is not part of the solution set.

EXAMPLE   Graph the solution set of $y - 3 \leq 1$.

Any number less than or equal to 4 is a solution. For example, 4, 2.1, −6 are all solutions.

Notice the shaded circle at 4. This tells you that 4 is one of the solutions.

CHECK YOUR UNDERSTANDING

Describe the solution set of the inequalities in Problems 1 and 2.
Graph the solution sets in Problems 3 and 4.

1. $b - 5 < 3$ **2.** $7 + f > 7$ **3.** $x \leq 10$ **4.** $-2 + y \geq 0$

Check your answers on page 379.

Formulas

A **formula** is a way of expressing a relationship between quantities. (A **quantity** is a number with a unit, usually a measurement or a count.) The quantities in a formula are represented by variables.

EXAMPLE What is the formula for the area of a parallelogram?

The variable A stands for the area,
b for the length of the base,
and h for the height of the parallelogram.

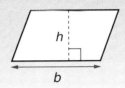

The formula for the area of a parallelogram is $A = b * h$.

Variables in Formulas

Often the symbol for a variable is the first letter of the quantity it represents.

EXAMPLES Write each formula using variables.

Area of parallelogram = base * height	$A = b * h$
circumference of circle = pi * diameter of circle	$c = \pi * d$

A letter variable can have different meanings depending on whether it is a capital or a lowercase (small) letter.

EXAMPLE The area of the shaded region in the figure at the right can be found by using the formula $A = S^2 - s^2$.

Note that S stands for the length of the side of the larger square and s for the length of the side of the smaller square.

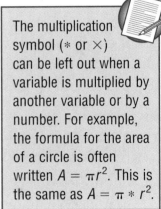

> **NOTE**
> The multiplication symbol ($*$ or $\times$) can be left out when a variable is multiplied by another variable or by a number. For example, the formula for the area of a circle is often written $A = \pi r^2$. This is the same as $A = \pi * r^2$.

Evaluating a Formula

To **evaluate** a formula means to find the value of one variable in the formula when the values of the other variables are given.

EXAMPLE Evaluate the formula for the area of the shaded region in the figure above when $S = 4$ cm and $s = 2$ cm.
$A = S^2 - s^2$
$A = (4 \text{ cm})^2 - (2 \text{ cm})^2$
$A = 16 \text{ cm}^2 - 4 \text{ cm}^2 = 12 \text{ cm}^2$
The area of the shaded region is 12 cm^2.

Units in Formulas

It is important that the **units** (hours, inches, meters, and so on) in a formula are consistent. An area formula will not give a correct result if one measurement is in millimeters and another is in centimeters.

> **EXAMPLE** Find the area of the rectangle.
>
> 7 mm
>
> 5 cm
>
> First, you need to change millimeters to centimeters or centimeters to millimeters. Then, use the formula $A = b * h$.
>
> Change centimeters to millimeters: 5 cm = 50 mm
> $A = 7$ mm $* 50$ mm $= 350$ mm^2
>
> Change millimeters to centimeters: 7 mm = 0.7 cm
> $A = 0.7$ cm $* 5$ cm $= 3.5$ cm^2
>
> The area of the rectangle is 350 mm^2 or 3.5 cm^2.

The formula $d = r * t$ gives the distance traveled in time, t, at a rate of travel (speed) r. If the value of r is in miles per hour, the value of t should be in hours. If the value of r is in meters per second, t should be in seconds.

> **EXAMPLE** Find the distance if $r = 50$ miles per hour and $t = 2$ hours. Use the formula $d = r * t$.
>
> If $r = 50$ miles per hour and $t = 2$ hours, then
> $d = 50$ miles per hour $* 2$ hours $= 100$ miles.

CHECK YOUR UNDERSTANDING

1. Find the area of rectangle $ABCD$.

   A ___ B
   16 inches
   D ___ 3 feet ___ C

2. If a car is traveling 80 feet per second, how far will it travel in one minute?

3. If $S = 6$ meters and $s = 2$ meters, what is the area of the shaded region in the diagram at the right?

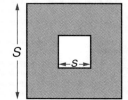

4. Express each of the following relationships with a formula.
   a. The volume of a cone (V) is equal to $\frac{1}{3}$ of the area of the base (B) times the height of the cone (h).
   b. The interest (i) earned on $1,000 deposited in a savings account is equal to $1,000 times the rate of interest (r) times the length of time the money is left in the account (t).

Check your answers on page 379.

Order of Operations

In many everyday situations, the order in which things are done is important. When you bake a cake, for example, you crack the eggs before adding them to the batter. In mathematics, too, many operations should be done in a certain order.

Rules for the Order of Operations

1. Do the operations inside **parentheses**. Follow rules 2–4.
2. Calculate all expressions with **exponents**.
3. **Multiply** and **divide** in order from left to right.
4. **Add** and **subtract** in order from left to right.

Some people remember the order of operations by memorizing this sentence:

Please **E**xcuse **M**y **D**ear **A**unt **S**ally.

Parentheses **E**xponents **M**ultiplication **D**ivision **A**ddition **S**ubtraction

---

EXAMPLE Evaluate. $5 * 4 - 6 * 3 + 2 = ?$

Multiply first.
Subtract next, then add.

$$5 * 4 - 6 * 3 + 2 = ?$$
$$20 - 18 + 2 = ?$$
$$2 + 2 = 4$$

$5 * 4 - 6 * 3 + 2 = 4$

EXAMPLE Evaluate. $5^2 + (3 * 4 - 2) / 5 = ?$

Clear parentheses first.
Calculate exponents next.
Divide, and then add.

$$5^2 + (3 * 4 - 2) / 5 = ?$$
$$5^2 + 10 / 5 = ?$$
$$25 + 10 / 5 = ?$$
$$25 + 2 = 27$$

$5^2 + (3 * 4 - 2) / 5 = 27$

CHECK YOUR UNDERSTANDING

Evaluate each expression.

1. $33 - 18 / 3 + 9$

2. $14 + (7 * 22) / 4$

3. $20 * 4 / 2 - 30$

4. $10 * (18 / 9 + 4) / 12 + 1$

Check your answers on page 379.

The Distributive Property

You have been using the **distributive property** for years, probably without knowing it.

The distributive property can be illustrated by finding the area of a rectangle.

> **EXAMPLE** Show how the distributive property works by finding the area of the rectangle in two different ways.
>
>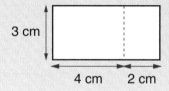
>
> **Method 1** Find the total width of the rectangle and multiply that by the height.
>
> $A = 3 \text{ cm} * (4 \text{ cm} + 2 \text{ cm})$
> $= 3 \text{ cm} * 6 \text{ cm}$
> $= 18 \text{ cm}^2$
>
> **Method 2** Find the areas of the two smaller rectangles, and then add them together.
>
> $A = (3 \text{ cm} * 4 \text{ cm}) + (3 \text{ cm} * 2 \text{ cm})$
> $= 12 \text{ cm}^2 + 6 \text{ cm}^2$
> $= 18 \text{ cm}^2$
>
> The area of the rectangle is 18 cm^2.
>
> Since both methods give the area of the rectangle, you know that $3 * (4 + 2) = (3 * 4) + (3 * 2)$. This is an example of the distributive property of multiplication over addition.

The distributive property of **multiplication over addition** can be stated in two ways:

$a * (x + y) = (a * x) + (a * y)$

$(x + y) * a = (x * a) + (y * a)$

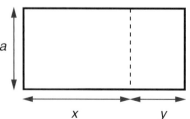

EXAMPLE   Show how the distributive property of multiplication over subtraction works by finding the area of the shaded part of the rectangle in two different ways.

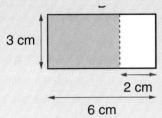

Method 1 Multiply the length of the shaded rectangle by its width.

$A = 3 \text{ cm} * (6 \text{ cm} - 2 \text{ cm})$
$\quad = 3 \text{ cm} * 4 \text{ cm}$
$\quad = 12 \text{ cm}^2$

Method 2 Subtract the area of the unshaded rectangle from the entire area of the whole rectangle.

$A = (3 \text{ cm} * 6 \text{ cm}) - (3 \text{ cm} * 2 \text{ cm})$
$\quad = 18 \text{ cm}^2 - 6 \text{ cm}^2$
$\quad = 12 \text{ cm}^2$

The area of the shaded part of the rectangle is 12 cm².

Since both methods give the area of the shaded part of the rectangle, you know that $3 \text{ cm} * (6 \text{ cm} - 2 \text{ cm}) =$ ($3 \text{ cm} * 6 \text{ cm}$) − ($3 \text{ cm} * 2 \text{ cm}$). This is an example of the distributive property of multiplication over subtraction.

The distributive property of multiplication over subtraction can also be stated in two ways:

$a * (x - y) = (a * x) - (a * y)$

$(x - y) * a = (x * a) - (y * a)$

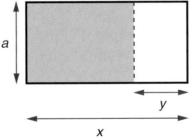

CHECK YOUR UNDERSTANDING

Use the distributive property to solve the problems.

1. $8 * (105 + 30)$ **2.** $(32 - 12) * 6$ **3.** $11 * (90 - 6)$

4. Use a calculator to verify that $1.23 * (456 + 789) = (1.23 * 456) + (1.23 * 789)$.

Check your answers on page 379.

Pan Balance Problems and Equations

If two different kinds of objects are placed in the pans of a balance so that they balance, then you can find the weight of one kind of object in terms of the other kind of object.

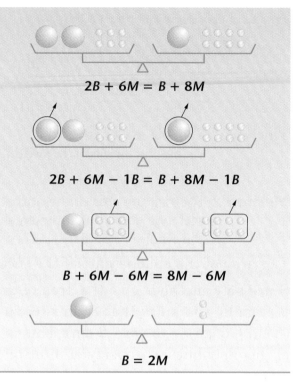

2B + 6M = B + 8M

2B + 6M − 1B = B + 8M − 1B

B + 6M − 6M = 8M − 6M

B = 2M

EXAMPLE   The pan balance at the right has 2 balls and 6 marbles in one pan and 1 ball and 8 marbles in the other pan. How many marbles weigh as much as 1 ball?

Step 1: If 1 ball is removed from each pan, the pan balance will remain balanced. One ball and 6 marbles will be left in the pan on the left and 8 marbles will be left in the pan on the right.

Step 2: If 6 marbles are removed from each pan, the pan balance will remain balanced. One ball will be left in the pan on the left and 2 marbles will be left in the pan on the right.

1 ball weighs as much as 2 marbles.

When solving a pan balance problem, the pans must balance after each step. If you do the same thing to the objects in both pans, then the pans will remain balanced. For example, you might remove the same number of the same kinds of objects from both pans, or you might remove half of each kind of object.

You can think of pan balance problems as models for equations. Suppose that B stands for the weight of 1 ball and M stands for the weight of 1 marble. The pan balance problem in the example above can then be expressed by the equation $2B + 6M = B + 8M$.

CHECK YOUR UNDERSTANDING

Write an equation for each pan balance problem.

1.

2.

6 □   2 ⫽   8 ⫽   3 □

Check your answers on page 379.

A Systematic Method for Solving Equations

Many equations with just one unknown can be solved using only addition, subtraction, multiplication, and division. If the unknown appears on both sides of the equal sign, you must change the equation to an equivalent equation with the unknown appearing on one side. You may also have to change the equation to one with all the constants on the other side of the equal sign.

> **NOTE**
>
> A **constant** is just a number, such as 3 or 7.5 or π. Constants don't change, or vary, the way variables do.

EXAMPLE   Solve $3y + 10 = 7y - 6$.

Step	Equation
1. Subtract $3y$ from each side. (S $3y$)	$3y + 10 = 7y - 6$ $\quad -3y \qquad\quad -3y$ $\overline{\qquad\quad 10 = 4y - 6}$
2. Add 6 to both sides. (A 6)	$10 = 4y - 6$ $+6 \qquad\quad +6$ $\overline{16 = 4y}$
3. Divide both sides by 4. (D 4)	$16 / 4 = 4y / 4$ $4 = y$

Check: Substitute the solution, 4, for y in the original equation:

$$3y + 10 = 7y - 6$$
$$3 * 4 + 10 = 7 * 4 - 6$$
$$12 + 10 = 28 - 6$$
$$22 = 22$$

Since $22 = 22$ is true, the solution, 4, is correct.
So, $y = 4$.

Like terms are terms that have exactly the same unknown or unknowns. The terms $4x$ and $2x$ are like terms because they both contain x. The terms 6 and 15 are like terms because they both contain no variables; 6 and 15 are both constants.

If an equation has parentheses, or if the unknown or constants appear on both sides of the equal sign, here is how you can **simplify** it.

- If an equation has parentheses, use the distributive property or other properties to write an equivalent equation without parentheses.

- If an equation has two or more like terms on one side of the equal sign, combine the like terms.

- If an equation has more than one constant on one side of the equal sign, combine the constants.

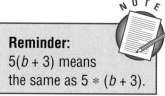

Reminder:
$5(b + 3)$ means the same as $5 * (b + 3)$.

EXAMPLE Solve $5(b + 3) - 3b + 5 = 4(b - 1)$.

Step	Equation
1. Use the distributive property to remove the parentheses.	$5b + 15 - 3b + 5 = 4b - 4$
2. Combine like terms.	$2b + 20 = 4b - 4$
3. Subtract 2b from both sides. (S 2b)	$\begin{array}{r} 2b + 20 = 4b - 4 \\ -2b \qquad\quad -2b \\ \hline 20 = 2b - 4 \end{array}$
4. Add 4 to both sides. (A 4)	$\begin{array}{r} 20 = 2b - 4 \\ +\,4 \qquad +\,4 \\ \hline 24 = 2b \end{array}$
5. Divide both sides by 2. (D 2)	$24 / 2 = 2b / 2$ $12 = b$

CHECK YOUR UNDERSTANDING

1. Check that 12 is the solution of the equation in the example above.

Solve.

2. $5x - 7 = 1 + 3x$　　　**3.** $5 * (s + 12) = 10 * (3 - s)$　　　**4.** $3(9 + b) = 6(b+3)$

Check your answers on page 380.

"What's My Rule?" Problems

Imagine a machine that works like this: When a number (the *input*, or "in" number) is dropped into the machine, the machine changes the number according to a rule, and a new number (the *output*, or "out" number) comes out the other end.

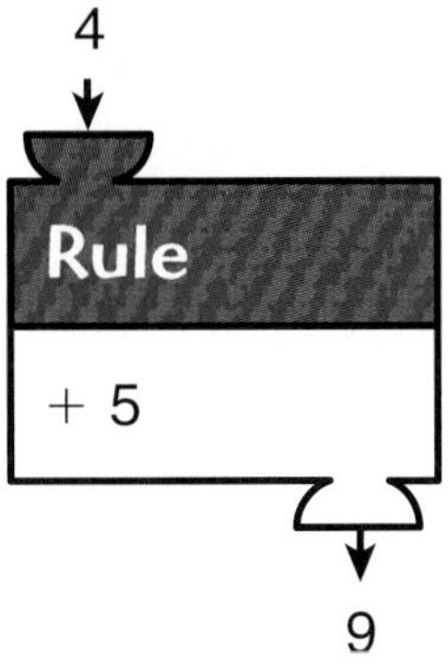

This machine adds 5 to any "in" number. Its rule is "+ 5."
- If 4 is dropped in, 9 comes out.
- If 7 is dropped in, 12 comes out.
- If 53 is dropped in, 58 comes out.
- If −6 is dropped in, −1 comes out.

"In" and "out" numbers can be displayed in table form as shown at the right.

To solve a "What's My Rule?" problem, you need to find the missing information. In the following examples, the solutions (the missing information) appear in color.

4 ↓

Rule

+ 5

↓ 9

in	out
x	x + 5
4	9
7	12
53	58
−6	−1

EXAMPLES

Find the "out" numbers.

Rule: subtract 7 from "in"

in	out
z	z − 7
9	2
27	20

9 − 7 = 2

27 − 7 = 20

Find the "in" numbers.

Rule: multiply "in" by 2

in	out
w	w * 2
4	8
24	48

4 * 2 = 8

24 * 2 = 48

Find the rule.

Rule: raise "in" to the second power

in	out
r	r^2
2	4
5	25

$2^2 = 4$

$5^2 = 25$

CHECK YOUR UNDERSTANDING

Solve the "What's My Rule?" problems.

1. *Rule:* divide "in" by 3

in	out
n	n / 3
9	
36	

2. *Rule:* subtract 4 from "in"

in	out
k	k − 4
	7
	24

3. *Rule:* ?

in	out
x	
4	120
10	300

Check your answers on page 380.

Rules, Tables, and Graphs

Many problems can be solved by showing relationships between
variables with rules, tables, or graphs.

EXAMPLE   Sara earns $6 per hour. Use a rule, a table,
and a graph to find how much Sara earns in $2\frac{1}{2}$ hours.

Rule: If h stands for the number of hours Sara works and
e stands for her earnings, then $e = 6 * h$.

$$e = 6 * h = 6 * 2\frac{1}{2}$$
$$= 15$$

Table:

Time (hours)	Earnings ($)
h	$6 * h$
0	0
1	6
2	12
3	18
...	...

Think of $2\frac{1}{2}$ hours as 2 hours + $\frac{1}{2}$ hour. For 2 hours, Sara
earns $12. For $\frac{1}{2}$ hour, Sara earns half of $6, or $3. In all,
Sara earns $12 + $3 = $15. Or note that $2\frac{1}{2}$ hours is halfway
between 2 hours and 3 hours, so her earnings will be
halfway between $12 and $18, which is $15.

Graph:

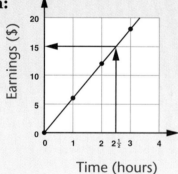

To use the graph, first find $2\frac{1}{2}$ hours on the horizontal axis.
Then go straight up to the line for Sara's earnings. Turn left
and go across to the vertical axis. You will end up at the
same answer as you did when you used the table, $15.

Sara earned $15 in $2\frac{1}{2}$ hours.

CHECK YOUR UNDERSTANDING

1. Christie types about 40 words per
minute. Use the graph to find how
many words she can type in
12.5 minutes.

2. Daniel earns $3.50 an hour. He
worked 9 hours. Use the rule to
find how much he earned. (e stands
for earnings; h stands for the number
of hours worked.) Rule: $e = \$3.50 * h$.

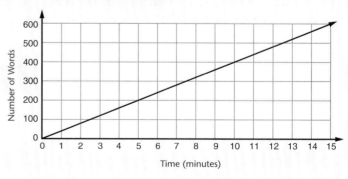

Check your answers on page 380.

Problem Solving

Mathematical Modeling

A **mathematical model** is a mathematical object that fits or describes something in the real world. A sphere, for example, is a model of a volleyball. The formula $d = (60 \text{ miles/hour}) * t$ is a model for the distance a car travels in t hours at 60 miles/hour. The graph at the right is a model for the cost of renting a bicycle at B & H Rentals, which charges $10 for the first hour and $2.50 for each additional half hour or fraction thereof.

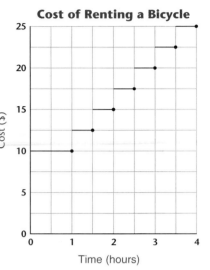

Cost of Renting a Bicycle

You have used mathematical models to solve problems for many years. Beginning in Kindergarten, you solved problems using physical models such as straws and connectors, base-10 blocks, counters, and pattern blocks. You have also learned to use pictures, diagrams, graphs, and number models to solve problems. As you continue studying mathematics, you will learn to make and use more powerful mathematical models.

Everyday Mathematics has many different kinds of problems. Some problems ask you to find something. Other problems ask you to make something. When you get older, some problems will ask you to prove things, which means giving convincing reasons why something is true or correct.

Problems to Find Something	Problems to Make Something
1. Five out of 8 students in Lane School play a musical instrument. A total of 140 students play an instrument. How many students attend Lane School? **2.** What are the missing numbers? 1, 3, 6, 10, __, 21, 28, __, __	**3.** Use pattern-block triangles and squares to make a semiregular tessellation. **4.** Use a compass and straightedge to construct a parallelogram that includes this angle: 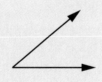

Problems you already know how to solve are often good practice for improving your skills. But the problems that will help you learn the most are the ones you can't solve right away. Learning to be a good problem solver means learning what to do when you don't know what to do.

A Guide for Solving Number Stories

Learning to solve problems is the main reason for studying mathematics. One way you learn to solve problems is by solving number stories. A **number story** is a story with a problem that can be solved with arithmetic.

A Guide for Number Stories
1. Understand the problem.
2. Plan what to do.
3. Carry out the plan.
4. Look back.

1. Understand the problem.
- Read the problem. Can you retell it in your own words?
- What do you know?
- What do you want to find out?
- Do you have all the information needed to solve the problem?

2. Plan what to do.
- Is the problem like one you solved before?
- Is there a pattern you can use?
- Can you draw a picture or a diagram?
- Can you write a number model or make a table?
- Can you use counters, base-10 blocks, or some other tool?
- Can you estimate the answer and check if you're right?

3. Carry out the plan.
- After you decide what to do, do it. Be careful.
- Make a written record of what you do.
- Answer the question.

4. Look back.
- Does your answer make sense?
- Does your answer agree with your estimate?
- Can you write a number model for the problem?
- Can you solve the problem in another way?

NOTE

Understanding the problem is the most important step. Good problem solvers spend most of their time making sure they really understand the problem.

NOTE

Sometimes it's easy to know what to do. Other times you need to be creative.

CHECK YOUR UNDERSTANDING

1. There are 20 students in Mr. Khalid's sixth grade class. Two out of 8 have no brothers or sisters. How many students have no siblings?

2. Your school ran a weekend car wash and raised $385. Your class received $\frac{2}{7}$ of this total. How much did your class receive?

Check your answers on page 380.

A Problem-Solving Diagram

Over the years, you have developed good skills for solving number stories. But problem solving is much more than just solving number stories. Problems from everyday life, science, and business are often more complicated than the number stories you solve in school. Sometimes the steps in the "Guide for Solving Number Stories" may not all be helpful.

Problem solving can be difficult because no single method works for every problem. However, there are some basic strategies that many good problem solvers use. These may not always help, but they can often be useful when you have a difficult problem.

- Try to understand the problem. Can you retell it in your own words? What do you know? What do you want to find out? Try to imagine what an answer might look like. People who go straight to doing arithmetic usually are not the best problem solvers.

- Study the data you have. Organize the data in a list or in some other way. Get rid of any data that you don't need. Look for more data if you need it.

- Play with the data. Try drawing a picture, a diagram, or a graph. Can you write a number model? Can you model the problem with counters or blocks?

- Do the math. Use arithmetic (perhaps with a calculator), geometry, or other mathematics to find an answer. Label the answer with units.

- Check your answer. Does it make sense? Compare your answer to a friend's answer. Review the problem to see whether the question you are trying to answer is the right question. Try the answer in the problem. If you need to, go back to the strategies above. Can you solve the problem another way?

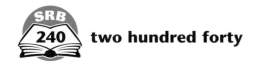

The diagram below shows another way to think about problem solving. This diagram is more complicated than a list, but it shows more accurately what people do when they solve problems in science and business. The arrows connecting the boxes are meant to show that you don't always do things in the same order.

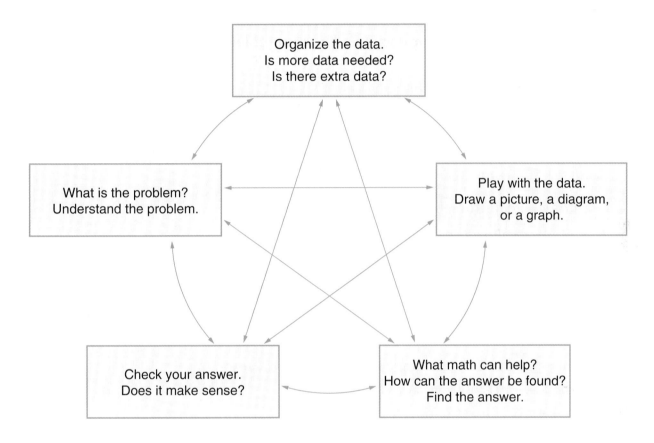

Organize the data.
Is more data needed?
Is there extra data?

What is the problem?
Understand the problem.

Play with the data.
Draw a picture, a diagram,
or a graph.

Check your answer.
Does it make sense?

What math can help?
How can the answer be found?
Find the answer.

CHECK YOUR UNDERSTANDING

Use the diagram to help you decide how you would answer the following question:

Walking at a normal pace, about how many steps would you take in 1 hour?

Check your answer on page 380.

Interpreting a Remainder in Division

Some number stories are solved by dividing whole numbers. You may need to decide what to do when there is a nonzero remainder.

There are three possible choices.
- Ignore the remainder. Just the quotient is the answer.
- Round the quotient up to the next whole number.
- Write the remainder as a fraction or decimal. The remainder is part of the answer.

EXAMPLES

- Suppose 3 people share 20 counters equally. How many counters will each person get?

  $20 / 3 \rightarrow 6\ R2$

Ignore the remainder. Just the quotient is the answer.

Each person will have 6 counters. Two counters are left over.

- Suppose 20 photos are placed in a photo album. How many pages are needed if 3 photos can fit on a page?

  $20 / 3 \rightarrow 6\ R2$

Round the quotient up to the next whole number. The album will have 6 pages filled and another page only partially filled.

So, 7 pages are needed.

- Suppose 3 friends share a 20-inch-long string of licorice. How long is each piece if the friends receive equal shares?

  $20 / 3 \rightarrow 6\ R2$

The answer, 6 R2, shows that if each person receives 6 inches of licorice, 2 inches remain to be divided. Imagine that this 2-inch remainder is divided into thirds. It can be divided into three $\frac{2}{3}$-inch pieces.

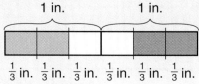

Write the remainder as a fraction. The remainder is part of the answer.

Each friend will get a $6\frac{2}{3}$-inch-long piece of licorice.

To rewrite a remainder as a fraction:

1. Make the remainder the *numerator* of the fraction.
2. Make the divisor the *denominator* of the fraction.

Problem	Answer	Remainder Rewritten as a Fraction	Answer Written as a Mixed Number	Answer Written as a Decimal
375 / 4	93 R3	$\frac{3}{4}$	$93\frac{3}{4}$	93.75

Making Estimates

In many situations, it is not necessary to find an exact answer; a "ballpark" answer, called an **estimate,** will do. For example, if you have $10 and you want to buy several cans of tennis balls that cost $2.89 per can, you don't need to find the exact cost to decide how many cans you can buy. Since $2.89 is almost $3, 3 cans will cost a little under $9, and 4 cans will cost under $12 but more than $10. So, you can buy at most 3 cans with $10.

Sometimes it is impossible to find an exact answer. It is impossible to get an exact population count for a city, for example, because the count changes constantly. Thus, when solving a problem, you must decide whether it is possible to find an exact answer and, even if it is possible, whether an exact answer is needed or if an estimate will do.

If you choose to estimate an answer, you must decide how accurate your estimate should be. Keep in mind that an estimate is *not* a guess. A guess is just an opinion that may not be based on much real information.

One kind of very rough estimate is called a **magnitude estimate.** When making a magnitude estimate, ask yourself "Is the answer in the tens? Hundreds? Thousands?" and so on. These are good questions to ask to check answers when using a calculator or to judge whether information you read or hear makes sense.

A more accurate estimate can be made by **rounding** the numbers in the problem.

EXAMPLE   Mr. Huber has started a new job at a salary of $1,957 a month. He expects to get a raise after 6 months. About how much can he expect to earn in the first 6 months?

To estimate the answer, round $1,957 to $2,000 and multiply the rounded number by 6.

Since 6 * $2,000 = $12,000, he can expect to earn a little under $12,000 in the first 6 months on the job.

When a range of possible values is more useful than just one estimated value, make an **interval estimate.** An interval estimate consists of two numbers. One number is less than the exact value, and the other number is greater than the exact value. For example: Most cars weigh between 2,000 and 4,000 pounds.

Rounding Numbers

In many situations, exact numbers are not needed. For example, Jupiter revolves around the sun every 4,332.6 Earth days, and Neptune revolves around the sun every 10,759.2 Earth days. To compare the length of a year on these two planets, round the numbers to the nearest thousand. A year on Jupiter is about 4,000 Earth days, and a year on Neptune is about 11,000 Earth days. Using the rounded numbers, you can see that a year on Neptune is almost 3 times as long as a year on Jupiter.

It is also useful to round numbers when estimating results of operations such as addition and multiplication.

EXAMPLES

1. Round 3,548 to the nearest hundred.
2. Round 86,721 to the nearest thousand.
3. Round 2,595 to the nearest ten.
4. Round 4.563 to the nearest tenth.

	Step 1: Find the digit in the place to which you are rounding.	Step 2: Rewrite the number, replacing all digits to the right of this digit with zeros. This is the lower number.	Step 3: Add 1 to the digit in the place to which you are rounding. If the sum is 10, write 0 and add 1 to the digit to its left. This is the higher number.	Step 4: Is the number you are rounding closer to the lower number or to the higher number?	Step 5: Round to the closer of the two numbers. If it is halfway between the higher and the lower number, round to the higher number.
1.	3,5<u>4</u>8	3,500	3,600	lower number	3,500
2.	86,<u>7</u>21	86,000	87,000	higher number	87,000
3.	2,5<u>9</u>5	2,590	2,600	halfway	2,600
4.	4.<u>5</u>63	4.500	4.600	higher number	4.600 = 4.6

CHECK YOUR UNDERSTANDING

Round 35,481.746 to the nearest:

1. hundred
2. ten thousand
3. thousand
4. hundredth

Check your answers on page 380.

Estimates and Significant Digits

All measurements are estimates. The accuracy of a measurement is limited by the accuracy of whatever measuring tool (ruler, scale, and so on) is used to obtain the measurement and by the skill of the humans who interpret the tool.

The only exact measurement relationships are those that are defined. For example, 1 inch is defined by international agreement to be exactly 2.54 centimeters.

The measurements in the table at the right are not only estimates, they are averages of other measurements. They have been rounded to two **significant digits.**

Planet	Average Diameter (miles)
Mercury	3,000
Venus	7,500
Earth	7,900
Mars	4,200
Jupiter	89,000
Saturn	75,000
Uranus	31,000
Neptune	31,000
Pluto	1,400

EXAMPLE In the measurement 7,900 miles, 7 and 9 are significant digits.

A significant digit is a digit from an actual measurement. We are sure that it accurately represents the quantity being measured. Nonzero digits are *always* significant. Zero is a significant digit if it is *between two significant digits* or *at the end of a decimal.* Usually, everyday measurements have, at most, two or three significant digits. Zeros at the end of whole numbers are sometimes significant and sometimes not.

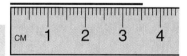

EXAMPLE The line segment in the diagram at the right is between 35 and 36 millimeters long. You would report its length as either 35 mm or 36 mm. That would be two significant digits. You would not report it as 35.2 mm since this particular measuring tool (the ruler) does not give a measurement that is this accurate.

> **NOTE**
> As you work with measurements, try not to report results that appear to be more accurate or precise than the original data. If the numbers you start with have only one or two significant digits, for example, your final answer should have only one or two significant digits.

EXAMPLE Earth travels about 600,000,000 miles per year in its orbit. What is its average speed of revolution in miles per hour?

Hours in 1 year: 365.25 days * 24 hours/day = 8,766 hours

600,000,000 miles ÷ 8,766 hours ≈ 68,446.2696 miles/hour

But 600,000,000 has only one significant digit, so round the answer to one significant digit. Round 68,446.2696 to the nearest ten thousand.

So, the average speed should be reported as about 70,000 miles per hour.

Venn Diagrams

A **Venn diagram** is a picture that uses circles to show relationships between sets.

EXAMPLE At Lincoln Middle School, every student is required to take music. Seventy-five students take either a band or an orchestra class. The remaining 300 students take a general music class.

The Venn diagram for this situation consists of two circles that do not overlap. Students who take band or orchestra classes do not take general music classes, and students who take general music classes do not take band or orchestra classes. The Venn diagram shows that there are 375 students in Lincoln Middle School.

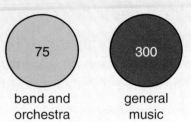

EXAMPLE Ms. Barrie teaches both math and science. There are 26 students in her math class and 24 students in her science class. Five of the students are in both her math and science classes.

The Venn diagram for this situation consists of two overlapping circles. The overlapping part of the diagram represents the students who are in both her math and science classes. The Venn diagram shows that there are 45 students in Ms. Barrie's classes: 21 students take math only, 19 students take science only, and 5 students take both math and science.

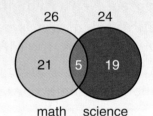

EXAMPLE Students recorded their TV viewing last week.

sports only: 9
comedy only: 6
drama only: 2

sports, comedy, and drama: 1
sports and comedy: 4 + 1 = 5
sports and drama: 3 + 1 = 4
comedy and drama: 2 + 1 = 3

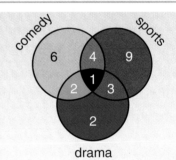

CHECK YOUR UNDERSTANDING

The Venn diagram at the right shows the results of a survey in which students were asked whether they write with their left hand or right hand.

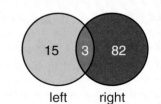

1. How many students were surveyed?
2. How many students can write with their left hand? With their right hand?
3. How many students can write with either hand?

Check your answers on page 380.

Calculators

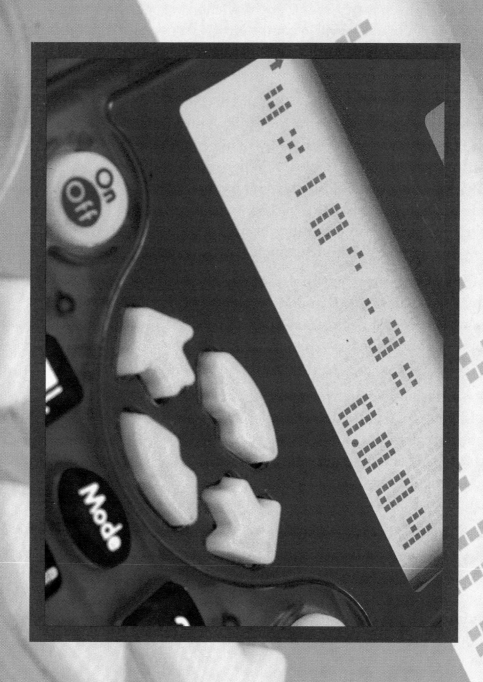

About Calculators

Throughout your study of mathematics you have used tools such as counters, rulers, tape measures, pattern blocks, compasses, protractors, and the Geometry Template. Since kindergarten, you have also used calculators. In earlier grades, you used calculators to help you learn to count. Now you use them for computations with whole numbers, fractions, decimals, and percents.

Although a calculator can help you compute quickly and accurately, you must know when and how to use it. You must decide whether it is best to solve a problem by using mental arithmetic, paper and pencil, or a calculator. When you choose to use a calculator, estimation should always be part of your work. You can use a magnitude estimate of the answer to check whether you have keyed in a wrong number or operation. Always ask yourself if the number in the display makes sense.

There are many different kinds of calculators. Simple four-function calculators do little more than add, subtract, multiply, and divide whole numbers and decimals. Other calculators also perform operations with fractions.

Rather than try to describe how various calculators work, we have chosen one calculator to which we refer throughout this book. If you have a different calculator, don't worry. There are many other calculators that work well with *Everyday Mathematics*. If the instructions in this book don't work for your calculator, you can refer to the directions that came with it, or you can ask your teacher for help.

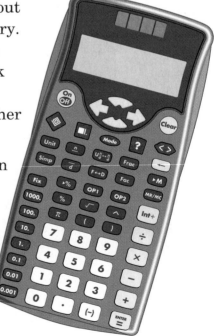

A reminder: Just as carpenters, dentists, and people in many other occupations must take care of their tools if they expect them to work properly, you must take care of your calculator. Dropping it, leaving it in the sun, or other kinds of carelessness may break it or make it less reliable.

Basic Operations

Pressing a key on a calculator is called "keying in" or "entering." In this book, calculator keys, except numbers, are shown in rectangular boxes: ⊕, (Enter), ⊗, and so on. A set of instructions for performing a calculation is called a "key sequence." The key sequences in this book are for the calculator shown on the previous page, but many of them also work for other calculators.

(On/Off) turns the calculator on and off. When you turn the calculator on, you will see a blinking triangle that looks like this: ◁. This is the cursor.

Simple Arithmetic: (On/Off), ⊕, ⊖, ⊗, ÷, (Enter)

You probably already know how to use a calculator for basic arithmetic operations. Usually, you can just enter the numbers and operations and press (Enter) to see the answer. Solve each problem below on your calculator.

253

Key	Problem	Key Sequence	Display
⊕	$4.7 + 6.8$	4 ⊙ 7 ⊕ 6 ⊙ 8 (Enter)	$4.7 + 6.8 = 11.5$
	$\frac{3}{8} + \frac{1}{4}$	3 (n) 8 (d) ⊕ 1 (n) 4 (d) (Enter)	$\frac{3}{8} + \frac{1}{4} = \frac{5}{8}$
⊖	$12.3 - 5.9$	12 ⊙ 3 ⊖ 5 ⊙ 9 (Enter)	$12.3 - 5.9 = 6.4$
	$\frac{7}{8} - \frac{1}{3}$	7 (n) 8 (d) ⊖ 1 (n) 3 (d) (Enter)	$\frac{7}{8} - \frac{1}{3} = \frac{13}{24}$
⊗	$3.5 * 7.4$	3 ⊙ 5 ⊗ 7 ⊙ 4 (Enter)	$3.5 \times 7.4 = 25.9$
	$\frac{4}{5} * \frac{3}{8}$	4 (n) 5 (d) ⊗ 3 (n) 8 (d) (Enter)	$\frac{N}{D} \rightarrow \frac{n}{d}$ $\frac{4}{5} \times \frac{3}{8} = \frac{12}{40}$
÷	$24.9 / 1.6$	24 ⊙ 9 ÷ 1 ⊙ 6 (Enter)	$24.9 \div 1.6 = 15.5625$
	$\frac{5}{6} / \frac{1}{2}$	5 (n) 6 (d) ÷ 1 (n) 2 (d) (Enter)	$\frac{N}{D} \rightarrow \frac{n}{d}$ $\frac{5}{6} \div \frac{1}{2} = 1\frac{4}{6}$

Correcting and Clearing: ⊖ , (Clear) , ⇐ , ⇒

⊖ erases the character to the left of the cursor.

EXAMPLE	Enter 123.444. Change it to 123.456.	

Key Sequence	Display
1 2 3 ⊙ 4 4 4	123.444
⊖ ⊖	123.4
5 6	123.456

You can use ⇐ and ⇒ to move the cursor to the left and right. This is useful for correcting mistakes in the middle of expressions you have entered without erasing numbers that are correct.

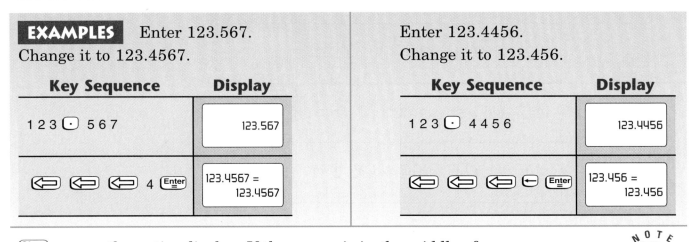

EXAMPLES	Enter 123.567. Change it to 123.4567.

Key Sequence	Display
1 2 3 ⊙ 5 6 7	123.567
⇐ ⇐ ⇐ 4 (Enter)	123.4567 = 123.4567

Enter 123.4456. Change it to 123.456.

Key Sequence	Display
1 2 3 ⊙ 4 4 5 6	123.4456
⇐ ⇐ ⇐ ⊖ (Enter)	123.456 = 123.456

(Clear) erases the entire display. If the cursor is in the middle of a display, you will need to press (Clear) twice to clear the entire display. Holding (On/Off) and (Clear) down together for a few moments will clear the calculator completely. Whenever you use the calculator, you should first clear it completely.

> **NOTE**
>
> The calculator remembers its settings and problems it has solved even when it is turned off. If you don't start by clearing it completely, it may not work properly.

Order of Operations and Parentheses: ⬤, ⬤

The calculator shown on page 248 follows the rules for the order of operations.

If you have a different calculator, check whether it follows the rules for the order of operations. To do so, key in 5 ⊞ 6 ⊠ 2 (Enter). If your calculator follows the order of operations, it will multiply first, then add, and the display will show 17. A calculator that does not follow the order of operations will probably do the operations in the order they are entered, adding first, then multiplying, and will display 22.

If you want the calculator to do operations in an order different from the usual order, use ⬤ and ⬤

EXAMPLE Evaluate. 7 − (2 + 1)

Key Sequence	Display
7 ⊖ ⬤ 2 ⊞ 1 ⬤ (Enter)	7 − (2 + 1) = 4

7 − (2 + 1) = 4

Sometimes expressions are given without all of the multiplication signs. Remember to press the multiplication key even when it is not written.

EXAMPLE Evaluate. 9 − 2(1 + 2)

Key Sequence	Display
9 ⊖ 2 ⊠ ⬤ 1 ⊞ 2 ⬤ (Enter)	9 − 2 × (1+2) = 3

9 − 2(1 + 2) = 3

CHECK YOUR UNDERSTANDING

Use your calculator to evaluate each expression.

1. 98 − (7 + 9)   **2.** 64 − 6(2 + 8)   **3.** 9(7 + 4) − 43   **4.** 8(34 − 21) + 24

Check your answers on page 380.

Negative Numbers: (–)

Use (–) to enter a negative number.

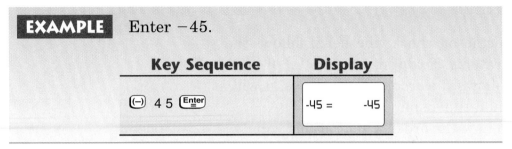

EXAMPLE Enter −45.

Key Sequence	Display
(–) 4 5 (Enter)	-45 = -45

Notice that (–) is not an operation. The key for subtraction is ⊖ . If you try to use (–) to do subtraction, you will get an error.

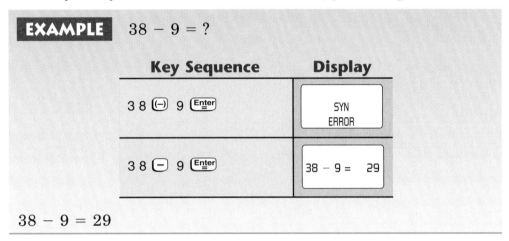

EXAMPLE 38 − 9 = ?

Key Sequence	Display
3 8 (–) 9 (Enter)	SYN ERROR
3 8 ⊖ 9 (Enter)	38 − 9 = 29

38 − 9 = 29

Division with Remainders: (Int÷)

The result of a division with whole numbers is often not a whole number. Most calculators display such a result as a decimal. Many calculators also have another division key, (Int÷), that displays the results of a division as a whole number quotient with a whole number remainder.

> **NOTE**
> *Int* stands for *integer.* This kind of division is known as "integer division."

EXAMPLE 39 ÷ 5 = ? Use the (Int÷) key.

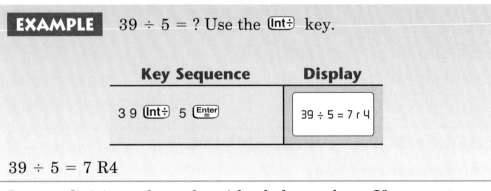

Key Sequence	Display
3 9 (Int÷) 5 (Enter)	39 ÷ 5 = 7 r 4

39 ÷ 5 = 7 R4

Integer division only works with whole numbers. If you try to use a negative number or a fraction, you will get an error.

Fractions and Percent

Certain calculators can handle fractions. Once fractions have been entered on such calculators, they can be added, subtracted, multiplied, and divided using the $\boxed{+}$, $\boxed{-}$, $\boxed{\times}$, and $\boxed{\div}$ keys.

Entering Fractions and Mixed Numbers: $\boxed{n}$, $\boxed{d}$, $\boxed{Unit}$, $\boxed{U\frac{n}{d} \leftrightarrow \frac{n}{d}}$

Use $\boxed{n}$, $\boxed{d}$, and $\boxed{Unit}$ to enter fractions and mixed numbers.

> **NOTE**
>
> You do not need to press $\boxed{d}$ after you enter the denominator.

EXAMPLE $\frac{3}{4} + \frac{7}{8} = ?$

Key Sequence	Display
3 $\boxed{n}$ 4 $\boxed{d}$ $\boxed{+}$ 7 $\boxed{n}$ 8 $\boxed{d}$ $\boxed{Enter}$	$\frac{3}{4} + \frac{7}{8} = 1\frac{5}{8}$

$\frac{3}{4} + \frac{7}{8} = 1\frac{5}{8}$

EXAMPLE $1\frac{1}{2} \div 2\frac{1}{2} = ?$

Key Sequence	Display
1 $\boxed{Unit}$ 1 $\boxed{n}$ 2 $\boxed{d}$ $\boxed{\div}$ 2 $\boxed{Unit}$ 1 $\boxed{n}$ 2 $\boxed{d}$	$\frac{N}{D} \rightarrow \frac{n}{d}$ $\quad 1\frac{1}{2} \div 2\frac{1}{2} = \frac{6}{10}$

$1\frac{1}{2} \div 2\frac{1}{2} = \frac{6}{10}$

Use $\boxed{U\frac{n}{d} \leftrightarrow \frac{n}{d}}$ to change between mixed numbers and improper fractions.

EXAMPLE

Key Sequence	Display
4 5 $\boxed{n}$ 7 $\boxed{d}$ $\boxed{Enter}$	$\frac{45}{7} = 6\frac{3}{7}$
$\boxed{U\frac{n}{d} \leftrightarrow \frac{n}{d}}$	$\frac{45}{7}$
$\boxed{U\frac{n}{d} \leftrightarrow \frac{n}{d}}$	$6\frac{3}{7}$

Simplifying Fractions: Simp, Fac

The calculator shown here does not simplify fractions automatically. The message $\frac{N}{D} \rightarrow \frac{n}{d}$ in the display means that the fraction shown is not yet in simplest form.

Use Simp to simplify fractions. When you press Simp Enter, the calculator divides the numerator and the denominator by a common factor. To see which number the calculator used, press Fac. You may have to press Simp Enter several times to put a fraction in simplest form.

The Simp key simplifies fractions.

The Fac key tells which common factor the calculator used when simplifying a fraction.

EXAMPLE Change $\frac{18}{24}$ to simplest form.

Key Sequence	Display
18 ⃞n 24 ⃞d Simp Enter	$\frac{18}{24} \vdash \vdots \quad \overset{\frac{N}{D} \rightarrow \frac{n}{d}}{\frac{9}{12}}$
Simp Enter	$\frac{9}{12} \vdash \vdots \quad \frac{3}{4}$
Fac	3

$$\frac{18}{24} = \frac{3}{4}$$

If you want to tell the calculator to divide the numerator and the denominator by a certain number, enter that number after you press Simp. If you use the greatest common factor of the numerator and the denominator, you can simplify the fraction in one step.

EXAMPLE Change $\frac{18}{24}$ to simplest form in one step by dividing the numerator and the denominator by their greatest common factor, 6.

Key Sequence	Display
18 ⃞n 24 ⃞d Simp 6 Enter	$\frac{18}{24} \vdash \vdots 6 \quad \frac{3}{4}$
Fac	6

Percent: %, ▸%

On the calculator shown here, % divides the number before it by 100. % can be used to change percents into decimals.

EXAMPLES

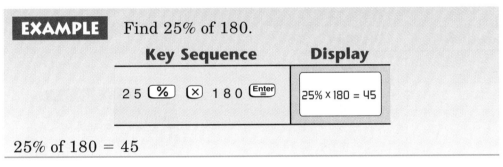

Key Sequence	Display
85 % Enter	85% = 0.85
250 % Enter	250% = 2.5
1 % Enter	1% = 0.01

The ▸% key multiplies a number by 100.

% can also be used to solve problems with percents.

EXAMPLE Find 25% of 180.

Key Sequence	Display
2 5 % × 1 8 0 Enter	25% × 180 = 45

25% of 180 = 45

▸% does the opposite of % . That is, ▸% multiplies the number before it by 100. ▸% can be used to change a number into an equivalent percent.

The % key divides a number by 100.

EXAMPLES

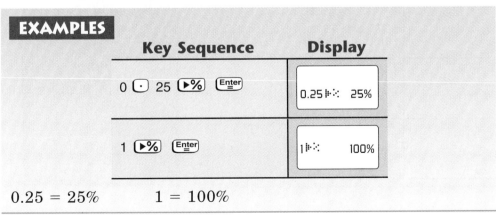

Key Sequence	Display
0 · 25 ▸% Enter	0.25 ▸∴ 25%
1 ▸% Enter	1 ▸∴ 100%

0.25 = 25%   1 = 100%

Fraction/Decimal/Percent Conversions: (F↔D)

Calculators can be used to convert between fractions, decimals, and percents. Conversions of fractions to decimals and percents can be done on any calculator. For example, to rename $\frac{3}{5}$ as a decimal, simply enter 3 ÷ 5 (Enter). The display will show 0.6. To rename a decimal as a percent, just multiply by 100.

Conversions of decimals and percents to fractions can only be done directly on calculators that have special keys to handle fractions. Such calculators usually have special keys for changing a fraction to its decimal equivalent or a decimal to an equivalent fraction.

Use (F↔D) to change between fractions and decimals. When decimals are changed to fractions, they may need to be simplified.

EXAMPLE Convert $\frac{3}{8}$ to a decimal and back to a fraction in simplest form.

Key Sequence	Display
3 (n) 8 (d) (Enter)	$\frac{3}{8} = \frac{3}{8}$
(F↔D)	0.375
(F↔D)	$\frac{N}{D} \rightarrow \frac{n}{d}$ $\frac{375}{1000}$
(Simp) (Enter)	$\frac{N}{D} \rightarrow \frac{n}{d}$ $\frac{375}{1000} \Vdash \frac{75}{200}$
(Simp) (Enter)	$\frac{N}{D} \rightarrow \frac{n}{d}$ $\frac{75}{200} \Vdash \frac{15}{40}$
(Simp) (Enter)	$\frac{15}{40} \Vdash \frac{3}{8}$

The table shows examples of various conversions. Although only one key sequence is shown for each conversion, there are other ways to do most of these conversions.

Conversion	Starting Number	Key Sequence	Display
Fraction to decimal	$\frac{3}{5}$	3 [n] 5 [d] [Enter] [F↔D]	0.6
Decimal to fraction	0.125	0 [.] 1 2 5 [Enter] [F↔D]	N/D → n/d $\frac{125}{1000}$
Decimal to percent	0.75	0 [.] 7 5 [▶%] [Enter]	0.75 ⊩∴ 75%
Percent to decimal	125%	1 2 5 [%] [Enter]	125% = 1.25
Fraction to percent	$\frac{5}{8}$	5 [n] 8 [d] [▶%] [Enter]	$\frac{5}{8}$ ⊩∴ 62.5%
Percent to fraction	35%	3 5 [%] [Enter] [F↔D]	N/D → n/d $\frac{35}{100}$

CHECK YOUR UNDERSTANDING

Use your calculator to convert between fractions, decimals, and percents.

1. $\frac{5}{16}$ to a decimal
2. 0.385 to a fraction
3. 0.009 to a percent
4. 458% to a decimal
5. $\frac{7}{16}$ to a percent
6. 58% to a fraction

Check your answers on page 380.

Advanced Operations

Your calculator can do more than simple arithmetic with whole numbers, fractions, and decimals. The following pages explain some of the other things your calculator can do.

Scrolling: ⬆ , ⬇

⬆ and ⬇ allow you to see previous entries and results. Moving up and down to previous displays is called **scrolling.** Small arrows in the display tell you in which directions you can scroll.

You can use ⬆ and ⬇ to see problems you entered before. Then you can use ⬅, ➡, and ⬅ to change those problems if you wish.

⬆ and ⬇ are also used with menus.

Menus: (Mode)

The calculator shown here has several menus for changing how it works. In each menu, the current choice is underlined. Use ⬅ and ➡ to change what is underlined. Then press (Enter) to make your new choice active. If you don't press (Enter), the old menu choice will still be active.

Most of the menus are reached by pressing (Mode). The fraction menus are reached by pressing (Frac).

Use the ⬆ and ⬇ keys to scroll through menus, entries, and results.

Key Sequence	Display	Purpose
(Mode)	N/d ÷	Controls whether quotients are shown as decimals or as mixed numbers.
(Mode) ⬇	+1 ? OP	Controls whether the operation is shown or hidden when (Op1) and (Op2) are used.
(Mode) ⬇ ⬇	OP1 OP2 CLEAR	Used for clearing a constant operation.
(Mode) ⬇ ⬇ ⬇	N Y RESET	Used for resetting the calculator.

Use the (Mode) key to browse menus.

EXAMPLE   Divide. Show the quotient as a mixed number.

$56 / 3 = ?$

Key Sequence	Display
(Mode) ⇒ (Enter)	$\frac{n}{d}$ ÷ · $\underline{n/d}$ ÷
(Mode)	$\frac{n}{d}$ ÷
5 6 ÷ 3 (Enter)	$\frac{n}{d}$ ÷ $56 ÷ 3 = 18\frac{2}{3}$

$56 / 3 = 18\frac{2}{3}$

EXAMPLE   Reset the calculator.

Key Sequence	Display
(Mode) ⇩ ⇩ ⇩ ⇒	n Y RESET
(Enter)	MEM CLEARED

Fraction Menus: (Frac)

There are two menus for changing how the calculator handles fractions. Use (Frac) to reach these menus. As with other menus, use (⇐) and (⇒) to change what is underlined. Then press (Enter) to make your new choice active. If you don't press (Enter), the old choice will still be active.

Key Sequence	Menu	Purpose
(Frac)	U n/d n/d	Controls whether results are shown as mixed numbers or improper fractions.
(Frac) ⇩	MAN AUTO	Controls whether simplifying fractions is done manually or automatically.

EXAMPLE   Solve $\frac{4}{5} * \frac{1}{2}$ with the calculator first in MAN mode, then in AUTO mode.

Key Sequence	Display
4 `n` 5 `d` `×` 1 `n` 2 `d` `Enter`	$\frac{4}{5} \times \frac{1}{2} = \overset{\frac{N}{D} \to \frac{n}{d}}{\frac{4}{10}}$
`Simp` `Enter`	$\frac{4}{10} \models \qquad \frac{2}{5}$
`Frac` `↓` `⇨` `Enter`	Auto MAN <u>AUTO</u>
`Frac` `Clear`	Auto
4 `n` 5 `d` `×` 1 `n` 2 `d` `Enter`	$\frac{4}{5} \times \frac{1}{2} = \overset{Auto}{\frac{2}{5}}$

$\frac{4}{5} * \frac{1}{2} = \frac{2}{5}$

EXAMPLE   Change to improper fraction mode and solve $\frac{5}{2} + \frac{8}{3}$. Then change the answer to a mixed number.

Key Sequence	Display
`Frac` `⇨` `Enter`	U n/d <u>n/d</u>
5 `n` 2 `d` `+` 8 `n` 3 `d` `Enter`	$\frac{5}{2} + \frac{8}{3} = \frac{31}{6}$
`U n/d ↔ n/d`	$5\frac{1}{6}$

$\frac{5}{2} + \frac{8}{3} = 5\frac{1}{6}$

Rounding

To set the calculator to round, press (Fix) and one of the numbers on the red keys below the (Fix) key.

The calculator can be set to round to any place from thousands (1000.) to thousandths (0.001). To turn off rounding, press (Fix) (·).

EXAMPLE Set the calculator to round to hundreds. Then round 1,376; 79; and 23 to the nearest hundred.

Key Sequence	Display
(Fix) (100.)	Fix
1376 (Enter)	Fix 1376 = 1400.
79 (Enter)	Fix 79 = 100.
23 (Enter)	Fix 23 = 000.

EXAMPLE Solve 73 * 19 and 1,568 + 399. Find the exact answer. Then find the answer rounded to the nearest hundred.

Key Sequence	Display
73 (×) 1 9 (Enter)	73 x 19 = 1387
1 5 6 8 (+) 3 9 9 (Enter)	1568 + 399 = 1967

Key Sequence	Display
(Fix) (100.)	Fix
7 3 (×) 19 (Enter)	Fix 73 x 19 = 1400.
1 5 6 8 (+) 3 9 9 (Enter)	Fix 1568 + 399 = 2000.

CHECK YOUR UNDERSTANDING

Use your calculator to round to the indicated place.

1. 78 to tens   **2.** 234 to tens   **3.** 1,258 to hundreds   **4.** 50,459 to thousands

Check your answers on page 380.

Powers and Square Roots: $\boxed{\wedge}$, $\boxed{\sqrt{}}$

$\boxed{\wedge}$ is used for raising numbers to powers on many calculators. Sometimes $[y^x]$ or some other key is used. Negative exponents are allowed, but be careful to use $\boxed{(-)}$ when you enter a negative number. If you use $\boxed{-}$, you may get an error.

> **NOTE**
>
> The symbol ^ is called a "caret." It is often used in computer programming for raising numbers to powers.
>
> 5^2 means
> $$5^2 = 5 * 5 = 25$$

EXAMPLES Find the value of 3^4 and 5^{-2}.

Problem	Key Sequence	Display
3^4	3 $\boxed{\wedge}$ 4 $\boxed{\text{Enter}}$	3 ^ 4 = 81
5^{-2}	5 $\boxed{\wedge}$ $\boxed{(-)}$ 2 $\boxed{\text{Enter}}$	5 ^ -2 = 0.04

To find the reciprocal of a number, raise the number to the -1 power.

EXAMPLES Find the reciprocals of 25 and $\frac{2}{3}$.

Key Sequence	Display
25 $\boxed{\wedge}$ $\boxed{(-)}$ 1 $\boxed{\text{Enter}}$	25 ^ -1 = 0.04
2 $\boxed{\text{n}}$ 3 $\boxed{\text{d}}$ $\boxed{\wedge}$ $\boxed{(-)}$ 1 $\boxed{\text{Enter}}$	$\frac{2}{3}$ ^ -1 = 1.5

Note: To see the reciprocal of $\frac{2}{3}$ as a fraction, use $\boxed{\text{F↔D}}$, $\boxed{\text{Simp}}$, $\boxed{\text{Enter}}$, and $\boxed{\text{U}\frac{n}{d}\text{↔}\frac{n}{d}}$. The reciprocal of $\frac{2}{3}$ written as a fraction is $\frac{3}{2}$.

Many calculators have a special key for finding square roots. Notice that before you press $\boxed{\text{Enter}}$, you have to press $\boxed{)}$.

EXAMPLES Find the square roots of 25 and 10,000.

> **NOTE**
>
> On some calculators the square root key $\boxed{\sqrt{}}$ is entered after the number, but sometimes it is entered before the number. On the calculator shown on page 248, the square root key is entered before the number.

Key Sequence	Display
$\boxed{\sqrt{}}$ 25 $\boxed{)}$ $\boxed{\text{Enter}}$	$\sqrt{(25)}$ = 5
$\boxed{\sqrt{}}$ 10000 $\boxed{)}$ $\boxed{\text{Enter}}$	$\sqrt{(10000)}$ = 100

Scientific Notation

On many calculators, numbers with more digits than will fit in the display are automatically shown in scientific notation. Calculators differ in the way they show scientific notation.

Scientific notation is a way of writing numbers in which a number is written as the product of a number and a power of 10. The number must be 1 or greater but less than 10. In scientific notation, 900,000 is written as $9 * 10^5$.

Some calculators can display raised exponents, but most cannot. Some calculators that have scientific notation do not bother to display the base, which is always 10, and use a space or letter to show the exponent. Others, like the one shown on this page, do show the base, but use a caret ^ to show the exponent.

EXAMPLES

Key Sequence	Display
7 ⊗ 1 0 ⌃ 4 Enter	7 x 10 ^ 4 = 70000
4 ⊙ 35 ⊗ 1 0 ⌃ 5 Enter	4.35 x 10 ^ 5 = 435000
4 ⊗ 1 0 ⌃ (-) 3 Enter	4 x 10 ^ -3 = 0.004

CHECK YOUR UNDERSTANDING

Use your calculator to convert the following to standard notation:

1. $5.8 * 10^{-4}$ **2.** $7.6 * 10^9$ **3.** $4.3 * 10^{-6}$ **4.** $2.3 * 10^8$

Check your answers on page 380.

Numbers with more than 10 digits can be entered in the calculator on page 248—the maximum number of digits allowed is 88—but answers with more than 10 digits are displayed in scientific notation.

EXAMPLE Write 123,123,123,123,123,123 in scientific notation.

Key Sequence	Display
1 2 3 1 2 3 1 2 3 1 2 3 1 2 3 1 2 3 (Enter)	1.231 x 10 ^ 17

$123{,}123{,}123{,}123{,}123{,}123 = 1.231 * 10^{17}$

EXAMPLE Write $1*2*3*4*5*6*7*8*9*10*11*12*13*14*15$ in scientific notation.

Key Sequence	Display
1 (×) 2 (×) 3 (×) 4 (×) 5 (×) 6 (×) 7 (×) 8 (×) 9 (×) 10 (×) 11 (×) 12 (×) 13 (×) 14 (×) 15 (Enter)	1.308 x 10 ^ 12

$1 * 2 * 3 * 4 * 5 * 6 * 7 * 8 * 9 * 10 * 11 * 12 * 13 * 14 * 15 = 1.308 * 10^{12}$

CHECK YOUR UNDERSTANDING

Write in scientific notation.

1. $995 * 7 * 54 * 65 * 659 * 807 * 468$

2. $956 * 859 * 760 * 862$

3. $527 * 32 * 987 * 424 * 77 * 145 * 195$

4. $15^9 * 13 * 996 * 558$

Convert from scientific notation to standard notation.

5. $9.867 * 10^{10}$

6. $4.32 * 10^8$

Check your answers on page 380.

Pi: π

The formulas for the circumference and area of circles involve pi (π). Pi is a number that is a little more than 3. The first few digits of π are 3.14159265.... Your calculator has a special key for pi, $\boxed{\pi}$. When you need to use π in a calculation, use $\boxed{\pi}$.

Note: To see a decimal for π, press $\boxed{\pi}$ $\boxed{Enter}$ $\boxed{F \leftrightarrow D}$.

EXAMPLE Find the area of a circle with a 4-foot radius. Use the formula $A = \pi r^2$.

Key Sequence	Display
$\boxed{\pi}$ $\boxed{\times}$ 4 $\boxed{\wedge}$ 2 $\boxed{Enter}$	$\Pi \times 4 \wedge 2 = 16\Pi$

Notice that the display answer is 16π. This is the exact area for a circle with a 4-foot radius. To see 16π as a decimal, press $\boxed{F \leftrightarrow D}$.

Key Sequence	Display
$\boxed{F \leftrightarrow D}$	50.26548246

This answer, 50.26548246 square feet, has more digits than are significant. Since you know the circle's radius only to one significant digit, it's not appropriate to have 10 digits in the area. You need to round the result to an appropriate number of decimal places. Here, you might say the area is 50 square feet or perhaps 50.3 square feet.

EXAMPLE Find the circumference of a circle with a 15-foot diameter. Use the formula $c = \pi d$.

Key Sequence	Display
$\boxed{\pi}$ $\boxed{\times}$ 15 $\boxed{Enter}$	$\Pi \times 15 = \qquad 15\Pi$
$\boxed{F \leftrightarrow D}$	47.1238898

The circumference is about 47 feet.

Memory: ▸M , MR/MC

The memory of a calculator is a place where a number can be stored while the calculator is working with other numbers. Later, when you need it, you can recall the number from memory. Most calculators display an "M" or similar symbol when there is a number other than 0 in the memory.

The ▸M key stores the number in the display.

Key Sequence	Purpose
▸M Enter	Stores the number in the display in the memory, *replacing* any number already in the memory.
MR/MC	Recalls the number stored in memory and shows it in the display.
MR/MC MR/MC	Clears the memory. (This really means that 0 is in the memory.)

The calculator's memory only works with numbers that are the result of calculations. This means that you must press Enter before you can store a number in the memory.

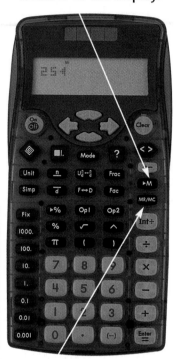

EXAMPLE Store 25 in the memory.

Key Sequence	Display
2 5 ▸M Enter	MEM ERROR

Press Clear twice to clear the "MEM ERROR" display.

Key Sequence	Display
2 5 Enter ▸M Enter	M 25 = 25
Clear	M
MR/MC	M 25

The MR/MC key recalls the number stored in the memory.

CHECK YOUR UNDERSTANDING

Store π in the memory. Clear the display. Then compute the area of a circle whose radius is 14 feet, without pressing the π key. (Area = πr^2)

Check your answers on page 380.

EXAMPLE Compute a 15% tip on a $25 bill. Store the tip in the memory, then find the total bill.

Key Sequence	Display
15 [%] [×] 25 (Enter)	15% × 25 = 3.75
(▶M) (Enter)	M 15% × 25 = 3.75
25 [+] (MR/MC) (Enter)	M 25 + 3.75 = 28.75

To clear the memory, press (MR/MC) twice. Do not press (MR/MC) more than twice.

Key Sequence	Display	Number in Memory
5 (Enter) (▶M) (Enter)	M 5 = 5	5
(MR/MC)	M 5	5
(MR/MC)	5	0

N O T E

If you press (MR/MC) more than twice, the calculator will "recall" 0 from the memory. A "0" will be written where the cursor is.

CHECK YOUR UNDERSTANDING

Use your calculator to solve each problem.

1. Compute a 15% tip on a $75 bill. Then find the total bill.

2. Compute a 20% tip on a $66.78 bill. Then find the total bill.

Check your answers on page 380.

You can use the memory of a calculator to solve problems that have several steps.

> **EXAMPLE** Marguerite ordered the following food at the food court: 2 hamburgers at $1.49 each and 3 hot dogs at $0.89 each. How much change will she receive from a $10 bill?

Key Sequence	Display
2 ⊠ 1 ⊡ 4 9 (Enter) (▶M) (Enter)	M 2 x 1.49 = 2.98
3 ⊠ ⊡ 8 9 (Enter) (▶M) (+)	M 3 x .89 = 2.67
1 0 ⊖ (MR/MC) (Enter)	M 10 − 5.65 = 4.35

Marguerite will receive $4.35 back.

> **EXAMPLE** Mr. Beckman bought 2 adult tickets at $8.25 each and 3 child tickets at $4.75 each. He redeemed a $5 gift certificate. How much did he pay for the tickets?

Key Sequence	Display
2 ⊠ 8 ⊡ 2 5 (Enter) (▶M) (Enter)	M 2 x 8.25 = 16.5
3 ⊠ 4 ⊡ 7 5 (Enter) (▶M) (+)	M 3 x 4.75 = 14.25
(MR/MC) ⊖ 5 (Enter)	M 30.75 − 5 = 25.75

Mr. Beckman paid $25.75 for the tickets.

Key Sequence	Function
▶M ⊕	Adds the number in the display to the number already in memory.
▶M ⊖	Subtracts the number in the display from the number already in memory.
▶M ⊗	Multiplies the number in the memory by the number in the display. The product is stored in the memory.
▶M ⊘	Divides the number in the memory by the number in the display. The quotient is stored in the memory.
▶M Int÷	Divides the number in the memory by the number in the display. The quotient is stored in the memory and the remainder is discarded.

EXAMPLE   Juan and his 6 friends bought the following tickets for a baseball game: 2 bleacher seats at $15.25 each and 5 mezzanine seats at $27.50 each. If everyone intends to split the costs evenly seven ways, how much does each person owe?

Key Sequence	Display
2 ⊗ 15 ⊙ 25 Enter ▶M Enter	M 2 × 15.25 = 30.5
5 ⊗ 27 ⊙ 50 Enter ▶M ⊕	M 5 × 27.50 = 137.5
MR/MC ⊘ 7 Enter	168 M÷ 7 = 24

Juan and his friends each paid $24.00 for the tickets.

CHECK YOUR UNDERSTANDING

Use your calculator to solve each problem.

1. How much would 2 shirts and 2 hats cost if shirts cost $18.50 each and hats cost $13.25 each?

2. How much would it cost to take a family of 2 adults and 2 children to a matinee if tickets cost $6.25 for adults and $4.25 for children?

Check your answers on page 380.

Repeating an Operation: Op1 , Op2

Most calculators have a way to let you repeat an operation. This is called the **constant function.** (*Constant* means *unchanging*.)

To use the constant function of your calculator, follow these steps.

1. Press Op1 .
2. Press the keys that define the constant function.
3. Press Op1 .
4. Enter a number.
5. Press Op1 .

You can repeat Steps 4 and 5 for as many different numbers as you wish.

The Op1 and Op2 keys allow you to program and repeat operations.

EXAMPLE Set up the calculator to multiply numbers by 7. Then multiply several numbers by 7.

Key Sequence	Display
Op1 ⊠ 7 Op1	Op1 × 7
8 Op1	Op1 8 × 7 1 56
20 Op1	Op1 20 × 7 1 140

Use Mode to clear the constant operation(s).

Key Sequence	Display
Mode ⬇ ⬇ Enter	Op1 Op2 CLEAR

In earlier grades, you may have used the constant function to practice counting by a certain number.

EXAMPLE Starting at 3, count by 7s.

Key Sequence	Display
(Op1) (+) 7 (Op1)	Op1 + 7
3 (Op1)	Op1 3 + 7 1 10
(Op1)	Op1 10 + 7 2 17
(Op1)	Op1 17 + 7 3 24
(Op1)	Op1 24 +7 4 31
(Op1)	Op1 31 + 7 5 38

N O T E

The number in the lower left corner of the display shows how many counts you have made.

You can use (Op2) to define a second constant operation. (Op2) works in exactly the same way as (Op1).

CHECK YOUR UNDERSTANDING

Use your calculator to do the following counts. Write five counts each.

1. Starting at 11, count by 7s.

2. Starting at 12, count by 11s.

Check your answers on page 380.

If you wish, you can hide the constant function. This makes the calculator like a function machine with a mystery rule. Press (Mode) to reach the menu for hiding the constant function.

The ◈ key provides a set of electronic flash cards to test addition, subtraction, multiplication, and division skills.

EXAMPLE

Key Sequence	Display
(Op1) (×) 3 (Op1)	Op1 × 3
(Mode) (⇩) (⇨) (Enter)	Op1 +1 ? OP
(Mode) 8 (Op1)	Op1 1 24
5 (Op1)	Op1 1 15
9 (Op1)	Op1 1 27

The ◨. key is for working with a place value. The (?) key can be used with ◈ to enter equations with unknowns.

Other Features

The calculator shown here has several features not discussed in this book. Most of these have to do with the red keys: ◈, ◨., (?), and so on. Some of these keys are for place value. Others make the calculator give you problems so you can practice arithmetic. For details, ask your teacher or read the instructions that came with the calculator.

Games

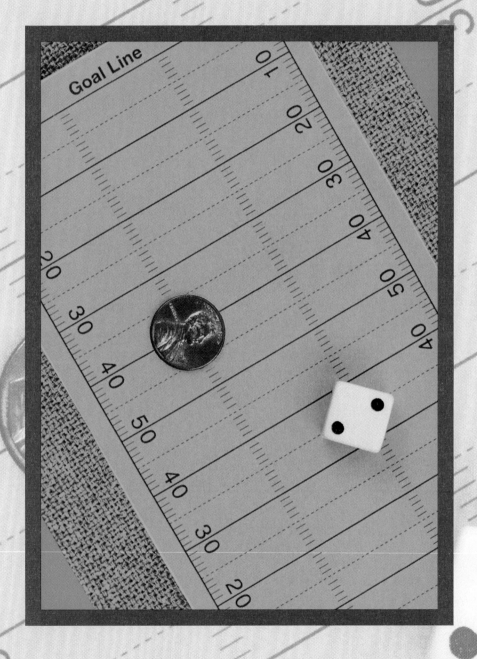

Games

Throughout the year, you will play games that help you practice important math skills. Playing mathematics games gives you a chance to practice math skills in a way that is different and enjoyable.

In this section of your *Student Reference Book,* you will find the directions for many games. The numbers in most games are generated randomly. This means that the games can be played over and over without repeating the same problems.

Many students have created their own variations to these games to make them more interesting. We encourage you to do this. We hope that you will play often and have fun!

Materials

You need a deck of number cards for many of the games. You can use an Everything Math Deck, a regular deck of cards, or make your own deck out of index cards.

An Everything Math Deck includes 54 cards. There are four cards each for the numbers 0–10. And there is one card for each of the numbers 11–20.

A deck of playing cards includes 54 cards (52 regular cards, plus 2 jokers). To create a deck of number cards from it, use a permanent marker to mark cards in the following way:

• Mark each of the four aces with the number 1.
• Mark each of the four queens with the number 0.
• Mark the four jacks and four kings with the numbers 11 through 18.
• Mark the two jokers with the numbers 19 and 20.

For some games you will have to make a game board, or a score sheet, or a set of cards that are not number cards. The instructions for doing this are included with the game directions. More complicated game boards and card decks are available from your teacher.

Game	Skill	Page
Algebra Election	Variable substitution, solving equations	276–277
Angle Tangle	Estimating and measuring angle size	278
Baseball Multiplication (1 to 6 Facts)	Multiplication facts 1 to 6	279
Baseball Multiplication (Advanced Versions)	Multiplication facts through 12s	280
Buzz Games	Finding multiples and common multiples	281
Credits/Debits Game	Addition and subtraction of positive and negative numbers	282
Credits/Debits Game (Advanced Version)	Addition and subtraction of positive and negative numbers	283
Division Dash	Division of 2-digit numbers by 1-digit numbers	284
Doggone Decimal	Estimating products of whole numbers and decimals	285
Estimation Squeeze	Estimating square roots	286
Exponent Ball	Converting exponential notation to standard notation, comparing probabilities	287
Factor Captor	Finding factors of a number	288
First to 100	Variable substitution, solving equations	289
Frac-Tac-Toe	Renaming fractions as decimals and percents	290–292
Fraction Action, Fraction Friction	Estimating sums of fractions	293
Fraction Top-It	Comparing fractions	294
Getting to One	Estimation	295
Hidden Treasure	Plotting ordered pairs, developing a search strategy	296
High-Number Toss	Place-Value, exponential notation	297
High-Number Toss: Decimal Version	Decimal place-value, subtraction and addition	298
Landmark Shark	Finding the range, mode, median, and mean	299–300
Name That Number	Naming numbers with expressions	301
Polygon Capture	Properties of polygons	302
Scientific Notation Toss	Converting from scientific notation to standard notation	303
Solution Search	Solving inequalities	304
Spoon Scramble	Fraction, decimal, and percent multiplication	305
Spreadsheet Scramble	Addition of positive and negative numbers	306
3-D Shape Sort	Properties of 3-D shapes	307
Top-It Games	Addition, subtraction, multiplication and division facts	308–309
Top-It with Positive and Negative Numbers	Addition and subtraction of positive and negative numbers	310

Algebra Election

Materials □ 32 *Algebra Election* Problem Cards (*Math Journal 2*, Activity Sheets 5 and 6)
□ Electoral Vote Map (*Math Masters*, pp. 102 and 103)
□ 1 six-sided die
□ 4 pennies or other small counters
□ calculator

Players 2 teams, each with 2 players

Object of the game Players move their counters on a map of the United States. For each state, or the District of Columbia (D.C.), that a player lands on, the player tries to win that state's electoral votes by solving a problem. The first team to collect 270 or more votes wins the election. Winning-team members become President and Vice President.

Directions

1. Each player puts a counter on Iowa.

2. One member of each team rolls the die. The team with the higher roll goes first.

3. Alternate turns between teams and partners: Team 1, Player 1; Team 2, Player 1; Team 1, Player 2; Team 2, Player 2.

4. Shuffle the Problem Cards. Place them facedown in a pile.

5. The first player rolls the die. The result tells how many moves the player must make from the current state. Each new state counts as one move. Moves can be in any direction as long as they pass between states that share a common border.

   Exceptions: Players can get to and from Alaska by way of Washington state and to and from Hawaii by way of California. Once a player has been in a state, the player may not return to that state on the same turn.

6. The player moves the counter and takes the top Problem Card. The state's number of electoral votes is substituted for the variable x in the problems on the card. The map names how many electoral votes the state has. The player solves the problem(s) and offers an answer. The other team checks the answer with a calculator.

Find: x squared x to the fourth power $1/x$	Find n. (*Hint: n* could be a negative number.) $1000 + n = x$ $1000 + n = -x$	Complete. $x * 10^6 =$ ___ million $x * 10^9 =$ ___ billion $x * 10^{12} =$ ___ ___	What is the value of n? $-20 + x = n$ $-100 + (-x) = n$
Insert parentheses in $10 * x - 10$ so that its value is greater than 0 and less than 100.	Find n. (*Hint: n* could be a negative number.) $n + 10 = x$ $n - 10 = x$	What is the value of n? $n = ((5 * x) - 4) / 2$	What is the value of n? $20 + (-x) = n$ $-20 - (-x) = n$
$T = B - (2 * \frac{H}{1000})$ If $B = 80$ and $H = 100x$, what does T equal?	Find n. $n = (2 * x) / 10$ $n + 1 = (2 * x)$	Suppose you earn x dollars per hour. Complete the table. Time / Earnings: 1 hr \$ / 2 hr \$ / 4 hr \$ / 10 hr \$	Which is greater: x^2 or 10^3? x^3 or 10^4?
Tell whether each is true or false. $10 * x > 100$ $\frac{1}{2} * x * 100 < 10^3$ $x^3 * 1000 > 4 * 10^4$	Which number is this? $x * 10^2$? $x * 10^5$?	A boulder dropped off a cliff falls approximately $16 * x^2$ feet in x seconds. How many feet is that?	Which is less: $\frac{x^3}{10}$ or $(x + 10)^2$? $10 * x^2$ or $(x + 10)^3$?

Is $1/x$ greater than, less than, or equal to $\frac{1}{10}$?	Is point (x, x) to the left of, to the right of, or on the line through points A and B?	Tell which is correct for each: <, =, or >. $x < = > 30 - x$ $x < = > 20 - x$ $x < = > 10 - x$	What is n? $5 + 2 * x = n + x$
Subtract. $x - 100 = ?$ $x - (-100) = ?$	What is the value of n? $10 + (-x) = n$ $-10 - (-x) = n$	Name a number n such that $x - n$ is a negative number greater than -10.	$\frac{x + \triangle}{}$ $\frac{200\ oz}{}$ $1 \triangle$ weighs ___ ounces.
Add. $-25 + x = ?$ $x + 3 - 10 = ?$	What is the median of 4, 8, 12, 13, and x?	Suppose you have 10 ⊞ markers and 2 * x ⊟ markers. What is your balance?	Insert parentheses so that the equation is true. $10 * x + 4 = 10 * x + 40$
Suppose you travel x miles per hour. Complete the table. Time / Distance: 1 hr / 2 hr / 4 hr / 10 hr	If $(2 * x) + n = 100$, what is the value of n?	Suppose you have x ⊞ markers and 40 ⊟ markers. What is your balance?	Is point (x, x) above, below, or on the line through points A and B?

7. If the answer is correct, the player's team wins the state's electoral votes. They do the following:
   - Write the state's name and its electoral votes on a piece of scratch paper.
   - Write their first initials in pencil on the state to show that they have won it.

   Once a state is won, it is out of play. The opposing team may land on the state, but they cannot get its votes.

NOTE: Alaska and Hawaii are not drawn to scale.

8. If the partners do not solve the problem(s) correctly, the state remains open. Players may still try to win its votes.

9. The next player rolls the die and moves his or her counter.

10. The first team to get at least 270 votes wins the election.

11. When all the Problem Cards have been used, shuffle the deck and use it again.

12. Each player begins a turn from the last state he or she landed on.

Notes

- "A state" means "a state or the District of Columbia (D.C.)."
- Partners may discuss the problem with one another. Each player, however, has to answer the problem on his or her own.
- If a player does not want to answer a Problem Card, the player may say "Pass," and draw another card. A player may "Pass" 3 times during a game.
- If a Problem Card contains several problems, a player must answer all the questions on a card correctly to win a state's votes.
- Suggested strategy: Look at the map to see which states have the most votes, then work with your partner to win those states.

Variations:

1. Agree on a time limit for answering problems.

2. Give one extra point if the player can name the capital of the state landed on.

3. A shorter version of the game can be played by going through all 32 cards just once. The team with the most votes at that time is the winner.

Angle Tangle

Materials ☐ protractor
☐ straightedge
☐ blank sheets of paper

Players 2

Directions

In each round:

1. Player 1 uses a straightedge to draw an angle on a sheet of paper.

2. Player 2 estimates the degree measure of the angle.

3. Player 1 measures the angle with a protractor. Players agree on the measure.

4. Player 2's score is the difference between the estimate and the actual measure of the angle. (The difference will be a 0 or a positive number.)

5. Players trade roles and repeat Steps 1–4.

Players add their scores at the end of five rounds. The player with the lower total score wins the game.

EXAMPLE

	Player 1			Player 2		
	Estimate	Actual	Score	Estimate	Actual	Score
Round 1	120°	108°	12	50°	37°	13
Round 2	75°	86°	11	85°	87°	2
Round 3	40°	44°	4	15°	19°	4
Round 4	60°	69°	9	40°	56°	16
Round 5	135°	123°	12	150°	141°	9
Total score			48			44

Player 2 has the lower total score. Player 2 wins the game.

Baseball Multiplication (1 to 6 Facts)

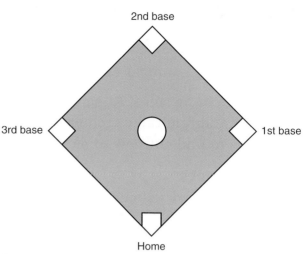

2nd base

3rd base

1st base

Home

Materials   □ *Baseball Multiplication* Game Mat
(*Math Masters*, p. 483)
□ 2 six-sided dice
□ 4 pennies
□ calculator or a
multiplication/division table

Players   2 or 2 teams

Object of the game To score the most runs in a
3-inning game.

Directions

Advance Preparation: Draw a diamond and label
Home plate, 1st base, 2nd base, and *3rd base.* Make a
Scoreboard sheet that looks like the one shown at
the right.

Inning		1	2	3	Total
Team 1	outs				
	runs				
Team 2	outs				
	runs				

Take turns being the *pitcher* and the *batter*. The rules
are similar to the rules of baseball, but this game lasts
only three innings.

1. At the start of the inning, the batter puts a penny on home
plate. The pitcher rolls the dice. The batter multiplies the
numbers rolled and gives the answer. The pitcher checks
the answer and may use a calculator to do so.

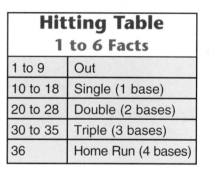

Hitting Table	
1 to 6 Facts	
1 to 9	Out
10 to 18	Single (1 base)
20 to 28	Double (2 bases)
30 to 35	Triple (3 bases)
36	Home Run (4 bases)

2. If the answer is correct, the batter looks up the product in
the Hitting Table at the right. If it is a hit, the batter
moves all pennies on the field the number of bases shown
in the table. If a product is not a hit, it is an out.

3. An incorrect answer is a strike and another pitch (dice roll)
is thrown. Three strikes make an out.

4. A run is scored each time a penny crosses home plate. The
batter tallies each run scored on the Scoreboard.

5. After each hit or out, the batter puts a penny on home plate.
A player remains the batter for three outs. Then the players
switch roles. The inning is over when both players have
made three outs.

The player who has more runs at the end of three innings wins
the game. If the game is tied at the end of three innings, play
continues into extra innings until one player wins.

Baseball Multiplication (Advanced Versions)

1 to 10 Facts
Materials ☐ number cards 1–10 (4 of each)

Follow the basic rules. At each turn, draw two cards from the deck and find their product. Use the Hitting Table at the right to find out how to move the pennies.

2 to 12 Facts
Materials ☐ 4 six-sided dice

Follow the basic rules. At each turn, the pitcher rolls four dice. The batter separates the dice into two pairs, adds the numbers in each pair, and multiplies the sums. Use the Hitting Table at the right.

How you pair the numbers can determine the kind of hit you get or whether you get an out. For example, suppose you roll a 1, 2, 3, and 5. You could add pairs in different ways and multiply as follows:

one way	a second way	a third way
1 + 2 = 3	1 + 3 = 4	1 + 5 = 6
3 + 5 = 8	2 + 5 = 7	2 + 3 = 5
3 * 8 = 24	4 * 7 = 28	6 * 5 = 30
Out	Single	Single

Three-Factors Game
Materials ☐ 3 six-sided dice

The pitcher rolls three dice. The batter multiplies the three numbers (factors) and uses the Hitting Table at the right.

10s * 10s Game
Materials ☐ 4 six-sided dice or number cards 1–10
(4 of each)

The rules for this game are the same as for the **2 to 12 Facts** game with two exceptions:

1. A sum 2 through 9 represents 20 through 90. A sum 10 through 12 represents itself.

   Roll 1, 2, 3, and 5. Get sums 6 and 5. Multiply 60 * 50.
   Roll 3, 4, 6, and 6. Get sums 12 and 7. Multiply 12 * 70.
2. Use the Hitting Table at the right.

Hitting Table
1 to 10 Facts

1 to 21	Out
24 to 45	Single (1 base)
48 to 70	Double (2 bases)
72 to 81	Triple (3 bases)
90 to 100	Home Run (4 bases)

Hitting Table
2 to 12 Facts

4 to 24	Out
25 to 49	Single (1 base)
50 to 64	Double (2 bases)
66 to 77	Triple (3 bases)
80 to 144	Home Run (4 bases)

Hitting Table
Three-Factors Game

1 to 54	Out
60 to 90	Single (1 base)
96 to 120	Double (2 bases)
125 to 150	Triple (3 bases)
180 to 216	Home Run (4 bases)

Hitting Table
10s * 10s Game

100 to 2,000	Out
2,100 to 4,000	Single (1 base)
4,200 to 5,400	Double (2 bases)
5,600 to 6,400	Triple (3 bases)
7,200 to 8,100	Home Run (4 bases)

Buzz Games

Buzz

Materials none
Players 5–10

Directions

1. Players sit in a circle and choose a leader. The leader names any whole number from 3 to 9. This number is the BUZZ number. The leader also chooses the STOP number. The STOP number should be at least 30.

2. The player to the left of the leader begins the game by saying "one." Play continues clockwise with each player saying either the next whole number or "BUZZ."

3. A player must say "BUZZ" instead of the next number if:
   • The number is the BUZZ number or a multiple of the BUZZ number; or
   • The number contains the BUZZ number as one of its digits.

4. If a player makes an error, the next player must start again with 1.

5. Play continues until the STOP number is reached.

6. For the next round, the player to the right of the leader becomes the new leader.

> **EXAMPLE** The BUZZ number is 4. Play should proceed as follows: 1, 2, 3, BUZZ, 5, 6, 7, BUZZ, 9, 10, 11, BUZZ, 13, BUZZ, 15, and so on.

Bizz-Buzz

Bizz-Buzz is played like *Buzz,* except the leader names two numbers: a BUZZ number and a BIZZ number.

Players say:

1. "BUZZ" if the number is a multiple of the BUZZ number.

2. "BIZZ" if the number is a multiple of the BIZZ number.

3. "BIZZ–BUZZ" if the number is a multiple of both the BUZZ number and the BIZZ number.

> **NOTE**
> The numbers 6 and 12 in the example below are replaced by the word "BIZZ-BUZZ" since 6 and 12 are multiples of both 6 and 3.

> **EXAMPLE** The BUZZ number is 6, and the BIZZ number is 3. Play should proceed as follows: 1, 2, BIZZ, 4, 5, BIZZ-BUZZ, 7, 8, BIZZ, 10, 11, BIZZ-BUZZ, 13, 14, BIZZ, 16, and so on.

Credits/Debits Game

Materials ☐ 1 complete deck of number cards
☐ recording sheet

Players   2

Directions

Pretend that you are an accountant for a business. Your job is to keep track of the company's current balance. The current balance is also called the "bottom line." As credits and debits are reported, you will record them and then adjust the bottom line.

Recording Sheet			
	Start	**Change**	**End/next start**
1	+$10		
2			
3			
4			
5			
6			
7			
8			
9			
10			

1. Shuffle the deck and lay it facedown between the players.

2. The black-numbered cards are the "credits," and the blue- or red-numbered cards are the "debits."

3. Each player begins with a bottom line of +$10.

4. Players take turns. On your turn, do the following:
   • Draw a card. The card tells you the dollar amount and whether it is a credit or debit to the bottom line. Record the credit or debit in the "Change" column.
   • Use the credit or debit to adjust the bottom line.
   • Record the result in the table.

EXAMPLES Ellen has a "Start" balance of +$20. She draws a black 9. This is a credit of $9, so she records +$9 in the "Change" column, she adds $9 to the bottom line: $20 + $9 = $29. Ellen then records +$29 in the "End" column. She also records +$29 in the "Start" column on the next line.

Larry has a "Start" balance of +$10. He draws a red 12. This is a debit of $12, so he records −$12 in the "Change" column. He subtracts $12 from the bottom line: $10 − $12 = −$2. Larry then records −$2 in the "End" column. He also records −$2 in the "Start" column on the next line.

Scoring: At the end of 10 draws each, the player with the most money is the winner of the round. If both players have negative dollar amounts, the player whose amount is closer to 0 wins.

Credits/Debits Game (Advanced Version)

Materials ☐ 1 complete deck of number cards
  ☐ 1 penny
  ☐ recording sheet for each player
    (*Math Masters*, p. 94)

Players 2

Directions

Pretend that you are an accountant for a business. Your job is to keep track of the company's current balance. The current balance is also called the "bottom line."

		Recording Sheet		
			Change	End, and
	Start	**Addition or Subtraction**	**Credit or Debit**	**next start**
1	+$10			
2				
3				
4				
5				
6				
7				
8				
9				
10				

1. Shuffle the deck and lay it facedown between the players.

2. The black-numbered cards are the "credits," and the blue- or red-numbered cards are the "debits."

3. The heads side of the coin tells you to **add** a credit to the bottom line. The tails side of the coin tells you to **subtract** a credit or debit from the bottom line.

4. Each player begins with a bottom line of +$10.

5. Players take turns. On your turn, do the following:
   • Flip the coin. This tells you whether to add or subtract.
   • Draw a card. The card tells you what amount in dollars (positive or negative) to add or subtract from the bottom line. Red or blue numbers are negative numbers.
   • Record the result in the table.

EXAMPLES Max has a new "Start" balance of $5. He draws a red 8 and records −$8 in the "Credit or Debit" column. His coin lands heads-side up and he records + in the "Addition or Subtraction" column. Max adds: $5 + (−$8) = −$3. He records −$3 in the "End" balance column. He also records −$3 in the "Start" column on the next line.

Beth has a new "Start" balance of −$20. Her coin lands tails-side up, which means subtract. She draws a black 11 (+$11). She subtracts: −$20 − (+$11) = −$31. Her "End" balance is −$31.

Scoring: After 10 turns each, the player with more money is the winner of the round. If both players have negative dollar amounts, the player whose amount is closer to 0 wins.

Division Dash

Materials □ calculator for each player
□ score sheet

Players 1 or 2

Object of the game To reach 100 in as few divisions
as possible.

Directions

Player 1		Player 2	
Quotient	Score	Quotient	Score

1. On a piece of paper, prepare a score sheet as shown
   at the right.

2. Players clear their calculator memories. Each
   player then chooses a number that is greater than
   1,000 and enters the following key sequence on
   their calculator:
   Op1 ∧ · 5 Op1 [selected number] Op1

3. Each player uses the final digit in the calculator display as a
   1-digit number, and the two digits before the final digit as a
   2-digit number.

4. Each player divides the 2-digit number by the 1-digit number
   and records the result. (This result is the quotient.
   Remainders are ignored.) Players calculate mentally or on
   paper, not on the calculator.

5. **Players do not clear their calculators.** They just press
   Op1 and repeat Steps 3 and 4 until the sum of one player's
   quotients is 100 or more. The winner is the first player to
   reach at least 100. If there is only one player, the object of the
   game is to reach 100 or more in as few turns as possible.

EXAMPLE

	Quotient	Score
First turn: Press Op1 ∧ · 5 Op1 5678 Op1 . On a 10-digit display, the result is 7 5 . 3 5 2 5 0 <u>4 9</u> <u>4</u>. Divide 49 by 4. The quotient is 12 with a remainder of 1.	12	12
Second turn: Press Op1 . The result is 8 . 6 8 0 5 8 2 <u>0 6</u> <u>2</u>. Divide 06, or 6, by 2. The quotient is 3.	3	15
Third turn: Press Op1 . The result is 2 . 9 4 6 2 8 2 <u>7 5</u> <u>3</u>. Divide 75 by 3. The quotient is 25.	25	40

Continue until one player has a total score of 100 or more.

Doggone Decimal

Materials ☐ number cards 0–9 (4 of each)
☐ 4 index cards labeled 0.1, 1, 10, and 100
☐ 2 counters or coins per player (to use as decimal points)
☐ calculator

Players 2

Object of the game To collect the most number cards.

Directions

1. One player shuffles the number cards and deals four cards facedown to each player.

2. The other player shuffles the index cards, places them facedown, and turns over the top card. The number that appears (0.1, 1, 10, or 100) is the **target number.**

3. Using four number cards and two decimal-point counters, each player forms two numbers. Numbers must have two digits and a decimal point.
   • Players try to form numbers whose product is as close as possible to the target number.
   • The decimal point can go anywhere in a number—for example:

4. Players compute the product of their numbers on a calculator.

5. The player whose product is closer to the target number wins all eight number cards.

6. Four new number cards are dealt to each player and a new target number is turned over. Repeat Steps 3–5 using the new target number.

7. The game ends when all target numbers have been used.

8. The player with the most number cards wins the game. In the case of a tie, reshuffle the index cards and turn over a target number. Play one tie-breaking round.

EXAMPLE   The target number is 10.

Briana is dealt 1, 4, 8, and 8. She forms the numbers 8.8 and 1.4.
Evelyn is dealt 2, 3, 6, and 9. She forms the numbers 2.6 and 3.9.
Briana's product is 12.32 and Evelyn's is 10.14.
Evelyn's product is closer to 10. She wins the round and the cards.

Estimation Squeeze

Materials ☐ calculator
Players 2

Object of the game To estimate the square root of a number without using the 🔲 key on the calculator.

Directions

1. Pick a number that is less than 600 and is NOT a perfect square. (See the table to the right.) This is the **target number.** Record the target number.

2. Players take turns. When it is your turn:

   • Estimate the square root of the target number and enter the estimate on the calculator.
   • Find the square of the estimate with the calculator and record it.

3. The first player who makes an estimate whose square is within 0.1 of the target number wins the game. For example, if the target number is 139, the square of the estimate must be greater than 138.9 and less than 139.1.

Perfect Squares

1	81	289
4	100	324
9	121	361
16	144	400
25	169	441
36	196	484
49	225	529
64	256	576

A perfect square is the square of a whole number.
$1 = 1 * 1$, $64 = 8 * 8$,
$400 = 20^2$

> **EXAMPLE** Use your calculator to square the number 13.5.
> Press 13 ⊙ 5 ⌃ 2 (Enter), or press 13 ⊙ 5 ⊗ 13 ⊙ 5 (Enter).
> Answer: 182.25.

4. Do not use the 🔲 key on the calculator. This key provides the best estimate of a square root that the calculator can calculate.

> **EXAMPLE** Target number: 139

	Estimate	Square of Estimate	
Nick	12	144	too large
Erin	11	121	too small
Nick	11.5	132.25	too small
Erin	11.8	139.24	too large
Nick	11.75	138.0625	too small
Erin	11.79	139.0041	between 138.9 and 139.1

Erin wins.

Exponent Ball

Materials   ☐ an *Exponent Ball* Gameboard (*Math Masters,* p. 25)
                 ☐ 1 six-sided die
                 ☐ penny or other counter
                 ☐ calculator

Players   2

Directions

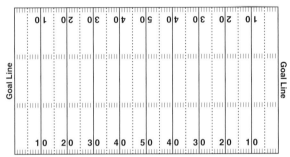

1. The game is similar to U.S. football. The player who goes first puts the ball (counter) on one of the 20-yard lines. The player's goal is to reach the goal line, 80 yards away. A turn consists of four chances to advance the counter to the goal line and score.

2. The first three chances must be runs on the ground. To run, the player rolls the die twice. The first roll names the **base,** the second roll names the **exponent.** For example, rolls of 5 and 4 name the number $5^4 = 625$.

3. The player calculates the value of the rolls. Use Table 1 on the gameboard page to find how far to move the ball forward ($+$) or backward ($-$).

4. If the player does not score in the first three chances, the player may choose to run or kick on the fourth chance. To kick, the player rolls the die once and multiplies the result by 10. The result is the distance the ball travels (Table 2 on the gameboard page).

5. If the ball reaches the goal line on a run, the player scores 7 points. If the ball reaches the goal line on a kick, the player scores 3 points.

6. If the ball does not reach the goal line in four chances, the turn ends. The second player starts where the first player stopped and moves toward the opposite goal line.

7. If the first player scores, the second player puts the ball on the 20-yard line and follows the directions above.

8. Players take turns. A round consists of four turns for each player. The player with more points wins.

Table 1: Runs		
Value of Roll	**Move Ball**	**Chances of Gaining on the Ground**
1	−15 yd	−15 yards: 1 out of 6 or about 17%
2 to 6	+10 yd	10 yards or more: 5 out of 6 or about 83%
8 to 81	+20 yd	20 yards or more: 4 out of 6 or about 67%
in the 100s	+30 yd	30 yards or more: 13 out of 36 or about 36%
in the 1,000s	+40 yd	40 yards or more: 7 out of 36 or about 19%
in the 10,000s	+50 yd	50 yards: 1 out of 18 or about 6%

Table 2: Kicks		
Value of Roll	**Move Ball**	**Chances of Kicking**
1	+10 yd	10 yards or more: 6 out of 6 or 100%
2	+20 yd	20 yards or more: 5 out of 6 or about 83%
3	+30 yd	30 yards or more: 4 out of 6 or about 67%
4	+40 yd	40 yards or more: 3 out of 6 or about 50%
5	+50 yd	50 yards or more: 2 out of 6 or about 33%
6	+60 yd	60 yards or more: 1 out of 6 or about 17%

N O T E

If a backward move should carry the ball behind the goal line, the ball (counter) is put on the goal line.

Factor Captor

Materials
- ☐ calculators for each player
- ☐ paper and pencil
- ☐ a *Factor Captor* grid—either Grid 1 or Grid 2 (*Math Masters,* pp. 484 and 485)
- ☐ coin-size counters (48 for Grid 1, 70 for Grid 2)

Players 2

Directions

1. To start the first round, Player 1 (James) chooses a 2-digit number on the number grid. James covers it with a counter, and records the number on scratch paper. This is James's score for the round.

2. Player 2 (Emma) covers all of the factors of James's number. Emma finds the sum of the factors, and records it on scratch paper. This is Emma's score for the round.

A factor may only be covered once during a round.

3. If Emma missed any factors, James can cover them with counters and add them to his score.

4. In the next round, players switch roles. Player 2 (Emma) chooses a number that is not covered by a counter. Player 1 (James) covers all factors of that number.

5. Any number that is covered by a counter is no longer available and may not be used again.

6. The first player in a round may not cover a number less than 10, unless no other numbers are available.

7. Play continues with players trading roles in each round, until all numbers on the grid have been covered. Players then use their calculators to find their total scores. The player with the higher total score wins the game.

1	2	2	2	2	2
2	3	3	3	3	3
3	4	4	4	4	5
5	5	5	6	6	7
7	8	8	9	9	10
10	11	12	13	14	15
16	18	20	21	22	24
25	26	27	28	30	32

1	2	2	2	2	3
3	3	3	3	4	4	4
4	5	5	5	5	6	6
6	7	7	8	8	9	9
10	10	11	12	13	14	15
16	17	18	19	20	21	22
23	24	25	26	27	28	30
32	33	34	35	36	38	39
40	42	44	45	46	48	49
50	51	52	54	55	56	60

EXAMPLE

Round 1: James covers 27 and scores 27 points. Emma covers 1, 3, and 9, and scores 1 + 3 + 9 = 13 points.

Round 2: Emma covers 18 and scores 18 points. James covers 2, 3, and 6, and scores 2 + 3 + 6 = 11 points. Emma covers 9 with a counter, because 9 is also a factor of 18. Emma adds 9 points to her score.

First to 100

Materials ☐ set of 32 *First to 100* Problem Cards
(*Math Journal 1*, Activity Sheets 3 and 4)
☐ 2 six-sided dice
☐ calculator

Players 2 to 4

Object of the game To solve problems and be the first
player to collect 100 points.

Directions

1. Shuffle the Problem Cards and place them facedown in
a pile.

2. Players take turns. When it is your turn:

   • Roll two dice and find the product of the numbers.

   • Turn over the top Problem Card and substitute the
   product for the variable x in the problem on the
   card.

   • Solve the problem mentally, or use paper and
   pencil. Then give the answer. (You have three
   chances to use a calculator to solve difficult
   problems during a game.) Other players check the
   answer with a calculator.

   • If the answer is correct, you win the number of
   points equal to the product that was substituted
   for the variable x. Some Problem Cards require
   two or more answers. In order to win any points,
   you must answer all parts of the problem correctly.

   • Put the used Problem Card at the bottom of the
   card pile.

3. The first player to get at least 100 points wins.

How many inches are there in x feet? How many centimeters are there in x meters? **1**	How many quarts are there in x gallons? **2**	What is the smallest number of x's you can add to get a sum greater than 100? **3**	Is $50 * x$ greater than 1,000? Is $\frac{x}{10}$ less than 1? **4**
$\frac{1}{2}$ of $x = ?$ $\frac{1}{10}$ of $x = ?$ **5**	$1 - x = ?$ $x + 998 = ?$ **6**	If x people share 1,000 stamps equally, how many stamps will each person get? **7**	What time will it be x minutes from now? What time was it x minutes ago? **8**
It is 102 miles to your destination. You have gone x miles. How many miles are left? **9**	What whole or mixed number equals x divided by 2? **10**	Is x a prime or a composite number? Is x divisible by 2? **11**	The time is 11:05 A.M. The train left x minutes ago. What time did the train leave? **12**
Bill was born in 1939. Freddy was born the same day, but x years later. In what year was Freddy born? **13**	Which is larger: $2 * x$ or $x + 50$? **14**	There are x rows of seats. There are 9 seats in each row. How many seats are there in all? **15**	Sargon spent x cents on apples. If she paid with a $5 bill, how much change should she get? **16**

The temperature was 25°F. It dropped x degrees. What is the new temperature? **17**	Each story in a building is 10 feet high. If the building has x stories, how tall is it? **18**	Which is larger: $2 * x$ or $\frac{100}{x}$? **19**	$20 * x = ?$ **20**
Name all of the whole-number factors of x. **21**	Is x an even or an odd number? Is x divisible by 9? **22**	Shalanda was born on a Tuesday. Linda was born x days later. On what day of the week was Linda born? **23**	Will had a quarter plus x cents. How much money did he have in all? **24**
Find the perimeter and area of this square. x cm **25**	What is the median of these weights? 5 pounds 21 pounds x pounds What is the range? **26**	**27**	$x^2 = ?$ 50% of $x^2 = ?$ **28**
$(3x + 4) - 8 = ?$ **29**	x out of 100 students voted for Ruby. Is this more than 25%, less than 25%, or exactly 25% of the students? **30**	There are 200 students at Wilson School. $x\%$ speak Spanish. How many students speak Spanish? **31**	People answered a survey question either Yes or No. $x\%$ answered Yes. What percent answered No? **32**

EXAMPLE Alice rolls a 5 and 6. The product is 30.

She turns over a Problem Card: $20 * x = ?$
She substitutes 30 for x and answers 600.

The answer is correct. Alice wins 30 points.

Frac-Tac-Toe

2-4-5-10 Frac-Tac-Toe

Materials
- number cards 0–10 (4 of each)
- *Number Card Board: (Math Masters, p. 67)*
- *Game Board: (Math Masters, p. 68)*
- *Counters:* Counters (2 colors) or pennies (one player using heads, the other using tails)
- calculator

Players   2

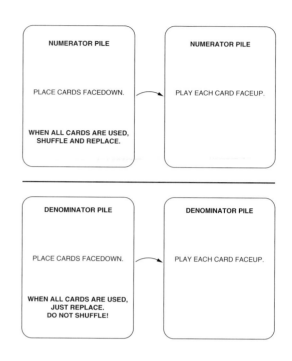

Advance Preparation: Separate the cards into two piles on the Number Card Board—a numerator pile and a denominator pile. For a 2-4-5-10 game, place two each of the 2, 4, 5, and 10 cards in the denominator pile. All other cards are placed on the numerator pile.

Shuffle the cards in each pile. Place the piles facedown in the left-hand spaces. When the numerator pile is completely used, reshuffle that pile, and place it facedown in the left-hand space. When the denominator pile is completely used, turn it over and place it facedown in the left-hand space without reshuffling it.

Directions

1. Players take turns. When it is your turn:
   - Turn over the top card from each pile to form a fraction (numerator card over denominator card).
   - Try to match the fraction shown with one of the grid squares on the Game Board. If a match is found, cover that grid square with your counter and your turn is over. If no match is found, your turn is over.

2. To change the fraction shown by the cards to a decimal, players may use either a calculator or the *Table of Decimal Equivalents for Fractions* on page 340.

Game Board for the 2-4-5-10 Decimal Version of Frac-Tac-Toe

>1.0	0 or 1	>2.0	0 or 1	>1.0
0.1	0.2	0.25	0.3	0.4
>1.5	0.5	>1.5	0.5	>1.5
0.6	0.7	0.75	0.8	0.9
>1.0	0 or 1	>2.0	0 or 1	>1.0

290   two hundred ninety

EXAMPLES

The cards show the fraction $\frac{4}{5}$. The player may cover the 0.8 square, unless that square has already been covered.

The cards show the fraction $\frac{0}{5}$. The player may cover any one of the four squares labeled "0 or 1" that has not already been covered.

The cards show the fraction $\frac{4}{2}$. The player may cover any square labeled "> 1.0" or "> 1.5" that has not been previously covered. The player may not cover a square labeled "> 2.0," because $\frac{4}{2}$ is equal to, but not greater than, 2.0.

3. **Scoring** The first player covering three squares in a row in any direction (horizontal, vertical, diagonal) is the winner.

Variation: Play a version of the *2-4-5-10* game using the percent game board shown at the right. Use *Math Masters*, page 69.

>100%	0% or 100%	>200%	0% or 100%	>100%
10%	20%	25%	30%	40%
>100%	50%	>200%	50%	>100%
60%	70%	75%	80%	90%
>100%	0% or 100%	>200%	0% or 100%	>100%

Play the *2-4-8*, or the *3-6-9* version of the game. Game boards for the different versions are shown below.

- For a *2-4-8* game, place two each of the *2, 4,* and *8* cards in the denominator pile. Use *Math Masters,* page 74 or 75.

- For a *3-6-9* game, place two each of the *3, 6,* and *9* cards in the denominator pile. Use *Math Masters,* page 72 or 73.

2-4-8 Frac-Tac-Toe

>2.0	0 or 1	>1.5	0 or 1	>2.0
1.5	0.125	0.25	0.375	1.5
>1.0	0.5	0.25 or 0.75	0.5	>1.0
2.0	0.625	0.75	0.875	2.0
>2.0	0 or 1	1.125	0 or 1	>2.0

2-4-8 Frac-Tac-Toe

>200%	0% or 100%	>150%	0% or 100%	>200%
150%	$12\frac{1}{2}$%	25%	$37\frac{1}{2}$%	150%
>100%	50%	25% or 75%	50%	>100%
200%	$62\frac{1}{2}$%	75%	$87\frac{1}{2}$%	200%
>200%	0% or 100%	$112\frac{1}{2}$%	0% or 100%	>200%

3-6-9 Frac-Tac-Toe

>1.0	0 or 1	$0.\overline{1}$	0 or 1	>1.0
$0.1\overline{6}$	$0.\overline{2}$	$0.\overline{3}$	0.3	$0.\overline{4}$
>2.0	$0.\overline{5}$	>1.0	$0.\overline{6}$	>2.0
$0.\overline{6}$	$0.\overline{7}$	$0.8\overline{3}$	$0.\overline{8}$	$1.\overline{3}$
>1.0	0 or 1	$1.\overline{6}$	0 or 1	>1.0

3-6-9 Frac-Tac-Toe

>100%	0% or 100%	11.1%	0% or 100%	>100%
$16\frac{2}{3}$%	22.2%	$33\frac{1}{3}$%	33.3%	44.4%
>200%	55.5%	>100%	66.6%	>200%
$66\frac{2}{3}$%	77.7%	$83\frac{1}{3}$%	88.8%	$133\frac{1}{3}$%
>100%	0% or 100%	$166\frac{2}{3}$%	0% or 100%	>100%

Fraction Action, Fraction Friction

Materials ☐ one set of 16 *Fraction Action, Fraction Friction* cards
(*Math Masters*, p. 486)
☐ one or more calculators

Players 2 or 3

Object of the game To gather a set of fraction cards
with a sum as close as possible to 2, without going over 2.

$\frac{1}{2}$	$\frac{1}{3}$	$\frac{2}{3}$	$\frac{1}{4}$
$\frac{3}{4}$	$\frac{1}{6}$	$\frac{1}{6}$	$\frac{5}{6}$
$\frac{1}{12}$	$\frac{1}{12}$	$\frac{5}{12}$	$\frac{5}{12}$
$\frac{7}{12}$	$\frac{7}{12}$	$\frac{11}{12}$	$\frac{11}{12}$

Directions

1. Shuffle the deck. Place the pile facedown between the players.

2. Players take turns.

   - On each player's first turn, he or she takes a card from the top of the pile, then places it faceup on the playing surface.

   - On each of the player's following turns, he or she announces one of the following:

   "Action" This means that the player wants an additional card. The player believes that the sum of the cards is not close enough to 2 to win the hand. The player thinks that another card will bring the sum of the cards closer to 2, without going over 2.

   "Friction" This means that the player does not want an additional card. The player believes that the sum of the cards is close enough to 2 to win the hand. The player thinks there is a good chance that taking another card will make the sum of the 2 cards greater than 2.

   Once a player says "Friction," he or she cannot say "Action" on any turn after that.

3. Play continues until all players have announced "Friction" or have a set of cards whose sum is greater than two. The player whose sum is closest to 2 without going over 2 is the winner of the hand. Players may check each other's sums on their calculators.

4. Reshuffle the cards and begin again. The winner of the game is the first player to win five hands.

Fraction Top-It

Materials   ☐ 1 deck of 32 Fraction Cards
(*Math Masters,* pp. 47 and 48)

Players   2 to 4

Object of the game To collect the most cards.

Directions

Advance Preparation: Before beginning the game, write the fraction for the shaded part on the back of each card.

Fraction Cards 1

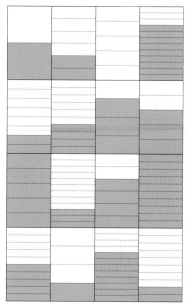

1. Deal the same number of cards, fraction-side up, to each player:
    • 16 cards each, if there are 2 players
    • 10 cards each, if there are 3 players
    • 8 cards each, if there are 4 players

2. Place the cards on the playing surface in front of each player, fraction-side up.

3. Starting with the dealer and going in a clockwise direction, each player plays one card.

Fraction Cards 2

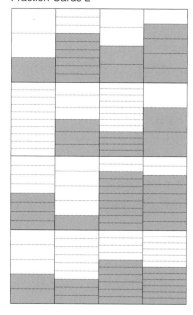

4. Place cards on the table with the fraction-side showing.

5. The player with the largest fraction wins the round and takes the cards. Players may check who has the largest fraction by turning over the cards and comparing the amount shaded.

6. If there is a tie for the largest fraction, each player plays another card. The player with the largest fraction takes all the cards.

7. The player who takes the cards starts the next round. The game is over when all cards have been played.

The player who takes the most cards wins.

Getting to One

Materials ☐ calculator
Players 2

Object of the game To guess a mystery number in as few tries as possible.

Directions

1. Player A chooses a mystery number that is less than 100. Suppose the mystery number is 65.

2. Player B guesses the mystery number.

3. Player A uses a calculator to divide the guessed number by the mystery number. Player A then reads the answer that appears in the calculator display. If the answer has more than two decimal places, only the first two decimal places are read.

4. Player B continues to guess until the result is 1. Player B keeps track of the number of guesses.

5. When Player B has guessed the mystery number, players trade roles and follow Steps 1–4. The player who guesses the mystery number in the fewest number of guesses wins the round. The first player to win three rounds wins the game.

EXAMPLE Player A chooses the mystery number 65.

Player B guesses: 55. Player A keys in: 55 ÷ 65 (Enter) . Answer: 0.846153   Too small.

Player B guesses: 70. Player A keys in: 70 ÷ 65 (Enter) . Answer: 1.076923   Too big.

Player B guesses: 65. Player A keys in: 65 ÷ 65 (Enter) . Answer: 1   Just right!

Advanced Version Allow mystery numbers up to 1,000.

Hidden Treasure

Materials ☐ Each player makes two playing grids on one sheet of graph paper. (See example at right.) (*Math Masters*, p. 44)

☐ pencil, red pen or crayon

Players 2

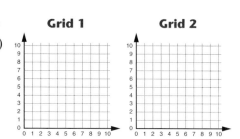

Object of the game Each player "hides" a point on a grid. Players try to "find" each other's hidden point.

Directions

1. Each player writes on his or her own pair of playing grids. Players sit so they cannot see what the other is writing.

2. Each player secretly marks a point on Grid 1. These are the "hidden" points.

3. Player 1 guesses the location of Player 2's hidden point by naming an ordered pair. To name (1,2), say "1 comma 2."

4. If Player 2's hidden point is at that location, Player 1 wins.

5. If the hidden point is not at that location, Player 2 marks the guess in pencil on Grid 1. Player 2 counts the least number of "square sides" needed to travel from the hidden point to the guessed point and tells it to Player 1. Repeat Steps 3–5 with Player 2 guessing and Player 1 answering.

EXAMPLE

Player 1 marks a hidden point at (2,5).   Player 2 marks a hidden point at (3,7).

Player 1

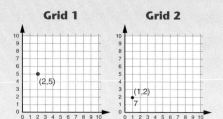

Player 2

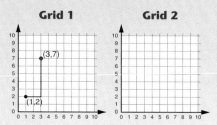

• Player 1 guesses that Player 2's hidden point is at (1,2) and marks it on Grid 2 in pencil.

• Player 2 marks the point (1,2) in pencil on Grid 1 and tells Player 1 that (1,2) is 7 units away from the hidden point.

• Player 1 writes 7 next to the point (1,2) on Grid 2.

Advanced Version Use a 4-quadrant grid with axes labeled from −7 to 7.

High-Number Toss

Materials ☐ 1 six-sided die
Players 2

Object of the game To make the largest number possible.

NOTE

If you don't have a die, you can use a deck of number cards. Use the numbers 1 through 6. Instead of rolling the die, draw the top card from the facedown deck.

Directions

1. Each player draws four blank lines on a sheet of paper to record the numbers that come up on the rolls of the die.

   Player 1: ____ ____ ____ | ____
   Player 2: ____ ____ ____ | ____

2. Player 1 rolls the die and writes the number on any one of his or her four blanks. It does not have to be the first blank—it can be any of them. *Keep in mind that the larger number wins!*

3. Player 2 then rolls the die and writes the number on one of his or her blanks.

4. Players take turns rolling the die and writing the numbers three more times each.

5. Each player then uses the four numbers on his or her blanks to build a number.

   • Numbers on the first three blanks are the first three digits of the number the player builds.
   • The number on the fourth blank tells the number of zeros that come after the first three digits.

6. Each player reads his or her number. (See the place-value chart below.) The player with the larger number wins the round. The first player to win four rounds wins the game.

Hundred-Millions	Ten-Millions	Millions	,	Hundred-Thousands	Ten-Thousands	Thousands	,	Hundreds	Tens	Ones

EXAMPLE

First three digits   Number of zeros

Player 1: <u>1</u> <u>3</u> <u>2</u> | <u>6</u> = 132,000,000 (132 million)

Player 2: <u>3</u> <u>5</u> <u>6</u> | <u>4</u> =   3,560,000 (3 million, 560 thousand)

Player 1 wins.

High-Number Toss: Decimal Version

Materials   ☐ number cards 0–9 (4 of each)

   ☐ scorecard for each player

Players   2

Object of the game To make the largest number possible.

Directions

1. Each player makes a scorecard like the one shown at the right. Players fill out their own scorecards.

2. Shuffle the cards and place the deck facedown on the playing surface.

3. In each round:

   • Player 1 draws the top card from the deck and writes that number on any one of the three blanks on the scorecard. It need not be the first blank—it can be any of them.

   • Player 2 draws the next card from the deck and writes the number on one of his or her blanks.

   • Players take turns doing this two more times. The player with the larger number wins the round.

4. **Scoring** The winner's score for a round is the difference between the two players' scores. The loser scores 0 points for the round.

Game 1	
Round 1	Score
0. ___ ___ ___	_____
Round 2	
0. ___ ___ ___	_____
Round 3	
0. ___ ___ ___	_____
Round 4	
0. ___ ___ ___	_____
Total:	_____

EXAMPLE

Player 1: 0 . 6 5 4
Player 2: 0 . 7 5 3

Player 2 has the larger number and wins the round.

Since 0.753 − 0.654 = 0.099, Player 2 scores 0.099 points for the round. Player 1 scores 0 points.

5. Players take turns starting a round. At the end of four rounds, they find their total scores. The player with the larger total score wins the game.

Landmark Shark

Materials   ☐ 1 complete deck of number cards
                 ☐ 1 each of *range, median,* and *mode* Landmark
                     Shark Cards for each player (*Math Masters,* p. 4)
                 ☐ score sheet (*Math Masters,* p. 5)

Players   2 or 3

Object of the game To get the most points possible.

Directions

1. To play a round:
   - The dealer shuffles the number cards and deals five cards facedown to each player.
   - Each player puts his or her cards in order from the smallest number to the largest.
   - There are three ways to score points for the hand.

Range: The player's score is the range of the hand.

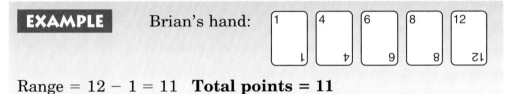

Range = 12 − 1 = 11   **Total points = 11**

Median: The player's score is the median of the hand.

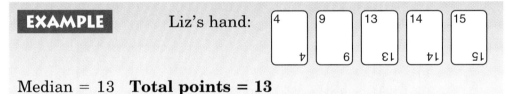

Median = 13   **Total points = 13**

Mode: The player must have at least two cards with the same number. The player's score is found by multiplying the mode of the hand by the number of modal cards. If there is more than one mode, the player uses the mode that will produce the most points.

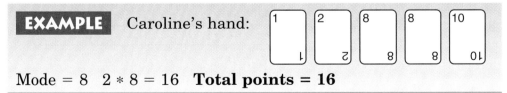

Mode = 8   2 ∗ 8 = 16   **Total points = 16**

2. Each player decides which landmark will yield the highest score for their hand. The player indicates the choice by placing one of the three landmark cards (range, median, or mode) on the table.

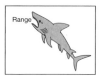

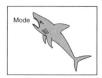

3. Players can try to improve their scores by exchanging up to three of their cards for new cards from the deck. However, the landmark card stays the same.

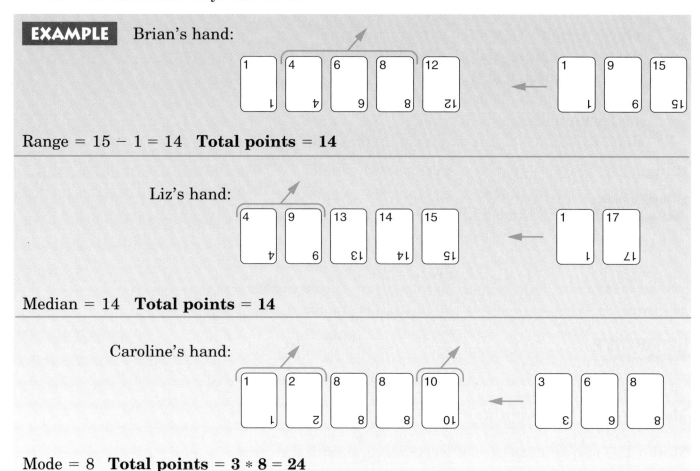

EXAMPLE   Brian's hand:

Range = 15 − 1 = 14   Total points = 14

Liz's hand:

Median = 14   Total points = 14

Caroline's hand:

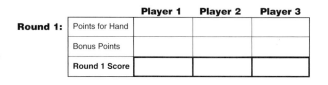

Mode = 8   Total points = 3 * 8 = 24

4. Players lay down their hands and record their scores on the score sheet.

5. **Bonus Points:** Each player calculates the *mean* of their cards to the nearest tenth. This value is then added to their score.

6. Repeat Steps 1–5 for each round. The winner is the player with the highest total after five rounds.

		Player 1	Player 2	Player 3
Round 1:	Points for Hand			
	Bonus Points			
	Round 1 Score			

Name That Number

Materials   ☐ 1 complete deck of number cards
Players   2 or 3

Object of the game To collect the most cards.

Directions

1. Shuffle the cards and deal five cards to each player. Place the remaining cards number-side down. Turn over the top card and place it beside the deck. This is the **target number** for the round.

2. Players try to match the target number by adding, subtracting, multiplying, or dividing the numbers on as many of their cards as possible. A card may only be used once.

3. Players write their solutions on a sheet of paper or a slate. When players have written their best solutions:

   - They set aside the cards they used to name the target number.
   - Replace them by drawing new cards from the top of the deck.
   - Put the old target number on the bottom of the deck.
   - Turn over a new target number, and play another hand.

4. Play continues until there are not enough cards left to replace all of the players' cards. The player who sets aside more cards wins the game.

EXAMPLE   Target number: 16

A player's cards:

Some possible solutions:

$$10 + 8 - 2 = 16 \text{ (three cards used)}$$

$$7 * 2 + 10 - 8 = 16 \text{ (four cards used)}$$

$$8 / 2 + 10 + 7 - 5 = 16 \text{ (all five cards used)}$$

The player sets aside the cards used to make a solution and draws the same number of cards from the top of the deck.

Polygon Capture

Materials   ☐ 1 set of *Polygon Capture* pieces
(*Math Masters*, p. 90)

☐ 1 set of *Polygon Capture* Property Cards
(*Math Masters*, p. 89)

Players   2 or two teams of 2

Object of the game To collect the most polygons.

Directions

1. Spread out the polygons on the playing surface. Shuffle the Property Cards and sort them facedown into ANGLE-card and SIDE-card piles. (The cards are labeled on the back.)

2. Players take turns doing the following:

   • Draw the top card from each pile of Property Cards.

> **EXAMPLE**   Liz has the cards "All angles are right angles" and "All sides are the same length." She may take all the squares (polygons A and H). Liz has "captured" these polygons.

   • Take all of the polygons that have both of the properties shown on the Property Cards.

   • If there are no polygons with both properties, draw one additional Property Card—either an ANGLE-card or a SIDE-card. Look for polygons that have this new property and one of the properties already drawn. Take these polygons.

   • At the end of a turn, if a player has not captured a polygon he or she could have taken, the other player can name and capture it.

3. When all the Property Cards have been drawn, shuffle the cards, and sort them again into two facedown piles. Continue playing.

4. The game ends when there are fewer than three polygons left.

5. The winner is the player with the most polygons.

There is only one right angle.	There are one or more right angles.	All angles are right angles.	There are no right angles.
There is at least one acute angle.	At least one angle is more than 90°.	All angles are right angles.	There are no right angles.
All opposite sides are parallel.	Only one pair of sides is parallel.	There are no parallel sides.	All sides are the same length.
All opposite sides are parallel.	Some sides have the same length.	All opposite sides have the same length.	**Wild Card:** Pick your own side property.

Scientific Notation Toss

Materials ☐ 2 six-sided dice
Players 2

Object of the game To create the largest number, written in scientific notation.

Directions

1. Each player rolls two dice. One number is used to name a power of 10, such as 10^2 or 10^4. The other number is used to multiply that power of 10.

EXAMPLES | A 5 and a 4 are rolled. | A 2 and a 3 are rolled.

Either $4 * 10^5$ or $5 * 10^4$ can be written. | Either $2 * 10^3$ or $3 * 10^2$ can be written.

2. Each player rolls the dice three times and writes each result in scientific notation.

3. Players convert their numbers from scientific notation to standard notation. Then they order the numbers from largest to smallest.

4. Players compare lists. The player who has the largest number wins. In case of a tie, they roll a fourth time.

EXAMPLE

Lisa   rolls: 2 and 4   5 and 3   1 and 6
           writes: $2 * 10^4$ $3 * 10^5$ $1 * 10^6$
                    $= 2 * 10,000$ $= 3 * 100,000$ $= 1 * 1,000,000$
                    $= 20,000$ $= 300,000$ $= 1,000,000$
           orders: 1,000,000,   300,000,   20,000

Luis   rolls: 5 and 5   2 and 1   4 and 3
           writes: $5 * 10^5$ $1 * 10^2$ $3 * 10^4$
                    $= 5 * 100,000$ $= 1 * 100$ $= 3 * 10,000$
                    $= 500,000$ $= 100$ $= 30,000$
           orders: 500,000,   30,000,   100

Lisa's highest number is greater than Luis's highest number. So Lisa wins.

Advanced Scientific Notation Toss

Use 2 twelve-sided dice or 4 six-sided dice. If you are using 4 dice, first add the results on pairs of dice. A dice roll of 11 and 9 can be either $9 * 10^{11}$ or $11 * 10^9$.

Solution Search

Materials ☐ 1 set of *Solution Search* cards
(*Math Masters*, p. 110)

☐ 1 complete deck of number cards

Players 3 or 4

Object of the game To discard all cards first.

$q + 2 > 20$	$m < 3.5$	$y^2 < 5$	$x > 9$
$b < 6$	$s \neq 5$	$100 / k > 25$	$(9 * z) + 2 > 65$
$49 \leq p^2$	$r / 2 \geq 5$	$w - 3 < 2$	$-2 + a \geq 5$
$\sqrt{25} \leq t$	$10 < 50 / d$	$c * 7 \leq 14$	$81 > f^2$

Directions

1. Shuffle the *Solution Search* cards and place them facedown in the center of the playing surface.

2. Shuffle the deck of playing cards and deal eight cards to each player. Place the remainder of the deck facedown in the center of the playing surface.

3. Player 1 begins the first round by turning over the top *Solution Search* card. For example, Player 1 may turn over $x > 9$. Player 1 then does one of the following:
   • Discards a card that is a solution to the inequality.
   • If Player 1 does not have a card that is a solution, he or she must continue to draw from the deck of number cards until a possible solution is drawn. Player 1 then discards this card.

4. Play continues in a clockwise direction. Each player must discard a solution card. The round is over when each player has had a turn.

5. Player 2 starts the next round by turning over the top *Solution Search* card. The round proceeds as above.

6. When a player completes a round, the player on his or her left starts the next round by turning over the top *Solution Search* card. The round proceeds as above.

7. When no more *Solution Search* cards remain, turn the pile facedown and, without shuffling, take the top *Solution Search* card.

8. The winner is the first player to discard all of his or her cards.

Variation: 2s and 7s are special cards: 2s are WILD. A player may choose to play a 2 card with its given value of 2, or a player may assign any value he or she wishes to the 2 card. The value of the 7 card is always 7. However, if a player plays the 7 card, the next player loses his or her turn.

Spoon Scramble

Materials ☐ one set of 32 *Spoon Scramble* Cards
(*Math Journal 1,* Activity Sheets 1 and 2)
☐ 3 spoons

Players 4

Object of the game To avoid getting all the letters in
the word *SPOONS.*

Directions

1. Place the spoons in the center of the table.
2. One player is the dealer. The dealer shuffles
   and deals four cards facedown to each player.
3. Players look at their cards. If a player has four
   cards of equal value, proceed to Step 5 below.
   Otherwise, each player chooses a card to discard
   and passes it, facedown, to the player on the left.
4. Each player picks up the new card and repeats
   Step 3. The passing of the cards should proceed as
   quickly as possible.
5. As soon as a player has four cards of equal value, the
   player places the cards faceup on the table and grabs
   a spoon.
6. The other players then try to grab one of the
   remaining spoons. The player left without a spoon in
   each round is assigned a letter from the word
   SPOONS, starting with the first letter. If a player
   incorrectly claims to have four cards of equal value,
   that player receives a letter instead of the player
   left without a spoon.
7. Players put the spoons back in the center of the table.
   The dealer shuffles and deals the cards. A new round begins. (Step 3 above.)
8. Play continues until three players get all the letters in the
   word *SPOONS.* The player who does not have all the letters is the winner.

Variations

- For three players: Eliminate one set of four equivalent *Spoon
  Scramble* Cards. Use only two spoons.
- Players can make their own deck of *Spoon Scramble* Cards.
  Each player writes four computation problems with equivalent
  answers on four index cards. Check to be sure the players
  have all chosen different values.

$\frac{1}{7}$ of 42	$\frac{24}{4} * \frac{5}{5}$	$\frac{54}{9}$	$2\frac{16}{4}$
$\frac{1}{5}$ of 35	$\frac{21}{3} * \frac{4}{4}$	$\frac{56}{8}$	$4\frac{36}{12}$
$\frac{1}{8}$ of 64	$\frac{48}{6} * \frac{3}{3}$	$\frac{32}{4}$	$3\frac{25}{5}$
$\frac{1}{4}$ of 36	$\frac{63}{7} * \frac{6}{6}$	$\frac{72}{8}$	$5\frac{32}{8}$

$1 \div 2$	$\frac{35}{70}$	$\frac{1}{8} * 4$	0.5
$\frac{1}{3}$	$\frac{1}{6} * 2$	$33\frac{1}{3}\%$	$\frac{1}{2} - \frac{1}{6}$
$\frac{26}{13}$	$(\frac{6}{9} * \frac{9}{6}) * 2$	2	$4 * \frac{1}{2}$
$\frac{3}{4}$	$\frac{600}{800}$	0.75	$3 \div 4$

Spreadsheet Scramble

Materials □ *Spreadsheet Scramble* Game Mat (*Math Masters,* p. 39)

Players   2

Object of the game To get the most points.

Directions

1. Player 1 uses the positive numbers 1, 2, 3, 4, 5, and 6. Player 2 uses the negative numbers −1, −2, −3, −4, −5, and −6.

2. Player 1 begins the game. Players take turns writing one of their numbers in a cell within the 4-by-3 rectangle outlined on the spreadsheet. Once a player has written a number, it cannot be used again.

	A	B	C	D	E	F
1						Total
2						
3						
4						
5	Total					

3. After all 12 numbers have been used, fill in Total cells F2, F3, and F4 by adding each row across. For example, F2 = B2 + C2 + D2 + E2. Fill in Total cells B5, C5, D5, and E5 by adding each column down. For example, C5 = C2 + C3 + C4.

4. Seven cells show row and column totals: F2, F3, F4, B5, C5, D5, and E5. Player 1 gets one point for each cell that contains a positive number. Player 2 gets one point for each cell that contains a negative number. Neither player gets a point for 0. The player with more points wins.

EXAMPLES

Game 1:

Player 1 gets 1 point each for cells F3, F4, and C5.

Player 2 gets 1 point each for F2 and E5.

Player 1 wins the game, 3 points to 2 points.

	A	B	C	D	E	F
1						Total
2		−1	−6	3	−5	−9
3		4	2	−4	6	+8
4		−3	5	1	−2	+1
5	Total	0	+1	0	−1	

Game 2:

Player 1 gets 1 point each for F2, F4, and C5.

Player 2 gets 1 point each for F3, B5, and E5.

The game is a tie, 3 points to 3 points.

	A	B	C	D	E	F
1						Total
2		−4	6	4	−5	+1
3		−1	−3	−6	−2	−12
4		3	5	2	1	+11
5	Total	−2	+8	0	−6	

3-D Shape Sort

Materials   ☐ 1 set of 12 Shape Cards
(*Math Masters*, p. 163)

☐ 1 set of 16 Property Cards
(*Math Masters*, p. 164)

Players   2, or two teams of 2

Object of the game To collect the most Shape Cards.

Directions

1. Spread out the Shape Cards faceup on the playing surface. Shuffle the Property Cards and sort them into VERTEX/EDGE-card and SURFACE-card piles.

2. Players take turns doing the following:

   • Draw the top card from each pile of Property Cards.

   • Take all the Shape Cards that have both of the properties shown on the Property Cards.

   • If there are no Shape Cards with both properties, draw one additional Property Card—either a VERTEX/EDGE Card or a SURFACE Card. Look for Shape Cards that have the new property and one of the properties drawn before. Take those Shape Cards.

   • When all the Property Cards have been drawn, shuffle the deck, and sort them again into two facedown piles. Continue playing.

   • At the end of a turn, if a player has not taken a Shape Card he or she could have taken, the other player may take it.

3. The game ends when there are fewer than three Shape Cards left. The winner is the player with the most Shape Cards.

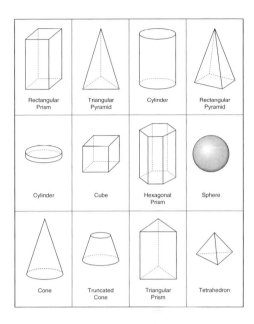

Rectangular Prism	Triangular Pyramid	Cylinder	Rectangular Pyramid
Cylinder	Cube	Hexagonal Prism	Sphere
Cone	Truncated Cone	Triangular Prism	Tetrahedron

I have an even number of vertices.	I have no vertices.	I have at least 2 edges that are parallel to each other.	I have an odd number of edges.
One of my vertices is formed by an even number of edges.	I have at least one curved edge.	I have fewer than 6 vertices.	I have at least 2 edges that are perpendicular to each other.
All of my surfaces are polygons.	I have at least one face (flat surface).	I have at least one curved surface.	All of my faces are triangles.
All of my faces are regular polygons.	At least one of my faces is a circle.	I have at least one pair of faces that are parallel to each other.	**Wild Card:** Pick your own surface property.

Top-It Games

The materials, number of players, and object of the game are the same for all games described below.

Materials ☐ number cards 1–10 (4 of each)
☐ calculator (optional)

Players 2 to 4

Object of the game To collect the most cards.

Addition Top-It
Directions

1. Shuffle the cards and place the deck number-side down.

2. Each player turns over two cards and calls out the sum of the numbers. The player with the highest sum takes all the cards. In case of a tie for the highest sum, each tied player turns over two more cards and calls out the sum. The player with the highest sum takes all the cards from both plays.

3. Check answers using an Addition Table or a calculator.

4. Play ends when not enough cards are left for each player to have another turn.

5. The player who took the most cards wins.

Variation: Each player turns over three cards and finds their sum.

Advanced Version Use only the number cards 1–9. Each player turns over four cards, forms two 2-digit numbers, and finds the sum. Players should carefully consider how they form their numbers since different arrangements have different sums. For example, 74 + 52 has a greater sum than 25 + 47.

Subtraction Top-It
Directions

1. Each player turns over three cards, finds the sum of any two of the numbers, then finds the difference between the sum and the third number.

2. The player with the largest difference takes all the cards.

EXAMPLE   A 4, an 8, and a 3 are turned over. There are three ways to form the numbers. Always subtract the smaller number from the larger one.

$4 + 8 = 12$ or	$3 + 8 = 11$ or	$3 + 4 = 7$
$12 - 3 = 9$	$11 - 4 = 7$	$8 - 7 = 1$

Advanced Version Use only the number cards 1–9. Each player turns over four cards, forms two 2-digit numbers, and finds their difference. Players should carefully consider how they form their numbers. For example, $75 - 24$ has a greater difference than $57 - 42$.

Multiplication Top-It
Directions

1. The rules are the same as for *Addition Top-It*, except that players find the product of the numbers instead of the sum.

2. The player with the largest product takes all the cards. Answers can be checked with a Multiplication Table or a calculator.

Variation: Use only the number cards 1–9. Each player turns over three cards, forms a 2-digit number, then multiplies the 2-digit number by the remaining number.

Division Top-It
Directions

1. Use only the number cards 1–9. Each player turns over three cards and uses them to generate division problems as follows:
   • Choose two cards to form the dividend.
   • Use the remaining card as the divisor.
   • Divide and drop the remainder.

2. The player with the largest quotient takes all the cards.

Advanced Version Use only the number cards 1–9. Each player turns over four cards, chooses three of them to form a 3-digit number, then divides the 3-digit number by the remaining number. Players should carefully consider how they form their 3-digit numbers. For example, $462 / 5$ is greater than $256 / 4$.

Top-It Games with Positive and Negative Numbers

Materials □ 1 complete deck of number cards
□ calculator (optional)

Players   2 to 4

Object of the game To collect the most cards.

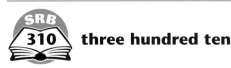

NOTE

Black cards (spades and clubs) are *positive numbers*.

Red cards (hearts and diamonds) or blue cards (Everything Math Deck) are *negative numbers*.

Addition Top-It with Positive and Negative Numbers
Directions

1. Shuffle the cards and place the deck number-side down.

2. Each player turns over two cards and calls out their sum. The player with the highest sum takes all the cards. In case of a tie, each tied player turns over two more cards and calls out the sum. The player with the highest sum takes all the cards from both plays. If necessary, check answers with a calculator.

3. Play continues until there are too few cards left for each player to have another turn. The player who took the most cards wins.

EXAMPLE   Lindsey turns over a red 5 and a black 7. $-5 + 7 = 2$

Fred turns over a red 3 and a red 4. $-3 + (-4) = -7$

Lindsey takes all four cards because 2 is greater than -7.

Variation: Each player turns over three cards and finds the sum.

Subtraction Top-It with Positive and Negative Numbers
Directions

1. The rules are the same as above except that players find differences instead of sums.

2. Each player turns over two cards, one at a time, and subtracts the second number from the first number. The player with the highest answer takes all the cards.

EXAMPLE   Lindsey turns over a black 2 first, then a red 3. $+2 - (-3) = 5$

Fred turns over a red 5 first, then a black 8. $-5 - (+8) = -13$

Lindsey takes all four cards because 5 is greater than -13.

Art & Design Activities

Perspective Drawing

Drawings are often used to represent real or imagined objects. Which of the drawings below do you think represents a cube?

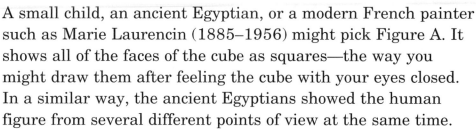

A small child, an ancient Egyptian, or a modern French painter such as Marie Laurencin (1885–1956) might pick Figure A. It shows all of the faces of the cube as squares—the way you might draw them after feeling the cube with your eyes closed. In a similar way, the ancient Egyptians showed the human figure from several different points of view at the same time.

Greek and Roman artists experimented with ways of making pictures that would resemble the way we actually see an object. Philosophers discussed how vision might be explained with geometry. They noticed several features of human sight:

- An object moving away from the viewer appears to get smaller.

- Parallel lines moving away from the viewer seem to get closer.

After the Roman period, European artists returned to a flat style of painting. When they did try to show depth, they often made a drawing like Figure B above to represent a cube.

In the late Middle Ages, artists and scholars rediscovered the writings of the Greek philosophers and mathematicians. They also began their own experiments with representing 3-dimensional space. Their first attempts looked something like Figures C and D.

During the next hundred years, many artists, especially those in Italy, experimented with these ideas. They created more and more realistic images. In 1425, architect and engineer Filippo Brunelleschi (1377–1446) demonstrated what is now known as geometric **perspective** (also called linear perspective or Renaissance perspective). This system uses geometry to produce an illusion of depth, as if the flat surface of a painting were a window looking onto a 3-dimensional scene.

Each part of the body was drawn from the direction that would make it most recognizable. The head, arms, and legs were drawn in profile (from the side); while the shoulders and chest were shown from the front.

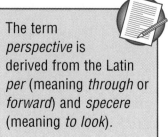

The term *perspective* is derived from the Latin *per* (meaning *through* or *forward*) and *specere* (meaning *to look*).

Brunelleschi discovered that to create a convincing illusion of three dimensions, objects should be drawn smaller the farther away they are from the viewer. Parallel lines moving away from the viewer should meet at a common point, which came to be called the **vanishing point.** Figure E on page 312 shows a cube drawn using this system. Later artists perfected a system using two vanishing points, as shown in Figure F on page 312.

In 1435, architect Leon Battista Alberti (1404–1472) wrote a book about painting that included detailed rules of perspective. Leonardo da Vinci (1452–1519) also experimented with perspective. Dissatisfied with Alberti's rules, he worked on a system of "natural" perspective that came closer to human vision. In his system, shapes were projected onto a curved surface, like the retina of the human eye, rather than onto the flat surface of a painting. These investigations and others that followed led to a branch of mathematics known as **projective geometry.**

The painting at the left above was made in the twelfth century. There is no illusion of depth. The ships in the distance (at the top of the painting) are the same size as the ones in the foreground (at the bottom of the painting).

The painting at the right above, *A View of the Grand Canal*, by Canaletto (1697–1768), shows a similar subject, this time using the rules of perspective to create an illusion of three dimensions. The building and ships in the foreground are larger than those in the background. The lines in the buildings meet at a vanishing point (at the middle-right side of the painting).

When German artist Albrecht Dürer (1471–1528) visited Italy, he was exposed to new ideas circulating among artists and scholars. He later wrote a manual on painting that included the woodcut below. It shows an easy way to make a drawing with correct perspective. (Some of Dürer's best-known works are woodcuts, a type of print that is made in the same way as designs printed with a rubber stamp.)

The artist looks through a grid made of threads set in a wooden frame. He copies what he sees onto a similar grid on paper. The object directly in front of the artist helps him keep his eye in the same position at all times.

Return to the question asked earlier: Which of the drawings below do you think represents a cube?

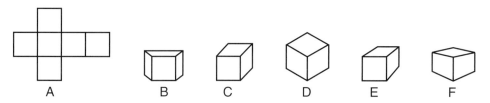

After reading the previous pages, your answer may be "They all do." Depending on your personal taste or how you want to use a drawing, any one of the above may be the "best" representation of a cube.

If you are interested in learning more about perspective drawing, look in an encyclopedia under topic headings such as *Mechanical Drawing, Greek Art, Human Perception, Medieval Art, Perspective, Projection, Projective Geometry, Renaissance Art,* and *Roman Art.*

Drawing a Rectangular Solid

Follow these steps to draw a rectangular solid or box.

Step 1: Draw a horizontal line segment as the horizon line. Mark a point on the horizon line to be the vanishing point.

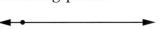

Step 2: Use your Geometry Template to draw a rectangle in front of the horizon line. This will be the front face of the box.

Step 3: Draw line segments from the four vertices of the rectangle to the vanishing point. These are called **vanishing lines.**

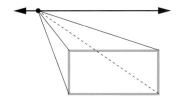

Step 4: Draw a line segment for the edge at the back of the box, parallel to the top edge of the front.

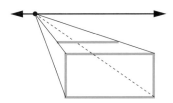

Step 5: Complete the top face of the box.

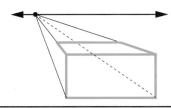

Step 6: Draw a side edge for the back of the box, parallel to the side edge of the front.

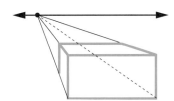

Step 7: Complete the side face of the box.

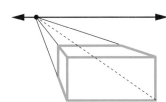

Drawing a Person

Materials
☐ piece of cardboard measuring at least $8\frac{1}{2}$ inches by 11 inches

☐ transparency with a 7-inch square grid (from your teacher)

☐ masking or transparent tape

☐ scissors

☐ Geometry Template

☐ dark-colored transparency marker

Directions

Step 1: Near the top of the piece of cardboard, draw a square with sides that are 6 inches long. Draw it so that its sides are at least 1 inch from the sides of the cardboard.

Step 2: Cut out the square, leaving a 6-inch "window" in the cardboard.

Step 3: Cut out the grid from the transparency. Be sure to cut along the dashed line segments as indicated. You will get a square piece about 7 inches on a side.

Step 4: Tape the grid to the cardboard so that it completely covers the cardboard window.

Step 5: Tape the bottom of the cardboard to a chair back so that the window is above the chair.

Step 6: Make a perspective drawing of your partner.

Your partner sits in a chair with his or her legs on a desk or tabletop.

Place the chair with the attached cardboard 3 to 4 feet in front of your partner's feet.

Sit or kneel and look at your partner through the grid in the window. Adjust your distance away from the window. Your partner should be completely visible (except for the part that is below the desk or tabletop) and should fill up most of the window.

Try to keep your head in the same position while drawing your partner's picture. Use the transparency marker to trace an outline of your partner on the plastic window.

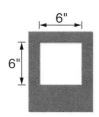

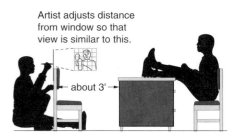

Artist adjusts distance from window so that view is similar to this.

about 3'

Drawing an Enlargement of a Picture

Use the following procedure to draw an enlargement.

Materials
- ☐ a picture with simple shapes and lines, such as a comic-strip character
- ☐ 1-inch grid paper
- ☐ sharp pencil with eraser
- ☐ colored pencils, markers, or crayons

Directions

Step 1: Use a ruler and pencil to draw a grid pattern of $\frac{1}{2}$-inch squares onto the picture you chose.

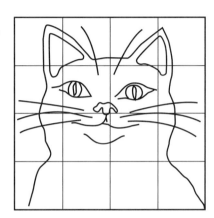

Step 2: Copy the part of the original picture in each grid square onto the corresponding grid square of the 1-inch grid. Notice where each line and shape begins and ends on the original grid, and locate its relative position on the 1-inch grid.

Try to reproduce all of the lines and shapes as accurately as you can. This method of drawing a copy is called **sighting.**

(Depending on the size of the picture you choose, you may need to tape several pieces of 1-inch grid paper together to create your enlargement.)

Step 3: After you complete the drawing in pencil, you may want to add color to fill in shapes or darken lines.

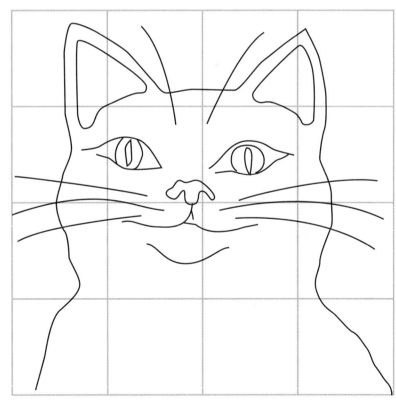

If you follow this procedure, you will draw a 2X enlargement of the original picture. Each $\frac{1}{2}$-inch length will be doubled. The size-change factor depends on the size of the grid squares on the original picture and the size of the grid onto which you make your drawing.

The Golden Ratio

Which of the following rectangles do you like best?

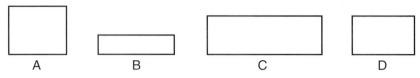

A   B   C   D

It has been shown that Rectangle D, called the **Golden Rectangle,** is chosen more often than any other rectangle. In a Golden Rectangle, the ratio of the length of the longer side to the length of the shorter side is about 1.618 to 1. This ratio is known as the **Golden Ratio.**

The popularity of the Golden Ratio dates back to the ancient Greeks who used it in many of their works of art and architecture. For example, the front of the Parthenon in Athens fits almost exactly into a Golden Rectangle.

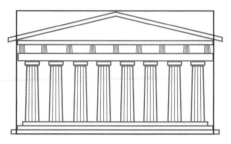

The Parthenon in Athens, Greece

The symbol for the Golden Ratio is the Greek letter ϕ (pronounced "phi"), perhaps chosen for the name of the famous Athenian sculptor Phidias (about 490–430 B.C.).

Throughout the ages, many artists have found that they could create a feeling of order in their works by using the Golden Ratio. For example, in the picture of St. Jerome, painted about the year 1483 by Leonardo da Vinci, the figure of St. Jerome fits perfectly into a Golden Rectangle. It is believed that this was not just a coincidence, but that da Vinci used the Golden Ratio because of his great interest in mathematics.

St. Jerome **by Leonardo da Vinci**

The mask shown at the right was made in the Benin Kingdom in western Africa in the early sixteenth century. It was worn by the Oba, which means "king." The Oba was a sacred figure, and many ceremonies took place in his honor. If you measure the sides of the rectangles that frame some of the features in the mask, you will find that the ratio of the length of the longer side to the length of the shorter side is the Golden Ratio, about 1.618 to 1. Notice also that the mask is perfectly symmetric.

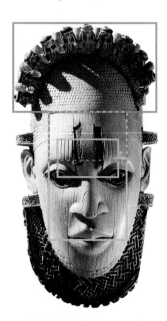

West African mask

A Classical Face

The Golden Ratio can be found in many of the sculptures that were made during the classical period of Greek art (about 480–350 B.C.). The picture at the right is a good example of a "classical Greek" face. It shows a sculpture of the head of the Greek goddess Hera. According to Greek mythology, Hera was queen of the Olympian gods and the wife of the god Zeus. The sculpture was found in a temple in Argos, a city of which Hera was a patron. It was probably completed about 420 B.C. The sculpture is currently owned by the National Museum in Athens.

Nine different parts of the face are indicated on the picture shown below. By measuring various parts of the face, you will find many examples of the Golden Ratio in the sculpture.

a = total width of head (including hair)

b = top of hair to pupils

c = top of eye to bottom of chin

d = top of hair to bottom of chin

e = distance from ear to ear

f = peak of hairline to bottom of chin

g = distance between outsides of eyes

h = pupil to chin

i = from inside of one eye to inside of other eye

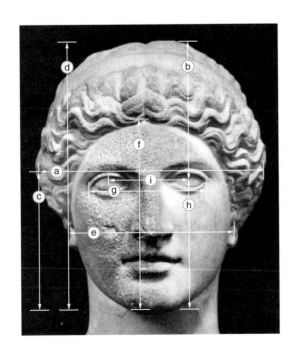

Constructing a Golden Rectangle

Step 1: Draw a square *ABCD* on grid paper.

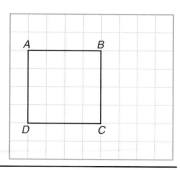

Step 2: Draw $\overline{EF}$ to divide the square in half.

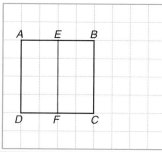

Step 3: Draw the diagonal $\overline{FB}$. Extend $\overline{DC}$.

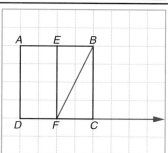

Step 4: Use your compass to draw an arc from point *F* through point *B* that intersects $\overrightarrow{DC}$ at point *G*. (Place the compass point on point *F* and the pencil point on point *B*. Draw the arc.)

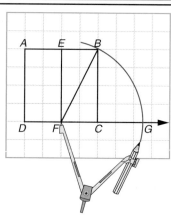

Step 5: Extend $\overline{AB}$. Draw a line segment perpendicular to $\overrightarrow{DC}$ at point *G* and intersecting the extension of $\overline{AB}$ at point *H*.

Rectangle *AHGD* is a Golden Rectangle.

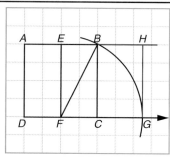

Rotation Symmetry
A Point-Symmetry Magic Trick

Setting the Stage Tell a friend that you will be able to guess which playing card, from a set of four, she or he turns upside down while you are not looking.

Materials ☐ four cards from a regular deck of playing cards:
- 1 card with point symmetry
- 3 cards without point symmetry

Performing the Trick

Step 1: Place the four playing cards in a row, faceup. Of the cards shown at the right, only the 10 of hearts has point symmetry. The other three cards do not.

Step 2: Turn your back to the four cards, but be sure to study the position of the figures on the cards before you do. Tell your friend to rotate one of the cards 180 degrees (turn it upside down).

Step 3: Turn around, study the cards, and tell which card your friend turned. If your friend has turned one of the three cards without point symmetry, it will be easy to determine that it was rotated. For example:

The middle spade is now pointing toward the bottom of the card.	The middle diamond is now at the bottom of the card.	The stem of the middle club is now pointing toward the bottom of the card.
original 180° position rotation	original 180° position rotation	original 180° position rotation

If none of the cards without point symmetry has been rotated, then the one card with point symmetry must have been rotated.

This may seem like a simple trick, but that's because you know how it works. Many cards look almost the same before and after they have been rotated 180°.

Drawing Shapes with Rotation Symmetry of a Given Order

Materials
☐ sharp pencil
☐ blank piece of paper
☐ protractor
☐ compass
☐ scissors
☐ index card
　 or other card stock

Directions

Step 1: On a blank piece of paper, use a sharp pencil to *lightly* draw three rays coming from one point. The rays should be separated by 120°, forming three 120° angles.

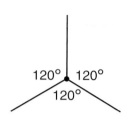

Step 2: Cut out any shape you wish from an index card. The first time that you try this activity, you might want to work with a simple shape. Once you have learned the procedure, you could try a more complicated shape.

Step 3: Draw a line anywhere through the shape.

Step 4: Push the point of your compass through the shape at any point along the line that you drew. Place the compass point on the paper with the three rays at the point where the rays intersect. Match the line on the shape with one of the rays.

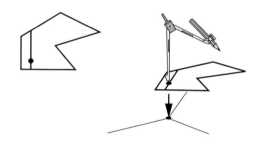

Step 5: When the shape is lined up properly, remove the compass. Hold the shape in place, and trace around it. Replace the compass point, and use it to rotate the shape so that the line on the shape matches up with the next ray. Remove the compass, and trace around the shape. Repeat the procedure for the third ray.

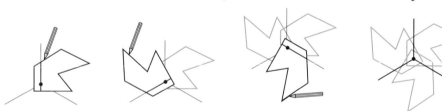

Step 6: Erase any interior lines. The outer edges of the three tracings form a shape with rotation symmetry of order 3. You might want to use tracing paper to copy your shape and check if it is symmetric.

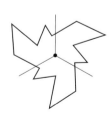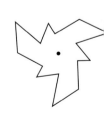

Use this procedure to create a shape with a rotation symmetry of order 2. Then create a shape with a rotation symmetry of order 5.

Tessellations

A **tessellation** is a pattern of shapes that completely covers a surface.

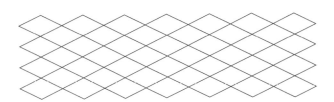

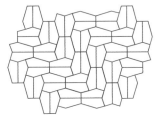

- The shapes in a tessellation do not overlap.

overlap

gap

- There are no gaps between the shapes.

A **vertex point** of a tessellation is a point where vertices of the shapes meet.

- The sum of the measures of the angles around a vertex point must be exactly 360°.

vertex point

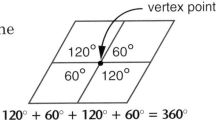

$120° + 60° + 120° + 60° = 360°$

- If the sum is less than 360°, there will be gaps between the shapes. The pattern is *not* a tessellation.

- If the sum is greater than 360°, the shapes will overlap. The pattern is *not* a tessellation.

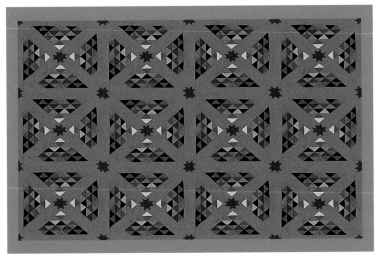

Many quilt designs use tessellation. The smaller triangles in the quilt at the left are tessellated.

three hundred twenty-three

SRB
323

Regular Tessellations

A tessellation that is made by repeating a single shape is called a **regular tessellation** if the shape used is a regular polygon.

For example, a regular tessellation can be made up of squares, regular hexagons, or equilateral triangles.

4.4.4.4

6.6.6

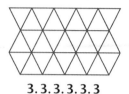

3.3.3.3.3.3

Regular tessellations are named by giving the number of sides of the polygons that meet at a vertex point. The numbers are separated by periods. For example, the name of the hexagon tessellation above is 6.6.6 because there are three 6-sided polygons around each vertex.

Semiregular Tessellations

Tessellations may involve more than one type of shape. (See at the right.) A tessellation is called a **semiregular tessellation** if it satisfies these conditions:

- It uses at least two different shapes.

- The shapes used are regular polygons.

- The same combination of regular polygons meets in the same order at each vertex.

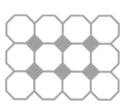

4.8.8

There are eight different semiregular tessellations. The octagon-square tessellation shown at the right is semiregular. Other semiregular tessellations are shown below.

Semiregular tessellations are named by listing the number of sides of the polygons around each vertex. You start with the polygon with the least number of sides and then list the number of sides of each polygon as you move clockwise around the vertex. The name of the octagon-square tessellation in the margin above is 4.8.8.

3.4.6.4

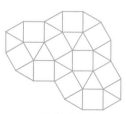

3.12.12

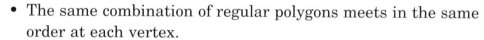

3.3.4.3.4

Escher Translation Tessellations

The graphic artist M. C. Escher (Maurits Cornelius Escher) was born on June 17, 1898, in Leeuwarden, a small town in the Netherlands. He became famous for his drawings that combined realistic details with optical illusions and distorted perspectives. The drawing at the right, *Hand with Reflecting Sphere,* is a self-portrait of Escher.

In 1936, Escher visited the Alhambra, a Moorish palace in Spain that was built in the thirteenth and fourteenth centuries. He was fascinated by the beautiful tiling patterns created from simple geometric shapes that covered the floors and walls. Escher was inspired by these intricate designs to create tessellations such as those at the bottom of this page.

Unlike the Islamic artists who decorated the Alhambra, Escher did not limit himself to purely geometric designs. He built tessellations from representations of objects such as birds, fish, reptiles, and humans. Escher used translations (slides), reflections (flips), and rotations (turns) to create unusual and fantastic designs.

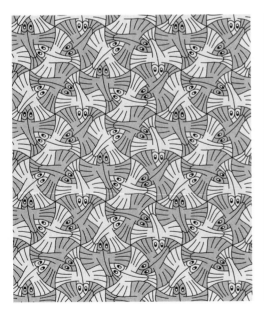

Creating an Escher-Type Translation Tessellation

Materials
- ☐ sharp pencil
- ☐ scissors
- ☐ markers, crayons, or colored pencils
- ☐ 3-inch by 3-inch square cut from card stock (such as an index card)
- ☐ tape
- ☐ large piece of white construction paper

Directions

Step 1: To create a template for your **translation tessellation,** begin with a 3-inch by 3-inch square of card stock.

Step 2: Draw a curve from point A to point B.

Step 3: Use scissors to cut along curve AB. Tape the cut-out edge of the square so that point A lines up with point D and point B lines up with point C.

Step 4: Draw a curve from point A to point D.

Step 5: Use scissors to cut along curve AD. Tape the cut-out edge of the square so that point A lines up with point B and point D lines up with point C.

Step 6: You now have a template for your tessellation. Begin by tracing your template onto the *center* of the construction paper. Continue tracing, interlocking each new tracing with the previous tracing, until you have filled the entire sheet.

Step 7: Use markers, crayons, or colored pencils to decorate your design.

M. C. Escher worked hard to create shapes that not only tessellated but also looked like birds, reptiles, insects, and other familiar objects. You may want to repeat Steps 1 to 5 several times until you create a recognizable shape.

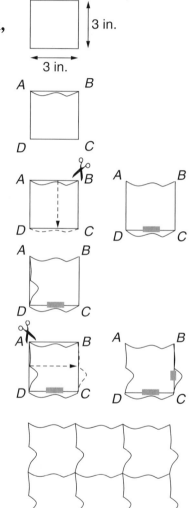

Constructing and Experimenting with Möbius Strips

*A mathematician confided
That a Möbius band is one-sided.
And you'll get quite a laugh,
If you cut one in half,
For it stays in one piece when divided.*

The above limerick was inspired by the work of August Ferdinand Möbius (1790–1868), a German mathematician and astronomer. Möbius examined the properties of one-sided surfaces. One such surface, easily made from a strip of paper, became known as a **Möbius strip,** or **Möbius band.** Möbius strips are studied in the branch of mathematics known as **topology.**

You may think that Möbius strips would only interest mathematicians and magicians. However, they also have practical uses. For example, Möbius strips have been used in the design of drive belts, such as fan belts and conveyor belts.

Friction would wear out an ordinary two-sided belt more quickly on the inside than on the outside. If a belt with a half-twist (a Möbius strip) is used, it wears more evenly and slowly because it has only one side.

Möbius strips are also recognized for their artistic properties. The artist M. C. Escher was intrigued not only by tessellations but also by Möbius strips. In his work *Möbius Strip II*, he depicts nine red ants endlessly crawling along a Möbius strip.

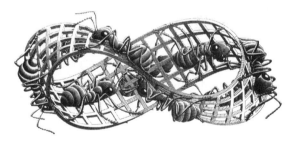

Construct a Möbius strip. Cut a strip of newspaper about $1\frac{1}{2}$ inches wide and as long as possible. Turn over one end of the strip (give one end a half-twist), and tape the two ends together to form a loop.

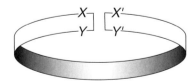

Now, poke your scissors through the paper, and cut the strip lengthwise all the way around. What happens? Is the limerick at the top of the page correct?

Designing a Paper Airplane
The First International Paper Airplane Competition

The First International Paper Airplane Competition was held during the winter of 1966–1967 and was sponsored by *Scientific American* magazine. The 11,851 entries (including an estimated 5,000 from children), from 28 different countries, were original designs for paper airplanes. These paper airplanes were entered into one or more of the following categories:

- duration aloft (The winning designs spent 9.9 and 10.2 seconds in the air.)
- distance flown (The winning designs flew 58 feet 2 inches and 91 feet 6 inches.)
- aerobatics (stunts performed in flight)
- origami (the traditional Japanese art or technique of folding paper into a variety of decorative or representational forms)

Contestants were permitted to use paper of any weight and size. The smallest entry received, entered in the distance category, measured 0.08 inch by 0.00003 inch. However, this entry was found to be made of foil, not paper. The largest entry received, also entered in the distance category, was 11 feet long. It flew two times its length when tested.

Scientific American awarded winners' trophies to two designers, a nonprofessional and a professional, in each category. Nonprofessionals were people not professionally involved in air travel. Professionals were "people employed in the air travel business and people who build nonpaper airplanes." Each winner received a trophy called *The Leonardo,* named after Leonardo da Vinci (1452–1519), whom *Scientific American* refers to as the "Patron Saint of Paper Airplanes."

Da Vinci, known for many accomplishments in the fields of painting and sculpture, was also an architect, engineer, and inventive builder. Studying the flight of birds, da Vinci believed that it would be possible to build a flying machine that would enable humans to soar through the air. He designed several wing-flapping machines; suggested the use of rotating wings similar to those of the modern helicopter; and invented the "air screw," similar to the modern propeller, to pull a machine through the air.

NOTE

More information about the First International Paper Airplane Competition, as well as templates and directions for making each of the winning designs, can be found in *The Great International Paper Airplane Book,* by Jerry Mander, George Dippel, and Howard Luck Gossage; Simon and Schuster Publishing, 1971.

The Leonardo

Leonardo da Vinci

A Winning Paper Airplane Design

The design plan shown below was submitted by Louis W. Schultz, an engineer. Schultz's paper airplane flew 58 feet 2 inches and was a winner in the distance category for nonprofessionals. The professional winner in the distance category was Robert Meuser. His paper airplane flew 91 feet 6 inches before it hit the rear wall of the testing site.

1. Follow the directions below to make an accurate copy of the design plan on an $8\frac{1}{2}$-inch by 11-inch sheet of paper.

   a. Use a ruler to find the midpoints at the top and bottom of the paper. Mark these points. Draw a line connecting the midpoints.

   b. Mark two points that are $\frac{1}{4}$ inch away from the midpoint at the top of the paper.

   c. Use a protractor to make two 45° angles as shown.

   d. Use a protractor to make two 82° angles as shown.

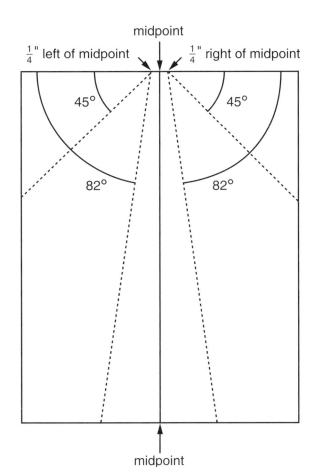

Louis W. Schultz's paper airplane design plan

2. Assemble the paper airplane as shown below. Be very careful to make precise folds. Make the folds on a table. When making a fold, first press down on the paper with your finger. Then, go over this fold with a pen or a ruler on its side. **Do not** use your fingernails to make folds.

a. Fold the paper back and forth along the center line to make a sharp crease. Then unfold.

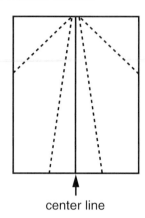

center line

b. Fold corners along the dashed lines as shown. Use a small piece of tape to secure each corner as shown in the sketch.

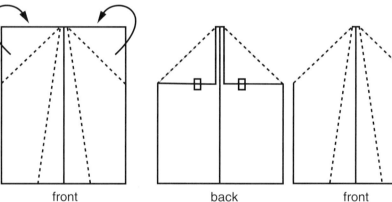

front　　　　　　back　　　　　　front

c. With the back of the paper facing you, fold the right side of the paper toward the center so that the edges highlighted in the sketch meet. Use a small piece of tape to secure the flap in the position shown in the sketch. Do the same to the other side.

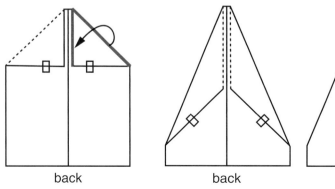

back　　　　　　back　　　　　　front

d. Flip the paper to the front side. Fold in half along the center line so that the front side is now in the inside. Your paper airplane should now look like this:

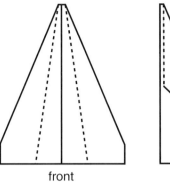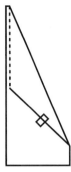

front

e. Take the top flap of the paper, and fold it outward along the dashed lines. (Look for these dashed lines on the inside of the plane.) Do the same to the other flap. Your paper airplane should now look like this:

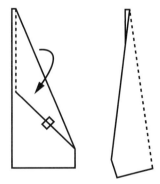

f. First, tape the wings together on top of the airplane. Then, tape the bottom as shown, making sure that all loose flaps are secured.

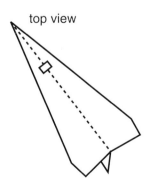

top view

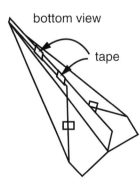

bottom view

tape

Air is a real substance, just as water, earth, and maple syrup are real substances. Because air is a substance, it offers **resistance,** or opposition, to the movement of objects through it.

Imagine dropping a penny into a bottle of maple syrup. The penny will eventually fall to the bottom of the bottle, but the maple syrup will slow its progress; the maple syrup offers resistance to the movement of the penny. Air works in much the same way; objects can move through it, but the air offers resistance to the movement of those objects.

Did you know that this resistance can serve a helpful purpose? Try the following experiments to see how resistance can be used to help an object, such as an airplane, move through the air more efficiently.

The "Kite Effect"

- Hold one end of an $8\frac{1}{2}$-inch by 11-inch sheet of paper as illustrated—forefinger on top, supported by the thumb and second finger on the bottom. Notice that the paper in the illustration is tilted slightly so that the opposite end of the paper is a bit higher than the end you are holding.

- *Push* the paper directly forward as illustrated.

You will notice that the end of the paper that is opposite the end you are holding tilts up. When the tilted surface of the paper pushes against the air, the air pushes back. This partially slows the paper down and partially lifts it up.

The sheet of paper has some of the characteristics of an airplane wing. The wing of an airplane is set at an angle so that its front edge is higher than its back edge. In this way, the lower surface of the airplane wing uses the air resistance to achieve a small amount of lift.

The "Vacuum Effect"

- Hold the small end of a 2-inch by 6-inch strip of paper between your thumb and forefinger as illustrated— thumb on top. The paper should fall forward in a curve.

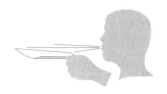

- Blow over the top of the paper as illustrated.

As you blow over the top of the paper, you will notice that the end of the paper that is opposite the end you are holding tilts up. Air rushing over the upper surface of the paper causes the air pressure on the upper surface to decrease. When the air pressure on the upper surface becomes less than the air pressure on the lower surface, the higher pressure underneath lifts the paper.

This sheet of paper also has some of the characteristics of an airplane wing. Only the lower surface of an airplane wing is flat; the upper surface is curved or arched. In this way, the upper surface of the airplane wing also uses the air resistance to achieve lift.

Both the "kite effect" and the "vacuum effect" contribute to the total lift of an airplane. However, the "vacuum effect" is responsible for about 80% of it.

Additional Sources of Information about Paper Airplanes

If you are interested in finding paper airplane designs, visit the following Web site:

http://www.pchelp.net/paper_ac.htm This site allows you to print out directions and templates for folding a variety of planes.

If you are interested in paper airplane software, tips for making and flying planes, and step-by-step directions for folding a variety of planes, visit the following site:

http://www4.gratisweb.com/byeomans

Keep in mind that Web sites come and go. The ones cited here may no longer exist, but there will probably be many new ones to take their place.

You can find many additional Web sites of interest by simply searching the Internet for the topic "paper airplanes."

> **NOTE**
> For more information about paper airplanes, read *The World Record Paper Airplane Book* by Ken Blackburn and Jeff Lammers; Workman Publishing Company, 1994. This book contains designs and instructions for folding and fine-tuning paper airplanes, details on throwing techniques, and ideas on the best places to fly paper airplanes.

How to Balance a Mobile

A **mobile** is a piece of sculpture constructed of rods and other objects that are suspended by wire, twine, or thread in midair. The rods and objects are connected in such a way that the sculpture is balanced when it is suspended.

The point at which the rod is suspended is called the fulcrum. The **fulcrum** may be the center point of the rod or some other point on the rod. The objects may be hung at the ends of the rods or at points between the ends of the rod and the fulcrum.

Suppose the fulcrum is the center point of a rod and you hang two objects from points on the rod, one on each side of the fulcrum.

Let W = the weight of one object
$\quad D$ = the distance of this object, W, from the fulcrum
$\quad w$ = the weight of the second object
$\quad d$ = the distance of this object, w, from the fulcrum

The mobile will balance if $W * D = w * d$.

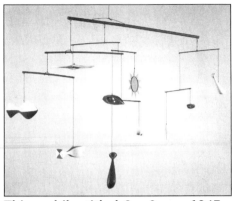

This mobile, titled *Sea Scape, 1947*, was made by Alexander Calder (1898–1976). It is made of painted wood, sheet metal, string, and wire; it is 60 inches wide.

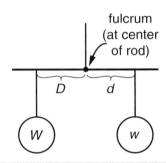

EXAMPLE   In the mobile at the right, what is the missing distance?

Replace the variables in the formula $W * D = w * d$ with the values shown in the diagram. Then, solve the equation.

$\quad W = 6 \qquad D = 7 \qquad w = 10 \qquad d = x$

Solution: $W * D = w * d$
$\qquad\quad 6 * 7 = 10 * x$
$\qquad\quad\ \ 42 = 10 * x$
$\qquad\quad\ 4.2 = x$

Therefore, the distance, x, to the fulcrum is 4.2 units.

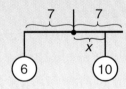

CHECK YOUR UNDERSTANDING

Decide whether the mobiles are in balance.

1.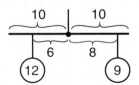

2.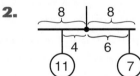

Check your answers on page 380.

Suppose the fulcrum is not the center point of the rod and you hang two objects from some points on the rod, one on each side of the fulcrum.

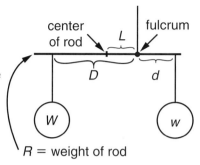

Let R = the weight of the rod
 L = the distance from the center of the rod to the fulcrum
 W = the weight of the object that is on the same side of the fulcrum as the center of the rod
 D = the distance of this object, W, from the fulcrum
 w = the weight of the other object
 d = the distance of this object, w, from the fulcrum

The mobile will balance if $(W * D) + (R * L) = w * d$.

EXAMPLE   In the mobile at the right, what is the missing weight?

Replace the variables in the formula $(W * D) + (R * L) = w * d$ with the values shown in the diagram. Then, solve the equation.

$$W = 7 \quad D = 10 \quad R = 25 \quad L = 2 \quad w = 5x \quad d = 6$$

Solution: $(W * D) + (R * L) = w * d$
$(7 * 10) + (25 * 2) = 5x * 6$
$70 + 50 = 30x$
$120 = 30x$
$4 = x$

Since $x = 4$, $5x = 5 * 4 = 20$.

Therefore, the weight of the object suspended to the right of the fulcrum is 20 units.

CHECK YOUR UNDERSTANDING

In Problems 1 and 2, decide whether the mobiles are in balance. In Problem 3, find the weight of the object on the left of the fulcrum.

1.
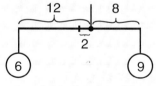
weight of rod = 10

2.
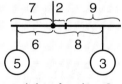
weight of rod = 3

3.
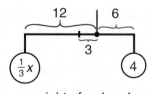
weight of rod = 4

Check your answers on page 380.

Place-Value Chart

Place	Value	Power
billions	1,000 millions	10^9
100 millions	100,000,000s	10^8
10 millions	10,000,000s	10^7
millions	1,000,000s	10^6
100 thousands	100,000s	10^5
10 thousands	10,000s	10^4
thousands	1,000s	10^3
hundreds	100s	10^2
tens	10s	10^1
ones	1s	10^0
.	.	.
tenths	0.1s	10^{-1}
hundredths	0.01s	10^{-2}
thousandths	0.001s	10^{-3}

Prefixes

uni-	one	tera-	trillion (10^{12})
bi-	two	giga-	billion (10^9)
tri-	three	mega-	million (10^6)
quad-	four	kilo-	thousand (10^3)
penta-	five	hecto-	hundred (10^2)
hexa-	six	deca-	ten (10^1)
hepta-	seven	uni-	one (10^0)
octa-	eight	deci-	tenth (10^{-1})
nona-	nine	centi-	hundredth (10^{-2})
deca-	ten	milli-	thousandth (10^{-3})
dodeca-	twelve	micro-	millionth (10^{-6})
icosa-	twenty	nano-	billionth (10^{-9})

Multiplication and Division Table

*,/	1	2	3	4	5	6	7	8	9	10	11	12
1	1	2	3	4	5	6	7	8	9	10	11	12
2	2	4	6	8	10	12	14	16	18	20	22	24
3	3	6	9	12	15	18	21	24	27	30	33	36
4	4	8	12	16	20	24	28	32	36	40	44	48
5	5	10	15	20	25	30	35	40	45	50	55	60
6	6	12	18	24	30	36	42	48	54	60	66	72
7	7	14	21	28	35	42	49	56	63	70	77	84
8	8	16	24	32	40	48	56	64	72	80	88	96
9	9	18	27	36	45	54	63	72	81	90	99	108
10	10	20	30	40	50	60	70	80	90	100	110	120
11	11	22	33	44	55	66	77	88	99	110	121	132
12	12	24	36	48	60	72	84	96	108	120	132	144

Rules for Order of Operations

1. Do operations within parentheses or other grouping symbols before doing anything else.
2. Calculate all powers.
3. Do multiplications or divisions in order, from left to right.
4. Then do additions or subtractions in order, from left to right.

Metric System

Units of Length

1 kilometer (km)	= 1,000 meters (m)
1 meter	= 10 decimeters (dm)
	= 100 centimeters (cm)
	= 1,000 millimeters (mm)
1 decimeter	= 10 centimeters
1 centimeter	= 10 millimeters

Units of Area

1 square meter (m^2)	= 100 square decimeters (dm^2)
	= 10,000 square centimeters (cm^2)
1 square decimeter	= 100 square centimeters
1 square kilometer	= 1,000,000 square meters

Units of Volume

1 cubic meter (m^3)	= 1,000 cubic decimeters (dm^3)
	= 1,000,000 cubic centimeters (cm^3)
1 cubic decimeter	= 1,000 cubic centimeters

Units of Capacity

1 kiloliter (kL)	= 1,000 liters (L)
1 liter	= 1,000 milliliters (mL)
1 cubic centimeter	= 1 milliliter

Units of Mass

1 metric ton (t)	= 1,000 kilograms (kg)
1 kilogram	= 1,000 grams (g)
1 gram	= 1,000 milligrams (mg)

System Equivalents

1 inch is about 2.5 cm (2.54)
1 kilometer is about 0.6 mile (0.621)
1 mile is about 1.6 kilometers (1.609)
1 meter is about 39 inches (39.37)
1 liter is about 1.1 quarts (1.057)
1 ounce is about 28 grams (28.350)
1 kilogram is about 2.2 pounds (2.205)

U.S. Customary System

Units of Length

1 mile (mi)	= 1,760 yards (yd)
	= 5,280 feet (ft)
1 yard	= 3 feet
	= 36 inches (in.)
1 foot	= 12 inches

Units of Area

1 square yard (yd^2)	= 9 square feet (ft^2)
	= 1,296 square inches ($in.^2$)
1 square foot	= 144 square inches
1 acre	= 43,560 square feet
1 square mile (mi^2)	= 640 acres

Units of Volume

1 cubic yard (yd^3)	= 27 cubic feet (ft^3)
1 cubic foot	= 1,728 cubic inches ($in.^3$)

Units of Capacity

1 gallon (gal)	= 4 quarts (qt)
1 quart	= 2 pints (pt)
1 pint	= 2 cups (c)
1 cup	= 8 fluid ounces (fl oz)
1 fluid ounce	= 2 tablespoons (tbs)
1 tablespoon	= 3 teaspoons (tsp)

Units of Weight

1 ton (T)	= 2,000 pounds (lb)
1 pound	= 16 ounces (oz)

Units of Time

1 century	= 100 years
1 decade	= 10 years
1 year (yr)	= 12 months
	= 52 weeks (plus one or two days)
	= 365 days (366 days in a leap year)
1 month (mo)	= 28, 29, 30, or 31 days
1 week (wk)	= 7 days
1 day (d)	= 24 hours
1 hour (hr)	= 60 minutes
1 minute (min)	= 60 seconds (sec)

Decimal and Percent Equivalents for "Easy" Fractions

"Easy" Fractions	Decimals	Percents
$\frac{1}{2}$	0.50	50%
$\frac{1}{3}$	$0.\overline{3}$	$33\frac{1}{3}\%$
$\frac{2}{3}$	$0.\overline{6}$	$66\frac{2}{3}\%$
$\frac{1}{4}$	0.25	25%
$\frac{3}{4}$	0.75	75%
$\frac{1}{5}$	0.20	20%
$\frac{2}{5}$	0.40	40%
$\frac{3}{5}$	0.60	60%
$\frac{4}{5}$	0.80	80%
$\frac{1}{6}$	$0.1\overline{6}$	$16\frac{2}{3}\%$
$\frac{1}{8}$	0.125	$12\frac{1}{2}\%$
$\frac{3}{8}$	0.375	$37\frac{1}{2}\%$
$\frac{5}{8}$	0.625	$62\frac{1}{2}\%$
$\frac{7}{8}$	0.875	$87\frac{1}{2}\%$
$\frac{1}{10}$	0.10	10%
$\frac{3}{10}$	0.30	30%
$\frac{7}{10}$	0.70	70%
$\frac{9}{10}$	0.90	90%

The Global Grid

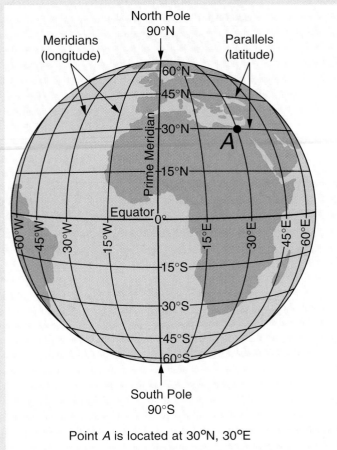

Point A is located at 30°N, 30°E

Fraction-Decimal Number Line

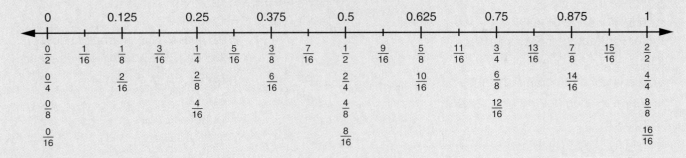

Fraction-Stick and Decimal Number-Line Chart

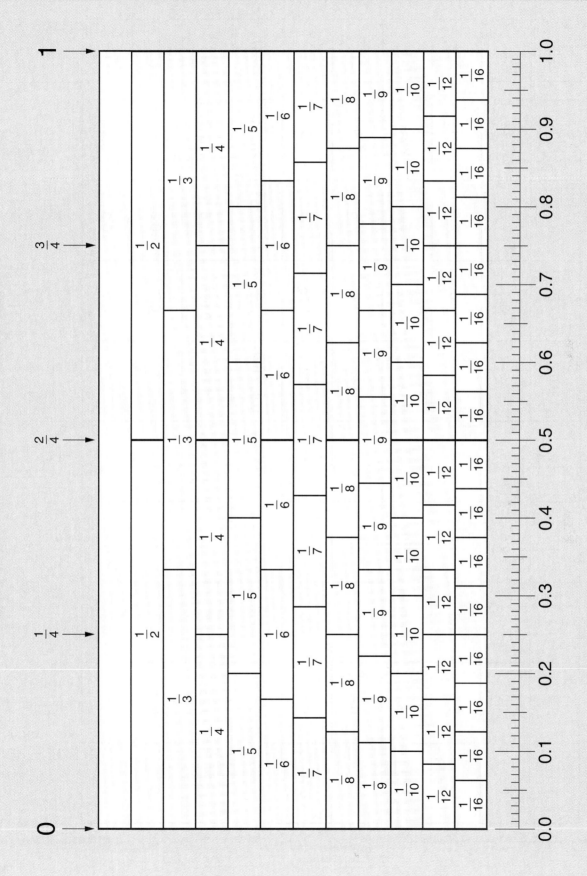

Tables and Charts

Table of Decimal Equivalents for Fractions

	Numerator 1	2	3	4	5	6	7	8	9	10
Denominator 1	1.0	2.0	3.0	4.0	5.0	6.0	7.0	8.0	9.0	10.0
2	0.5	1.0	1.5	2.0	2.5	3.0	3.5	4.0	4.5	5.0
3	$0.\overline{3}$	$0.\overline{6}$	1.0	$1.\overline{3}$	$1.\overline{6}$	2.0	$2.\overline{3}$	$2.\overline{6}$	3.0	$3.\overline{3}$
4	0.25	0.5	0.75	1.0	1.25	1.5	1.75	2.0	2.25	2.5
5	0.2	0.4	0.6	0.8	1.0	1.2	1.4	1.6	1.8	2.0
6	$0.1\overline{6}$	$0.\overline{3}$	0.5	$0.\overline{6}$	$0.8\overline{3}$	1.0	$1.1\overline{6}$	$1.\overline{3}$	1.5	$1.\overline{6}$
7	$0.\overline{142857}$	$0.\overline{285714}$	$0.\overline{428571}$	$0.\overline{571428}$	$0.\overline{714285}$	$0.\overline{857142}$	1.0	$1.\overline{142857}$	$1.\overline{285714}$	$1.\overline{428571}$
8	0.125	0.25	0.375	0.5	0.625	0.75	0.875	1.0	1.125	1.25
9	$0.\overline{1}$	$0.\overline{2}$	$0.\overline{3}$	$0.\overline{4}$	$0.\overline{5}$	$0.\overline{6}$	$0.\overline{7}$	$0.\overline{8}$	1.0	$1.\overline{1}$
10	0.1	0.2	0.3	0.4	0.5	0.6	0.7	0.8	0.9	1.0

Equivalent Fractions, Decimals, and Percents

															Decimal	Percent
$\frac{1}{2}$	$\frac{2}{4}$	$\frac{3}{6}$	$\frac{4}{8}$	$\frac{5}{10}$	$\frac{6}{12}$	$\frac{7}{14}$	$\frac{8}{16}$	$\frac{9}{18}$	$\frac{10}{20}$	$\frac{11}{22}$	$\frac{12}{24}$	$\frac{13}{26}$	$\frac{14}{28}$	$\frac{15}{30}$	0.5	50%
$\frac{1}{3}$	$\frac{2}{6}$	$\frac{3}{9}$	$\frac{4}{12}$	$\frac{5}{15}$	$\frac{6}{18}$	$\frac{7}{21}$	$\frac{8}{24}$	$\frac{9}{27}$	$\frac{10}{30}$	$\frac{11}{33}$	$\frac{12}{36}$	$\frac{13}{39}$	$\frac{14}{42}$	$\frac{15}{45}$	$0.\overline{3}$	$33\frac{1}{3}\%$
$\frac{2}{3}$	$\frac{4}{6}$	$\frac{6}{9}$	$\frac{8}{12}$	$\frac{10}{15}$	$\frac{12}{18}$	$\frac{14}{21}$	$\frac{16}{24}$	$\frac{18}{27}$	$\frac{20}{30}$	$\frac{22}{33}$	$\frac{24}{36}$	$\frac{26}{39}$	$\frac{28}{42}$	$\frac{30}{45}$	$0.\overline{6}$	$66\frac{2}{3}\%$
$\frac{1}{4}$	$\frac{2}{8}$	$\frac{3}{12}$	$\frac{4}{16}$	$\frac{5}{20}$	$\frac{6}{24}$	$\frac{7}{28}$	$\frac{8}{32}$	$\frac{9}{36}$	$\frac{10}{40}$	$\frac{11}{44}$	$\frac{12}{48}$	$\frac{13}{52}$	$\frac{14}{56}$	$\frac{15}{60}$	0.25	25%
$\frac{3}{4}$	$\frac{6}{8}$	$\frac{9}{12}$	$\frac{12}{16}$	$\frac{15}{20}$	$\frac{18}{24}$	$\frac{21}{28}$	$\frac{24}{32}$	$\frac{27}{36}$	$\frac{30}{40}$	$\frac{33}{44}$	$\frac{36}{48}$	$\frac{39}{52}$	$\frac{42}{56}$	$\frac{45}{60}$	0.75	75%
$\frac{1}{5}$	$\frac{2}{10}$	$\frac{3}{15}$	$\frac{4}{20}$	$\frac{5}{25}$	$\frac{6}{30}$	$\frac{7}{35}$	$\frac{8}{40}$	$\frac{9}{45}$	$\frac{10}{50}$	$\frac{11}{55}$	$\frac{12}{60}$	$\frac{13}{65}$	$\frac{14}{70}$	$\frac{15}{75}$	0.2	20%
$\frac{2}{5}$	$\frac{4}{10}$	$\frac{6}{15}$	$\frac{8}{20}$	$\frac{10}{25}$	$\frac{12}{30}$	$\frac{14}{35}$	$\frac{16}{40}$	$\frac{18}{45}$	$\frac{20}{50}$	$\frac{22}{55}$	$\frac{24}{60}$	$\frac{26}{65}$	$\frac{28}{70}$	$\frac{30}{75}$	0.4	40%
$\frac{3}{5}$	$\frac{6}{10}$	$\frac{9}{15}$	$\frac{12}{20}$	$\frac{15}{25}$	$\frac{18}{30}$	$\frac{21}{35}$	$\frac{24}{40}$	$\frac{27}{45}$	$\frac{30}{50}$	$\frac{33}{55}$	$\frac{36}{60}$	$\frac{39}{65}$	$\frac{42}{70}$	$\frac{45}{75}$	0.6	60%
$\frac{4}{5}$	$\frac{8}{10}$	$\frac{12}{15}$	$\frac{16}{20}$	$\frac{20}{25}$	$\frac{24}{30}$	$\frac{28}{35}$	$\frac{32}{40}$	$\frac{36}{45}$	$\frac{40}{50}$	$\frac{44}{55}$	$\frac{48}{60}$	$\frac{52}{65}$	$\frac{56}{70}$	$\frac{60}{75}$	0.8	80%
$\frac{1}{6}$	$\frac{2}{12}$	$\frac{3}{18}$	$\frac{4}{24}$	$\frac{5}{30}$	$\frac{6}{36}$	$\frac{7}{42}$	$\frac{8}{48}$	$\frac{9}{54}$	$\frac{10}{60}$	$\frac{11}{66}$	$\frac{12}{72}$	$\frac{13}{78}$	$\frac{14}{84}$	$\frac{15}{90}$	$0.1\overline{6}$	$16\frac{2}{3}\%$
$\frac{5}{6}$	$\frac{10}{12}$	$\frac{15}{18}$	$\frac{20}{24}$	$\frac{25}{30}$	$\frac{30}{36}$	$\frac{35}{42}$	$\frac{40}{48}$	$\frac{45}{54}$	$\frac{50}{60}$	$\frac{55}{66}$	$\frac{60}{72}$	$\frac{65}{78}$	$\frac{70}{84}$	$\frac{75}{90}$	$0.8\overline{3}$	$83\frac{1}{3}\%$
$\frac{1}{7}$	$\frac{2}{14}$	$\frac{3}{21}$	$\frac{4}{28}$	$\frac{5}{35}$	$\frac{6}{42}$	$\frac{7}{49}$	$\frac{8}{56}$	$\frac{9}{63}$	$\frac{10}{70}$	$\frac{11}{77}$	$\frac{12}{84}$	$\frac{13}{91}$	$\frac{14}{98}$	$\frac{15}{105}$	0.143	14.3%
$\frac{2}{7}$	$\frac{4}{14}$	$\frac{6}{21}$	$\frac{8}{28}$	$\frac{10}{35}$	$\frac{12}{42}$	$\frac{14}{49}$	$\frac{16}{56}$	$\frac{18}{63}$	$\frac{20}{70}$	$\frac{22}{77}$	$\frac{24}{84}$	$\frac{26}{91}$	$\frac{28}{98}$	$\frac{30}{105}$	0.286	28.6%
$\frac{3}{7}$	$\frac{6}{14}$	$\frac{9}{21}$	$\frac{12}{28}$	$\frac{15}{35}$	$\frac{18}{42}$	$\frac{21}{49}$	$\frac{24}{56}$	$\frac{27}{63}$	$\frac{30}{70}$	$\frac{33}{77}$	$\frac{36}{84}$	$\frac{39}{91}$	$\frac{42}{98}$	$\frac{45}{105}$	0.429	42.9%
$\frac{4}{7}$	$\frac{8}{14}$	$\frac{12}{21}$	$\frac{16}{28}$	$\frac{20}{35}$	$\frac{24}{42}$	$\frac{28}{49}$	$\frac{32}{56}$	$\frac{36}{63}$	$\frac{40}{70}$	$\frac{44}{77}$	$\frac{48}{84}$	$\frac{52}{91}$	$\frac{56}{98}$	$\frac{60}{105}$	0.571	57.1%
$\frac{5}{7}$	$\frac{10}{14}$	$\frac{15}{21}$	$\frac{20}{28}$	$\frac{25}{35}$	$\frac{30}{42}$	$\frac{35}{49}$	$\frac{40}{56}$	$\frac{45}{63}$	$\frac{50}{70}$	$\frac{55}{77}$	$\frac{60}{84}$	$\frac{65}{91}$	$\frac{70}{98}$	$\frac{75}{105}$	0.714	71.4%
$\frac{6}{7}$	$\frac{12}{14}$	$\frac{18}{21}$	$\frac{24}{28}$	$\frac{30}{35}$	$\frac{36}{42}$	$\frac{42}{49}$	$\frac{48}{56}$	$\frac{54}{63}$	$\frac{60}{70}$	$\frac{66}{77}$	$\frac{72}{84}$	$\frac{78}{91}$	$\frac{84}{98}$	$\frac{90}{105}$	0.857	85.7%
$\frac{1}{8}$	$\frac{2}{16}$	$\frac{3}{24}$	$\frac{4}{32}$	$\frac{5}{40}$	$\frac{6}{48}$	$\frac{7}{56}$	$\frac{8}{64}$	$\frac{9}{72}$	$\frac{10}{80}$	$\frac{11}{88}$	$\frac{12}{96}$	$\frac{13}{104}$	$\frac{14}{112}$	$\frac{15}{120}$	0.125	$12\frac{1}{2}\%$
$\frac{3}{8}$	$\frac{6}{16}$	$\frac{9}{24}$	$\frac{12}{32}$	$\frac{15}{40}$	$\frac{18}{48}$	$\frac{21}{56}$	$\frac{24}{64}$	$\frac{27}{72}$	$\frac{30}{80}$	$\frac{33}{88}$	$\frac{36}{96}$	$\frac{39}{104}$	$\frac{42}{112}$	$\frac{45}{120}$	0.375	$37\frac{1}{2}\%$
$\frac{5}{8}$	$\frac{10}{16}$	$\frac{15}{24}$	$\frac{20}{32}$	$\frac{25}{40}$	$\frac{30}{48}$	$\frac{35}{56}$	$\frac{40}{64}$	$\frac{45}{72}$	$\frac{50}{80}$	$\frac{55}{88}$	$\frac{60}{96}$	$\frac{65}{104}$	$\frac{70}{112}$	$\frac{75}{120}$	0.625	$62\frac{1}{2}\%$
$\frac{7}{8}$	$\frac{14}{16}$	$\frac{21}{24}$	$\frac{28}{32}$	$\frac{35}{40}$	$\frac{42}{48}$	$\frac{49}{56}$	$\frac{56}{64}$	$\frac{63}{72}$	$\frac{70}{80}$	$\frac{77}{88}$	$\frac{84}{96}$	$\frac{91}{104}$	$\frac{98}{112}$	$\frac{105}{120}$	0.875	$87\frac{1}{2}\%$
$\frac{1}{9}$	$\frac{2}{18}$	$\frac{3}{27}$	$\frac{4}{36}$	$\frac{5}{45}$	$\frac{6}{54}$	$\frac{7}{63}$	$\frac{8}{72}$	$\frac{9}{81}$	$\frac{10}{90}$	$\frac{11}{99}$	$\frac{12}{108}$	$\frac{13}{117}$	$\frac{14}{126}$	$\frac{15}{135}$	$0.\overline{1}$	$11\frac{1}{9}\%$
$\frac{2}{9}$	$\frac{4}{18}$	$\frac{6}{27}$	$\frac{8}{36}$	$\frac{10}{45}$	$\frac{12}{54}$	$\frac{14}{63}$	$\frac{16}{72}$	$\frac{18}{81}$	$\frac{20}{90}$	$\frac{22}{99}$	$\frac{24}{108}$	$\frac{26}{117}$	$\frac{28}{126}$	$\frac{30}{135}$	$0.\overline{2}$	$22\frac{2}{9}\%$
$\frac{4}{9}$	$\frac{8}{18}$	$\frac{12}{27}$	$\frac{16}{36}$	$\frac{20}{45}$	$\frac{24}{54}$	$\frac{28}{63}$	$\frac{32}{72}$	$\frac{36}{81}$	$\frac{40}{90}$	$\frac{44}{99}$	$\frac{48}{108}$	$\frac{52}{117}$	$\frac{56}{126}$	$\frac{60}{135}$	$0.\overline{4}$	$44\frac{4}{9}\%$
$\frac{5}{9}$	$\frac{10}{18}$	$\frac{15}{27}$	$\frac{20}{36}$	$\frac{25}{45}$	$\frac{30}{54}$	$\frac{35}{63}$	$\frac{40}{72}$	$\frac{45}{81}$	$\frac{50}{90}$	$\frac{55}{99}$	$\frac{60}{108}$	$\frac{65}{117}$	$\frac{70}{126}$	$\frac{75}{135}$	$0.\overline{5}$	$55\frac{5}{9}\%$
$\frac{7}{9}$	$\frac{14}{18}$	$\frac{21}{27}$	$\frac{28}{36}$	$\frac{35}{45}$	$\frac{42}{54}$	$\frac{49}{63}$	$\frac{56}{72}$	$\frac{63}{81}$	$\frac{70}{90}$	$\frac{77}{99}$	$\frac{84}{108}$	$\frac{91}{117}$	$\frac{98}{126}$	$\frac{105}{135}$	$0.\overline{7}$	$77\frac{7}{9}\%$
$\frac{8}{9}$	$\frac{16}{18}$	$\frac{24}{27}$	$\frac{32}{36}$	$\frac{40}{45}$	$\frac{48}{54}$	$\frac{56}{63}$	$\frac{64}{72}$	$\frac{72}{81}$	$\frac{80}{90}$	$\frac{88}{99}$	$\frac{96}{108}$	$\frac{104}{117}$	$\frac{112}{126}$	$\frac{120}{135}$	$0.\overline{8}$	$88\frac{8}{9}\%$

Note: The decimals for sevenths have been rounded to the nearest thousandth.

Symbols

+	plus or positive
−	minus or negative
∗, ×	multiplied by
÷, /	divided by
=	is equal to
≠	is not equal to
<	is less than
>	is greater than
≤	is less than or equal to
≥	is greater than or equal to
≈	is about equal to
x^n, $x \wedge n$	nth power of x
$\sqrt{x}$	square root of x
%	percent
$a{:}b$, a/b, $\frac{a}{b}$	ratio of a to b or a divided by b or the fraction $\frac{a}{b}$
$a \, [bs]$	a groups, b in each group
$n/d \rightarrow a \, \mathrm{R}b$	n divided by d is a with remainder b
{ }, ( ), [ ]	grouping symbols
∞	infinity
$n!$	n factorial
°	degree
(a,b)	ordered pair
$\overleftrightarrow{AS}$	line AS
$\overline{AS}$	line segment AS
$\overrightarrow{AS}$	ray AS
∟	right angle
⊥	is perpendicular to
‖	is parallel to
△ABC	triangle ABC
∠ABC	angle ABC
∠B	angle B
≅	is congruent to
∼	is similar to
≡	is equivalent to

Probability Meter

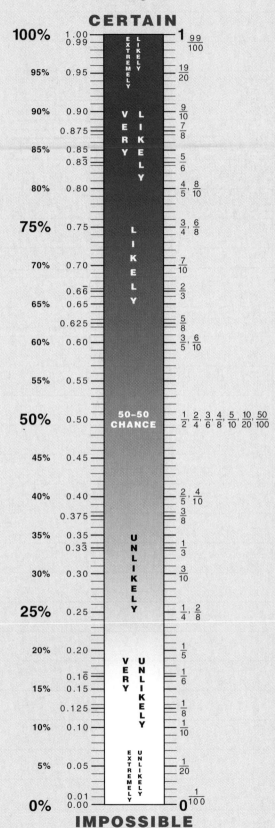

Formulas	**Meaning of Variables**
Rectangles • Perimeter: $p = (2 * l) + (2 * w)$ • Area: $A = (b * h)$	p = perimeter; l = length; w = width A = area; b = length of base; h = height
Squares • Perimeter: $p = 4 * s$ • Area: $A = s^2$	p = perimeter; s = length of side A = area
Parallelograms • Area: $A = b * h$	A = area; b = length of base; h = height
Triangles • Area: $A = \frac{1}{2} * b * h$	A = area; b = length of base; h = height
Regular Polygons • Perimeter: $p = n * s$	p = perimeter; n = number of sides; s = length of side
Circles • Circumference: $c = \pi * d$, or $c = 2 * \pi * r$ • Area: $A = \pi * r^2$	c = circumference; d = diameter; r = radius A = area
Pick's Formula for the Area of Polygons • Area: $A = (\frac{1}{2} * P) + I - 1$	A = area; P = number of grid points on polygon; I = number of grid points in the interior
Polyhedrons • Euler's Formula: $e = (f + v) - 2$	e = number of edges; f = number of faces; v = number of vertices
Mobiles • Fulcrum at center: $W * D = w * d$ • Fulcrum not at center: $(W * D) + (R * L) = w * d$	W = weight of object farthest from fulcrum D = distance of this object from the fulcrum w = weight of object closest to fulcrum d = distance of this object from the fulcrum R = weight of rod L = distance from center to fulcrum

Formulas	Meaning of Variables
Rectangular Prisms • Volume: $V = B * h$, or $V = l * w * h$ • Surface area: $S = 2 * ((l * w) + (l * h) + (w * h))$	V = volume; B = area of base; l = length; w = width; h = height S = surface area
Cubes • Volume: $V = e^3$ • Surface area: $S = 6 * e^2$	V = volume; e = length of edge S = surface area
Cylinders • Volume: $V = B * h$, or $V = \pi * r^2 * h$ • Surface area: $S = (2 * \pi * r^2) + ((2 * \pi * r) * h)$	V = volume; B = area of base; h = height; r = radius of base S = surface area
Pyramids • Volume: $V = \frac{1}{3} * B * h$	V = volume; B = area of base; h = height
Cones • Volume: $V = \frac{1}{3} * B * h$, or $V = \frac{1}{3} * \pi * r^2 * h$	V = volume; B = area of base; h = height; r = radius of base
Spheres • Volume: $V = \frac{4}{3} * \pi * r^3$	V = volume; r = radius
Temperatures • Fahrenheit to Celsius conversion: $C = \frac{5}{9} * (F - 32°)$ • Celsius to Fahrenheit conversion: $F = (\frac{9}{5} * C) + 32°$	C = degrees Celsius; F = degrees Fahrenheit
Distances • $d = r * t$	d = distance traveled; r = rate of speed; t = time of travel

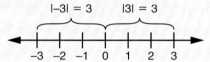

Absolute value The distance between a number and 0 on the number line. The absolute value of a positive number is the number itself. The absolute value of a negative number is the *opposite* of the number. For example, the absolute value of 3 is 3, and the absolute value of −6 is 6. The absolute value of 0 is 0. The notation for the absolute value of a number *n* is |*n*|.

|−3| = 3 |3| = 3

$$-3 \quad -2 \quad -1 \quad 0 \quad 1 \quad 2 \quad 3$$

Abundant number A number whose *proper factors* add up to more than the number itself. For example, 12 is an abundant number because the sum of its proper factors is 1 + 2 + 3 + 4 + 6 = 16, and 16 is greater than 12. See also *proper factor, deficient number,* and *perfect number.*

Acre In the U.S. customary system of measurement, a unit of *area* equal to 43,560 square feet. An acre is roughly the size of a football field. A square mile is 640 acres.

Addend One of two or more numbers that are added. For example, in 5 + 3 + 1, the addends are 5, 3, and 1.

Adjacent angles Angles that are next to each other; adjacent angles have a common side but no other overlap. In the diagram,

Angles 1 and 2 are adjacent angles. So are Angles 2 and 3, Angles 3 and 4, and Angles 4 and 1.

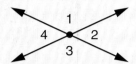

Algebraic expression An expression that contains a variable. For example, if Maria is 2 inches taller than Joe and if the variable *M* represents Maria's height, then the algebraic expression *M* − 2 represents Joe's height. See also *expression.*

Algorithm A set of step-by-step instructions for doing something, such as carrying out a computation or solving a problem.

Angle A figure that is formed by two rays or two line segments with a common endpoint. The common endpoint is called the *vertex* of the angle. An *acute angle* has a measure greater than 0° and less than 90°. An *obtuse angle* has a measure greater than 90° and less than 180°. A *reflex angle* has a measure greater than 180° and less than 360°. A *right angle* measures 90°. A *straight angle* measures 180°. See also *endpoint, ray,* and *vertex.*

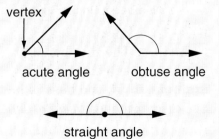

acute angle   obtuse angle

straight angle

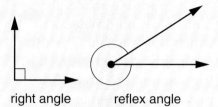

right angle   reflex angle

Apex In a pyramid or a cone, the vertex opposite the base. See also *base of a pyramid or a cone.*

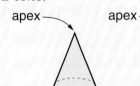

apex   apex

Arc Part of a circle, from one point on the circle to another. For example, a *semicircle* is an arc whose endpoints are the endpoints of a diameter of the circle.

arcs

Area The amount of surface inside a closed boundary. Area is measured in square units, such as square inches or square centimeters.

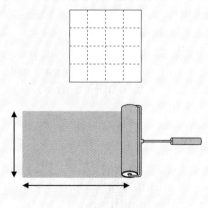

Two ways to model area

Area model A model for multiplication problems in which the length and width of a rectangle represent the factors, and the area of the rectangle represents the product. Also, a model for showing fractions as parts of circles, rectangles, or other geometric figures.

$3 * 5 = 15$

Array An arrangement of objects in a regular pattern, usually rows and columns. Arrays can be used to model multiplication. For example, the array below is a model for $3 * 5 = 15$. See also *rectangular array*.

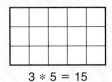

Associative property A property of addition and multiplication (but not of subtraction or division) that says when you add or multiply three numbers, it doesn't matter which two are added or multiplied first. For example:
$(4 + 3) + 7 = 4 + (3 + 7)$
and $(5 * 8) * 9 = 5 * (8 * 9)$.

Average A typical value for a set of numbers. The word *average* usually refers to the *mean* of a set of numbers, but there are other averages. See also *mean, median,* and *mode*.

Axis (plural: **axes**) (1) Either of the two number lines that intersect to form a *coordinate grid*.

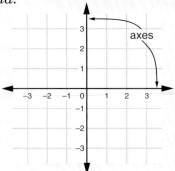

axes

(2) A line about which a solid figure rotates.

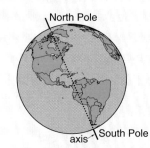

North Pole

axis South Pole

B

Bar graph A graph that uses horizontal or vertical bars to represent data.

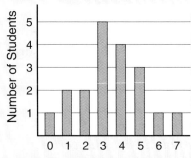

Number of Students

Number of Books Read

Base (in exponential notation) The number that is raised to some power. For example, in 5^3, the base is 5. See also *exponential notation*.

Base of a polygon A side on which a polygon "sits." The

height of a polygon may depend on which side is called the base. See also *height of a parallelogram* and *height of a triangle*.

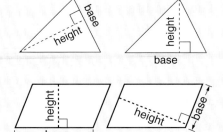

base
height
height
base

height
base
height
base

Base of a prism or a cylinder Either of the two parallel and congruent faces that define the shape of a prism or a cylinder.

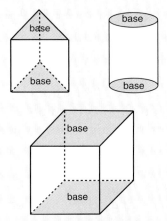

base
base
base

base
base

base
base

Base of a pyramid or a cone The face of a pyramid or a cone that is opposite its apex.

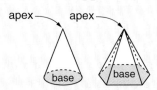

apex apex
base base

Base-10 The feature of our system for writing numbers that results in each place having a value 10 times the place to its right. See also *place value*.

Benchmark A well-known count or measure that can be used to check whether other counts, measures, or estimates make sense. For example, a benchmark for land area is that a football field is about one acre. A benchmark for length is that the width of a man's thumb is about one inch.

Bisect To divide a segment, an angle, or another figure into two equal parts.

Ray *BD* bisects Angle *ABC*.

Bisector A line or ray that divides a segment or an angle into two equal parts. See also *bisect*.

Broken-line graph A graph in which data points are connected by line segments. Same as *line graph*.

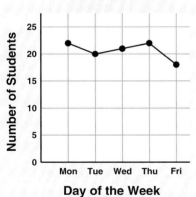

Attendance for the First Week of School

Capacity The amount a container can hold. Also, the heaviest weight a scale can measure.

Change diagram A diagram used in *Everyday Mathematics* to represent situations in which quantities are increased or decreased.

Start	Change	End
14	−5	9

Circle The set of all points in a plane that are a given distance from a given point in the plane. The given point is the *center* of the circle, and the given distance is the *radius*.

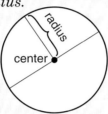

Circle graph A graph in which a circle and its interior are divided into parts to show the parts of a set of data. The whole circle represents the whole set of data. Same as *pie graph*.

Circumference The distance around a circle or a sphere; the perimeter of a circle.

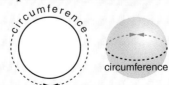

Column-addition method A method for adding numbers in which the

addends' digits are first added in each place-value column separately and then 10-for-1 trades are made until each column has only one digit. Lines are drawn to separate the place-value columns.

```
    100s 10s  1s
      2   4   8
  +   1   8   7
 ────────────────
      3  12  15
      3  13   5
      4   3   5
```

Column-division method A division procedure in which vertical lines are drawn between the digits of the dividend. The lines make the procedure easier to carry out.

```
       1 │  7 │  2
  5│  8  │  6 │  3
  − 5    │    │
       3 │ 36 │ 13
         │−35 │
       3 │  1 │−10
         │    │  3
```

863 / 5 → 172 R3

Common denominator Any number, except 0, that is a multiple of the denominators of two or more fractions. For example, the fractions $\frac{1}{2}$ and $\frac{2}{3}$ have the common denominators 6, 12, 18, and so on. See also *denominator*.

Common factor Any number that is a factor of two or more numbers. For example, 4 is a common factor of 8 and 12.

Commutative property A property of addition and multiplication (but not of subtraction or division) that says that changing the order of the numbers being added or multiplied doesn't change the answer. For example: 5 + 10 = 10 + 5 and 3 ∗ 8 = 8 ∗ 3.

Comparison diagram A diagram used in *Everyday Mathematics* to represent situations in which two quantities are compared.

Quantity
12

Quantity	Difference
9	?

Complementary angles Two angles whose measures total 90°.

∠ 1 and ∠ 2 are complementary.

Composite number A whole number that has more than two factors. For example, 4 is a composite number because it has three factors: 1, 2, and 4.

Concave polygon A polygon in which at least one vertex is "pushed in." Not every line segment with endpoints on different sides of a concave polygon is inside the polygon. Same as *nonconvex polygon*.

Concentric circles Circles that have the same center but radii of different lengths.

Cone A 3-dimensional shape that has a circular *base*, a curved surface, and one vertex, which is called the *apex*. The points on the curved surface of a cone are on straight lines connecting the apex and the circumference of the base.

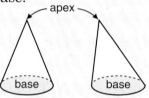

Congruent Having exactly the same shape and size.

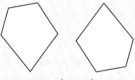

congruent pentagons

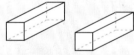

congruent prisms

Consecutive angles Two angles in a polygon that share a common side.

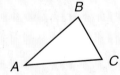

Angles *A* and *B*, *B* and *C*, and *C* and *A* are consecutive angles.

Constant A quantity that does not change.

Contour line A curve on a map through places where a certain measurement (such as temperature or elevation) is the same. Often contour lines separate regions that have been colored differently to show a range of conditions.

Contour map A map that uses *contour lines* to show a particular feature (such as elevation or climate).

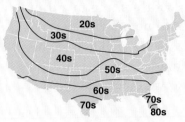

Convex polygon A polygon in which all vertices are "pushed outward." Any line segment with endpoints on different sides of a convex polygon lies inside the polygon.

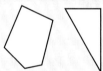

Coordinate A number used to locate a point on a number line or one of two numbers used to locate a point on a coordinate grid.

Coordinate grid A device for locating points in a plane using *ordered number pairs*, or *coordinates*. A *rectangular coordinate grid* is formed by two number lines that intersect at right angles at their zero points. See also *ordered number pair*.

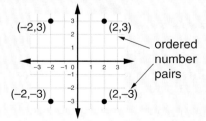

Corresponding Having the same relative position in *similar* or *congruent figures.* In the diagram, pairs of corresponding sides are marked with the same number of slash marks and corresponding angles are marked with the same number of arcs.

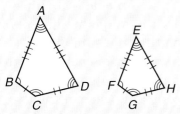

corresponding sides and angles

Counting numbers The numbers used to count things. The set of counting numbers is {1, 2, 3, 4, ...}. Sometimes 0 is considered to be a counting number.

Cover-up method A method for solving equations by covering up key expressions.

Cross multiplication The process of finding the cross products of two fractions. Cross multiplication can be used in solving proportions.

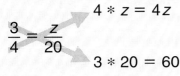

$$\frac{3}{4} = \frac{z}{20}$$

$$4 * z = 4z$$
$$3 * 20 = 60$$

Cross products The cross products of two fractions are found by multiplying the numerator of each fraction by the denominator of the other fraction.

$$\frac{2}{3} = \frac{6}{9}$$

$$3 * 6 = 18$$
$$2 * 9 = 18$$

Cross section A shape formed by the intersection of a plane and a geometric solid.

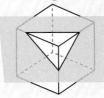

cross section of a cube

Cube A polyhedron with 6 square faces. A cube has 8 vertices and 12 edges.

Cubic centimeter A metric unit of volume equal to the volume of a cube that is 1 cm on each side. $1 \text{ cm}^3 = 1 \text{ mL}$.

Cubic unit A unit used in measuring volume, such as cubic centimeters or cubic feet.

Cubit An ancient unit of length, measured from the point of the elbow to the end of the middle finger. A cubit is about 18 inches. The Latin word *cubitum* means "elbow."

Curved surface A surface that is rounded rather than flat.

Cylinder A 3-dimensional shape that has two circular or elliptical bases that are parallel and congruent and are connected by a curved surface. The points on the curved surface of a cylinder are on straight lines connecting corresponding points on the bases. A can is shaped like a cylinder.

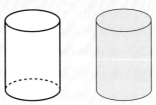

Data Information that is gathered by counting, measuring, questioning, or observing.

Decimal A number that contains a decimal point, such as 2.54. See also *standard notation.*

Decimal point A dot used to separate the ones and tenths places in decimal numbers.

Deficient number A number whose proper factors add up to less than the number itself. For example, 10 is a deficient number because the sum of its proper factors is $1 + 2 + 5 = 8$, and 8 is less than 10. See also *proper factor, abundant number,* and *perfect number.*

Degree (°) A unit of measure for angles based on dividing a circle into 360 equal parts. Also, a unit of measure for temperature. A small raised circle (°) is used to show degrees.

Denominator The number below the line in a fraction. In a fraction where a whole is divided into equal parts, the denominator represents the number of equal parts into which the whole (the ONE or unit) is divided. In the fraction $\frac{a}{b}$, b is the denominator.

Density A *rate* that compares the *mass* of an object with its *volume*. For example, suppose a ball has a mass of 20 grams and a volume of 10 cubic centimeters. To find its density, divide its mass by its volume: 20 g/10 cm³ = 2 g/cm³, or 2 grams per cubic centimeter.

Diameter A line segment that passes through the center of a circle or sphere and has endpoints on the circle or sphere; also, the length of this line segment. The diameter of a circle or sphere is twice the length of its radius.

Difference The result of subtracting one number from another.

Digit One of the number symbols 0, 1, 2, 3, 4, 5, 6, 7, 8, 9.

Discount The amount by which the regular price of an item is reduced.

Distributive property A property that relates multiplication and addition or subtraction. This property gets its name because it "distributes" a factor over terms inside parentheses. Distributive property of multiplication over addition: $a * (b + c) = (a * b) + (a * c)$, so $2 * (5 + 3) = (2 * 5) + (2 * 3) = 10 + 6 = 16$

Distributive property of multiplication over subtraction: $a * (b - c) = (a * b) - (a * c)$, so $2 * (5 - 3) = (2 * 5) - (2 * 3) = 10 - 6 = 4$

Dividend The number in division that is being divided. For example, in $35 \div 5 = 7$, the dividend is 35.

Divisibility test A test to find out whether a whole number is *divisible by* another whole number without actually doing the division. A divisibility test for 5, for example, is to check the digit in the 1s place: if that digit is 0 or 5, then the number is divisible by 5.

Divisible by One whole number is divisible by another whole number if there is no remainder when the larger number is divided by the smaller number. For example, 28 is divisible by 7 because 28 divided by 7 is 4 with a remainder of 0.

Division of Fractions Property The principle that says that division by a fraction is equivalent to multiplication by that fraction's *reciprocal*. For example, since the reciprocal of $\frac{1}{2}$ is 2, the division problem $4 \div \frac{1}{2}$ is equivalent to the multiplication problem $4 * 2$.

Divisor In division, the number that divides another number. For example, in $35 \div 5 = 7$, the divisor is 5.

Edge A line segment where two faces of a polyhedron meet.

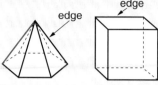

Ellipse An oval. An ellipse is the set of all points in a plane such that the sum of the distances from each point to two fixed points in the plane is constant. Each of the two fixed points is called a focus of the ellipse.

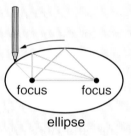

ellipse

Endpoint A point at the end of a line segment or ray. A line segment is normally named using the letter labels of its endpoints. See *line segment* and *ray*.

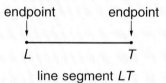

line segment *LT*

Enlarge To increase the size of an object or a figure. See also *size-change factor*.

Equation A number sentence that contains an equal sign. For example, $15 = 10 + 5$ is an equation.

Equilateral triangle A triangle with all three sides equal in length. In an equilateral triangle, all three angles have the same measure.

Equivalent Equal in value but possibly in a different form. For example, $\frac{1}{2}$, 0.5, and 50% are all equivalent.

Equivalent equations Equations that have the same *solution*. For example, $2 + x = 4$ and $6 + x = 8$ are equivalent equations because the solution to both is $x = 2$.

Equivalent fractions Fractions that have different denominators but name the same amount. For example, $\frac{1}{2}$ and $\frac{4}{8}$ are equivalent fractions.

Equivalent rates *Rates* that make the same comparison. For example, the rates $\frac{60 \text{ miles}}{1 \text{ hour}}$ and $\frac{1 \text{ mile}}{1 \text{ minute}}$ are equivalent.

Equivalent ratios *Ratios* that make the same comparison. Equivalent ratios can be expressed by *equivalent fractions*. For example, the ratios 12 to 20, 6 to 10, and 3 to 5 are equivalent ratios because $\frac{12}{20} = \frac{6}{10} = \frac{3}{5}$.

Estimate An answer that is close to an exact answer. As a verb, *to estimate* means to calculate an answer that is close to the exact answer.

Evaluate To find a value for. To evaluate a mathematical expression, replace the variables (if there are any) with numbers, then carry out the operations. See also *expression*.

Even number A whole number that can be divided by 2 with no remainder. The even numbers are 2, 4, 6, 8, and so on. 0 may also be considered even.

Exponent A small raised number in *exponential notation* that tells how many times the base is to be multiplied by itself. For example, in 5^3, the exponent is 3. See also *base*.

Exponential notation A way to show repeated multiplication by the same factor. For example, 2^3 is exponential notation for $2 * 2 * 2$. The small raised 3 is the exponent. It tells how many times the number 2, called the base, is used as a factor.

$$2^3 \longleftarrow \text{exponent}$$
$$\uparrow$$
$$\text{base}$$

Expression A group of mathematical symbols that represents a number—or can represent a number if values are assigned to any variables in the expression.

Extended multiplication fact A multiplication fact involving multiples of 10, 100, and so on. In an extended multiplication fact, each factor has only one digit that is not 0. For example, $6 * 70$, $60 * 7$, and $60 * 70$ are extended multiplication facts.

F

Face A flat surface on a 3-dimensional shape.

Fact family A set of related addition and subtraction facts or related multiplication and division facts. For example, $5 + 6 = 11$, $6 + 5 = 11$, $11 - 5 = 6$, and $11 - 6 = 5$ are a fact family. $5 * 7 = 35$, $7 * 5 = 35$, $35 \div 5 = 7$, and $35 \div 7 = 5$ are another fact family.

Factor One of two or more numbers that are multiplied to give a product. The numbers that are multiplied are called *factors* of the product. For example, 4 and 3 are factors of 12 because $4 * 3 = 12$. As a verb, *to factor* means to find two (or more) smaller numbers whose product equals a given number. For example, 15 can be factored as $5 * 3$.

$$4 * 3 = 12$$
$$\uparrow \quad \uparrow \qquad \uparrow$$
$$\text{factors} \quad \text{product}$$

Factor pair Two whole-number factors of a number whose product is the number. A number may have more than one factor pair. For example, the factor pairs for 18 are 1 and 18, 2 and 9, and 3 and 6.

Factor rainbow A way to show factor pairs in a list of all the factors of a number. A factor rainbow can be used to check whether a list of factors is correct.

factor rainbow for 24

Factor string A number written as a product of at least two whole-number factors. For example, a factor string for the number 24 is 2 * 3 * 4. This factor string has three factors, so its length is 3. The number 1 is never part of a factor string.

Factor tree A way to get the *prime factorization* of a number. The original number is written as a product of factors; then each of these factors is written as a product of factors, and so on, until the factors are all prime numbers. A factor tree looks like an upside-down tree, with the root (the original number) at the top and the leaves (the factors) beneath it. See *prime factorization.*

Factorial A product of a whole number and all the smaller whole numbers except 0. An exclamation point, !, is used to write factorials. For example, "three factorial" is written as 3! and

is equal to 3 * 2 * 1 = 6. 10! = 10 * 9 * 8 * 7 * 6 * 5 * 4 * 3 * 2 * 1 = 3,628,800.

Fair Free from bias. Each side of a fair die or coin will come up about equally often.

Fair game A game in which every player has the same chance of winning.

False number sentence A number sentence in which the relation symbol does not accurately relate the two sides. For example, 8 = 5 + 5 is a false number sentence.

Fathom A unit used by people who work with boats and ships to measure depths underwater and lengths of cables. A fathom is now defined as 6 feet.

Figurate numbers Numbers that can be shown by specific geometric patterns. Square numbers and triangular numbers are examples of figurate numbers.

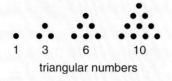

1   3   6   10
triangular numbers

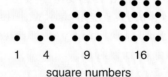

1   4   9   16
square numbers

Formula A general rule for finding the value of something. A formula is often written using letters, called *variables,* that stand for the quantities involved. For example, the formula for the area of a rectangle may be written as A = l * w, where A represents

the area of the rectangle, *l* represents its length, and *w* represents its width.

Fraction A number in the form $\frac{a}{b}$ or a/b. Fractions can be used to name parts of a whole, to compare quantities, or to represent division. For example, $\frac{2}{3}$ can be thought of as 2 divided by 3. See also *numerator* and *denominator.*

Fraction-stick A diagram used in *Everyday Mathematics* to represent simple fractions.

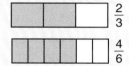

Fulcrum A point on a mobile at which a rod is suspended. In general, the point or place around which a lever pivots.

Genus In *topology,* the number of holes in a geometric shape. Shapes with the same genus are *topologically equivalent.* For example, a donut and a teacup are both genus 1. See also *topology.*

Geometric solid A 3-dimensional shape, such as a prism, pyramid, cylinder, cone, or sphere. Despite its name, a geometric solid is hollow; it does not contain the points in its interior.

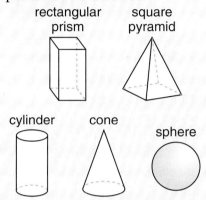

rectangular prism   square pyramid

cylinder   cone   sphere

Geometry Template An *Everyday Mathematics* tool that includes a millimeter ruler, a ruler with sixteenth-inch intervals, half-circle and full-circle protractors, a percent circle, pattern-block shapes, and other geometric figures. The Template can also be used as a compass.

Golden Ratio A ratio of approximately 1.618 to 1. The Golden Ratio is sometimes denoted by the Greek letter *phi:* **φ**. The Golden Ratio is an irrational number.

Golden Rectangle A rectangle in which the ratio of the length of the longer side to the length of the shorter side is the *Golden Ratio,* or about 1.618 to 1. A 5-inch by 3-inch index card is nearly a Golden Rectangle.

Great span The distance from the tip of the thumb to the tip of the little finger (pinkie) when the hand is stretched as far as possible. Also called *hand span.*

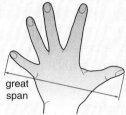

great span

Greatest common factor (GCF) The largest factor that two or more numbers have in common. For example, the common factors of 24 and 36 are 1, 2, 3, 4, 6, and 12; the greatest common factor of 24 and 36 is 12.

Grouping symbols Symbols such as parentheses ( ), brackets [ ], and braces { } that tell the order in which operations in an expression are to be done. For example, in the expression (3 + 4) ∗ 5, one should do the operation in the parentheses first. The expression then becomes 7 ∗ 5 = 35.

●●●●●● **H** ●●●●●●

Height of a parallelogram The shortest length between the base of a parallelogram and the line containing the side opposite its base. The height is perpendicular to the base. See also *base of a polygon.*

height   base   height   base

Height of a prism or a cylinder The shortest length from a base of a prism or a cylinder to the plane containing the opposite base. See also *base of a prism or a cylinder.*

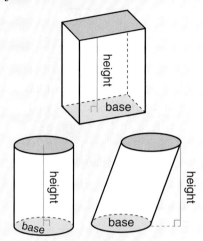

height   base

height   base   height   base

Height of a pyramid or a cone The shortest length from the vertex of a pyramid or a cone to the plane containing its base. See also *base of a pyramid or a cone.*

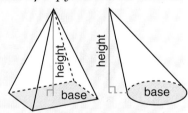

height   base   height   base

Height of a triangle The shortest length between the line containing a base of a triangle and the vertex opposite that base. See also *base of a polygon.*

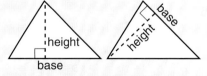

height   base   base   height

Hemisphere Half of Earth's surface. Also, half of a sphere.

Heptagon A polygon with seven sides.

Hexagon A polygon with six sides.

Hexagram A 6-pointed star formed by extending the sides of a regular hexagon.

Horizon Where the earth and sky appear to meet; if nothing is in the way, as when looking out to sea, the horizon looks like a line.

Horizontal In a left-right orientation; parallel to the horizon.

Hypotenuse In a right triangle, the side opposite the right angle.

Image The reflection of an object that you see when you look in a mirror. Also, a figure that is produced by a *transformation* (a *reflection, translation,* or *rotation,* for example) of another figure. See also *preimage.*

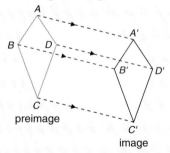

Improper fraction A fraction whose numerator is greater than or equal to its denominator. For example, $\frac{4}{3}$, $\frac{5}{2}$, $\frac{4}{4}$, and $\frac{24}{12}$ are improper fractions. In *Everyday Mathematics,* improper fractions are sometimes called "top-heavy" fractions.

Indirect measurement Determining heights, distances, and other quantities that cannot be measured directly.

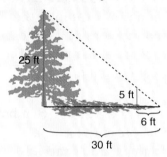

25 ft
5 ft
6 ft
30 ft

Inequality A number sentence with $>$, $<$, $\geq$, $\leq$, or $\neq$. For example, the sentence $8 < 15$ is an inequality.

Inscribed polygon A polygon whose vertices are all on the same circle.

inscribed square

Integer A number in the set $\{..., -4, -3, -2, -1, 0, 1, 2, 3, 4, ...\}$; a *whole number* or the *opposite* of a whole number.

Interior The inside of a closed 2-dimensional or 3-dimensional figure. The interior is usually not considered to be part of the figure.

Intersect To meet or cross.

Intersecting Meeting or crossing one another. Lines, segments, rays, and planes can intersect.

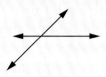

intersecting   intersecting
lines   planes

Interval (1) The set of numbers between two numbers a and b, which may include a or b or both. (2) A part of a line, including all points between two specific points.

interval
0 1 2 3 4 5 6 7 8

Interval estimate An estimate that places an unknown quantity in a range. For example, an interval estimate of a person's weight might be "between 100 and 110 pounds."

Irrational number A number that cannot be written as a fraction, where both the numerator and the denominator are *integers* and the denominator is not zero. For example, π is an irrational number.

Isometry transformation A transformation such as a *translation* (slide), *reflection* (flip), or *rotation* (turn) that changes the position or orientation of a figure but does not change its size or shape.

slide   flip   turn

Isosceles triangle A triangle with at least two sides that are the same length. In an isosceles triangle, at least two angles have the same measure.

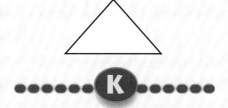

Kite A quadrilateral with two pairs of adjacent equal sides. The four sides cannot all have the same length, so a rhombus is not a kite.

Landmark A notable feature of a data set. Landmarks include the *median, mode, maximum, minimum,* and *range.*

Latitude A measure, in degrees, of the distance of a place north or south of the equator.

Lattice method A very old way to multiply multidigit numbers.

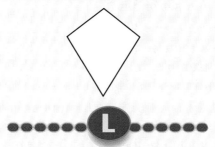

256 ∗ 57 = 14,592

Least common denominator (LCD) The *least common multiple* of the denominators of every fraction in a given collection. For example, the least common denominator of $\frac{1}{2}$, $\frac{4}{5}$, and $\frac{3}{8}$ is 40. See also *least common multiple.*

Least common multiple (LCM) The smallest number that is a multiple of two or more numbers. For example, while some common multiples of 6 and 8 are 24, 48, and 72, the least common multiple of 6 and 8 is 24.

Leg of a right triangle A side of a right triangle that is not the *hypotenuse.* See also *hypotenuse.*

Like The same. The fractions $\frac{2}{5}$ and $\frac{3}{5}$ have like denominators. The measurements 23 cm and 52 cm have like units.

Like terms In an *algebraic expression,* either the constant terms or any terms that contain the same variable(s) raised to the same power(s). For example, $4y$ and $7y$ are like terms in the expression $4y + 7y - z$.

Line A straight path that extends infinitely in opposite directions.

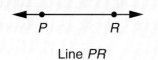

Line *PR*

Line graph See *broken-line graph.*

Line of reflection (mirror line) A line halfway between a figure (preimage) and its reflected image. In a reflection, a figure is "flipped over" the line of reflection. See also *reflection.*

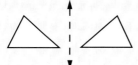

Line of symmetry A line drawn through a figure that divides it into two parts that look exactly alike but are facing in opposite directions. See also *line symmetry.*

Line plot A sketch of data in which check marks, Xs, or other marks above a labeled line show the frequency of each value.

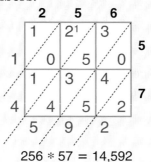

Number of Siblings

Line segment A straight path joining two points. The two points are called the *endpoints* of the segment.

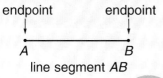

line segment *AB*

Line symmetry A figure has line symmetry if a line can be drawn through it so that it is divided into two parts with both parts looking exactly alike but facing in opposite directions. See also *line of symmetry*.

Lines of latitude Lines that run east-west on a map or globe and indicate the location of a place with reference to the equator, which is also a line of latitude. Lines of latitude are called *parallels* because each one is parallel to the equator.

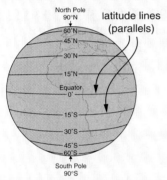

Lines of longitude Lines that run north-south on a map or globe and indicate the location of a place with reference to the prime meridian, which is also a line of longitude. Lines of longitude are semicircles that meet at the North and South Poles. They are also called meridians.

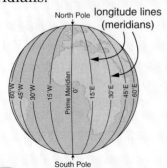

Longitude A measure, in degrees, of how far east or west of the prime meridian a place is. See also *prime meridian*.

Lowest terms See *simplest form*.

Magnitude estimate A very rough estimate. A magnitude estimate tells whether an answer should be in the tens, hundreds, thousands, ten-thousands, and so on.

Map legend (map key) A diagram that explains the symbols, markings, and colors on a map.

Map scale A tool that helps you estimate real distances between places shown on a map by relating distances on the map to distances in the real world. For example, a map scale may show that 1 inch on a map represents 100 miles in the real world. See also *scale*.

Maximum The largest amount; the greatest number in a set of data.

Mean The sum of a set of numbers divided by the number of numbers in the set. The mean is often referred to simply as the *average*.

Median The middle value in a set of data when the data are listed in order from smallest to largest. If there is an even number of data points, the median is the *mean* of the two middle values.

Metric system of measurement A measurement system based on the base-ten numeration system. It is used in most countries around the world.

Midpoint A point halfway between two other points. The midpoint of a line segment is the point halfway between the endpoints.

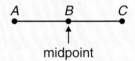

Minimum The smallest amount; the smallest number in a set of data.

Minuend The number that is reduced in subtraction. For example, in $19 - 5 = 14$, the minuend is 19.

Mixed number A number that is written using both a whole number and a fraction. For example, $2\frac{1}{4}$ is a mixed number equal to $2 + \frac{1}{4}$.

Möbius strip (Möbius band) A shape with only one side and one edge. The Möbius strip is named for the mathematician August Ferdinand Möbius.

Mode The value or values that occur most often in a set of data.

Multiple of a number, *n*
(1) A product of *n* and a counting number. The multiples of 7, for example, are 7, 14, 21, 28, … . (2) A product of *n* and an integer. The multiples of 7 are …, −21, −14, −7, 0, 7, 14, 21, … .

Multiplication counting principle A way of determining the total number of possible outcomes for two or more separate choices. Suppose, for example, you roll a die and then flip a coin. There are 6 choices for which face of the die shows and 2 choices for which side of the coin shows. Then there are 6 * 2, or 12 possible outcomes altogether: (1,H), (1,T), (2,H), (2,T), (3,H), (3,T), (4,H), (4,T), (5,H), (5,T), (6,H), (6,T).

Multiplication diagram A diagram used for problems in which there are several equal groups. The diagram has three parts: a number of groups, a number in each group, and a total number. Also called *multiplication/ division diagram*. See also *rate diagram*.

rows	chairs per row	total chairs
15	25	?

Multiplication property of −1 A property of multiplication that says that for any number *a*, $(-1) * a =$ (OPP) *a*, or −*a*. For example, for $a = 5$: $5 * (-1) = $ (OPP) 5 $= -5$. For $a = -3$: $-3 * (-1) = $ (OPP) $-3 = -(-3) = 3$.

Multiplicative inverses
Two numbers whose product is 1. For example, the multiplicative inverse of 5 is $\frac{1}{5}$, and the multiplicative inverse of $\frac{3}{5}$ is $\frac{5}{3}$. Multiplicative inverses are also called *reciprocals* of each other.

Mystery plot An unlabeled graph or plot. The viewer is challenged to find a situation that the plot or graph might represent.

Name-collection box A diagram that is used for writing equivalent names for a number.

25	37 − 12	20 + 5
⊦⊦⊦⊦ ⊦⊦⊦⊦ ⊦⊦⊦⊦ ⊦⊦⊦⊦ ⊦⊦⊦⊦		
twenty-five		*veinticinco*

Negative number A number that is less than zero; a number to the left of zero on a horizontal number line or below zero on a vertical number line.

***n*-gon** A polygon with *n* sides. For example, a 5-gon is a pentagon, and an 8-gon is an octagon.

Nonagon A polygon with nine sides.

Nonconvex polygon See *concave polygon*.

Normal span The distance from the tip of the thumb to the tip of the first (index)

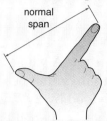

normal span

finger of an outstretched hand. Also called *span*.

***n*-to-1 ratio** A ratio with 1 in the denominator.

Number-and-word notation A way of writing a number using a combination of numbers and words. For example, *27 billion* is number-and-word notation for 27,000,000,000.

Number model A number sentence that models or fits a number story or situation. For example, the story, *Sally had $5, and then she earned $8*, can be modeled as $5 + 8 = 13$.

Number sentence At least two numbers or expressions separated by a relation symbol ($=, >, <, \geq, \leq, \neq$). Most number sentences contain at least one operation symbol ($+, -, \times, *, \bullet, \div, /$). Number sentences may also have grouping symbols, such as parentheses and brackets.

Number story A story with a problem that can be solved using arithmetic.

Numerator The number above the line in a fraction. In a fraction where a whole is divided into equal parts, the numerator represents the number of equal parts being considered. In the fraction $\frac{a}{b}$, *a* is the numerator.

Octagon A polygon with eight sides.

Odd number A whole number that cannot be evenly divided by 2. When an odd number is divided by 2, there is a remainder of 1. The odd numbers are 1, 3, 5, and so on.

ONE See *whole*.

Open sentence A *number sentence* which is neither true nor false because one or more *variables* hold the places of missing numbers. For example, $5 + x = 13$ is an open sentence. See also *number sentence* and *variable*.

Operation symbol A symbol used to stand for a particular mathematical operation. The most widely used operation symbols are $+$, $-$, $\times$, $*$, $\bullet$, $\div$, and $/$.

Opposite angles (1) of a *quadrilateral*: Angles that do not share a common side.

Angles *A* and *C* and Angles *B* and *D* are pairs of opposite angles.

(2) of a *triangle*: An angle is opposite the side of a triangle that is not one of the sides of the angle.

Angle *C* is opposite side *AB*.

(3) of two lines that *intersect*: the angles that do not share a common side are opposite angles. Opposite angles have equal measures. Same as *vertical angles*.

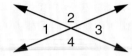

Angles 2 and 4 and Angles 1 and 3 are pairs of opposite, or vertical, angles.

Opposite of a number A number that is the same distance from 0 on the number line as a given number but on the opposite side of 0. The opposite of a number *n* may be written (OPP)(*n*) or $-n$. For example, the opposite of $+3$ is (OPP)($+3$) or -3, and the opposite of -5 is (OPP)(-5) or $+5$.

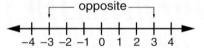

Order of operations Rules that tell in what order to perform operations in arithmetic and algebra. The order of operations is

1. Do the operations in parentheses first. (Use rules 2–4 inside the parentheses.)
2. Calculate all the expressions with exponents.
3. Multiply and divide in order from left to right.
4. Add and subtract in order from left to right.

Ordered number pair Two numbers that are used to locate a point on a *coordinate grid*. The first number gives the position along the horizontal axis, and the second number gives the position along the vertical axis. The numbers in an ordered pair are called *coordinates*. Ordered pairs are usually written inside parentheses: (5,3). See *coordinate grid* for an illustration.

Origin The 0 point on a number line or in a coordinate grid.

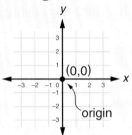

Outcome A possible result of a random process. For example, heads and tails are the two possible outcomes of tossing a coin.

Pan balance A tool used to weigh objects or compare weights.

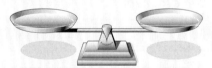

Parabola The curve formed by the intersection of a right circular cone with a plane that is parallel to a line on the cone.

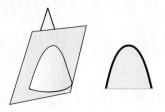

Parallel Never meeting and always the same distance apart. Lines, line segments, rays in a plane, and planes are parallel if they never meet, no matter how far they are extended. The symbol ∥ means "is parallel to."

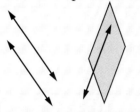

| parallel lines | line parallel to a plane | parallel planes |

Parallelogram A quadrilateral with two pairs of parallel sides. Opposite sides of a parallelogram are congruent.

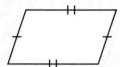

Parentheses Grouping symbols, ( ), used to tell which parts of an expression should be calculated first.

Partial-differences method A way to subtract in which differences are computed for each place (ones, tens, hundreds, and so on) separately. The partial differences are then added to give the final answer.

$$
\begin{array}{r}
9\ 3\ 2 \\
-\ 3\ 5\ 6 \\
\end{array}
$$

$900 - 300$	$\rightarrow$	6 0 0
$30 - 50$	$\rightarrow$	$-$ 2 0
$2 - 6$	$\rightarrow$	$-$ 4
$600 - 20 - 4$	$\rightarrow$	5 7 6

Partial-products method A way to multiply in which the value of each digit in one factor is multiplied by the value of each digit in the other factor. The final product is the sum of the several partial products.

$$
\begin{array}{r}
6\ 7 \\
\times\quad 5\ 3 \\
\end{array}
$$

50×60	$\rightarrow$	3 0 0 0
50×7	$\rightarrow$	3 5 0
3×60	$\rightarrow$	1 8 0
3×7	$\rightarrow$	+ 2 1
		3, 5 5 1

Partial-quotients method A way to divide in which the dividend is divided in a series of steps and the quotients for each step (called partial quotients) are added to give the final answer.

6)1010	
$-$ 600	100
410	
$-$ 300	50
110	
$-$ 60	10
50	
$-$ 48	8
2	168

↑ Remainder   ↑ Quotient

$1,010 \div 6 \rightarrow 168$ R2

Partial-sums method A way to add in which sums are computed for each place (ones, tens, hundreds, and so on) separately and are then

added to give the final answer.

$$
\begin{array}{r}
2\ 6\ 8 \\
+\ 4\ 8\ 3 \\
\end{array}
$$

Add the 100s.	$\rightarrow$	6 0 0
Add the 10s.	$\rightarrow$	1 4 0
Add the 1s.	$\rightarrow$	+ 1 1
Add partial sums.	$\rightarrow$	7 5 1

Parts-and-total diagram A diagram used in *Everyday Mathematics* to represent situations in which two or more quantities are combined.

Total	
13	
Part	**Part**
8	?

parts-and-total diagram for $13 = 8 + n$

Part-to-part ratio A *ratio* that compares a part of a whole to another part of the same whole. For example, the statement "There are 8 boys for every 12 girls" expresses a part-to-part ratio. See also *ratio* and *part-to-whole ratio*.

Part-to-whole ratio A *ratio* that compares a part of a whole to the whole. For example, the statements "8 out of 20 students are boys" and "12 out of 20 students are girls," both express part-to-whole ratios. See also *ratio* and *part-to-part ratio*.

Pentagon A polygon with five sides.

Percent (%) Per hundred or out of a hundred. For example, "48% of the students in the school are boys" means that 48 out of every 100 students in the school are boys.

Percent Circle A tool on the *Geometry Template* that is used to measure and draw figures that involve percents (such as circle graphs). See also *Geometry Template*.

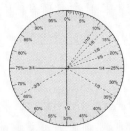

Perfect number A number whose proper factors add up to the number itself. For example, 6 is a perfect number because the sum of its proper factors is $1 + 2 + 3 = 6$. See also *proper factor, abundant number,* and *deficient number*.

Perimeter The distance around a closed 2-dimensional shape. A formula for the perimeter of a rectangle is $P = 2 * (l + w)$, where *l* represents the length and *w* represents the width of the rectangle.

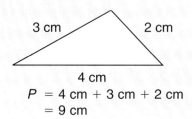

$$P = 4 \text{ cm} + 3 \text{ cm} + 2 \text{ cm}$$
$$= 9 \text{ cm}$$

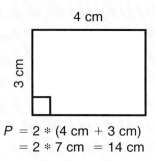

$$P = 2 * (4 \text{ cm} + 3 \text{ cm})$$
$$= 2 * 7 \text{ cm} = 14 \text{ cm}$$

Perpendicular Meeting at right angles. Lines, rays, line segments, and planes that meet at right angles are perpendicular. The symbol ⊥ means "is perpendicular to."

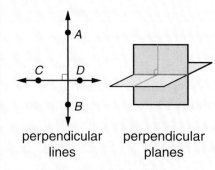

perpendicular   perpendicular
lines   planes

Perspective drawing A method of drawing that realistically represents a 3-dimensional object on a 2-dimensional surface.

Per-unit rate A *rate* with 1 in the denominator. Per-unit rates tell how many of one thing there are for one of another thing. For example, "2 dollars per gallon" is a per-gallon rate. "12 miles per hour" and "4 words per minute" are also examples of per-unit rates.

Pi (π) The ratio of the *circumference* of a circle to its *diameter*. Pi is also the ratio of the area of a circle to the square of its radius. Pi is the same for every circle and is an irrational number that is approximately equal to 3.14. (π is the sixteenth letter of the Greek alphabet.)

Pictograph A graph constructed with pictures or icons. A pictograph allows you to compare at a glance the relative amounts of two or more counts or measures.

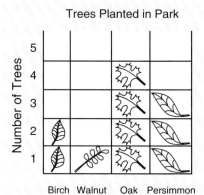

Trees Planted in Park

Pie graph See *circle graph*.

Place value A system that values a digit according to its position in a number. In our system for writing numbers, each place has a value that is ten times that of the place to its right and one-tenth the value of the place to its left. For example, in the number 456, the 4 is in the hundreds place and has a value of 400.

Plane A flat surface that extends forever.

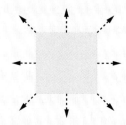

Point An exact location in space. The center of a circle is a point.

Point symmetry The property of balance in a figure that can be rotated 180° about a point in such a way that the resulting figure (the *image*) exactly matches the original figure (the *preimage*). Point symmetry is *rotation symmetry* in which the turn is 180°. See also *rotation symmetry.*

Polygon A closed 2-dimensional figure that is made up of line segments joined end-to-end. The line segments of a polygon may not cross.

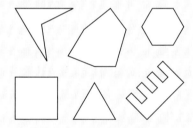

Polyhedron A closed 3-dimensional figure whose surfaces, or faces, are all formed by polygons and their interiors.

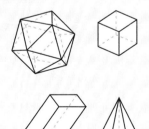

Population In data collection, the collection of people or objects that is the focus of study.

Power of a number Usually, a product of factors that are all the same. For example, 5 * 5 * 5 (or 125) is called "5 to the third power" or "the third power of 5" because 5 is a factor three times. 5 * 5 * 5 can also be written as 5^3.

Power of 10 A whole number that can be written using only 10s as factors. For example, 100 is equal to 10 * 10, or 10^2. 100 can be called the second power of 10 or 10 to the second power. Negative powers of 10 are numbers that can be written using only $\frac{1}{10}$ as a factor.

Precise In everyday language, a fine measurement or scale. The smaller the unit or fraction of a unit used, the more precise the measurement or scale. For example, a measurement to the nearest inch is more precise than a measurement to the nearest foot. A ruler with $\frac{1}{16}$-inch markings is more precise than a ruler with $\frac{1}{4}$-inch markings.

Preimage A geometric figure that is somehow changed (by a *reflection, rotation,* or *translation,* for example) to produce another figure. See also *image.*

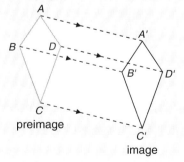

preimage

image

Prime factorization A whole number expressed as a product of prime factors. Every whole number greater than 1 has a unique prime factorization. For example, the prime factorization of 24 is 2 * 2 * 2 * 3.

Prime meridian An imaginary semicircle on Earth that connects the North and South Poles and passes through Greenwich, England.

Prime number A whole number that has exactly two *factors*: itself and 1. For example, 5 is a prime number because its only factors are 5 and 1.

Prism A solid with two parallel *faces*, called *bases*, that are congruent polygons and other *faces* that are all parallelograms. The points on the lateral faces of a prism are all on lines connecting corresponding points on the bases. Prisms get their names from the shape of their bases.

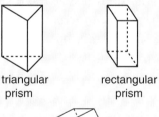

triangular prism   rectangular prism

hexagonal prism

Probability A number from 0 to 1 that tells the chance that an event will happen. The closer a probability is to 1, the more likely the event is to happen.

Probability tree diagram A drawing used to analyze the possible outcomes in a random situation. For example, the "leaves" of the probability tree diagram below represent the four equally likely outcomes when one coin is flipped two times.

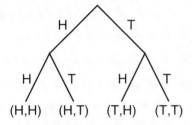

Product The result of multiplying two numbers called *factors*. For example, in $4 * 3 = 12$, the product is 12.

Proper factor Any whole-number *factor* of a number except the number itself. For example, the *factors* of 10 are 1, 2, 5, and 10, but the *proper factors* of 10 are 1, 2, and 5.

Proper fraction A fraction in which the numerator is less than the denominator; a proper fraction names a number that is less than 1. For example, $\frac{3}{4}$, $\frac{2}{5}$, and $\frac{12}{24}$ are proper fractions.

Proportion A number model that states that two fractions are equal. Often the fractions in a proportion represent rates or ratios. For example, the problem *Alan's speed is 12 miles per hour. At the same speed, how far can he travel in 3 hours?* can be modeled by the proportion

$$\frac{12 \text{ miles}}{1 \text{ hour}} = \frac{n \text{ miles}}{3 \text{ hours}}.$$

Protractor A tool for measuring and drawing angles. A half-circle protractor can be used to measure and draw angles up to 180°; a full-circle protractor, to measure and draw angles up to 360°.

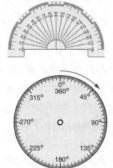

Pyramid A solid in which one face, the *base,* is any polygon and all the other *faces* are triangles that come together at a point called the *vertex,* or *apex.* Pyramids get their names from the shape of their bases.

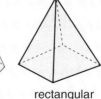

hexagonal pyramid   rectangular pyramid

Pythagorean theorem The following famous theorem: If the *legs of a right triangle* have lengths a and b and the *hypotenuse* has length c, then $a^2 + b^2 = c^2$.

●●●●●●●**Q**●●●●●●

Quadrangle A polygon that has four angles. Same as *quadrilateral.*

Quadrilateral A polygon that has four sides. Same as *quadrangle.*

Quick common denominator The product of the denominators of two or more fractions. For example, the quick common denominator of $\frac{1}{4}$ and $\frac{3}{6}$ is $4 * 6$, or 24. As the name suggests, this is a quick way to get a *common denominator* for a collection of fractions, but it does not necessarily give the *least common denominator.*

Quotient The result of dividing one number by another number. For example, in $35 \div 5 = 7$, the quotient is 7.

●●●●●●●**R**●●●●●●

Radius A line segment from the center of a circle (or sphere) to any point on the circle (or sphere); also, the length of such a line segment.

Random number A number that has the same chance of appearing as any other number. Rolling a *fair* die will produce random numbers.

Random sample A *sample* that gives all members of the *population* the same chance of being selected.

Range The difference between the *maximum* and the *minimum* in a set of data.

Rate A comparison by division of two quantities with unlike units. For example, a speed such as 55 miles per hour is a rate that compares distance with time. See also *ratio*.

Rate diagram A diagram used to model rate situations. See also *multiplication diagram*.

number of pounds	cost per pound	total cost
3	79¢	$2.37

Rate table A way of displaying *rate* information. See also *rate*.

miles	35	70	105
gallons	1	2	3

Ratio A comparison by division of two quantities with like units. Ratios can be expressed with fractions, decimals, percents, or words. Sometimes they are written with a colon between the two numbers that are being compared. For example, if a team wins 3 games out of 5 games played, the ratio of wins to total games can be written as $\frac{3}{5}$, 0.6, 60%, 3 to 5, or 3:5. See also *rate*.

Rational number A number that can be written as a fraction using only whole numbers and their opposites.

Ray A straight path that extends infinitely from a point called its *endpoint*.

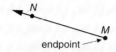

Ray *MN*

Real number Any *rational* or *irrational* number.

Reciprocal Same as *multiplicative inverse*.

Rectangle A parallelogram with four right angles.

Rectangle method A method for finding area in which rectangles are drawn around a figure or parts of a figure. The rectangles form regions that are rectangles or triangular halves of rectangles. The area of the original figure can be found by adding or subtracting the areas of these regions.

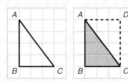

Rectangular array An arrangement of objects in rows and columns such that each row has the same number of objects and each column has the same number of objects.

Rectangular prism A *prism* with rectangular bases. See also *prism*.

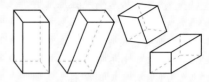

Reduce To make an object or a shape smaller. See also *size-change factor* Also, to put a fraction in *simpler form*.

Reflection The "flipping" of a figure over a line (the *line of reflection*) so that its image is the mirror image of the original. A reflection of a solid figure is a "flip" over a plane.

Regular polygon A polygon whose sides are all the same length and whose angles are all equal.

Regular polyhedron A polyhedron whose faces are formed by a single kind of congruent *regular polygon* and in which every vertex looks exactly the same as every other vertex. There are five regular polyhedrons:

tetrahedron	4 faces, each formed by an equilateral triangle
cube	6 faces, each formed by a square
octahedron	8 faces, each formed by an equilateral triangle
dodecahedron	12 faces, each formed by a regular pentagon
icosahedron	20 faces, each formed by an equilateral triangle

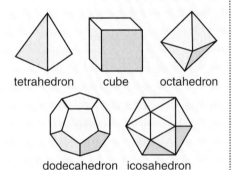

tetrahedron   cube   octahedron

dodecahedron icosahedron

Regular tessellation A *tessellation* made up of only one kind of regular polygon. There are only three regular tessellations.

the three regular tessellations

Relation symbol A symbol used to express a relationship between two quantities.

symbol	meaning
=	"is equal to"
≠	"is not equal to"
>	"is greater than"
<	"is less than"
≥	"is greater than or equal to"
≤	"is less than or equal to"

Remainder An amount left over when one number is divided by another number. For example, in $38 \div 5 \rightarrow 7$ R3 R3 stands for the remainder.

Repeating decimal A *decimal* in which one digit or a group of digits is repeated without end. For example, 0.3333... and $0.\overline{147}$ are repeating decimals. See also *decimal* and *terminating decimal*.

Rhombus A quadrilateral whose sides are all the same length.

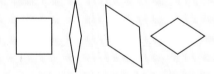

Right angle A 90° angle.

Right prism or **cylinder** A prism or cylinder whose bases are perpendicular to its other faces or surfaces.

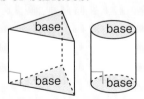

Right pyramid or **cone** A pyramid or cone whose apex is directly above the center of its base.

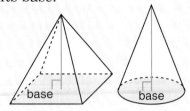

Right triangle A triangle that has a right angle.

Rotation A movement of a figure around a fixed point, or axis; a "*turn.*"

Rotation symmetry A figure has rotation symmetry if it can be rotated less than a full turn around a point or an axis so that the resulting figure (the *image*) exactly matches the original figure (the *preimage*).

Center of symmetry

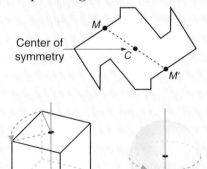

shapes with rotation symmetry

Round To adjust a number to make it easier to work with, or to make it better reflect the level of precision of the data. Often numbers are rounded to the nearest multiple of 10, 100, 1,000, and so on. For example, 12,964 rounded to the nearest thousand is 13,000.

Rubber-sheet geometry See *topology*.

Sample A part of a group chosen to represent the whole group.

Scale The *ratio* of a distance on a map, globe, drawing, or model to an actual distance. See also *map scale*.

Scale drawing A drawing of an object or a region in which all parts are drawn to the same *scale*. Architects and builders use scale drawings.

Scale factor The *ratio* between the size of an object and the size of a drawing or model of that object (such as a *scale drawing* or a *scale model*).

Scale model A model of an object in which all parts are in the same proportions as in the actual object. For example, many model trains and airplanes are scale models of actual vehicles.

Scalene triangle A triangle with sides of three different lengths. In a scalene triangle, all three angles have different measures.

Scientific notation A system for writing numbers in which a number is written as the product of a *power of 10* and a number that is at least 1 and less than 10. Scientific notation allows you to write big and small numbers with only a few symbols. For example, $4 * 10^{12}$ is scientific notation for 4,000,000,000,000.

Scroll To move through previous displays using the ⬆ and ⬇ keys on a calculator.

Sector A region bounded by an *arc* and two *radii* of a circle. A sector resembles a slice of pizza. The word *wedge* is sometimes used instead of *sector*.

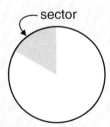

Semicircle Half of a circle. Sometimes the diameter joining the endpoints of the circle's arc is included.

Semiregular tessellation A *tessellation* with more than one kind of tile in which every tile is a regular polygon and the angles around every vertex point are all congruent. There are 8 semiregular tessellations. See also *regular tessellation*.

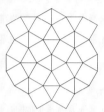

Side One of the line segments that makes up a polygon.

Significant digits The *digits* in a number that convey useful and reliable information. A number with more significant digits is more *precise* than a number with fewer significant digits.

Similar Exactly the same shape but not necessarily the same size.

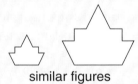

similar figures

Simpler form A fraction can be put in simpler form by dividing its numerator and denominator by a whole number that is greater than 1. For example, $\frac{18}{24}$ can be put in simpler form by dividing the numerator and denominator by 2. The result, $\frac{9}{12}$, is in simpler form than $\frac{18}{24}$.

Simplest form A fraction less than 1 is in simplest form if there is no number other than 1 that divides its numerator and denominator evenly. A *mixed number* is in simplest form if its fractional part is in simplest form.

Simplify (1) a fraction: To express in *simpler form*. (2) an equation or expression: To rewrite by removing parentheses and combining like terms and constants. For example, $7y + 4 + 5 + 3y$ can be simplified as $10y + 9$, and $2(a + 4) = 4a + 1 + 3$ can be simplified as $2a + 8 = 4a + 4$.

Simulation A model of a real situation. For example, a fair coin can be used to simulate a series of games between two evenly matched teams.

Size-change factor A number that tells the amount of enlargement or reduction. See also *enlarge* and *reduce*.

Skew lines Lines in space that do not lie in the same plane. Skew lines do not *intersect* and are not *parallel*. For example, an east-west line on the floor and a north-south line on the ceiling are skew.

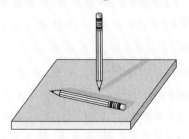

Slanted prism or **cylinder** A prism or cylinder whose bases are not perpendicular to all of its other faces or surfaces.

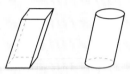

Slanted pyramid or **cone** A pyramid or cone whose apex is not directly above the center of its base.

Slide See *translation*.

Slide rule A tool used to perform calculations.

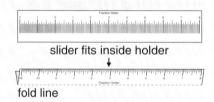

slider fits inside holder

↓

fold line

Solution of an open sentence A value for the variable in an *open sentence* that makes the sentence true. For example, 7 is the solution of $5 + n = 12$.

Solution set The set of all solutions of an equation or inequality. For example, the solution set of $x^2 = 25$ is $\{5, -5\}$ since substitution of either 5 or -5 for x makes the sentence true.

Speed A rate that compares a distance traveled with the time taken to travel that distance. For example, if a car travels 100 miles in 2 hours, then its speed is 100 mi / 2 hr, or 50 miles per hour.

Sphere The set of all points in space that are a given distance from a given point. The given point is the center of the sphere, and the given distance is the radius.

center • radius

Spreadsheet program A computer application in which numerical information is arranged in cells in a grid. The computer can use the information in the grid to perform mathematical operations, evaluate formulas, and relate data quickly. When a value in a cell changes, the computer automatically changes the values in any other cells that depend on the first cell.

	A	B	C	D
		Class Picnic ($$)		
1		budget for class picnic		
2				
3	quantity	food items	unit price	cost
4	6	packages of hamburgers	2.79	16.74
5	5	packages of hamburger buns	1.29	6.45
6	3	bags of potato chips	3.12	9.36
7	3	quarts of macaroni salad	4.50	13.50
8	4	bottles of soft drinks	1.69	6.76
9			subtotal	52.81
10			8% tax	4.22
11			total	57.03

Square number A number that is the product of a counting number multiplied by itself. For example, 25 is a square number because $25 = 5 * 5$. The square numbers are 1, 4, 9, 16, 25, and so on.

Square of a number The product of a number multiplied by itself. For example, 81 is the square of 9 because $81 = 9 * 9$.

Square root of a number The square root of a number n is a number that, when multiplied by itself, gives the number n. For example, 4 is the square root of 16 because $4 * 4 = 16$.

Square unit A unit used in measuring area, such as square centimeters or square feet.

Standard notation The most familiar way of representing whole numbers, integers, and decimals. In standard notation, the value of each digit depends on where the digit is. For example, standard notation for three hundred fifty-six is 356. See also *place value*.

Stem-and-leaf plot A display of data in which digits with larger *place values* are "stems" and digits with smaller *place values* are "leaves."
Data List: 24, 24, 25, 26, 27, 27, 31, 31, 32, 32, 36, 36, 41, 41, 43, 45, 48, 50, 52

Stems (10s)	Leaves (1s)
2	4 4 5 6 7 7
3	1 1 2 2 6 6
4	1 1 3 5 8
5	0 2

Step graph A graph that looks like steps because the values are the same for an interval, then change (or "step") for the next interval.

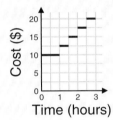

Straightedge A tool used to draw line segments. A straightedge does not have measure marks on it, so if you use a ruler as a straightedge, you should ignore the measurement marks on it.

Substitute To replace one thing with another. In a formula, to replace variables with numerical values.

Subtrahend In subtraction, the number that is being taken away from another number. For example, in $19 - 5 = 14$, the subtrahend is 5.

Sum The result of adding two or more numbers. For example, in $5 + 3 = 8$, the sum is 8.

Supplementary angles Two angles whose measures total 180°.

∠1 and ∠2 are supplementary

Surface (1) The outside boundary of an object; the part of an object that is next to the air. Common surfaces include the top of a body of water, the outermost part of a ball, and the topmost layer of ground that covers the Earth. (2) Any 2-dimensional layer, such as a *plane* or the faces of a *polyhedron*.

Surface area A measure of the surface of a 3-dimensional figure.

Survey A study that collects data.

Symmetric Having the same size and shape on either side of a line, or looking the same when turned by some amount less than 360°. See also *line symmetry*, *point symmetry*, and *rotation symmetry*.

Tally chart A table that uses marks, called tallies, to show how many times each value appears in a set of data.

Number of Pull-Ups	Number of Children
0	ǁǁǁ /
1	ǁǁǁ
2	////
3	//

Term In an *algebraic expression,* a number or a product of a number and one or more *variables.* For example, in the expression $5y + 3k - 8$, the terms are $5y$, $3k$, and 8.

Terminating decimal A decimal that ends. For example, 0.5 and 0.125 are terminating decimals. See also *decimal* and *repeating decimal.*

Tessellate To make a *tessellation;* to tile.

Tessellation An arrangement of shapes that covers a surface completely without overlaps or gaps. Also called a tiling.

Test number A number used to replace a variable when solving an equation using the *trial-and-error method.* Test numbers are useful for "closing in" on an exact solution. See also *trial-and-error method.*

Tetrahedron A triangular pyramid.

Theorem A mathematical statement that can be proved to be true; or sometimes a statement that is proposed and needs to be proved.

3-dimensional (3-D) Solid objects that take up volume. 3-dimensional objects have length, width, and thickness.

Time graph A graph that is constructed from a story that takes place over time. A time graph shows what has happened through a progression of time.

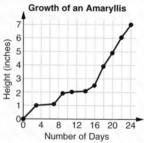

Topological properties Properties of a figure that are not changed by *topological transformations.* See also *topology.*

Topological transformation A shrinking, stretching, twisting, bending, or other operation that doesn't change what points are next to each other in a shape. See also *topology.*

Topologically equivalent In *topology,* a term for shapes that can be transformed into each other by a *topological transformation.* See also *topology* and *genus.*

Topology The study of the properties of shapes that are unchanged by shrinking, stretching, twisting, bending, and similar transformations. (Tearing, breaking, and sticking together are not allowed.)

Trade-first subtraction method A subtraction method in which all trades are done before any subtractions are carried out.

Transformation Something done to a geometric figure that produces a new figure. The most common transformations are *translations* (slides), *reflections* (flips), and *rotations* (turns). See also *isometry transformation* and *topological transformation.*

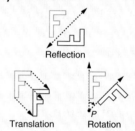

Transformation geometry The study of *transformations.*

Translation A movement of a figure along a straight line; a "slide."

Transversal A line that intersects two or more other lines.

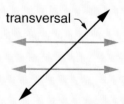

Trapezoid A quadrilateral that has exactly one pair of parallel sides.

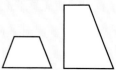

Tree Diagram A diagram such as a factor tree or probability tree. A tree diagram is a network of points connected by line segments. One special point is the root of the tree and closed loops are not allowed. Tree diagrams can be used to factor numbers and to represent probability situations in which there is a series of events.

prime factorization of 30

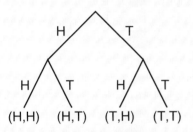

flipping a coin twice

Trial-and-error method A method for finding the solution of an equation by trying several *test numbers*. See also *test number*.

Triangle A polygon with three sides.

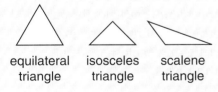

equilateral   isosceles   scalene
triangle   triangle   triangle

Triangular numbers Numbers that can be shown by triangular arrangements of dots. The triangular numbers are 1, 3, 6, 10, 15, 21, 28, 36, 45, and so on.

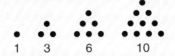

1   3   6   10

Triangular prism A prism whose bases are triangles.

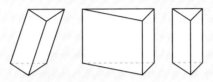

Triangular pyramid A pyramid in which all faces are triangles, any one of which can be called the base; also called a *tetrahedron*. If all of the faces are equilateral triangles, the pyramid is a regular tetrahedron.

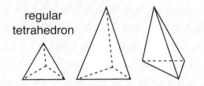

regular
tetrahedron

True number sentence A number sentence in which the relation symbol accurately relates the two sides. For example, 15 = 5 + 10 and 25 > 20 + 3 are both true number sentences.

Truncate (1) To replace all of the digits to the right of a particular place with 0s. For example, 3,654 can be truncated to 3,650 or 3,600 or 3,000. Truncation is similar to rounding but is easier and always makes the number smaller (unless all

the truncated digits are 0s). (2) To cut off a vertex of a solid figure.

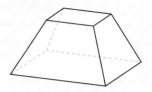

truncated pyramid

Turn See *rotation*.

Turn-around facts A pair of multiplication (or addition) facts in which the order of the factors (or addends) is reversed. For example, 3 * 9 = 27 and 9 * 3 = 27 are turn-around multiplication facts and 4 + 5 = 9 and 5 + 4 = 9 are turn-around addition facts. There are no turn-around facts for subtraction or division.

Turn-around rule A rule for solving addition and multiplication problems based on the *commutative property*. For example, if you know that 6 * 8 = 48, then, by the turn-around rule, you also know that 8 * 6 = 48. See *commutative property*.

Twin primes Two *prime numbers* that are separated by just one *composite number*. For example, 3 and 5 are twin primes; 11 and 13 are also twin primes.

2-dimensional (2-D) Having length and width but not thickness. 2-dimensional shapes have area but not volume. Circles and polygons are 2-dimensional.

Unit A label used to put a number in context. In measuring length, for example, inches and centimeters are units. In "5 apples," the word *apples* is the unit. See also *whole*.

Unit fraction A fraction whose numerator is 1. For example, $\frac{1}{2}$, $\frac{1}{3}$, $\frac{1}{8}$, and $\frac{1}{20}$ are unit fractions.

Unit percent One percent (1%).

Unit rate A *rate* with 1 in the numerator.

Unlike denominators Denominators that are different, as in $\frac{1}{2}$ and $\frac{1}{3}$.

"Unsquaring" a number Finding the *square root* of a number.

U.S. customary system of measurement The measuring system most frequently used in the United States.

Vanishing line A line connecting a point on a figure in a *perspective drawing* with the *vanishing point*.

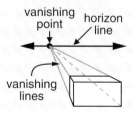

Vanishing point In a *perspective drawing,* the point at which parallel lines moving away from the viewer seem to converge. It is located on the horizon line. See also *vanishing line.*

Variable A letter or other symbol that represents a number. A variable can represent one specific number or it can stand for many different numbers.

Variable term A *term* that contains at least one variable.

Venn diagram A picture that uses circles or rings to show relationships between sets.

Girls on Sports Teams

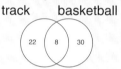

Vertex (plural: **vertices**) The point where the rays of an angle, the sides of a polygon, or the edges of a polyhedron meet.

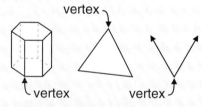

Vertex point A point where corners of shapes in a *tessellation* meet. See also *tessellation.*

Vertical Upright; perpendicular to the horizon.

Vertical (or **opposite**) **angles** When two lines intersect, the angles that do not share a common side.

Vertical angles have equal measures.

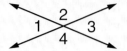

Angles 1 and 3 and Angles 2 and 4 are pairs of vertical angles.

Volume The amount of space inside a 3-dimensional object. Volume is usually measured in cubic units, such as cubic centimeters or cubic inches. Sometimes volume is measured in units of capacity, such as gallons or liters.

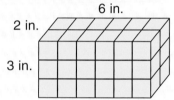

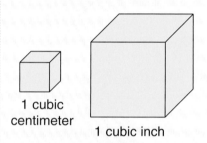

1 cubic centimeter

1 cubic inch

"What's My Rule?" Problem A type of problem that asks for a rule for relating two sets of numbers. Also, a type of problem that asks for one of the sets of numbers, given a rule and the other set of numbers.

Whole (or **ONE** or **unit**) The entire object, collection of objects, or quantity being considered—the ONE, the unit, 100%.

Whole number Any of the numbers 0, 1, 2, 3, 4 . . .

Page 4
1. 6,000
2. 600,000
3. 60
4. 60,000

Page 6
1. 25
2. 27
3. 100,000
4. 8
5. 119,025
6. 20,736

Page 8
1. $5.0 * 10^5$
2. $1.0 * 10^{10}$
3. $7.5 * 10^8$
4. $8.0 * 10^{-5}$
5. $4.5 * 10^{-2}$
6. 300,000,000
7. 41,000,000
8. 70,900,000,000
9. 0.004
10. 0.0906

Page 9
1. false
2. true
3. false
4. false

Page 10
1. 1, 2, 5, 10
2. 1, 3, 9, 27, 81
3. 1, 3, 7, 9, 21, 63
4. 1, 2, 3, 4, 6, 8, 12, 16, 24, 48
5. 1, 17
6. 1, 2, 4, 5, 10, 20, 25, 50, 100

Page 11
1. 240: 2, 3, 5, 6, 10
2. 7,260: 2, 3, 5, 6, 10
3. 427: none
4. 531: 3, 9
5. 14,850: 2, 3, 5, 6, 9, 10

Page 12
Sample answers:

1.
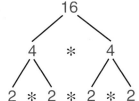

2.
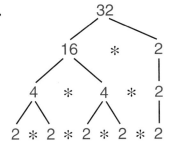

3.
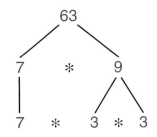

4.
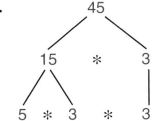

5.
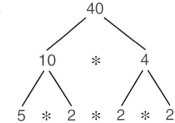

6.
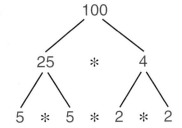

Page 14
1. 387
2. 113
3. 965
4. 1,809
5. 9,023

Page 15
1. 46
2. 391
3. 361
4. 71
5. 3,445

Page 16
1. 182
2. 52
3. 889
4. 131

Page 17
1. 496
2. 625
3. 175
4. 3,499

Page 18
1. 700
2. 98,000
3. 6,300
4. 81,000
5. 210,000
6. 48,000

Page 19
1. 3,227   **2.** 34,155   **3.** 5,238
4. 4,664   **5.** 4,991

Page 20
1.

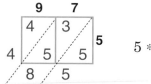

5 * 97 = 485

2.

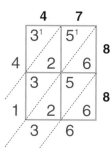

88 * 47 = 4,136

3.

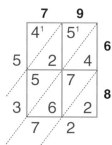

68 * 79 = 5,372

4.

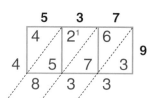

9 * 537 = 4,833

5.

987 * 7 = 6,909

Page 21
1. 97   **2.** 7,000   **3.** 90   **4.** 90

Page 23
1. 14 R2   **2.** 171   **3.** 91   **4.** 234 R2

Page 28
1. 2 tenths
2. 1 and 36 hundredths
3. 948 thousandths
4. 19 and 7 hundredths
5. 6 thousandths
6. 74 and 82 thousandths

Page 30
1. 0.25   **2.** 0.8   **3.** 2.5
4. 0.65   **5.** 0.16

Page 31
1. 0.3   **2.** about 0.87 or 0.88   **3.** about 4.3
4. 0.75   **5.** about 1.78   **6.** about 0.29

Page 33
1. 0.375   **2.** 0.167   **3.** 0.5556

Page 34
1. 0.125   **2.** 0.8333...   **3.** 0.888...

Page 35
1. 0.125   **2.** $0.\overline{6}$ **3.** $0.41\overline{6}$
4. $0.8\overline{3}$ **5.** $0.\overline{7}$ **6.** 0.1875

Page 37
1. a. 20%   **b.** 70%   **c.** 62.5%
   d. 125%   **e.** $33\frac{1}{3}$%, or about 33.3%
2. a. $\frac{60}{100}$, $\frac{6}{10}$, or $\frac{3}{5}$ **b.** $\frac{35}{100}$, or $\frac{7}{20}$
   c. $\frac{250}{100}$, or $2\frac{50}{100}$, or $2\frac{1}{2}$
3. a. $\frac{8}{10}$, or $\frac{4}{5}$ **b.** $\frac{25}{100}$, or $\frac{1}{4}$
   c. $3\frac{32}{100}$, or $3\frac{8}{25}$ **d.** $\frac{28}{1,000}$, or $\frac{7}{250}$

Page 41
1. 9.02   **2.** 21.6   **3.** 11.66

Page 42
1. 7.3 meters
2. a. About 4.7 m   **b.** About 0.02 sec

Page 44
1. 345   **2.** 0.0345   **3.** 1,600
4. 0.509   **5.** 0.00055   **6.** $5,500
7. 10.8   **8.** 0.327

Page 46
1. 22.23   **2.** 26.52   **3.** 2.5452
4. 0.0081

Page 47
1.

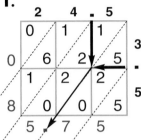

$24.5 * 3.5 = 85.75$

2.

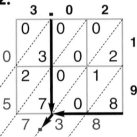

$3.02 * 19 = 57.38$

3.

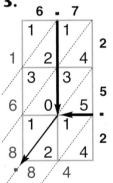

$6.7 * 25.2 = 168.84$

Page 48
1. 6.78   **2.** 678   **3.** 0.0054
4. $0.29   **5.** 7,750   **6.** 0.004
7. 3,750   **8.** 20

Page 49
1. 6.78   **2.** 678   **3.** 0.0054
4. $0.29   **5.** 7,750   **6.** 0.004
7. 3,750   **8.** 20

Page 51
1. 3   **2.** 3.2   **3.** 568   **4.** 0.625

Page 54
1. 5.8, 5.79, 5.795
2. 3.2, 3.21, 3.208
3. 1.0, 1.03, 1.030

Page 57
1. $32.40   **2.** $1.95

Page 58
$200

Page 60
1. $36   **2.** 21 free throws

Page 66
1. $\frac{5}{3}$ **2.** $\frac{9}{2}$ **3.** $\frac{15}{4}$
4. $\frac{5}{2}$ **5.** $\frac{17}{5}$ **6.** Sample answer: $\frac{16}{4}$

Page 67
1. $1\frac{1}{5}$ **2.** $2\frac{5}{8}$ **3.** 4
4. $5\frac{1}{2}$ **5.** $3\frac{3}{4}$ **6.** $6\frac{2}{3}$

Page 68
Sample answers:
1. $\frac{2}{8}$ **2.** $\frac{8}{16}$ **3.** $\frac{6}{4}$
4. $\frac{3}{4}$ **5.** $\frac{4}{5}$ **6.** $\frac{4}{5}$

Page 69
Answers vary for Problems 1–3. Sample answers:
1. $\frac{2}{4}$, or $\frac{1}{2}$ **2.** $\frac{6}{8}$, or $\frac{3}{4}$ **3.** $\frac{10}{12}$, or $\frac{5}{6}$
4. $\frac{3}{4}$ **5.** $\frac{2}{3}$ **6.** $\frac{5}{6}$

Page 70
1. >   **2.** <   **3.** <   **4.** >

Page 72
Answers vary for Problems 1–5. Sample answers:
1. $\frac{1}{2}$ **2.** $\frac{1}{3}$ **3.** $\frac{6}{8}$ **4.** $\frac{5}{8}$
5. $\frac{2}{3}$ **6.** $\frac{1}{10}$ **7.** $\frac{3}{7}$ **8.** $\frac{11}{12}$
9. $\frac{5}{9}$ **10.** $\frac{5}{8}$

Page 73

Sample answers:
1. $\frac{4}{6}$ and $\frac{1}{6}$ 2. $\frac{5}{20}$ and $\frac{8}{20}$ 3. $\frac{3}{10}$ and $\frac{5}{10}$
4. $\frac{15}{20}$ and $\frac{14}{20}$ 5. $\frac{12}{24}$ and $\frac{18}{24}$

Page 74

1. 12 2. 20 3. 12
4. 24 5. 18 6. 45

Page 76

1. 15 posters 2. 12 counters

Page 77

1. 1 2. 2 3. 8
4. 7 5. 6 6. 3

Page 78

1. $\frac{6}{9}$ 2. $\frac{3}{4}$ 3. $\frac{7}{12}$
4. $\frac{1}{12}$ 5. $\frac{19}{24}$

Page 80

1. 11 2. $5\frac{9}{10}$ 3. $10\frac{1}{12}$ 4. $22\frac{22}{63}$

Page 82

1. $2\frac{4}{15}$ 2. $3\frac{3}{8}$
3. $2\frac{3}{9}$, or $2\frac{1}{3}$ 4. $3\frac{4}{6}$, or $3\frac{2}{3}$

Page 83

1. 9 2. 27 3. 16
4. Gina gets $10, Robert gets $5.

Page 84

1. $\frac{5}{2}$, or $2\frac{1}{2}$ 2. $\frac{18}{4}$, or $4\frac{1}{2}$ 3. $\frac{12}{5}$, or $2\frac{2}{5}$

Page 85

1. $\frac{1}{6}$ 2. $\frac{3}{20}$ 3. $\frac{15}{60}$, or $\frac{1}{4}$
4. $\frac{0}{64}$, or 0 5. $\frac{18}{12}$, or $1\frac{1}{2}$

Page 86

1. $\frac{6}{4}$, or $1\frac{1}{2}$ 2. $\frac{72}{3}$, or 24 3. $\frac{162}{10}$, or $16\frac{1}{5}$

Page 88

1. $6 \div \frac{1}{2} = \frac{12}{2} \div \frac{1}{2} = 12$, 12 people
2. $8 \div \frac{1}{2} = \frac{16}{2} \div \frac{1}{2} = 16$, 16 bracelets
3. $5 \div \frac{1}{2} = \frac{10}{2} \div \frac{1}{2} = 10$

Page 90

1. $\frac{12}{5}$, or $2\frac{2}{5}$ 2. $\frac{15}{5}$, or 3 3. $\frac{7}{21}$, or $\frac{1}{3}$
4. $\frac{8}{12}$, or $\frac{2}{3}$ 5. $\frac{14}{5}$, or $2\frac{4}{5}$

Page 92

1. -2 2. -8 3. 3 4. -4

Page 93

1. -6 2. 3 3. 7 4. -4

Page 94

1. -15 2. 24 3. -0.4 4. -18
5. -4 6. -3 7. -10 8. 17

Page 95

1. -30 2. -270 3. -72
4. -7 5. -6 6. 5

Page 96

1. 0 2. 0 3. 0 4. No solution

Page 99

1. 1, 2, 3, 4 2. -1, 0, 1, 2, 3, 4
3. yes 4. yes
5. yes 6. yes
7. 1.166..., $1.1\overline{6}$, or $1\frac{1}{6}$;
   1.333..., $1.\overline{3}$, or $133\frac{1}{3}\%$;
   1.5, or $1\frac{3}{6}$;
   1.666..., $1.\overline{6}$, or $166\frac{2}{3}\%$
8. yes
9. $\tan 30°$, $\sqrt{2}$, $\sqrt{3}$, $\sqrt{5}$, e, π, $\sqrt{12}$

Page 101

1. for $r = 1$: $2 * (1) + (1) = 3 * (1)$
   for $r = -1$: $2 * (-1) + (-1) = 3 * (-1)$
   for $r = 0$: $2 * (0) + (0) = 3 * (0)$
2. for $b = 1$: $1 + (1 + 1) + (1 + 2) = 3 * (1 + 1)$
   for $b = 2$: $2 + (2 + 1) + (2 + 2) = 3 * (2 + 1)$
   for $b = 0$: $0 + (0 + 1) + (0 + 2) = 3 * (0 + 1)$
3. $x + y = y + x$
4. $\frac{x}{y} * \frac{y}{x} = 1$, x and y may not be 0.

Page 107

1. 4 dollars/hour, or $\frac{4\ dollars}{1\ hour}$

dollars	4	8	12	16	20	24	28
hours	1	2	3	4	5	6	7

2. 35 words/minute, or $\frac{35\ words}{1\ minute}$

words	35	70	105	140	175	210	245
minutes	1	2	3	4	5	6	7

Page 110

1. 18 ft **2.** $5 **3.** $30 **4.** 25 laps

Page 113

1. $t = 40$ **2.** $x = 8$ **3.** $m = 1.5$

Page 115

1. 12.5 cups **2.** 20 cousins

Page 118

1. $\frac{money\ spent}{total\ allowance} = \frac{3}{5}$ **2.** $\frac{money\ saved}{money\ spent} = \frac{2}{3}$

3. 1.5 times **4.** 40%

Page 121

1. a. 7.5 cm **b.** 30 cm

2. 600 miles

Page 124

1. About 5,000 miles

Page 128

1.

Number of Hits	Number of Players
0	////
1	///
2	///
3	/
4	/

2.

Number of Players

$$
\begin{array}{l}
\times \\
\times \\
\times \quad\quad \times \quad\quad \times \\
\times \quad\quad \times \quad\quad \times \\
\times \quad\quad \times \quad\quad \times \quad\quad \times \quad\quad \times
\end{array}
$$

| 0 | 1 | 2 | 3 | 4 |

Number of Hits

Page 129

1.

Ages of Space Travelers	Number of Travelers
20–29	////
30–39	##//
40–49	/

2. **Ages of Space Travelers**

Stems (10s)	Leaves (1s)
2	7 5 8 6
3	7 2 1 9 6
4	3

Page 130

min = 0; max = 4; range = 4; mode = 2; median = 1.5

Page 131

Megan's mean (average) is 80.91.

Page 132

Popular Pets in the United States

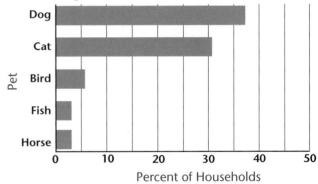

Page 134

Average Temperatures for Boston, Massachusetts

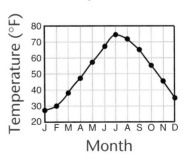

Page 135
1. **a.** $2.00   **b.** $3.50   **c.** $3.50
   d. $6.50   **e.** $6.50
2. **a.** $2.00   **b.** $1.50

Page 138
1. labels
2. 4.50; a number representing the unit price of 1 qt of macaroni salad
3. B1
4. 5; a number representing the quantity of packages of hamburger buns
5. A4, A5, A6, A7, A8, C4, C5, C6, C7, C8
6. Column D

Page 139
3rd grade represents 62% – 45%, or 17%;
4th grade represents 85% – 62%, or 23%;
5th grade represents 100% – 85%, or 15%

Page 140

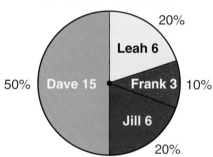

Points Scored

Page 141

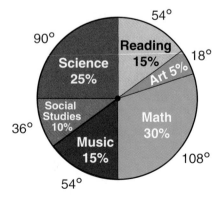

Page 144

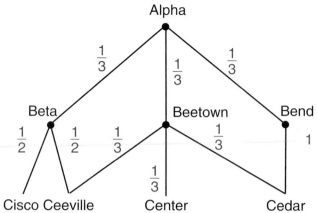

1. $\frac{1}{6}$
2. $\frac{1}{6} + \frac{1}{9} = \frac{5}{18}$
3. $\frac{1}{9}$
4. $\frac{1}{9} + \frac{1}{3} = \frac{4}{9}$

Page 149
Sample answers:

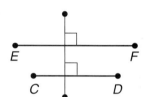

1.   2.

Page 150
Sample answers:

1.   2.

3.   4.

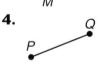

5.   6.

Page 151
1. **a.** same measure **b.** supplementary
   c. supplementary **d.** supplementary
   e. same measure **f.** same measure
2. **a.** 120° **b.** 60° **c.** 120°

Page 153
1. **a.** octagon
   b. quadrangle or quadrilateral
   c. hexagon
2. Sample answers:
   a. 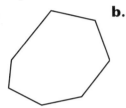 **b.**

3. The sides of the notebook paper are not all the same length.

Page 154
Sample answers:
1. *JLK, KLJ, KJL, LJK, LKJ*

2.

3.

Page 156
1. Sample answer:
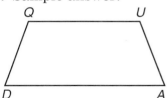

2. no
3. *UADQ, ADQU, DQUA, QDAU, AUQD, UQDA, DAUQ*

Page 157
Sample answers:
1. All four sides of a rhombus are equal. The sides of a rectangle do not all have to be the same length.
2. A trapezoid has exactly 1 pair of parallel sides. All four sides can be different lengths. A square has 2 pairs of parallel sides that are all the same length.
3. A kite has no parallel sides. A parallelogram has two pairs of parallel sides.

Page 159
Sample answers:
1. **a.** They do not have any vertices.
   b. A cylinder has three surfaces; a sphere has one. A cylinder has two edges. A sphere has no edges.
2. **a.** They each have at least one vertex. They each have a flat base.
   b. A cone has a curved surface; a pyramid has only flat surfaces. A cone has only one vertex. A pyramid has at least four vertices.

Page 160
1. **a.** 7 **b.** 1
2. **a.** 8 **b.** 2
3. rectangular prism

Page 161
1. **a.** 7 **b.** 15 **c.** 10
2. octagonal prism

Page 162
1. **a.** 5 **b.** 8 **c.** 5
2. triangular pyramid
3. Sample answers:
   a. They each have flat surfaces. The shape of their base is used to name them.
   b. A prism has at least 2 parallel faces (the bases); a pyramid has no parallel faces.

Page 163
1. a. 6   **b.** 4
2. Sample answers:
    a. All of their faces are equilateral triangles.
    b. A tetrahedron has four faces; an icosahedron has twenty faces. A tetrahedron has four vertices; an icosahedron has twelve vertices.

Page 166
1. C

Page 167
1. 10 inches   **2.** 15 inches

Page 169
1. WHAT   **2.** $A'(6,15)$; $T'(11,11)$ **3.** A

Page 170
1.

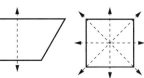

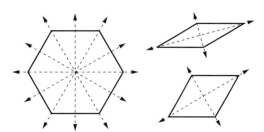

2. infinite; any line drawn directly through its center is a line of symmetry

Page 171
Sample answers:
1.
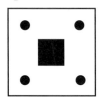
     2.

Page 173
1. a. false   **b.** false   **c.** true
    d. false   **e.** true

2. Sample answer:

Pages 176–188
Answers vary.

Page 191
1. millimeter, gram, kilometer, and decimeter
2. a. one thousand (1,000)   **b.** 0.002 kg

Page 194
1. 26 ft   **2.** 72 yd

Page 195
1. 25 mm   **2.** about 78.5 mm   **3.** 43.98 in.

Page 197
1. 6 square units   **2.** 90 in.^{2}
3. 49 m^2

Page 198
1. 88 ft^2 **2.** 108 in.^{2} **3.** 10.4 cm^2

Page 199
1. 24 in.^{2} **2.** 48 cm^2 **3.** 10.8 yd^2

Page 200
1. about 21 mm   **2.** about 10.5 mm
3. about 346 mm^2

Page 203
1. 336 yd^3 **2.** 1,728 cm^3 **3.** 2,304 ft^3

Page 205
1. 144 in.^{3} **2.** 640 cm^3 **3.** 800 ft^3

Page 206
1. about 33.5 in.^{3} **2.** about 268.1 cm^3

Page 207
1. 1,360 cm^2 **2.** 432 in.^{2} **3.** $\frac{3}{8}$ ft^2

Page 208
376.8 in.^{2}, or 377.0 in.^{2}

Page 210
1. 180 grams; 170.1 grams   **2.** 366 ounces

Page 214
1. 60°   **2.** 290°   **3.** 75°

Sample answers:

4.

70°

5.

280°

6.

55°

Page 215
1. a. 2   **b.** 3   **c.** 6   **d.** 10

2. 540°   **3.** 135°

4. number of sides of a polygon − 2
= number of triangles into which it can
be divided

Page 216
1–4.
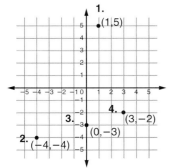

Page 221
1. $2n = 30$ **2.** $n - 8 = 12$

3. $157\frac{1}{2}$ miles   **4.** 3 minutes

Page 222
1. $(m - 2)$ inches   **2.** $2H$ minutes

3. $\$0.50 * R + \$2$

Page 223
1. true   **2.** true   **3.** false

4. true   **5.** false   **6.** false

Page 225
1. $c = 12$ **2.** $7 = z$ **3.** $f = 10.5$

4. $20 = 11.49 + C$, or $20 - 11.49 = C$

5. $10 * W = 70$

Page 226
1. $b < 8$ **2.** $f > 0$

3.

```
  +--+--+--+--+--+--+--+--+--●--+--+--+--+→
  0  1  2  3  4  5  6  7  8  9  10 11 12 13
```

4.

```
  +--+--●--+--+--+--+--+--+--+--+--+--+→
  0  1  2  3  4  5  6  7  8  9  10 11 12 13
```

Page 228
1. 576 in.^{2}, or 4 ft^2 **2.** 4,800 ft

3. 32 m^2

4. a. $V = \frac{1}{3} * B * h$ **b.** $i = 1,000 * r * t$

Page 229
1. 36   **2.** 52.5   **3.** 10   **4.** 6

Page 231
1. $(8 * 105) + (8 * 30) = 840 + 240 = 1,080$

2. $(32 * 6) - (12 * 6) = 192 - 72 = 120$

3. $(11 * 90) - (11 * 6) = 990 - 66 = 924$

4. $1.23 * (456 + 789) =$
$(1.23 * 456) + (1.23 * 789)$
$1.23 * 1245 \stackrel{?}{=} 560.88 + 970.47$
$1,531.35 = 1,531.35$

Page 232
1. $4S + 2T = 1T + 8S$

2. $6C + 2P = 8P + 3C$

Page 234

1. Both sides of the equation are equal to 44.

$$5(12 + 3) - 3(12) + 5 = 4(12 - 1)$$
$$5(15) - 36 + 5 = 4(11)$$
$$75 - 36 + 5 = 44$$
$$44 = 44$$

2. $x = 4$ **3.** $s = -2$ **4.** $b = 3$

Page 235

1.

in	out
n	$n / 3$
9	3
36	12

2.

in	out
k	$k - 4$
11	7
28	24

3. *Rule:* multiply "in" by 30

in	out
x	$x * 30$
4	120
10	300

Page 236

1. 500 words   **2.** Dan earned $31.50.

Page 239

1. 5 students   **2.** $110

Page 241

Answers vary.

Page 244

1. 35,500   **2.** 40,000
3. 35,000   **4.** 35,481.75

Page 246

1. 100 students   **2.** 18 students; 85 students
3. 3 students

Page 251

1. 82   **2.** 4   **3.** 56   **4.** 128

Page 257

1. 0.3125   **2.** $\frac{385}{1,000}$, or $\frac{77}{200}$ **3.** 0.9%

4. 4.58   **5.** 43.75%   **6.** $\frac{58}{100}$, or $\frac{29}{50}$

Page 261

1. 80   **2.** 230   **3.** 1,300
4. 50,000

Page 263

1. 0.00058   **2.** 7,600,000,000
3. 0.0000043   **4.** 230,000,000

Page 264

1. $6.085 * 10^{15}$ **2.** $5.380 * 10^{11}$
3. $1.537 * 10^{16}$ **4.** $2.778 * 10^{17}$
5. 98,670,000,000   **6.** 432,000,000

Page 266

about 615.75 ft^2

Page 267

1. $11.25; $86.25   **2.** $13.36; $80.14

Page 269

1. $63.50   **2.** $21.00

Page 271

1. 18, 25, 32, 39, 46
2. 23, 34, 45, 56, 67

Page 334

1. balanced   **2.** unbalanced

Page 335

1. unbalanced   **2.** balanced   **3.** 1